# WRITING ENGLISH

## The Canadian Handbook

*Diff- b/w homism and humanism.*

William E. Messenger | Jan de Bruyn
Judy Brown | Ramona Montagnes

OXFORD
UNIVERSITY PRESS

**OXFORD**
UNIVERSITY PRESS

Oxford University Press is a department of the University of Oxford.
It furthers the University's objective of excellence in research, scholarship,
and education by publishing worldwide. Oxford is a registered trade mark of
Oxford University Press in the UK and in certain other countries.

Published in Canada by
Oxford University Press
8 Sampson Mews, Suite 204,
Don Mills, Ontario  M3C 0H5 Canada

www.oupcanada.com

Copyright © Oxford University Press Canada 2012

The moral rights of the author have been asserted

Database right Oxford University Press (maker)

First Edition published in 2012

Previous Edition published in 2005.

**Library and Archives Canada Cataloguing in Publication**
Writing English : the Canadian handbook / William E. Messenger ...
[et al.].

Includes index.
ISBN 978-0-19-544658-6

1. English language—Rhetoric—Handbooks, manuals, etc.
2. English language—Canada.  I. Messenger, William E., 1931–

PE1408.W75 2011          808'.042          C2010-907902-7

Printed and bound in Canada.

5 6 7  –  18 17 16

# CONTENTS

# PREFACE

Writers who have a good command over the English language possess an enviable skill: the ability to write with confidence. Crafting a piece of writing can take on many forms; you may be writing to instruct, convince or persuade, or inform. Regardless of your purpose, your sentences and paragraphs should be coherent and well structured, communicating your ideas and arguments clearly to your reader.

This book guides individuals looking to improve their formal writing skills. Chapters I–II detail the mechanics of English as it is used in Canada today, providing an overview of sentence structure and parts of speech. With the intricacies of the language firmly established, the later chapters demonstrate various ways to construct strong sentences and paragraphs with techniques such as emphasis and organization, and by avoiding common pitfalls in spelling, punctuation, and usage.

The breadth of this book's coverage, from specific placement of a comma to the overall structure of your work, makes it useful to a wide variety of readers. You might be a professional looking to make your report writing more polished, a writer seeking guidance on documentation, or someone new to the English language who is interested in the nuts and bolts of sentence organization. Each potential user will have different strengths and weaknesses, and will look to different parts of this book depending on his or her individual needs. Like most reference books, this one isn't designed to be read cover-to-cover. Use the detailed table of contents and index to locate the sections that address your areas of interest.

Throughout these pages you will find several helpful features. Cross-references, to entire sections or to specific sub-sections, point you to other areas in the book that expand on the subject and offer exceptions to a rule. Each section is filled with numerous examples to clarify and demonstrate common Canadian usage. Examples marked with an **✗** demonstrate incorrect usage to help you avoid common errors—often shown alongside an example that illustrates the correct usage. Within examples you will also notice words, phrases, or entire clauses in italics to emphasize the point being made in the text.

While it is easy to look at the directions throughout these pages as hard and fast rules, try to approach the content, rather, as guidelines. Remember that writing is often at its best when it's not stiff and mechanical; depending on your purpose, your writing might be intimately personal or filled with colourful phrasing. Sometimes breaking a rule is the most effective way to create emphasis and meaning. Being able to manipulate and control language, however, begins with a firm understanding of how its parts work together. With this knowledge in hand, along with practice, you will be able to write effectively and confidently for a variety of purposes.

THE PUBLISHERS

# CHAPTER I
# Understanding Sentences

1. Sentence Patterns and Conventions

# INTRODUCTION
## The Conventions of Language

Words are the building blocks we use to put together language structures that enable us to communicate. Combinations of words produce sentences; combinations of sentences produce paragraphs; combinations of paragraphs can form stories, detailed expositions, descriptions, summaries, arguments.

When we write, we represent speech sounds with symbols called letters, which combine to form the units called words. Those who share a familiarity with a particular language are able to communicate because each person knows the meaning of the sounds. If you said "Look" when you meant "Listen," you would fail to communicate. The success of the process depends upon the conventions, the shared acceptance of what particular words mean.

Putting words together to make sentences is also subject to conventions. We use particular word orders and other standard ways of showing how words are related to each other; and since writing represents speech, we use certain visual devices to help clarify meaning and make communication easier. The conventions governing the arrangement of words and the relations between them constitute the grammar of a language. The techniques that help us "hear" writing as something like speaking constitute the conventions of punctuation.

The first four chapters (I–IV) of this book describe and illustrate these conventions of language and ways of avoiding errors in their use. Although on occasion we use terms like "rules" and "right" and "wrong," try to think of yourself as studying not the "rules" of grammar and punctuation but their conventions; and think not in terms of what is "right" or "correct" but in terms of what is conventional—that is, mutually agreed upon, and therefore understandable, and therefore effective.

## Grammar

The term *grammar* is virtually equivalent to the term *syntax*, which refers to the relations among words and the order of words in individual sentences. The first four chapters (I–IV) are about sentences, the primary units of communication: how they work, what goes into them, what their varieties are, how their parts are arranged, and how they are punctuated. You may be able to write fairly well without knowing much about these grammatical principles. But if you have any difficulties writing correct and effective sentences, you'll find it much easier to overcome them if you know how sentences work. And you'll find an understanding of sentence grammar especially helpful in improving the effectiveness of your punctuation.

Don't be intimidated by the thought that you're studying "grammar." After all, if you can read and understand these sentences, you already know a great deal of grammar; chances are you absorbed it, unconsciously, as part of everyday life. Now you need only raise some of that understanding into consciousness so that you can use it to help you stick to the conventions and make your writing more effective. You may often be able to trust your intuitive grasp of the way English words and sentences work; but if you find yourself having trouble, especially if you are multilingual and English isn't your first language, you may want to consult the principles more often and apply them more consciously.

We use the vocabulary of traditional grammar both because it has, for many, the virtue of simplicity and familiarity and because it is usually the vocabulary used to study another language. It is also the vocabulary used by dictionaries and other reference books in their definitions and discussions of usage. Learning these terms shouldn't be difficult. If you find the going rough, you may be making it unnecessarily hard for yourself; if you fight the material, it may well fight back. But if you approach it with interest and a desire to learn, you'll find that it will co-operate and that the quality of your writing will improve as you increase your mastery of the conventions. Further, you will not only be learning to follow "rules" in order to produce "correct" sentences but also be learning how to choose one form or usage or order rather than another. Good writing is often a result of being able to make intelligent choices from the alternatives available to you.

This chapter introduces the basic elements and patterns of English sentences and defines and classifies different kinds of sentences.

Awareness of these patterns and an ability to recognize phrases and clauses will increase your understanding of sentence grammar.

# 1. SENTENCE PATTERNS AND CONVENTIONS

Before getting into the nuts and bolts of sentence structure, it is helpful to understand the meaning of the term *sentence*. Most standard definitions are unsatisfactory and unrealistic. One of them, for example, says that a sentence is a group of words with a subject and a verb. However, some sentences lack one or the other or both:

> Now or never.
> Who, me?
> Call me Ishmael.

Out of context, such sentences don't tell us much, but they are clearly acceptable units. Moreover, some groups of words do contain a subject–verb combination but are still not sentences: an opening capital letter and a closing period don't make a subordinate clause a sentence:

✘ I decided to make a list. Before I went shopping.

✘ They bought me the bike. Which I had stared at in the store the week before.

The second clause in each of these is a fragment (see 1.24).

Another common definition claims that a sentence is a complete thought. But *Yes* and *No* aren't satisfyingly complete without the questions that prompted them, nor are some of the other examples without their respective contexts. Nor is there anything necessarily "incomplete" about such words as *dog*, *hand*, *chair*, *freedom*, *love*— yet these words are not normally thought of as sentences.

Remember that language is primarily spoken. It is more realistic to define a sentence as *a satisfyingly complete pattern of intonation or expression*: that is, a complete utterance. Your voice and natural tone should tell you whether a certain group of words is or is not a sentence. Make it a practice to read your written work aloud, or at least to sound it out in your mind. Doing so will help you avoid ambiguity.

All sentences have a purpose, namely to communicate ideas and/ or feelings. And there are conventional ways to convey these ideas and feelings. For example, if someone tells you,

> I am writing an article on student-centred learning.

you know that the sentence is stating a fact, or a supposed fact. If the same person then says,

> Are you familiar with the term *student-centred learning*?

you know that you are being asked a question and that you are expected to give an answer. If your co-worker then says,

> Give me your opinion of my article.

you know you are being asked to do something, being given a mild command. And when your co-worker says,

> What an ambitious article!

you know you are hearing an emphatic expression of strong feeling.

We know how to interpret these different kinds of utterances because we understand and accept the conventions of the way sentences communicate. Sentences are classified according to the kind of purpose each has. Sentences that make statements of fact or supposed fact are called declarative:

> The United States is Canada's largest trading partner

> *Anne of Green Gables* is tremendously popular in Japan.

> This seminar deals with the effects of globalization on education.

Sentences that ask questions are interrogative; in speech, they often (but not always) end with a rise in the pitch of one's voice; in writing, they end with a question mark:

> Is this computer virus affecting your email?

> Are you going to the opera?

> Why? What's the reason?

Sentences that give commands or make requests, that expect action or compliance, are imperative:

> Please print the document.

> Don't forget to file your income tax return.

> Edit your work carefully before submitting it.

Sentences that exclaim, that express strong feeling with vigour or emphasis, are called exclamatory; they customarily end with an exclamation point:

> That was an unforgettable race!

> Not if I can help it!

> Amazing!

Like many other traditional categories, however, the ones we've described aren't always so simple or obvious. For example, a sentence may include both interrogative and declarative elements:

> "Should the voting age be raised?" the candidate asked.

or both imperative and declarative elements:

> Please contact me about your project: I have information that's relevant.

or be both imperative and exclamatory:

> Slow down!

And many imperative sentences, especially those that make requests, are at least implicitly interrogative even though they don't end with a question mark:

> Please forward this message. (Will you please forward this message?)

Sometimes the same basic sense can be expressed in all four ways:

> I need your help.
> Will you help me?
> Help me with this.
> Help!

Nevertheless, you're seldom in doubt about the purpose of sentences you hear or read, and you're seldom, if ever, in doubt about the purpose or purposes of any sentence you speak or write. Your awareness of the conventions guides you: you know almost instinctively how to frame a sentence to make it do what you want.

But a more conscious grasp of the way sentences work will help you frame them even more effectively. It will help you when you're in doubt. And it will help you not only to avoid weaknesses and errors but also to revise and correct them when they do occur.

Since most sentences in formal writing are declarative, their patterns are the ones you need to understand first. Most of the rest of this chapter, then, deals with the basic elements and patterns of declarative sentences.

## 1.1 Subject and Predicate, Noun and Verb

A standard declarative sentence consists of two parts: a subject and a predicate. The subject is what acts or is talked about; the predicate is what the subject does or what is said about it. For example:

| subject | predicate |
|---------|-----------|
| Grass | grows. |
| Birds | fly. |
| I | disagree. |

The essential element of the subject part of a sentence is a noun (*Grass, Birds*) or a pronoun (*I*) (see sections 2 and 3); the essential element of the predicate part of a sentence is a verb (*grows, fly, disagree*) (see section 6).

## 1.2 Articles and Other Modifiers

Few sentences, however, consist of only a one-word subject and a one-word predicate. Frequently, for example, nouns are preceded by articles (*a, an, the*) (see 8.3):

| subject | predicate |
|---------|-----------|
| *The* child | toddled. |

And both subject and predicate often include modifiers, words that change or limit the meaning of nouns and verbs. Nouns are modified by adjectives (see section 8):

| subject | predicate |
|---------|-----------|
| The *young* child | toddled. |
| A *caged* bird | will sing. |

Verbs are modified by adverbs (see section 9):

| subject | predicate |
|---------|-----------|
| The young child | toddled *triumphantly*. |
| They | flew *south*. |

## 1.3–1.11 Basic Sentence Patterns

Such single-word modifiers as those in the example above account for only part of the richness of many sentences, which may feature impressive arrays of modifying phrases and clauses (see, for example, the sentences discussed in section 15). Yet complicated as they may seem, almost all English sentences use only a few basic patterns, or combinations of them. If you can recognize and understand these few simple patterns, you are well on your way to being able to analyze any sentence you write—or read.

### 1.3 Sentence Pattern 1

This is the pattern you've already looked at and imitated. The subject, consisting of a noun (with its modifiers) or a pronoun, is followed by the predicate, consisting of a verb (with its modifiers):

| subject | predicate |
|---------|-----------|
| The Cheshire cat | smiled mysteriously. |
| Birds | fly. |
| These large, ungainly birds | can fly quite gracefully. |
| They | soar majestically. |

## 1.4 Sentence Pattern 2A

subject + verb + direct object

In this pattern we expand the basic sentence core by adding a direct object to the predicate. A direct object, like a subject, must be either a noun or a pronoun, and the verb must be transitive—that is, it must be able to take a direct object (see 6.1):

| subject | predicate | |
| --- | --- | --- |
| noun or pronoun | transitive verb | direct object |
| I | paint | urban landscapes. |
| Sandra | enjoys | opera. |
| It | intrigues | him. |
| Pierre | is reading | scripts. |
| Impatient journalists | pursue | tight-lipped celebrities. |

In this pattern the subject acts, the verb indicates the action, and the direct object is the product (*landscapes*) or the receiver (*opera*, *celebrities*) of the action. Note that direct objects can, like subject-nouns, be modified by adjectives (*urban*, *tight-lipped*).

## 1.5 Sentence Pattern 2B (Passive Voice)

subject (receiver of the action) + passive voice verb (+ 'by' phrase: agent/performer of the action)

In this pattern the order of the main elements of Pattern 2A is reversed. That is, the former direct object becomes the subject, and the former subject moves to the end of the sentence, after the preposition *by* (see section 11). The verb stays in the middle but changes to the passive voice—a form of the verb *be* followed by a past participle (see 10.4). Use the passive voice strategically—that is, when you want to emphasize the receiver rather than the performer of an action. Make your choice knowing that overuse of the passive can sometimes make writing wordy and unclear. Consider a crime scenario in which a detective might say, using Pattern 2A,

Poison killed him. (active voice)

But in the circumstances it would be more natural to say

He was killed by poison. (passive voice)

Similarly, you can write some of the sentences under Pattern 2A according to Pattern 2B:

| subject | predicate | |
|---|---|---|
| noun or pronoun | verb | prepositional phrase |
| Urban landscapes | are painted | by me. |
| Scripts | are read | by Pierre. |
| Tight-lipped celebrities | are pursued | by impatient journalists. |

But you can see that such alternatives would be preferable only in unusual circumstances, for example if you wanted special emphasis on *urban landscapes* or *scripts* or *tight-lipped celebrities*. Note that in this pattern the *by*-phrase is often omitted as unnecessary or unknown:

He has been poisoned (by someone).

See also 6.15–6.16 and 18.6.

## 1.6 Sentence Pattern 3

subject + verb + indirect object + direct object

A sentence with a direct object sometimes also includes an indirect object, a noun or pronoun identifying *to* or *for* whom or what the action of the verb is carried out. The indirect object comes before the direct object:

| subject | predicate | | |
|---|---|---|---|
| noun or pronoun | transitive verb | indirect object | direct object |
| He | sent | his employer | an email message. |
| Grace | lent | Ari | her lecture notes. |
| Jason | offered | his guests | sushi. |

Note that you can usually vary this pattern, and still say essentially the same thing, by changing the indirect object to a prepositional phrase that comes after the direct object:

| subject | predicate | | |
|---|---|---|---|
| noun or verb | transitive verb | direct object | prepositional phrase |
| He | sent | an email message | to his employer. |
| Jason | offered | sushi | to his guests. |

## 1.7 Sentence Pattern 4A

**subject + linking verb + subjective complement (predicate adjective)**

Some verbs—called linking verbs (see 6.1)—require something other than an object to complete the idea, something called a complement. And since the complement is linked to the subject, it is sometimes called a subjective complement. The principal linking verb is *be* in its various forms (see 6.6). In Pattern 4A, the verb links the subject with an adjectival modifier in the predicate part of the sentence; the modifier is therefore called a predicate adjective:

| subject | predicate | |
|---|---|---|
| noun or pronoun | linking verb | subjective complement (predicate adjective) |
| She | is | curious. |
| Computers | have become | indispensable. |
| Samosas | taste | spicy. |

## 1.8 Sentence Pattern 4B

**subject + linking verb + subjective complement (predicate noun)**

In this pattern, a verb links the subject with a noun or pronoun acting as a subjective complement and called a predicate noun:

| subject | predicate | |
|---|---|---|
| noun or pronoun | linking verb | subjective complement (predicate noun) |
| This | is | it. |
| Lynn Coady | is | a talented writer. |
| Raw vegetables | make | good snacks. |

## 1.9 Sentence Pattern 5A

subject + verb + direct object + objective complement (adjective)

Such verbs as *appoint, believe, call, consider, declare, designate, elect, find, judge, make, name, nominate, select,* and *think* are sometimes followed by a direct object and an objective complement—a complement describing the object rather than the subject. In Pattern 5A, as in Pattern 4A, the complement is an adjective:

| subject | predicate | | |
|---|---|---|---|
| noun or pronoun | transitive verb | direct object | objective complement (adjective) |
| The committee | considered | the proposal | unworkable. |
| The jury | found | them | guilty as charged. |
| They | made | themselves | comfortable. |

## 1.10 Sentence Pattern 5B

subject + verb + direct object + objective complement (noun)

In this variation, the objective complement that completes the meaning of the direct object is a noun:

| subject | predicate | | |
|---|---|---|---|
| noun or pronoun | transitive verb | direct object | objective complement (noun) |
| The party | named | her | interim leader. |
| The critic | declared | the artist | a failure. |
| We | judged | the party | a success. |

## 1.11 Sentence Pattern 6 (Expletive)

*there* or *it* + linking verb (+ complement) + subject

This final pattern is, like the passive voice in Pattern 2B, something that you should use judiciously: the expletive pattern. In such sentences the word *There* or *It* appears at the beginning, in the place usually occupied by the subject; then comes a linking verb, usually a form of the verb *be*; and then comes the subject. When used strategically, *There* and *It* enable you to make certain kinds of statements in a more natural way or with a different emphasis than you could otherwise. For example, instead of having to say

| subject | predicate |
| --- | --- |
| That life begins at forty | may be true. |
| No solutions | existed. |
| No plumbing | was in the cabin. |

you can, using Pattern 6, say

| expletive | linking verb | complement | subject |
| --- | --- | --- | --- |
| It | may be | true | that life begins at forty. |
| There | were | | no solutions. |
| There | was | | no plumbing in the cabin. |

Here are some further examples of Pattern 6:

> There were several protesters waiting to heckle the premier.
>
> It is easy to follow this recipe.
>
> It is challenging to study Sanskrit.
>
> There wasn't a cloud in the sky.

See also 7.5, 18.6, and 60.1.

## 1.12 Other Elements: Structure Words

Most declarative sentences use one or more of the above patterns. And the elements in those patterns—subjects, verbs, modifiers, objects, and complements—make up the substance of all sentences.

Many sentences also include words like *and, but, for, of, under, with*. Such words are important because they connect other elements in various ways that establish meaningful relations between them. Such words are sometimes called structure words or function words; most of them belong to two other classes of words, or parts of speech, conjunctions (see section 12) and prepositions (see section 11). All of these elements are discussed and illustrated at greater length in chapters II and III.

# 1.13–1.18 Clauses and Phrases

Before you go on to chapter II, you need to understand the differences between clauses and phrases and how they work in sentences. Clauses and phrases are groups of words that function as grammatical units or elements within sentences but that—except for independent clauses—cannot stand alone as sentences.

### 1.13 Independent (Main) Clauses

A clause is a group of words containing both a subject and a predicate. If it is an independent clause, it can, as the term indicates, stand by itself as a sentence. Each of the sample sentences in the preceding sections is an independent clause, since each contains the minimum requirement: a noun or pronoun as subject and a verb functioning in the predicate; each is a simple sentence (see 1.25).

But an independent clause can also function as only part of a sentence. For example, if you start with two separate independent clauses—that is, two simple sentences:

> The exam ended.

> The students submitted their papers.

you can combine them to form a compound sentence (see 1.25):

> The exam ended; the students submitted their papers.

> The exam ended, and the students submitted their papers.

> The exam ended; therefore the students submitted their papers.

Each of the two halves of these sentences is an independent clause; each could stand alone as a sentence.

### 1.14 Subordinate (Dependent) Clauses

A subordinate clause, unlike an independent clause, usually cannot stand by itself. Even though, as a clause, it contains a subject and a predicate, it is by definition subordinate, depending on an independent clause for its meaning. It therefore must be treated as only part of a sentence, as in the following examples (the subordinate clauses are in italics); these are called complex sentences (see 1.25):

*When the exam ended*, the students submitted their papers.

The students submitted their papers *as the exam ended*.

The students submitted the papers *that they had written during the exam*.

The exam ended, *which meant that the students had to submit their papers*.

Note that subordinate clauses often begin with such words as *when*, *as*, *that*, and *which*, called subordinators, which often clearly signal the presence of a subordinate clause as opposed to an independent clause (see 12.3).

(Subordinate clauses can be used separately, for example in dialogue or as answers to questions, where the context is clear: Why did the students submit their papers? *Because the exam had ended.* Except in such circumstances, a subordinate clause should not stand by itself as if it were a sentence. See 1.23 and 1.24.)

## 1.15 Functions of Subordinate Clauses

Like a phrase (see 1.16), a subordinate clause functions as a grammatical unit in its sentence. That is, a subordinate clause can occupy several of the slots in the sentence patterns illustrated just above. For example, a noun clause can serve as the subject of a sentence:

*That free speech matters* is evident. (Pattern 4A)

as a direct object:

Azin knows *what she is doing.* (Pattern 2A)

or as a predicate noun:

The question is *what we should do next.* (Pattern 4B)

Adjectival clauses (also called relative clauses; see 3.4) modify nouns or pronouns, such as a direct object:

The reporter questioned the police officer *who had found the missing child.* (Pattern 2A) or a subject:

The project *that I am working on* is proceeding smoothly. (Pattern 1)

Adverbial clauses usually modify main verbs:

We left *because we were utterly bored*. (Pattern 1)

## 1.16 Phrases

A phrase is a group of words lacking a subject and/or predicate but functioning as a grammatical unit in a sentence. For example, a verb phrase (see 6.5) acts as the verb in this Pattern 1 sentence:

Most of the wedding guests *will be arriving* in the morning.

A prepositional phrase (see section 11) can be an adjectival modifier:

Most *of the wedding guests* will be arriving in the morning.

or an adverbial modifier:

Most of the wedding guests will be arriving *in the morning*.

The words *Most of the wedding guests* constitute a noun phrase functioning as the subject of the sentence. Any noun or pronoun along with its modifiers—so long as the group doesn't contain a subject–predicate combination—can be thought of as a noun phrase. Similarly, a gerund phrase (see 10.6) can function as a subject:

*Bungee jumping* can be risky. (Pattern 4A)

or as a direct object:

She tried *bungee jumping*. (Pattern 2A)

A participial phrase—always adjectival (see 10.4)—can modify a subject:

*Trusting her instincts*, Jane gave the candidate her support. (Pattern 3)

or a direct object:

I am reading an article *discussing human cloning*. (Pattern 2A)

An infinitive phrase (see l0.1) can function as a direct object (noun):

> This organization wants *to reduce poverty*. (Pattern 2A)

or as a subject (noun):

> It may be impossible *to eradicate poverty*. (Pattern 6)

It can also function as an adjective, for example one modifying the subject:

> Their desire *to eradicate poverty* is idealistic. (Pattern 4A)

or it can function as an adverb, for example one modifying the verb:

> They arranged the agenda *to highlight the literacy campaign*. (Pattern 2A)

Adverbial infinitive phrases can also act as sentence modifiers (see 9.1 and 9.4 [Sentence modifiers]), modifying not the verb or any other single word but rather all the rest of the sentence:

> *To be honest*, the meeting ended shortly after you left.

> *To tell the truth*, the meeting ended shortly after you left.

## 1.17 Appositives

Two other kinds of phrases you should be familiar with are the appositive and the absolute.

An appositive is a word or group of words that renames or restates, in other terms, the meaning of a neighbouring word. For example, if you start with two simple sentences,

> Marc is our lawyer. He looks after our business dealings.

you can turn the first into an appositive by reducing it and combining it with the second:

> Marc, *our lawyer*, looks after our business dealings.

The noun phrase *our lawyer* is here said to be in apposition to *Marc*.

Most appositives are nouns or noun phrases that redefine, usually in more specific terms, the nouns they follow. But occasionally an appositive precedes the other noun:

> *A skilful lawyer*, Marc looks after our business dealings.

And occasionally another part of speech can function as an appositive, for example a participial (adjectival) phrase:

> Searching frantically, *tossing books and papers everywhere*, they failed to find the missing document.

or a verb phrase:

> Document *(provide details of your sources for)* this argument.

An appositive can also be a single word, often a name:

> Our lawyer, *Marc*, looks after our business dealings.

And, rarely, even a subordinate clause can function as an appositive:

> How she travelled—*whether she journeyed alone or not*—remains a mystery.

Note that an appositive is grammatically equivalent to the term it defines and could replace it in the sentence:

> Our lawyer looks after our business dealings.

> A skilful lawyer looks after our business dealings.

> Marc looks after our business dealings.

> Tossing books and papers everywhere, they failed to find the missing document.

> Provide details of your sources for this argument.

> Whether she journeyed alone or not remains a mystery.

(For the punctuation of appositives, see 37.2 and 44.7.)

## 1.18 Absolute Phrases

An absolute phrase has no direct grammatical link with what it modifies; it depends simply on juxtaposition, in effect modifying the rest of the sentence by hovering over it like an umbrella. Most absolute phrases amount to a sentence with the verb changed to a participle (see 10.4). Instead of using two sentences,

> The intermission had ended. The last act finally began.

you can reduce the first to an absolute phrase modifying the second:

> *The intermission having ended*, the last act finally began.

If the original verb is a form of *be*, the participle can often be omitted:

> *The thunderstorm (being) over*, the tennis match resumed.

> In this experiment, careful measurement is a must, *the results (being) dependent on this kind of due attention.*

Sometimes, especially with certain common expressions, the participle isn't preceded by a noun:

> There were a few rough spots, but *generally speaking* the rehearsal was a success.

> *Judging by the census*, we have become a multicultural nation.

And sometimes infinitive phrases (see 1.16 and 10.1) function as absolutes:

> *To say the least*, the campaign was not a success.

You can also think of many absolutes as *with* phrases from which the preposition has been dropped:

> *(With) the thunderstorm over*, the tennis match resumed.

> Careful measurement is a must, *(with) the results dependent on this kind of due attention.*

And you can think of most absolute phrases as functioning much like an adverb modifying the rest of the sentence (see 9.1 and 9.4 [Sentence modifiers]):

> *All things considered*, it was a fair exam. (absolute phrase)

> *Unfortunately*, I hadn't studied hard enough. (adverb)

See also 10.9.

## 1.19 Order of Elements in Declarative Sentences

Even if you didn't know the names of some of the bits and pieces, chances are that the samples presented earlier in this section to illustrate the basic sentence patterns felt natural to you; they're the familiar kinds of sentences you use every day without even thinking about their structure. Note that the natural order of the elements in almost all the patterns is the same:

subject—verb
subject—transitive verb—object(s)—(objective complement)
subject—linking verb—subjective complement

The only exception is Pattern 6, the expletive, in which the subject follows the verb (see 1.11).

This conventional order of "subject—verb—object or complement" has proven itself the most direct and forceful pattern of expression:

War is hell.

Humpty Dumpty had a great fall.

We are such stuff as dreams are made on.

We shall defend every village, every town, and every city.

But this order can be altered to create special stylistic effects or special emphasis, and to introduce pleasing variations:

| direct object | subject | transitive verb |
| --- | --- | --- |
| Their generosity | I | have never doubted for a moment. |

| subjective complement | linking verb | subject |
| --- | --- | --- |
| Long | was | the introduction to this otherwise short speech. |

Such inversions aren't wrong, for conventions (or rules) are made to be broken as well as followed; but their very unconventionality demands that they be used judiciously. They are most at home in poetry or highly oratorical prose:

> Thirty days hath September . . .

> And now abideth faith, hope, and charity, these three; but the greatest of these is charity.

> Never in the field of human conflict was so much owed by so many to so few.

Elsewhere such variations are rare, since any unusual pattern almost automatically calls attention to itself, something seldom appropriate in expository prose. But used occasionally, and appropriately, they can be highly effective.

## 1.20 Order of Elements in Interrogative Sentences

The conventional order used in interrogative sentences usually differs from that used in declarative sentences. It is, of course, possible to use the declarative order for a question—for example in speaking, when one can use stress and end with the rising or falling intonation that usually indicates a question:

> They're getting married tomorrow?

thereby conveying a meaning something like:

> Do you mean to tell me that they are actually getting married so soon rather than waiting and planning a more formal ceremony? How surprising!

Unless you're recording or imitating dialogue, you won't use this technique too often in your writing.

. Usually, an interrogative sentence, besides ending with the conventional question mark, will take one of the following patterns. If the verb is a single-word form of *be*, it precedes the subject:

| verb | subject | subjective complement |
|------|---------|----------------------|
| Is | Nunavut | a province? |

With all other single-word verbs, it is necessary to supply a form of the auxiliary verb *do* before the subject; the main part of the verb then follows the subject in the normal way:

| auxiliary verb | subject | main verb | |
| --- | --- | --- | --- |
| Does | Nunavut | have | provincial status? |

If the verb is already a verb phrase, the first auxiliary comes before the subject:

| auxiliary verb | subject | second auxiliary | main verb |
| --- | --- | --- | --- |
| Are | you | | daydreaming? |
| Will | Max | speak | first? |
| Have | you | been | meditating? |

If the question includes a negative, the *not* goes before or after the subject, depending on whether one uses the less formal, contracted form:

> Aren't you going?

> Are you not going?

With questions using expletives (Pattern 6; see 1.11), the expletive and the verb are reversed:

> Were there many people at the orientation?

> Was it easy to follow her argument?

With so-called tag questions, a statement is followed by a verb–pronoun question; note also that a *not* appears in one or the other of the two parts:

> Maria has been hiking, hasn't she?

> Maria hasn't been hiking, has she?

All the above questions invite a yes or no answer, perhaps extended by a short clause made up of the appropriate pronoun (or expletive) and auxiliary, such as:

Yes, she was.      Yes I am.        No, I haven't.

Yes, there were.   No, it wasn't.   No, he hasn't.    No, he has not.

Note that the negative answers include a *not* in the clause.

The only other common form of question begins with a question word, one of the interrogative adverbs or pronouns; these invite answers beyond a mere yes or no. When a question begins with an interrogative adverb (see 9.1), a form of *do* or another already present auxiliary comes before the subject:

Why *did* he say that?

Where (When) *are* you going?

If an interrogative pronoun (see 3.3) functions as subject, the sentence retains standard declarative word order:

Who will speak first?

If the opening pronoun is the object of the verb or a preposition, it is followed by the added auxiliary *do* or the first part of a verb phrase, the subject, and the rest of the verb, just as in the yes or no pattern:

Whom did you invite?

To whom did you address the invitation?

A similar reversal occurs when an interrogative pronoun functions as a possessive or other adjective (see 8.1):

Whose (Which, What) political platform do you favour?

To what (which, whose) problems will the speaker address herself?

See also 11.2, on the placement of prepositions in questions.

## 1.21 The Structure of Imperative Sentences

Although it is possible, especially with emphatic commands, to use the full structure of a declarative sentence:

| subject | predicate |
| --- | --- |
| You | take that back! |
| You two in the corner | please join the rest of the group. |

the conventional form of imperative sentences uses only the predicate, omitting the subject (an understood *you*):

> Come into the garden, Maud. (*Maud* is not the subject, but a noun of address; see 2.2.)

> Stretch before you run.

> Close the door.

> Edit carefully.

> Enjoy.

Sometimes, especially in dialogue or informal contexts, even the verb can be omitted; a complement alone does the job:

> Careful. Easy, now. Steady.

You may think you'll have little use for imperative sentences in your writing. But if you ever want to write a set of instructions, you'll need to use a great many of them. And they can provide useful variety in other contexts as well, just as questions can. Declarative sentences are unquestionably the mainstay of written expression, but interrogative and imperative sentences are also useful. So consider using them.

# 1.22–1.24 Major Sentences, Minor Sentences, and Fragments

Sentences—that is, acceptable patterns of expression—are of two kinds, which we call major and minor. Though this and similar books deal almost exclusively with major sentences, and though you generally won't have much use for minor sentences, you should understand what minor sentences are so that you can use them occasionally for emphasis or other rhetorical effects, or when you are writing a piece of dialogue. And you need to be able to distinguish between the minor sentence, which is acceptable in some formal writing, and the fragmentary expression, which is not.

## 1.22 Major Sentences

A major sentence is a grammatically independent group of words containing at least two essential structural elements: a subject and a finite verb (see 1.1 and 6.2). Major sentences constitute 99 per cent or more of most formal writing. They are the sentences whose basic patterns are illustrated in sections 1.3–1.11.

## 1.23 Minor Sentences

A minor sentence is an acceptable pattern of expression that nevertheless lacks either a subject or a finite verb, or both. But it is easy to supply the missing element or elements from context; for whereas major sentences can usually stand by themselves, most minor sentences need a context of one or more nearby sentences in order to make sense—most obviously, for example, as answers to questions. The minor sentence, however, like the major, is grammatically independent.

Minor sentences are usually one of the following four kinds:

1.  Exclamations

    Oh!      Well, I never!      Heavens!
    Wow!    Incredible!

2.  Questions or responses to questions

    When? Tomorrow.      How many? Seven.
    Why? What for?        How come? Really?
    Yes. No.               Perhaps. Certainly.

3.  Common proverbial or idiomatic expressions

    Easy come, easy go.      Now or never.
    Better late than never.    Down the hatch.

4.  Minor sentences used for rhetorical or stylistic effect: These are more common in narrative and descriptive writing, but they can be effective in other contexts as well. Here is how Charles Dickens begins *Bleak House*:

    London. Michaelmas Term lately over, and the Lord Chancellor sitting in Lincoln's Inn Hall. Implacable November weather. As

> much mud in the streets, as if the waters had but newly retired from the face of the earth, and it would not be wonderful to meet a Megalosaurus, forty feet long or so, waddling like an elephantine lizard up Holborn Hill.

And so on, for three long paragraphs: not a major sentence in sight.

Clearly the beginning of a piece of writing is a good place to try the effects of a minor sentence or two. A writer might begin a work in these ways:

> Time, time, time. It is our constant companion and our greatest nemesis.

> One of the best times of the year in Vancouver is the spring. You know, those weeks in early April brimming with sunshine and new growth. Gardens and parks filled with crocuses, cherry trees in bloom, newborn birds in their nests.

## 1.24 Fragments

Don't mistake an unacceptable fragment for an acceptable minor sentence:

> ✘  I didn't see the film. *Because I felt that it would be too violent for my taste.*

The *Because*-clause is a fragment. The period after *film* should be deleted so that the subordinate clause can take its rightful place in the sentence. (But note that this *Because*-clause, like many other fragments, would be acceptable as an answer to a question just before it.)

> ✘  It was a hilarious moment. *One that I'll never forget.*

The clause beginning with *One* should be linked to the preceding independent clause with a comma, not separated from it by a period. It can then take its rightful place as a noun clause in apposition to *moment*.

> ✘  He gave me half his sandwich. *Being of a generous nature.*

The participial phrase beginning with *Being* is not a separate sentence but an adjective modifying *He*; it should be introduced by a comma, or even moved to the beginning of the sentence:

> Being of a generous nature, he gave me half his sandwich.

Note that fragments tend to occur after the independent clauses that they should be attached to.

## 1.25 Kinds of Major Sentences

Sentences can be classified grammatically as simple, compound, complex, and compound-complex.

### Simple sentences

A simple sentence has one subject and one finite verb, and therefore contains only one clause, an independent clause:

> s   v
> Denis works.

>     s   v
> The boat leaks.

>    |   s   |   v
> The new museum opened on the weekend.

The subject or the verb, or both, can be compound—that is, consist of more than one part—but the sentence containing them will still be simple:

> *Claude and Kim* left early. (compound subject)

> She *watched and waited.* (compound verb)

> *The sergeant and his men moved* down the hill *and crossed* the river.
> (compound subject)    (compound verb)

### Compound sentences

A compound sentence consists of two or more simple sentences—that is, independent clauses—linked by coordinating conjunctions (see 12.1), by punctuation, or by both:

>    |   s   |   v        s   v
> The conductor's baton fell, and the concert ended.

>    s   v                          s   v
> The clouds massed thickly against the hills; soon the rain fell in torrents.

> s   v                  s   v
> We wanted to hear jazz, but they played bluegrass instead.

I               s            I v              v
Gabriel's patience and persistence paid off; he not only won the prize
                    v
but also earned his competitors' respect.

      s    v           s    v              s    v
The day was warm, the breeze was mild, and everyone had a good time.

## Complex sentences

A complex sentence consists of one independent clause and one or more subordinate clauses; in the following examples, the subordinate clauses are italicized:

We believe *that we have some original plans for the campaign.* (noun clause as direct object)

The strike was averted *before we reported for picket duty.* (adverbial clause modifying *was averted*)

This course is the one *that calls for the most field research.* (adjectival clause modifying *one*)

Marco Polo, *who left his native Venice as a teenager*, returned home after twenty-five years of adventure. (adjectival clause modifying *Marco Polo*)

*When the film ended*, the audience burst into applause *which lasted several minutes*. (adverbial clause modifying *burst*, adjectival clause modifying *applause*)

*Although it seems premature*, the government is proceeding with third reading of the legislation. (adverbial clause of concession, in effect modifying the rest of the sentence)

Note that when the meaning is clear, the conjunction *that* introducing a noun clause, or the relative pronouns *that* and *which*, can be omitted:

He claimed he was innocent.

. . . the suitcase he had brought with him.

## Compound-complex sentences

A compound-complex sentence consists of two or more independent clauses and one or more subordinate clauses:

> Because the architect knows that the preservation of heritage buildings is vital, she is consulting widely, but as delays have developed, she has grown impatient, and therefore she is thinking of pulling out of a project that represents everything important to her.

We can analyze this example as follows:

Because the architect knows (adverbial clause)

that the preservation of heritage buildings is vital (noun clause)

she is consulting widely (independent clause)

but (coordinating conjunction)

as delays have developed (adverbial clause)

she has grown impatient (independent clause)

and (coordinating conjunction)

therefore (conjunctive adverb)

she is thinking of pulling out of a project (independent clause)

that represents everything important to her. (adjective clause)

# CHAPTER II
# Parts of Speech

# INTRODUCTION

## The Parts of Speech and How They Work in Sentences

As you saw in chapter I, word order helps determine whether a sentence is asking a question or making a statement. But word order is important in another and even more basic way. The order of elements in Pattern 2A (see 1.4), for example—subject, verb, direct object—determines meaning:

Editors need writers.

Clear enough. We know, from standard English word order, that *Editors* is the subject, *need* the verb, and *writers* the direct object. Reversing the order reverses the meaning:

Writers need editors.

Now we know that *Writers* are doing the *needing* and that *editors* are the objects of the need. If you know a language like German or Latin, you know how different—and in some ways more difficult—they can be; for in such languages it is the form of the words, rather than their position, that determines meaning. For example the following sentence would, in English, not only sound awkward but also be ambiguous:

Editors writers need.

But the same three words in Latin would be clear because the forms of the two nouns would show which was subject and which was object.

The change in a word's form is called inflection. Some words in modern English must be inflected in order for sentences to communicate clearly. If, for example, you want the noun *boy* to denote more than one young male, you change it—inflect it—by adding an *s* to make it plural: *boys*. If you want to use the verb *see* to denote the act of seeing in some past time, you change its form so that you can say, for example, *I saw* or *I have seen* or *I was seeing*.

English words fall traditionally into eight categories called parts of speech. Five of these can be inflected in one or more ways:

- noun
- pronoun
- verb

- adjective
- adverb

The other three are not inflected:

- preposition
- conjunction

- interjection

For example the preposition *in* is always *in*; the conjunction *but* is always *but*. (The only exceptions occur when words are referred to as words, as in "There are too many *and*s in that sentence" and "I don't want to hear any *if*s, *and*s, or *but*s," or in informal or idiomatic usages such as "She knows all the *in*s and *out*s of the process," where such words function as nouns rather than as structure words, prepositions, and conjunctions.)

Note that the term *inflection* applies only to the change of a word's form within its part of speech. That is, when the noun *boy* is inflected to make it plural, the new form, *boys*, is still a noun; when the pronoun *they* is inflected to *them* or *theirs*, the new forms are still pronouns. (Again there is an exception: When you inflect a noun or pronoun for the possessive case before a noun—the *boy's* coat, *their* idea—you turn it into an adjective; some people, however, thinking of form rather than function, prefer to call these inflected forms "possessive nouns" and "possessive pronouns.")

Many words can be changed so that they function as different parts of speech. For example the noun *centre* can be made into the adjective *central*, or the noun *meaning* into the adjective *meaningful*, or the verb *vacate* into the noun *vacation*. Such changes, however, are not inflections but derivations; a word can be derived from a word of a different part of speech, often by the addition of one or more suffixes: *trust, trustful, trustfully, trustfulness*. And many words, even without being changed, can serve as more than one part of speech; consider for example the word *cool*:

She is cool under pressure. (adjective)

Relations between the two may cool now that they're apart. (verb)

He knows how to keep his cool in a crisis. (noun)

The word *word* itself can be a noun ("Use this *word* correctly"), a verb ("How will you *word* your reply?"), or an adjective ("*Word* games are fun"). The word *right* can be a noun (his legal *right*), an adjective (the *right* stuff), an adverb (turn *right*, do it *right*), or a verb (*right* an overturned canoe). Or consider the versatility of the common word *over*:

At least we have a roof over our heads. (preposition)

The game is over. (adjective)

Write that page over. (adverb)

"Roger. Message received. Over." (interjection)

The form of a word, then, doesn't always determine its function. What part of speech a word is depends on its function in a particular sentence.

The rest of this chapter discusses the eight parts of speech—their inflections (if any) and other grammatical properties; their subcategories; how they work with other words in sentences; and some of their important derivatives (verbals)—and calls attention to some of their potential trouble spots, such as agreement and a verb's tenses.

# 2. NOUNS

A noun (from the Latin *nomen*, meaning "name") is a word that names or stands for a person, place, thing, class, concept, quality, or action: *woman, character, city, country, citizen, boat, garden, machine, silence, vegetable, road, freedom, beauty, river, spring, investigation.* Proper nouns are names of specific persons, places, or things and begin with a capital letter: *Dorothy, Rumpelstiltskin, Winnipeg, England,* the *Titanic.* All the others, called common nouns, are capitalized only if they begin a sentence:

Freedom is a precious commodity.

Spring is my favourite season.

or form part of a proper noun:

> Spring Garden Road
>
> the Peace Arch
>
> the Ottawa River

or are personified or otherwise emphasized, for example in poetry:

> Our noisy years seem moments in the being
> Of the eternal Silence . . .
>
> > (Wordsworth)

(See section 47, on capitalization.)

One can also classify nouns as either concrete, for names of tangible objects (*doctor, elephant, utensil, book, barn*), or abstract, for names of intangible things or ideas (*freedom, honour, happiness, history*). (See section 55.)

Collective nouns are names of collections or groups often considered as units: *army, committee, family, herd, flock.* (See 4.5 and 7.6.)

## 2.1 Inflection of Nouns

Nouns can be inflected in only two simple ways: for number and for possessive case.

### For number

Most common concrete nouns that stand for countable things are either singular (naming a single thing) or plural (naming more than one thing). And though proper nouns supposedly name specific persons, places, or things, they too can sometimes logically be inflected for the plural; for example:

> There are many John Smiths in the telephone book.
>
> There are several Londons. (e.g. the one in England and the one in Ontario)
>
> Since 1948 there have been two Koreas.

Most singular nouns are inflected to indicate the plural by the addition of *s* or *es*: *boy, boys; box, boxes.* But some are made plural in other ways: *child, children; stimulus, stimuli.* (For more on the formation of plurals, see 51.20.)

Some concrete nouns, however, called mass nouns, name materials that are measured, weighed, or divided, rather than items that are counted—for example *gold, oxygen, rice, sand,* and *pasta.* As uncountable or noncountable nouns, these are not inflected for the plural. Also uncountable are abstract nouns and nouns that stand for ideas, activities, and states of mind or being; for example, *honour, journalism, skiing, happiness.*

Some nouns, however, can be either countable or uncountable, depending on context. For example:

The butcher sells *meat.* (uncountable)

The delicatessen offers several delicious smoked *meats.* (countable, equivalent to *kinds of smoked meat)*

They insisted on telling the truth as a matter of *honour.* (uncountable)

Many *honours* were heaped upon the returning hero. (countable, since an *honour* here is not an abstract quality but designates a specific thing like a medal, a citation, or at least one or another sort of verbal recognition)

See also 4.3, 7.7, and 8.3 #6.

### For possessive case

As we saw earlier, in English, whether a noun is a subject (subjective case) or an object (objective case) is shown by word order rather than by inflection. But nouns are inflected for possessive case. By adding an apostrophe and an *s,* or sometimes only an apostrophe, you inflect a noun so that it shows possession or ownership:

my mother's job

the children's toys

the workers' pensions

See also 51.23.

## 2.2 Grammatical Function of Nouns

Nouns function in sentences in the following ways:

- as the subject of a verb (see 1.1):

  *Lawyers* work hard.

- as the direct object of a verb (see 1.4):

  Our team won the *championship*.

- as the indirect object of a verb (see 1.6):

  We awarded *Beverly* the prize.

- as the object of a preposition (see 1.6 and section 11):

  We gave the prize to *Beverly*. It was a book about *mountain-climbing*.

- as a predicate noun after a linking verb (see 1.8):

  Genevieve is an *accountant*.

- as an objective complement (see 1.10):

  The judges declared Beverly the *winner*.

- as an appositive to any other noun (see 1.17):

  Andre, the *chef*, stopped Roger, the *dishwasher*.

  We gave Beverly the prize, a *book* about mountain-climbing.

  My brother, *Masoud*, graduated last year.

Nouns in the possessive case function as adjectives (see 8.1):

  *Maria's* coat is expensive. (Which coat? Maria's.)

  I did a *day's* work. (How much work? A day's.)

or as predicate nouns, after a linking verb:

  The expensive-looking coat is *Maria's*.

Even without being inflected for possessive case, many nouns can also function as adjectives: the *school* paper, an *evening* gown, the *automobile* industry, the *dessert* course (see 60.7).

A noun (or pronoun) referring to someone being directly addressed, as in dialogue or in a letter, is called a noun of address. Such nouns, usually proper names, are not directly related to the syntax of the rest of the sentence and are set off with punctuation:

> *Yuki*, are you feeling well?

> Soon, *Steve*, you'll see what I mean.

# 3. PRONOUNS

A pronoun, as its name indicates, is a word that stands for (*pro*) or in place of a noun, or functions like a noun in a sentence. Most pronouns refer to nouns that come earlier, their antecedents (from Latin for "coming before"):

> Joshua offered an opinion, but he didn't feel confident about it.

Here, *Joshua* is the antecedent of the pronoun *he*, and *opinion* is the antecedent of the pronoun *it*. Occasionally an antecedent can come after the pronoun that refers to it, especially if the pronoun is in a subordinate clause and if the context is clear—that is, if the pronoun couldn't refer to some other noun (see also 5.4):

> Although he offered an opinion, Joshua didn't feel confident about it.

There are eight kinds of pronoun:

- personal
- impersonal
- interrogative
- relative
- demonstrative
- indefinite
- reflexive (or intensive)
- reciprocal

Generally, pronouns perform the same functions as nouns: they are most often subjects of verbs, direct and indirect objects, and objects of prepositions; some can also function as appositives and predicate nouns. Some pronouns are inflected much more than nouns, and some require particular care in their use.

The following sections discuss the different kinds of pronoun; their inflections; their grammatical functions in phrases, clauses, and sentences; and the special problems of case (see 3.5), agreement (see section 4), and reference (see section 5).

## 3.1 Personal Pronouns

Personal pronouns refer to specific persons or things. They are inflected in four ways:

**For person**
First-person pronouns (*I*, *we*, etc.) refer to the person or persons doing the speaking. Second-person pronouns (*you*, *yours*) refer to the person or persons being spoken to. Third-person pronouns (*he*, *she*, *it*, *they*, etc.) refer to the person(s) or thing(s) being spoken about.

**For number**
Singular pronouns (*I*, *she*, etc.) refer to individuals:

> I am writing. She is writing.

Plural pronouns (*we*, *they*, etc.) refer to groups:

> We are writing. They are writing.

(Note that the second-person pronoun *you* can be either singular or plural.)

**For gender (2nd- and 3rd-person pronouns)**
Masculine pronouns (*he*, *him*, *his*) refer to males. Feminine pronouns (*she*, *her*, *hers*) refer to females. The neuter pronoun (*it*) refers to ideas or things, and sometimes to animals. (Note that in the plural forms—*we*, *you*, *they*, etc.—there is no indication of gender.)

**For case (see also 3.5)**
Pronouns that function as subjects must be in the subjective case:

> I paint.

> She paints.

> They are painting.

Pronouns that function as objects must be in the objective case:

> The idea hit them. Give her the book. Give it to me.

Pronouns that indicate possession or ownership must be in the possessive case:

> That turtle is his. This turtle is mine. Where is yours?

(Note that pronouns in the possessive case—*yours, theirs, its, hers,* etc.—do not require an apostrophe before the *s* to indicate possession.)

The following chart shows all the inflections of personal pronouns:

|          |            | subject | object | possessive pronoun | possessive adjective |
|----------|------------|---------|--------|--------------------|----------------------|
| singular | 1st person | I       | me     | mine               | my                   |
|          | 2nd person | you     | you    | yours              | your                 |
|          | 3rd person | he      | him    | his                | his                  |
|          |            | she     | her    | hers               | her                  |
|          |            | it      | it     |                    | its                  |
| plural   | 1st person | we      | us     | ours               | our                  |
|          | 2nd person | you     | you    | yours              | your                 |
|          | 3rd person | they    | them   | theirs             | their                |

Possessive (or pronominal) adjectives always precede nouns (*My* car is in the shop); possessive pronouns may function as subjects, objects, and predicate nouns (Let's take *yours*).

Note that *you* and *it* are inflected only for possessive case, that *his* serves as both possessive pronoun and possessive adjective, and that *her* serves as both objective case and possessive adjective.

## 3.2 Impersonal Pronouns

Especially in relatively formal contexts, the impersonal pronoun *one,* meaning essentially "a person," serves in place of a first-, second-, or third-person pronoun:

> One must be careful when choosing course electives.

> One must keep one's priorities straight.

The pronoun *it* is also used as an impersonal pronoun in such sentences as the following; note that impersonal *it* is usually the subject of some form of *be* (see 6.6) and that it usually refers to time, distance, weather, and the like:

> It is getting late. It's almost four o'clock.
>
> It's warm. It feels warmer than it did yesterday.
>
> It was just one of those things.
>
> It is a mile and a half from here to the station.

## Proofreading Tip

### On Using the Impersonal Pronoun "It"

You may want to edit your work to avoid overuse of the impersonal pronoun "it." The sentences that are formed using this pattern are known as weak expletives and sometimes delay unnecessarily the true subject of the sentence. The last example could easily be revised to read *The station is a mile and a half from here.*

## 3.3 Interrogative Pronouns

Interrogative pronouns are question words used usually at or near the beginning of interrogative sentences (see 1.20). *Who* is inflected for objective and possessive case, *which* for possessive case only:

| subjective | objective | possessive |
|---|---|---|
| who | whom | whose |
| which | which | whose |
| what | what | |

*Who* refers to persons, *which* and *what* to things; *which* sometimes also refers to persons, as in *Which of you is going?* The compound forms *whoever* and *whatever*, and sometimes even *whichever* and *whomever*, can also function as interrogative pronouns. Here are some examples showing interrogative pronouns functioning in different ways:

- as a subject:

    Who said that?

    Which of these books is best?

    What is the baby's name?

- as the direct object of verb:

    Whom do you recommend for the job?

    What did you give Aunt Jane for her birthday?

- as the object of a preposition (see also section 11):

    To whom did you give the book?

    To what do I owe this honour?

- as an objective complement:

    What did you call me?

    You've named the baby what?

In front of a noun, an interrogative word functions as an interrogative adjective:

Whose book is this?

Which car shall we take?

See also 3.5 for more on *who* and *whom*.

## 3.4 Relative Pronouns

A relative pronoun usually introduces an adjective clause—called a relative clause—in which it functions as subject, object, or object of a preposition. The pronoun links, or relates, the clause to an antecedent in the same sentence, a noun or pronoun that the whole clause modifies.

The principal relative pronouns are *who*, *which*, and *that*. *Who* and *which* are inflected for case:

| subjective | objective | possessive |
| --- | --- | --- |
| who | whom | whose |
| which | which | whose |
| that | that | |

*Who* refers to persons (and sometimes to animals thought of as persons), *which* to things, and *that* to either persons or things. Consider some examples of how relative pronouns function:

> Margaret, who is leaving in the morning, will call us later tonight. (*who* as subject of verb *is*; clause modifies *Margaret*)

> Joel described the woman whom he had met at the party. (*whom* as direct object; clause modifies *woman*)

> At midnight Tanya began to revise her report, which was due in the morning. (*which* as subject of verb *was*; clause modifies *report*)

> She avoided working on the report that she was having trouble with. (*that* as object of preposition *with*; clause modifies *report*)

A relative clause is either restrictive and unpunctuated, or nonrestrictive and set off with punctuation. It is restrictive if it gives us information that is essential to identifying the antecedent (e.g. *whom he had met at the party*); it is nonrestrictive if the information it gives us is not essential to identifying the antecedent and could be left out of the sentence (e.g. *who is leaving in the morning*). (See also section 37.)

If the relative pronoun in a restrictive clause is the object of a verb or a preposition, it can usually be omitted:

> Joel described the woman [whom or that] he had met.

> She avoided working on the report [that or which] she was having trouble with.

But if the preposition is placed before the pronoun (e.g. *with which*), the pronoun cannot be omitted:

> She was working on the report with which she was having trouble.

When *whose* precedes and modifies a noun in a relative clause, it functions as what is called a relative adjective:

> His mother was the one whose advice he most valued.

And sometimes a relative adverb, often *when* or *where*, introduces a relative clause (see also 9.1):

> Here's an aerial photo of the town where I live. (The clause *where I live* modifies the noun *town*.)

> My parents told me about the time when I learned to walk. (The *when* clause modifies the noun *time*.)

Sometimes *what* and the *ever* compounds (*whatever, whoever, whomever, whichever*) are also considered relative pronouns, even though they introduce noun clauses (e.g. "Remember *what I said*." "Take *whichever one you want*."). *Who, whom*, and *which* may also introduce such noun clauses.

For more on *who* and *whom*, see 3.5. For more on adjective clauses, see section 8 and 15.1.

### 3.5 Case (See also 3.1 [For case].)

Choosing the correct case of personal, interrogative, and relative pronouns is sometimes difficult. The main problem is limited to deciding between subjective and objective case, in only a few kinds of sentences, and only in formal writing. In everyday speech and informal writing, things like "Who did you lend the book to?" and "It's me" and "That's her" upset few people. But in formal writing and strictly formal speech, you should use the correct forms: "To w*hom* did you lend the book?" "It is *she*." If you know how a pronoun is functioning grammatically, you will know which form to use. Here are some guidelines to help you with the kinds of sentences that sometimes cause problems:

**A pronoun functioning as the subject should be in the subjective case.** Whenever you use a pronoun as part of a compound subject (see 1.25), make sure it is in the subjective case. Someone who wouldn't say, "Me am going to the store," could slip and say something like, "Susan and me worked on the presentation" instead of the correct:

> Susan and I worked on the presentation.

If you're not sure, remove the other part of the subject; then you'll know which pronoun sounds right:

> [Susan and] I worked on the presentation.

But even a one-part subject can lead someone astray:

> ✘   Us citizens should stand up for our rights.
>
> We citizens should stand up for our rights.

The pronoun *We* is the subject; the word *citizens* is an appositive (see 1.17) further identifying it, as if saying, "We, the citizens, should . . .".

**A pronoun functioning as a direct or indirect object should be in the objective case.**

Again, errors most often result from the use of a two-part structure—here, a compound object. Someone who would not say, "The club asked I for my opinion," could slip and say, "They asked Ingrid and I to take part in the bookclub." When you use a pronoun as part of a compound object, make sure it's in the objective case. Again, test by removing the other part:

> They asked [Ingrid and] me to take part in the bookclub.

## Proofreading Tip

### On Hypercorrection of Pronouns

Don't slip into what is called "hypercorrection." Since many people say things like "Jake and me went camping," others—not understanding the grammar but wishing to seem correct—use the "and I" form even for an object, when it should be "and me." For example, you would say, "The new tent was for Jake and me," not "The new tent was for Jake and I."

**A pronoun functioning as the object of a preposition should be in the objective case.**

✘    This information is between you and I.

This information is between you and me.

Speakers and writers who have learned not to use *me* as part of a compound subject sometimes overcorrect in cases such as this and use *I*; but the objective *me* is correct in this instance, for it is the object of the preposition *between*.

**A pronoun functioning as a predicate noun (see 1.8 and 14.4) after a linking verb should be in the subjective case.**
In other words, if the pronoun follows the verb *be*, it takes the subjective form:

It is *they* who must decide, not *we*.

The swimmer who won the prize is *she*, over there by the pool.

It is *I* who will carry the greater burden.

If such usages sound stuffy and artificial to you—as they do to many people—find another way to phrase your sentences; for example:

They, not we, must decide.

The swimmer over by the pool is the one who won the prize.

First prize went to that girl, over there by the pool.

I will be the one carrying the greater burden.

Again, watch out for compound structures:

✘    The nominees are Yashmin and me.

The nominees are Yashmin and I.

**Pronouns following the conjunctions *as* and *than* in comparisons should be in the subjective case if they are functioning as subjects, even if their verbs are not expressed but left understood:**

Roberta is brighter than *they* [are].

> Aaron has learned less than *I* [have].

> Hiroshi is as tall as *I* [am].

If, however, the pronouns are functioning as objects, they should be in the objective case:

> *I* trust *her* more than [*I* trust] *him*.

See also section 61 (so . . . as).

**Use the appropriate case of the interrogative and relative pronouns *who* and *whom*, *whoever* and *whomever*.**
Although *who* is often used instead of *whom* in speech and informal writing, you should know how to use the two correctly when you want to write or speak more formally.

Use the subjective case for the subject of a verb in a question or a relative clause:

> *Who* is going?

> Dickens was a novelist *who* was extremely popular.

Use the objective case for the object of a verb or preposition:

> *Whom* do you prefer in that role?

> He is the candidate *whom* I most admire.

> She is the manager for *whom* the employees have the most respect.

If such usages with *whom* seem to you unnatural and stuffy, avoid them by rephrasing your sentence:

> She is the manager that the employees respect most.

In noun clauses, the case of the pronoun is determined by its function in its clause, not by other words:

> How can you tell *who won*?

> I'll give the prize to *whomever the judges declare the winner*.

See also 10.8 for the possessive case of pronouns with gerunds.

### 3.6 Demonstrative Pronouns

Demonstrative pronouns, which can be thought of as pointing to the nouns they refer to, are inflected for number:

| singular | plural |
| --- | --- |
| this | these |
| that | those |

*This* and *these* usually refer to something nearby or something just said or about to be said; *that* and *those* usually refer to something farther away or more remote in time or longer in duration; but there are no precise rules:

> Try some of this.
>
> The clerk was helpful; this was what pleased her the most.
>
> These are the main points I will cover in today's lecture.
>
> That looks appetizing.
>
> That was the story he told us the next morning.
>
> Those were his exact words.
>
> Those are the cities you should visit on your holiday.

## Proofreading Tip

### Avoiding Vagueness in Using Demonstrative Pronouns

Useful as demonstrative pronouns can be, however, employ them sparingly in writing, for they are often vague in their reference. Instead, consider this alternative: When followed by nouns, these words function as demonstrative adjectives, and then there's no risk of vagueness: *this* belief, *that* statement, *these* buildings, *those* arguments. See 5.3 and section 28.

These pronouns also often occur in prepositional phrases with *like* and *such as*:

> Someone who wears an orange shirt like that has an unusual fashion sense.

> I need more close friends like those.

> A cute house such as this will sell immediately.

## 3.7 Indefinite Pronouns

Indefinite pronouns refer to indefinite or unknown persons or things, or to indefinite or unknown quantities of persons or things. The only major issue with these words is whether they are singular or plural. Think of indefinite pronouns as falling into four groups:

Group 1: compounds ending with *body*, *one*, and *thing*. These words function like nouns—that is, they need no antecedents—and they are almost always considered singular:

| | | | |
|---|---|---|---|
| anybody | everybody | nobody | somebody |
| anyone | everyone | no one | someone |
| anything | everything | nothing | something |

Group 2: a few other indefinite pronouns that are almost always singular:

| | | | |
|---|---|---|---|
| another | each | either | much |
| neither | one | other | |

Group 3: a few that are always plural:

| | | | |
|---|---|---|---|
| both | few | many | several |

Group 4: a few that can be either singular or plural, depending on context and intended meaning:

| | | | |
|---|---|---|---|
| all | any | more | most |
| none | some | | |

For discussions of the important matter of grammatical agreement with indefinite pronouns, and examples of their use in sentences, see 4.3 and 7.4.

Only *one* and *other* can be inflected for number, by adding *s* to make them plural: *ones, others.* Several indefinite pronouns can be inflected for possessive case; unlike personal pronouns, they take *'s,* just as nouns do (or, with *others',* just an apostrophe):

| | | | |
|---|---|---|---|
| anybody's | anyone's | everybody's | everyone's |
| nobody's | no one's | somebody's | someone's |
| one's | other's | another's | others' |

The remaining indefinite pronouns must use *of* to show possession; for example:

That was the belief *of many* who were present.

When in the possessive case, indefinite pronouns function as adjectives. In addition, all the words in Groups 2, 3, and 4, except *none,* can also function as adjectives (see 8.1):

| | | |
|---|---|---|
| any boat | some people | few people |
| more money | each day | either direction |

The adjective expressing the meaning of *none* is *no:*

Send no attachments.

Sometimes the cardinal and ordinal numbers (*one, two, three,* etc., and *first, second, third,* etc.) are also classed as indefinite pronouns, for they often function similarly, both as pronouns and as adjectives:

How many ducks are on the pond? I see *several.* I see *seven.* I see *ten.*

Do you like these stories? I like *some,* but not *others.* I like the *first* and the *third.*

He owns *two* boats.

Stay tuned for the *second* thrilling episode.

## 3.8 Reflexive and Intensive Pronouns

Reflexive and intensive pronouns are formed by adding *self* or *selves* to the possessive form of the first- and second-person personal pronouns, to the objective form of third-person personal pronouns, and to the impersonal pronoun *one* (see 3.1 and 3.2).

| singular | plural |
|----------|--------|
| myself | ourselves |
| yourself | yourselves |
| himself | |
| herself | themselves |
| itself | |
| oneself | |

A reflexive pronoun is used as an object when that object is the same person or thing as the subject:

> He treated *himself* to bubble tea. (direct object)

> One should pamper *oneself* a little. (direct object)

> She gave *herself* a treat. (indirect object)

> We kept the idea to *ourselves*. (object of preposition)

These pronouns are also used as intensive pronouns to emphasize a subject or object. An intensive pronoun comes either right after the noun it emphasizes or at the end of the sentence:

> Although he let the others choose their positions, Angelo *himself* is going to pitch.

> The professor told us to count up our scores *ourselves*.

## Proofreading Tip

### On the Use of Intensive and Reflexive Pronouns

Do not use this form of pronoun as a substitute for a personal pronoun:

> The team and I [not *myself*] played a great game tonight.

Especially don't use *myself* simply to avoid having to decide whether *I* or *me* is correct in a compound subject or object (see 3.5).

They are also used in prepositional phrases with *by* to mean *alone* or *without help*:

> I can do this job by *myself.*

### 3.9 Reciprocal Pronouns

Like a reflexive pronoun, a reciprocal pronoun refers to the subject of a sentence, but this time the subject is always plural. The two reciprocal pronouns themselves are singular, and consist of two words each:

> each other (referring to a subject of two)

> one another (referring to a subject of three or more)

They can be inflected for possessive case by adding *'s*:

> each other's    one another's

These pronouns express some kind of mutual interaction between or among the parts of a plural subject:

> The president and the prime minister praised *each other's* policies.

> The computers in this office in effect speak to *one another*, even though the employees never do.

See also section 61 (each other, one another).

# 4. AGREEMENT OF PRONOUNS AND ANTECEDENTS

Any pronoun that refers to or stands for an antecedent (see section 3) must agree with—i.e. be the same as—that antecedent in person (1st, 2nd, or 3rd), number (singular or plural), and gender (masculine, feminine, or neuter). For example:

> *Joanne* wants to go to university so that *she* will be educated to take *her* place in the world.

Since the proper noun *Joanne*, the antecedent, is in the third person, singular, and feminine, any pronouns that refer to it must also be third-person, singular, and feminine: *she* and *her* thus agree grammatically with their antecedent.

The following sections (4.1–4.6) point out the most common sources of error in pronoun agreement. Note that these circumstances are similar to those affecting subject–verb agreement (see section 7). Note also that these errors all have to do with number—whether a pronoun should be singular or plural. Mistakes in gender and person are rare (but see 26.4, on shifts).

## 4.1 Antecedents Joined by *and*

When two or more singular antecedents are joined by *and*, use a plural pronoun:

> The manager and the accountant compared *their* figures.

> Both Jennifer and Chinmoy contributed *their* know-how.

If such a compound is preceded by *each* or *every*, however, the pronoun should be singular:

> Each book and magazine in the library has *its* own catalogue number.

## 4.2 Antecedents Joined by *or* or *nor*

When two or more antecedents are joined by *or* or *nor*, use a singular pronoun if the antecedents are singular:

> The dog or the cat is sure to make *itself* heard.

> Either David or Jonathan will bring *his* car.

> Neither Maylin nor her mother gave *her* consent.

If one antecedent is masculine and the other feminine, rephrase the sentence (see 4.4).

Use a plural pronoun if the antecedents are plural:

> Neither the players nor the coaches did *their* jobs properly.

If the antecedents are mixed singular and plural, a pronoun should agree with the nearest one. But if you move from a plural to a singular antecedent, the sentence will almost inevitably sound awkward; try to construct such sentences so that the last antecedent is plural:

> ✘ Neither the actors nor *the director* could control *his* temper.

> Neither the director nor *the actors* could control *their* tempers.

Note that the awkwardness of the first example extends to gender: if the actors included both men and women, neither *his* nor *her* would be appropriate (see 4.4). For more information on agreement of verbs with compound subjects joined by *or* or *nor*, see 7.3.

### 4.3 Indefinite Pronoun as Antecedent

If the antecedent is an indefinite pronoun (see 3.7), you'll usually use a singular pronoun to refer to it. The indefinite pronouns in Group 1 (the compounds with *body*, *one*, and *thing*) are singular, as are those in Group 2 (*another, each, either, much, neither, one, other*):

> *Each* of the boys worked on *his* own project.

> *Either* of *these women* is likely to buy that sports car for *herself*.

> *Everything* has *its* proper place.

Indefinite pronouns from Group 3 (*both, few, many, several*) are always plural:

> Only a *few* returned *their* ballots.

The indefinite pronouns in Group 4 (*all, any, more, most, none, some*) can be either singular or plural; the intended meaning is usually clearly either singular or plural:

> *Some* of the food on the menu could be criticized for *its* lack of nutrients.

> *Some* of the ships in the fleet had been restored to *their* original beauty.

Here the mass noun *food* demands the singular sense for *some*, and the countable noun *ships*, in the plural, demands the plural sense (see 3.7). But confusion sometimes arises with the indefinite pronoun *none*. (See also 7.4.) Although *none* began by meaning *no one* or *not one*, it now commonly has the plural sense:

> *None* of the professors knew how to fix *their* cars.

With a mass noun, or if your intended meaning is *not a single one*, treat *none* as singular:

> *None* of the food could be praised for *its* quality.

> *None* of the professors knew how to fix *his* car. (Here, you could perhaps even change *None* to *Not one*.)

When any of these words function as adjectives, the same principles apply:

> *Each* boy worked on *his* own project.

> *Either* woman may buy the car for *herself.*

> Only a *few* people returned *their* ballots.

> *Some* food can be praised for *its* nutritional value.

> *Some* ships had been restored to *their* original beauty.

Note: The word *every* used as an adjective requires a singular pronoun:

> *Every* boy has *his* own project.

## 4.4 Pronouns and Inclusive Language: Avoiding Gender Bias

Several indefinite pronouns and indefinite nouns like *person*, as well as many other nouns used in a generalizing way, present an additional problem: avoiding gender bias.

In the past, if a singular antecedent had no grammatical gender but could refer to either male or female, it was conventional to use the masculine pronoun *he* (*him, his, himself*) in a generic sense, meaning any person, male or female.

Today this practice is regarded as inappropriate and inaccurate, since it implies that no women are included in the statement. Such usages reveal the unconsidered assumption that males are the norm. And merely substituting *she* or *her* in all such instances is no solution, since it represents gender bias as well.

You can avoid biased language. Colloquially and informally, many writers simply use a plural pronoun:

> ✘   *Everyone* present at the lecture raised *his* hand.

> ✘   *A writer* should be careful about *his* diction.

> *Anyone* who doesn't pay *their* taxes is asking for trouble.

But this practice may be seen by some readers as fostering errors in agreement, and it is unacceptable to some who care about the traditions of language, for it is grammatically incorrect. (Note in the example above the clash between the plural pronoun *their* and the singular verb *is*.)

There are better solutions:

1.  If you are referring to a group or class consisting entirely of either men or women, it is only logical to use the appropriate pronoun, whether masculine or feminine:

    *Everyone* in the room raised *his* hand.
    *Everyone* in the room raised *her* hand.

    If the group is mixed, try to avoid the problem, for example by using the indefinite article:

    *Everyone* in the room raised *a* hand.

2.  Often the simplest technique is to make the antecedent itself plural: then the plural pronoun referring to it is grammatically appropriate, and no problem of gender arises:

    *All those* in the room raised *their* hands.
    *Writers* should be careful about *their* diction.

3.  If your purpose and the formality of the context permit, you can use the impersonal pronoun *one*:

    If one is considerate of others' feelings, one will get along better.

    But if this sounds too formal, consider using the less formal second-person pronoun *you* (but see 5.5; you need to be careful when you address the audience directly):

    If you are considerate of others' feelings, you will get along better.

4.  Another option is to revise a sentence so that no gendered pronoun is necessary:

    Everyone's hand went up.

    Sometimes the pronoun can simply be omitted:

    A writer should be careful about diction.

5. But if a sentence doesn't lend itself to such changes, or if you want to keep its original structure for some other reason, you can still manage. Don't resort to strings of unsightly devices such as *he/she*, *him/her*, *her/his*, *him/herself*, or *s/he*. But an occasional *he or she* or *she or he* and the like is acceptable:

> If anyone falls asleep, he or she will be asked to leave.
>
> A writer should be careful about her or his diction.

But do this only occasionally; used often, such repetitions become tedious and cluttering. See also section 61 (man, woman, lady, etc. and person, persons, people).

## 4.5 Collective Noun as Antecedent

If the antecedent is a collective noun (see section 2), use either a singular or a plural pronoun to refer to it, depending on context and desired meaning. If the collective noun stands for the group seen as a unit, use a singular pronoun:

> The *team* worked on *its* power play during the practice.
>
> The *committee* announced *its* decision.

If the collective noun stands for the members of the group seen as individuals, use a plural pronoun:

> The *team* took up *their* starting positions.
>
> The *committee* had no sooner taken *their* seats than *they* began chatting among *themselves*.

## 4.6 Agreement with Demonstrative Adjectives

Demonstrative adjectives must agree in number with the nouns they modify (usually *kind* or *kinds* or similar words):

> ✘  These kind of doctors work especially hard.
>
> This kind of doctor works especially hard.
>
> These kinds of doctors work especially hard.

# 5. REFERENCE OF PRONOUNS

A pronoun's reference to an antecedent must be clear. The pronoun or the sentence will not be clear if the antecedent is remote, ambiguous, vague, or missing.

## 5.1 Remote Antecedent

An antecedent should be close enough to the pronoun to be unmistakable; your reader shouldn't have to pause and search for it. An antecedent should seldom appear more than one sentence before its pronoun within a paragraph. For example:

> ✘ People who expect to experience happiness in material things alone may well discover that the life of the mind is more important than the life filled with possessions. Material prosperity may seem fine at a given moment, but in the long run its delights have a way of fading into inconsequential boredom and emptiness. *They* then realize, too late, where true happiness lies.

The word *People* is too far back to be a clear antecedent for the pronoun *They*. If the second sentence had also begun with *They*, the connection would be clearer. Or the third sentence might begin with a more particularizing phrase, like "Such people . . .".

## 5.2 Ambiguous Reference

A pronoun should refer clearly to only one antecedent:

> ✘ When Donna's mother told her that *she* had won a grand piano, *she* was obviously delighted.

Each *she* could refer either to Donna (*her*) or to Donna's mother. When revising such a sentence, don't just insert explanatory parentheses; rephrase the sentence:

> ✘ When Donna's mother told her that she (her mother) had won a grand piano, she (Donna) was obviously delighted.
>
> Donna was obviously delighted when her mother told her about winning a grand piano.
>
> Donna's mother had won a grand piano, and she was obviously delighted when she told Donna about it.
>
> Donna was obviously delighted when her mother said, "I won a grand piano!"

Another example:

> ✗ His second film was far different from his first. It was an adventure story set in Australia.

A pronoun like *it* often refers to the subject of the preceding independent clause, here *second film*, but *it* is also pulled toward the closest noun or pronoun, here *first*. The problem is easily solved by combining the two sentences, reducing the second to a subordinate element:

> His second film, an adventure story set in Australia, was far different from his first.

> His second film was far different from his first, which was an adventure story set in Australia.

## 5.3 Vague Reference

Vague reference is usually caused by the demonstrative pronouns *this* and *that* and the relative pronoun *which*:

> ✗ It was an exciting opening day for the store, and her cheerful partners were waiting for her. *This* made Shelagh enthusiastic about the meeting with the loan officer at the bank.

Another way of writing this would be to change *This*, after a comma, to *which*:

> ✗ It was an exciting opening day for the store, and her cheerful partners were waiting for her, *which* made Shelagh enthusiastic about meeting with the loan officer.

In both sentences there is a problem with vague reference. *This* in the first example and *which* in the second seem to refer to the entire content of the preceding sentence, but they also seem to refer specifically to the fact that Shelagh's cheerful partners were waiting for her. Revision is necessary:

> The excitement of the opening day for the store and her waiting partners' cheerfulness made Shelagh enthusiastic about the meeting with the loan officer at the bank.

> The store had an exciting opening day and her cheerful partners were waiting for her. These circumstances made Shelagh enthusiastic about the meeting with the loan officer at the bank.

A *this* or *which* can be adequate if the phrasing and meaning are appropriate:

> It was not only the exciting opening day for the store which made Shelagh enthusiastic about the meeting with the loan officer at the bank, but it was also the thought of her cheerful partners waiting for her.

Another example:

> ✘    Othello states many times that he loves Iago and that he thinks he is a very honest man; Iago uses *this* to his advantage.

The third *he* is possibly ambiguous, but more problematic is the vague reference of *this*. Changing *this* to *this opinion*, *these feelings*, *this attitude*, *these mistakes*, *this blindness of Othello's*, or even Othello's blindness makes the reference clearer. Even the *his* is slightly ambiguous: *Iago takes advantage of* would be better—or just omit *his*.

And don't catch the "this" virus; sufferers from it are driven to begin a large proportion of their sentences and other independent clauses with a *this*. Whenever you catch yourself beginning with a *this*, look carefully to see:

- if the reference to the preceding clause or sentence or paragraph is as clear on paper as it may be in your mind;
- if the *this* could be replaced by a specific noun or noun phrase, or otherwise avoided (for example by rephrasing or subordinating);
- whether, if you decide to keep *this*, it is an ambiguous demonstrative pronoun; if so, try to make it a demonstrative adjective, giving it a noun to modify—even if no more specific than "This *idea*," "This *fact*," or "This *argument*" (see 3.6 and section 28).

And always check if an opening *This* looks back to a noun that is in fact singular; it may be that *These* ideas, facts, or arguments would be more appropriate.

## 5.4 Missing Antecedent

Sometimes a writer may have an antecedent in mind but fail to write it down:

> ✘    In the early seventeenth century the Renaissance attitude was concentrated mainly on the arts rather than on developing the scientific part of *their* minds.

The writer was probably thinking of "the people of the Renaissance." Simply changing *their* to *people's* would clear up the difficulty.

> ✗    After the mayor's speech *he* agreed to answer questions from the audience.

The implied antecedent of *he* is *mayor*, but it isn't there, for the possessive *mayor's* functions as an adjective rather than a noun. Several revisions are possible:

> When the mayor finished his speech, he agreed to answer questions from the audience.
>
> After speaking, the mayor agreed to answer questions from the audience.
>
> At the end of his speech, the mayor agreed to answer questions from the audience.

Note that in this last version, *his* comes before its supposed antecedent, *mayor*—an unusual pattern, but one that is acceptable if the context is clear (for example, if no other possible antecedent for *his* occurred in the preceding sentence) and if the two are close together.

> ✗    Whenever a student assembly is called, *they* are required to attend.

Since *student* here functions as an adjective, it cannot serve as an antecedent for *they*. It is necessary to replace *they* with *students*—and then one would probably want to omit the original *student*. Or one could change "student assembly" to "an assembly of students" and retain *they*.

> ✗    Over half the guests left the party, but *it* did not stop the band from playing.

Again, no antecedent. Change *it* to *their departure*.

## 5.5 Indefinite *you*, *they*, and *it*

In formal writing, avoid the pronouns *you*, *they*, and *it* when they are indefinite:

> ✗    In order to practice law, *you* must pass the bar exam.
>
> In order to practice law, a lawyer must pass the bar exam.

(The impersonal *one* would be all right, but perhaps not as effective because it is less specific and more formal.)

> ✘    In some cities *they* do not have enough recycling facilities.
>
> Some cities do not have enough recycling facilities.
>
> Some cities' recycling facilities are inadequate.

Although it is correct to use the expletive or impersonal *it* (see 1.11 and 18.6) and write, "*It* is raining," "*It* is hard to get up in the morning," "*It* is seven o'clock," and so on, avoid such indefinite uses of *it* as the following:

> ✘    It states in this book that we should be careful how we use the pronoun *it*.
>
> This book states that we should be careful how we use the pronoun *it*.

# 6. VERBS

Verbs are core parts of speech. A verb is the focal point of a sentence or a clause. As you saw in chapter I, standard sentences consist of subjects and predicates: every subject has a predicate, and the heart of every predicate is its verb.

Verbs are often called "action" words; yet many verbs express little or no action. Think of verbs as expressing not only action but also occurrence, process, and condition or state of being. All verbs assert or ask something about their subjects, sometimes by linking a subject with a complement. Some verbs are single words; others are phrases consisting of two or more words. Here are some sentences with the verbs italicized:

> He *throws* curves.
>
> I *thought* for a while.
>
> Karen *is* a lawyer.
>
> Something *happened* last night.
>
> I *am cooking* pasta.
>
> In a week I *will have driven* two thousand kilometres.

*Are* you *listening?*

The two columns of figures *came out* even.

Will you *be needing* this DVD later?

The fresh bread *smells* delicious.

They *will set out* for Egypt in June.

(For a discussion of such two-part verbs as *come out* and *set out*, see 11.4–11.5.)

## 6.1 Kinds of Verbs: Transitive, Intransitive, and Linking

Verbs are classified according to the way they function in sentences.

A verb normally taking a direct object is considered a transitive verb. A transitive verb makes a transition, conveys a movement, from its subject to its object:

She *has* good taste.

He *introduced* me to his uncle.

Greg never *neglects* his homework.

She *expresses* her ideas eloquently.

He *stuffed* himself with pizza.

Where *did* you *put* that book?

A direct object answers the question consisting of the verb and *what* or *whom*: Introduced *whom?* Me. Never neglects *what?* Work. Expresses *what?* Ideas. Stuffed *whom?* Himself. Did put *what* where? Book. (See also 1.4, 1.6, 1.9, and 1.10.)

A verb that normally occurs without a direct object is considered intransitive (see also 1.3):

When *will* you *arrive?*

What *has happened* to the beluga whale?

The earthquake *occurred* during the night.

You *should rest* for a while.

He *gossiped* with his roommate.

Please *stay.*

Many verbs, however, can be either transitive or intransitive, depending on how they function in particular sentences:

I ran the business effectively. (transitive)

I ran to the store. (intransitive)

I can see the parade better from the balcony. (transitive)

I can see well enough from here. (intransitive)

He wished that he were home in bed. (transitive)

She wished upon a star. (intransitive)

In fact, few verbs are exclusively either transitive or intransitive, as a good dictionary will show you. Verbs felt to be clearly intransitive can often also be used transitively, and vice versa:

She *slept* the sleep of the just. (In this sentence, *slept* takes the object *sleep* and therefore is transitive.)

He leaned back in the chair and *remembered*. (In this sentence, *remembered* takes no object and therefore is intransitive.)

A third kind of verb is called a linking or copulative verb. The main one is *be* in its various forms. Some other common linking verbs are *become, seem, remain, act, get, feel, look, appear, smell, sound*, and *taste*.

Linking verbs don't have objects, but are yet incomplete; they need a subjective complement. A linking verb is like an equal sign in an equation: something at the right-hand (predicate) end is needed to balance what is at the left-hand (subject) end. The complement will be either a predicate noun or a predicate adjective (see also 1.7 and 1.8). Some examples:

Angela *is* a lawyer. (predicate noun: *lawyer*)

Angela *is* not well. (predicate adjective: *well*)

Martin *became* a pilot. (predicate noun: *pilot*)

Martin *became* uneasy. (predicate adjective: *uneasy*)

The winner *is* Nathan. (predicate noun: *Nathan*)

The band *sounds* good. (predicate adjective: *good*)

The surface *felt* sticky. (predicate adjective: *sticky*)

Occasionally a complement precedes the verb, for example in a question or in a sentence or clause inverted for emphasis:

How *sick* are you?

However *happy* he may have been, he did not let his feelings show to the other contestants.

Like an object, a subjective complement answers the question consisting of the verb and *what* or *whom*, or perhaps *how*: Is what? A lawyer. Became what? Uneasy. Is whom? Nathan. Sounds how? Good. It differs from an object in that it is the equivalent of the subject or says something about it.

Such verbs as *act, sound, taste, smell,* and *feel* can of course also function as transitive verbs: She *acted* the part. He *sounded* his horn. He *smelled* the hydrogen sulphide. I *tasted* the soup. He *felt* the bump on his head.

Similarly, many of these verbs can also function as regular intransitive verbs, sometimes accompanied by adverbial modifiers (see section 9): We *looked* at the painting. Santa *is* on the roof. Teresa *is* at home. We *are* here. But whenever one of these verbs is accompanied by a predicate noun or a predicate adjective, it is functioning as a linking verb.

## 6.2 Inflection of Verbs: Principal Parts

As well as being important, verbs are also the most complex, the most highly inflected, of the eight parts of speech. Verbs are inflected

- for person and number, in order to agree with a subject (see 6.4);
- for tense, in order to show an action's time—present, past, or future—and character (see 6.7);
- for mood, in order to show the kind of sentence a verb is in—indicative, imperative, or subjunctive (see 6.12–6.13);
- for voice, in order to show whether a subject is active (performing an action) or passive (being acted upon) (see 6.15–6.16).

Every verb (except some auxiliaries; see 6.5) has what are called its principal parts:

1.  its basic form (the form a dictionary uses)

2.  its past-tense form

3.  its past participle

4.  its present participle

Verbs regularly form both the past tense and the past participle simply by adding *ed* to the basic form:

| basic form | past-tense form | past participle |
|---|---|---|
| push | pushed | pushed |
| cook | cooked | cooked |

If the basic form already ends in *e*, however, only *d* is added:

| basic form | past-tense form | past participle |
|---|---|---|
| move | moved | moved |
| agree | agreed | agreed |

Present participles are regularly formed by adding *ing* to the basic form:

| basic form | present participle |
|---|---|
| push | pushing |
| cook | cooking |
| agree | agreeing |

But verbs ending in an unpronounced *e* usually drop it before adding *ing*:

| basic form | present participle |
|---|---|
| move | moving |
| skate | skating |

And some verbs double a final consonant before adding *ed* or *ing*:

| basic form | past participle | present participle |
|---|---|---|
| grin | grinned | grinning |
| stop | stopped | stopping |

For more on these and other irregularities, see 51.4–51.6. Further, good dictionaries list any irregular principal parts, ones not formed by simply adding *ed* or *ing* (and see 6.3).

It is from these four parts—the basic form and the three principal inflections of it—that all other inflected forms of a verb are made.

Note: The basic form of a verb is sometimes called the infinitive form, meaning that it can be preceded by *to* to form an infinitive: *to be*, *to push*, *to agree*. Infinitives, participles, and gerunds are called non-finite verbs, or verbals; they function not as verbs but as other parts of speech (see 10.1–10.6). Finite verbs, unlike non-finite forms, are restricted or limited by person, number, tense, mood, and voice; they function as the main verbs in sentences.

## 6.3 Irregular Verbs

Some of the most common English verbs are irregular in the way they make their past-tense forms and their past participles. Whenever you aren't certain about the principal parts of a verb, check your dictionary, or use the following list, which contains most of the common irregular verbs with their past-tense forms and their past participles (where two or more are given, the first is the more common). If you need to, memorize these forms; practise by composing sentences using each form (for example: *Choose* the one you want. I *chose* mine yesterday. Haven't you *chosen* yet?). If you're looking for a verb that is a compound or that has a suffix, look for the main verb: for *misread*, *proofread*, or *reread*, look under *read*:

| basic or present form | past-tense form | past participle |
|---|---|---|
| arise | arose | arisen |
| awake | awoke | awoken |
| bear | bore | borne (born *for "given birth to"*) |

| basic or present form | past-tense form | past participle |
|---|---|---|
| beat | beat | beaten, beat |
| become | became | become |
| begin | began | begun |
| bend | bent | bent |
| bet | bet, betted | bet, betted |
| bid | bid | bid |
| bind | bound | bound |
| bite | bit | bitten, bit |
| bleed | bled | bled |
| blow | blew | blown |
| break | broke | broken |
| breed | bred | bred |
| bring | brought | brought |
| broadcast | broadcast, broadcasted | broadcast, broadcasted |
| build | built | built |
| burst | burst | burst |
| buy | bought | bought |
| cast | cast | cast |
| catch | caught | caught |
| choose | chose | chosen |
| cling | clung | clung |
| come | came | come |
| cost | cost | cost |
| creep | crept | crept |
| cut | cut | cut |
| deal | dealt | dealt |
| dig | dug | dug |
| dive | dived, dove | dived |
| draw | drew | drawn |
| dream | dreamed, dreamt | dreamed, dreamt |
| drink | drank | drunk |
| drive | drove | driven |
| eat | ate | eaten |
| fall | fell | fallen |
| feed | fed | fed |
| feel | felt | felt |
| fight | fought | fought |
| find | found | found |
| fit | fit, fitted | fit, fitted |
| flee | fled | fled |

| basic or present form | past-tense form | past participle |
|---|---|---|
| fling | flung | flung |
| fly | flew | flown |
| forbid | forbade, forbad | forbidden |
| forecast | forecast, forecasted | forecast, forecasted |
| foresee | foresaw | foreseen |
| foretell | foretold | foretold |
| forgive | forgave | forgiven |
| forget | forgot | forgotten |
| forgo | forwent | forgone |
| forsake | forsook | forsaken |
| freeze | froze | frozen |
| frolic | frolicked | frolicked |
| get | got | got, gotten |
| give | gave | given |
| go | went | gone |
| grind | ground | ground |
| grow | grew | grown |
| hang | hung (hanged *for* "*execute*") | hung, hanged |
| hear | heard | heard |
| hide | hid | hidden |
| hit | hit | hit |
| hold | held | held |
| hurt | hurt | hurt |
| input | input, inputted | input, inputted |
| keep | kept | kept |
| kneel | knelt, kneeled | knelt, kneeled |
| knit | knitted, knit | knitted, knit |
| know | knew | known |
| lay | laid | laid |
| lead | led | led |
| leap | leaped, leapt | leaped, leapt |
| leave | left | left |
| lend | lent | lent |
| let | let | let |
| lie ("recline") | lay | lain |
| light | lit, lighted | lit, lighted |
| lose | lost | lost |
| make | made | made |
| mean | meant | meant |
| meet | met | met |

| basic or present form | past-tense form | past participle |
|---|---|---|
| mimic | mimicked | mimicked |
| mislead | misled | misled |
| mistake | mistook | mistaken |
| misunderstand | misunderstood | misunderstood |
| mow | mowed | mowed, mown |
| offset | offset | offset |
| overcome | overcame | overcome |
| overdo | overdid | overdone |
| panic | panicked | panicked |
| partake | partook | partaken |
| pay | paid | paid |
| prove | proved | proven, proved |
| put | put | put |
| quit | quit | quit |
| read | read (*changes pronunciation*) | read (*changes pronunciation*) |
| rid | rid | rid |
| ride | rode | ridden |
| ring | rang | rung |
| rise | rose | risen |
| run | ran | run |
| say | said | said |
| see | saw | seen |
| seek | sought | sought |
| sell | sold | sold |
| send | sent | sent |
| set | set | set |
| sew | sewed | sewn, sewed |
| shake | shook | shaken |
| shed | shed | shed |
| shine | shone (shined *for "polished"*) | shone, shined |
| shoot | shot | shot |
| show | showed | shown, showed |
| shrink | shrank, shrunk | shrunk |
| shut | shut | shut |
| sing | sang | sung |
| sink | sank, sunk | sunk |
| sit | sat | sat |
| slay | slew | slain |
| sleep | slept | slept |

| basic or present form | past-tense form | past participle |
|---|---|---|
| slide | slid | slid |
| sling | slung | slung |
| slink | slunk | slunk |
| slit | slit | slit |
| sneak | snuck, sneaked | snuck, sneaked |
| sow | sowed | sown, sowed |
| speak | spoke | spoken |
| speed | sped, speeded | sped, speeded |
| spend | spent | spent |
| spin | spun | spun |
| spit | spat, spit | spat, spit |
| split | split | split |
| spread | spread | spread |
| spring | sprang, sprung | sprung |
| stand | stood | stood |
| steal | stole | stolen |
| stick | stuck | stuck |
| sting | stung | stung |
| stink | stank, stunk | stunk |
| stride | strode | stridden |
| strike | struck | struck |
| string | strung | strung |
| strive | strove, strived | striven, strived |
| swear | swore | sworn |
| sweep | swept | swept |
| swell | swelled | swollen, swelled |
| swim | swam | swum |
| swing | swung | swung |
| take | took | taken |
| teach | taught | taught |
| tear | tore | torn |
| tell | told | told |
| think | thought | thought |
| thrive | thrived | thrived |
| throw | threw | thrown |
| thrust | thrust | thrust |
| traffic | trafficked | trafficked |
| tread | trod | trodden, trod |
| uphold | upheld | upheld |
| upset | upset | upset |
| wake | woke, waked | woken, waked |

| basic or present form | past-tense form | past participle |
|---|---|---|
| wear | wore | worn |
| weave | wove | woven |
| weep | wept | wept |
| wet | wet, wetted | wet, wetted |
| win | won | won |
| wind | wound | wound |
| withdraw | withdrew | withdrawn |
| wring | wrung | wrung |
| write | wrote | written |

## 6.4 Inflection for Person and Number

In order to agree with its subject (see section 7), a verb is inflected for person and number. To illustrate, here are four verbs inflected for person and number in the present tense, using personal pronouns as subjects (see 3.1):

| singular | | | | |
|---|---|---|---|---|
| lst person | I walk | I move | I push | I fly |
| 2nd person | you walk | you move | you push | you fly |
| 3rd person | he walks | he moves | he pushes | he flies |
|  | she walks | she moves | she pushes | she flies |
|  | it walks | it moves | it pushes | it flies |
| **plural** | | | | |
| 1st person | we walk | we move | we push | we fly |
| 2nd person | you walk | you move | you push | you fly |
| 3rd person | they walk | they move | they push | they fly |

Note that the inflection occurs only in the third-person singular, and that you simply add *s* or *es* to the basic form (first changing final *y* to *i* where necessary; see 51.5).

## 6.5 Auxiliary Verbs

Auxiliary or helping verbs go with other verbs to form verb phrases indicating tense, voice, and mood. The auxiliary *do* helps in forming questions (see 1.20), forming negative sentences, and expressing emphasis:

> *Did* you arrive in time?
>
> I *did not* arrive in time.
>
> She *doesn't* care for asparagus.
>
> I *did* wash my face!
>
> I *do* admire that man.

*Do* works only in the simple present and simple past tenses (see 6.7). The principal auxiliary verbs—*be*, *have*, *will*, and *shall*—enable us to form tenses beyond the simple present and the simple past, as illustrated in 6.7 and 6.8. *Be* and *have* go with main verbs and with each other to form the perfect tenses and the progressive tenses; *will* and *shall* (see 6.8 [Simple future]) help form the various future tenses. *Be* also combines with main verbs to form the passive voice (see 6.15–6.16).

## Modal auxiliaries

Modal auxiliaries combine with main verbs and other auxiliaries to express such meanings as ability, possibility, obligation, and necessity. The principal modal auxiliaries are *can*, *could*, *may*, *might*, *must*, *should*, and *would*.

> I *can* understand that.
>
> There *could* be thunderstorms tomorrow.
>
> I *would* tell you the answer if I *could*.
>
> The instructor *may* decide to cancel the quiz.
>
> I *might* attend, but then again I *might* not.
>
> You *should* have received the letter by now.
>
> *Must* we wear our uniforms?

The equivalent phrases *able to* (*can*), *ought to* (*should*), and *have to* (*must*) also function as modal auxiliaries.

- **could, might:** *Could* and *might* also serve as the past-tense forms of *can* and *may*, for example if demanded by the sequence of tenses after a verb in the past tense (see 6.9):

  He *was* sure that I *could* handle the project.

  She *said* that I *might* watch the rehearsal if I *was* quiet.

- **might, may:** *Might* and *may* are sometimes interchangeable when expressing possibility:

  She *may* (*might*) challenge the committee's decision.

  He *may* (*might*) have finished the job by now.

Usually there is a difference, with *may* indicating a stronger possibility, *might* a somewhat less likely one.

> Since more rain is forecast, the flood waters *may* rise overnight. (That is, flood waters *may very well* rise.)

> The weather report forecasts sunshine, but the river *might* still rise overnight. (That is, flood waters *could* rise but probably won't.)

(For the distinction between *can* and *may*, see section 61 [can, may]. For *should* and *would* as past-tense forms, see 6.9 [Past tense in independent clauses].)

To express a condition contrary to fact (see 6.13 #2), *might* is the right word:

> If you had edited your report, you *might* [not *may*] have received better feedback.

That is, you *didn't* edit carefully, and you *didn't* get good feedback. *Might* is necessary for clear expression of a hypothetical as opposed to a factual circumstance. Consider the difference in meaning between the following two sentences:

> Reducing his speed might have prevented the accident.

> Reducing his speed may have prevented the accident.

In the first sentence, *might* is used again to express a condition contrary to fact: the driver did not reduce his speed and the accident was not prevented, but the writer suggests the accident could have been prevented had the driver reduced his speed. The substitution of *may* for *might* in the second sentence changes the situation: in this case, the accident was prevented, and the writer is speculating that this fortunate occurrence may be attributable to the driver's having reduced his speed. See also section 61 (may, might).

Like forms of *do*, modal auxiliaries can join with the contraction *n't*: *can't, couldn't, shouldn't, wouldn't, mustn't*. In addition, *can* can join with the word *not*: *cannot*. Unlike other verbs (see 6.4), modal auxiliaries are not inflected for third-person singular:

> I can go.

> You can go.

> He or she or it can go.

Nor do these verbs have any participial forms, or an infinitive form (one cannot say *to can*; instead, one must use another verb phrase, *to be able*). But modal auxiliaries can work as parts of perfect tenses as well as of simple present and simple past tenses (see 6.7). (For more on modal auxiliaries, see 6.14.)

## 6.6 Inflection of *do*, *be*, and *have*

*Do*, *be*, and *have* are different from the other auxiliaries in that they can also function as main verbs. As a main verb, *do* most often has the sense of *perform*, *accomplish*:

> I *do* my job. He *did* what I asked. She *does* her best.

*Have* as a main verb most often means *own*, *possess*, *contain*:

> I *have* enough money. July *has* thirty-one days.

And *be* as a main verb can mean *exist* or *live* (a sense seldom used: "I think; therefore I *am*"), but most often means *occur*, *remain*, *occupy a place*:

> The meeting *is* today. I won't *be* more than an hour. The car *is* in the garage.

(See your dictionary for other meanings of these verbs.)

Even when functioning as auxiliaries, these verbs are fully inflected. Here are the inflections for *do* and *have*, which, as you can see, are irregular:

| singular | | |
|---|---|---|
| 1st person | I do | I have |
| 2nd person | you do | you have |
| 3rd person | he does | he has |
| | she does | she has |
| | it does | it has |

| plural | | |
|---|---|---|
| 1st person | we do | we have |
| 2nd person | you do | you have |
| 3rd person | they do | they have |
| | | |
| past-tense form | did | had |
| past participle | done | had |
| present participle | doing | having |

The most common verb of all, *be*, is also the most irregular:

| singular | present tense | past tense |
|---|---|---|
| 1st person | I am | I was |
| 2nd person | you are | you were |
| 3rd person | he / she / it is | he / she / it was |

| plural | | |
|---|---|---|
| 1st person | we are | we were |
| 2nd person | you are | you were |
| 3rd person | they are | they were |
| | | |
| past participle | been | |
| present participle | being | |

For a fuller discussion of tense, see 6.7–6.8.

## 6.7 Time and the Verb: Inflection for Tense

Even though verbs must agree with their subjects in person and number (see 6.4 and section 7), they are still the strongest elements in sentences because they not only indicate action but also control time. The verb by its inflection indicates the time of an action, event, or condition. Through its tense a verb shows when an action occurs:

> Yesterday, I *practised*. (past tense)

> Today, I *practise*. (present tense)

> Tomorrow, I *will practise*. (future tense)

Here the adverbs emphasize the time of the action, but the senses of past, present, and future are clear without them:

> I practised. I practise. I will practise.

## 6.8 The Functions of the Different Tenses

Following are brief descriptions and illustrations of the main functions of each tense. Although these points are sometimes oversimplifications of very complex matters, and although there are other exceptions and variations than those listed, these guidelines should help you to use the tenses properly and to take advantage of the possibilities they offer for clear expression.

| tense | verb form | |
|---|---|---|
| simple present | I / you | dance |
| | he / she / it | dances |
| | we / you / they | dance |
| simple past | I / you / he / she / it / we / you / they | danced |
| simple future | I / you / he / she / it / we / you / they | will dance |
| present perfect | he / she / it | has danced |
| | I / you / we / you / they | have danced |
| past perfect | I / you / he / she / it / we / you / they | had danced |

| tense | verb form | |
|---|---|---|
| future perfect | I / you / he / she / it / we / you / they | will have danced |
| present progressive | I | am dancing |
| | you | are dancing |
| | he / she / it | is dancing |
| | we / you / they | are dancing |
| past progressive | I | was dancing |
| | you | were dancing |
| | he / she / it | was dancing |
| | we / you / they | were dancing |
| future progressive | I / you / he / she / it / we / you / they | will be dancing |
| present perfect progressive | I / you | have been dancing |
| | he / she / it | has been dancing |
| | we / you / they | have been dancing |
| past perfect progressive | I / you / he / she / it / we / you / they | had been dancing |
| future perfect progressive | I / you / he / she / it / we / you / they | will have been dancing |

## Simple present

Generally, use this tense to describe an action or condition that is happening now, at the time of the utterance:

> The pitcher *throws*. The batter *swings*. It *is* a high fly ball.

> The day *is* very warm. I *am* uncomfortable. *Are* you all right? I *can* manage.

But this tense has several other common uses. It can indicate a general truth or belief:

> Ottawa *is* one of the coldest capitals in the world.

> Cheetahs *can* outrun any other animal.

> The bigger they *are* the harder they *fall*.

or describe a customary or habitual or repeated action or condition:

> I *paint* pictures for a living.

> Anne *spells* her name with an *e*.

I always *eat* breakfast before going to work.

Snow *starts* falling before Halloween.

or describe the characters or events in a literary or other work, or what an author does in such a work (see 6.11):

Oedipus *searches* for the truth almost like a modern detective.

In a famous children's book, owls *deliver* the mail to the school.

Dante with the help of Virgil *ascends* to paradise.

or even express future time, especially with the help of an adverbial modifier of time (see also present progressive, below):

He *arrives* tomorrow. (adverbial modifier: *tomorrow*)

We *leave* for London next Sunday. (adverbial modifier: *next Sunday*)

## Simple past

Use this tense for a single or repeated action or condition that began and ended in the past (compare present perfect, below):

She *earned* a lot of money last year.

I *was* happy when I received my paycheque.

I *painted* a picture yesterday.

I *painted* pictures last year.

He *went* to Paris three times last year.

## Simple future

Although there are other ways to indicate future time (see, for example, simple present [above] and present progressive [below]), the most common and straightforward is to use the simple future, putting *will* or *shall* before the basic form of the verb:

She *will arrive* tomorrow morning.

I *will paint* pictures next year.

We'*ll have* a nice picnic if it doesn't rain.

*Shall*, once considered the correct form to use with a first-person subject (*I*, *we*), is now restricted largely to expressing emphasis or determination or to first-person questions asking for agreement or permission or advice, where *will* would sound unidiomatic:

> Shall we go?

With negatives, the contracted forms of *will not* and *shall not* are *won't* and *shan't*:

> *Won't* we *arrive* on time?

> No, I *shan't be able* to attend.

Note, however, that *shan't* is uncommon in Canadian English.

### Present perfect
Use this tense for an action or condition that began in the past and that continues to the present (compare simple past, above); though considered "completed" as of the moment, some actions or conditions referred to in this tense could continue after the present:

> I *have earned* a lot of money this year.

> James Bond *has* just *entered* the casino.

> The weather *has been* lovely lately.

> The training course *has lasted* for two months.

You can use this tense for something that occurred entirely in the past if you feel that it somehow impinges on the present—that is, if you intend to imply the sense of "before now" or "so far" or "already":

> I *have painted* a picture; take a look at it.

> She *has told* us how she wants our reports done.

> I *have visited* Greece three times.

> We *have beaten* them seven out of ten times.

### Past perfect
Use this tense for an action completed in the past before a specific past time or event. Notice that there are at least two actions taking place in the past:

I *had painted* a picture just before they arrived.

Though I *had seen* the film twice before, I went again last week.

They got to the station only a minute late, but the train *had* already *left*.

## Future perfect

Use this tense for an action or condition that will be completed before a specific future time or event:

By this time next week I *will have painted* a picture.

I *will* already *have eaten* when you arrive.

Sometimes simple future works as well as future perfect:

Some experts predict that by the year 2010 scientists *will have found* a cure for diabetes.

## Present progressive

Use this tense for an action or condition that began at some past time and is continuing now, in the present:

I *am writing* my rough draft.

Global warming *is getting* worse.

Sometimes the simple and the progressive forms of a verb say much the same thing:

We *hope* for snow. We *are hoping* for snow.

I *feel* ill. I *am feeling* ill.

But usually the progressive form emphasizes an activity, or the singleness or continuing nature of an action, rather than a larger condition or general truth:

A tax hike *hurts* many people.
The tax hike *is hurting* many people.

I *walk* to work.
I *am walking* to work.

Like the simple present, the present progressive tense can also express future time, especially with adverbial help:

They *are arriving* early tomorrow morning.

You can also express future time with a form of *be* and *going* before an infinitive (see 10.1):

They *are going* to walk around Stanley Park on New Year's day.

## Past progressive

Use this tense for an action that was in progress during some past time, especially if you want to emphasize the continuing nature of the action:

I remember that I *was painting* a picture that day.

He *was driving* very fast.

They *were protesting* the council's decision.

Sometimes the past progressive tense describes an interrupted action or an action during which something else happens:

When the telephone rang I *was making* tempura.

Just as he *was stepping* off, the bus started moving.

## Future progressive

Use this tense for a continuing action in the future or for an action that will be occurring at some specific time in the future:

I *will be painting* pictures as long as I can hold a brush.

You *will be learning* things for the rest of your life.

They *will be arriving* on the midnight plane.

## Present perfect progressive

Use this tense to emphasize the continuing nature of a single or repeated action that began in the past and that has continued at least up to the present:

I *have been working* on this picture for an hour.

The dollar *has been declining* in value.

Our book club *has been meeting* once a week since January.

## Past perfect progressive

Use this tense to emphasize the continuing nature of a single or repeated past action that was completed before or interrupted by some other past action:

> I *had been painting* pictures for three years before I finally sold one.

> We *had all been expecting* something quite different.

> I *had been pondering* the problem for an hour when suddenly the solution popped into my head.

## Future perfect progressive

This tense is seldom used in formal writing. Use it to emphasize the continuing nature of a future action before a specific time in the future or before a second future action:

> If she continues to dance, by the year 2013 she *will have been dancing* for over half her life.

> You *will* already *have been driving* for about nine hours before you even get to the border.

## 6.9 Sequence of Tenses

When two or more verbs occur in the same sentence, they will sometimes be of the same tense, but often they will be of different tenses.

## Compound sentences

In a compound sentence, made up of two or more independent clauses (see 1.25), the verbs can be equally independent; use whatever tenses the sense requires:

> I *am leaving* [present progressive] now, but she *will leave* [future] in the morning.

> The polls *have closed* [present perfect]; the clerks *will* soon *be counting* [future progressive] the ballots.

> He *had made* [past perfect] his promise, and the committee *decided* [past] to hold him to it; therefore they *expect* [present] his co-operation in the weeks ahead.

## Past tense in independent clauses

In complex or compound-complex sentences, if the verb in an independent clause is in any of the past tenses, the verbs in any clauses subordinate to it will usually also be in one of the past tenses. For example:

> I *told* her that I *was* sorry.

> They *agreed* that this time the newly elected treasurer *would* not be a gambler.

Refer to a time *earlier* than that of the main verb in the past tense by using the past perfect tense:

> By Monday, Maria *had finished* the speed reading book that I lent her on Friday.

But there are exceptions. When the verb in the subordinate clause states a general or timeless truth or belief, or something characteristic or habitual, it stays in the present tense:

> Einstein *showed* that space, time, and light *are* linked.

> They *discovered* the hard way that money *doesn't guarantee* happiness.

And the context of the sentence sometimes dictates that other kinds of verbs in subordinate clauses should not be changed to a past tense. If you feel that a tense other than the past would be clearer or more accurate, use it; for example:

> I *learned* yesterday that I *will be* able to get into the new program in the fall.

The rule calls for *would*, but *will* is logical and clear. Notice that the adverbial marker "in the fall" tells us the action will occur in the future.

> In an interview yesterday, Smith *said* that he *is* determined to complete the series of concerts.

To use *was* rather than *is* here would be ambiguous, implying that Smith's determination was a thing of the past; if it definitely was past, then *had been* would be clearer.

And here is one more example of a sentence in which the "sequence of tenses" rule is best ignored:

> The secretary *told* me this morning that my boss is ill and *will not be attending* work this afternoon.

## 6.10 Verb Phrases in Compound Predicates

When a compound predicate consists of two verb phrases in different tenses, don't omit part of one of them:

**✘** The leader has never and will never practise nepotism.

Rather, include each verb in full or rephrase the sentence:

> The leader has never practised and will never practise nepotism.

> The leader has never practised nepotism and will never do so.

## 6.11 Tenses in Writing about Literature

When discussing or describing the events in a literary work, it is customary to use the present tense (see also 6.8 [Simple present]):

> While he *is* away, Hamlet *arranges* to have Rosencrantz and Guildenstern put to death. He *holds* Yorick's skull and *watches* Ophelia being buried. He *duels* with Laertes and dies. Without a doubt, death *is* one of the principal themes in the play.

For the tenses of infinitives and participles, see 10.2 and 10.5.

## Proofreading Tip

### On Verb Tense and Conventions of Literary Analysis

It is also customary to speak even of a long-dead author in the present tense when one is discussing a particular work; another example:

> In *Pride and Prejudice*, Austen *shows* the consequences of making hasty judgments of others.

## 6.12 Mood

English verbs are usually considered to have three moods. The mood of a verb has to do with the nature of the expression in which it's being used. The ordinary mood is the indicative, which is used for statements of fact or opinion and for questions:

> The weather forecast for tomorrow *sounds* promising.

> Shall we *proceed* with our plans?

The imperative mood is used for most commands and instructions (see 1.21):

> *Put* the picnic hamper in the trunk.

> *Don't forget* the bubbly.

The subjunctive mood in English is less common, but it presents some difficulty. It is discussed below.

## 6.13 Using the Subjunctive

The subjunctive has almost disappeared from contemporary English. It survives in some standard expressions or idioms such as "*Be* that as it may"; "*Come* what may"; "Heaven *forbid*!" and "Long *live* the Queen!" Otherwise, you need consider only two kinds of instances where the subjunctive still functions.

1. Use the subjunctive in a *that*-clause after verbs expressing demands, obligations, requirements, recommendations, suggestions, wishes, and the like:

   > The doctor recommended that she *take* a sea voyage.

   > Ruth asked that the door *be* left open.

   > I wish [that] I *were* in Paris.

2. Use the subjunctive to express conditions that are hypothetical or impossible—often in *if*-clauses or their equivalents:

He looked as if he *were* going to explode. (But he didn't explode, we hope.)

If Lise *were* here she *would* back me up. (But she isn't here.)

An *as if* or *as though* clause almost always expresses a condition contrary to fact, but not all *if*-clauses do; don't be misled into using a subjunctive where it's not appropriate:

✘    He said that if there *were* another complaint he would resign.

The verb should be *was*, for the condition could turn out to be true: there may be another complaint.

Since only a few subjunctive forms differ from those of the indicative, they are easy to learn and remember. The third person singular form loses its *s*:

I like the way she *paints*. (indicative)

I suggested that she *paint* my portrait. (subjunctive)

The subjunctive forms of the verb *be* are *be* and *were*:

He *is* friendly. (I *am*, you / we / they *are*) (indicative)

The judge asked that she *be* excused. (that I / you / we / they *be*) (subjunctive)

I know that I *am* in Edmonton. (indicative)

I wish that I *were* in Florence. (subjunctive)

Note that both *be* and *were* function with either singular or plural subjects. Note also that the past tense form *were* functions in present tense expressions of wishes and contrary-to-fact conditions. Other verbs also use their past tense as a subjunctive after a present-tense wish:

I wish that I *shopped* less.

After a past-tense wish, use the standard past perfect form:

He wished that he *had been* more attentive.

She wished that she *had played* better.

## 6.14 Using Modal Auxiliaries and Infinitives Instead of Subjunctives

The *modal auxiliaries* (see 6.5) offer common alternatives to many sentences using subjunctives; they express several of the same moods.

> The doctor told her she *should* [*ought to*] live in a less polluted area.
>
> I wish that I *could* be in Paris.
>
> He looked as if he *might* explode.
>
> If Lise *could have* been here, she would back me up.

Another alternative uses the *infinitive* (see 10.1):

> It is necessary for us *to be* there before noon.
>
> The judge ordered Ralph *to attend* the hearing.
>
> Ruth asked us *to leave* the door open.

## 6.15 Voice

There are two voices, active and passive. The active voice is direct: *I made this toy boat.* The passive voice is less direct, reversing the normal subject–verb–object pattern: *This toy boat was made by me* (see 1.5). Passive voice is easy to recognize; the verb uses some form of *be* followed by a past participle: *was made.* What in active voice would be a direct object (*boat*) in passive voice becomes the subject of the verb. And passive constructions often leave unmentioned the agent of the action or state they describe: *The toy boat was made* (by whom isn't specified).

## 6.16 The Passive Voice

Using the passive voice, some people can promise action without committing themselves to perform it, and they can admit error without accepting responsibility:

> Be assured [by whom?] that action will be taken [by whom?]. (passive)
>
> I assure you that I will act. (active)
>
> It is to be regretted [by whom?] that an error has been made [by whom?]. (passive)
>
> I am sorry we made an error in your account. I will look into the matter and correct it immediately. (active)

Although the passive voice has its uses, it is not often preferable to the active voice. When possible, use the direct and more vigorous active voice. Here are some examples of weak uses of the passive voice:

> ✘    All of this *is communicated* by Tolkien by means of a poem rather than prose. The poetry *is shown* as a tool which Tolkien employs in order to foreshadow events and establish ideas which otherwise *could not be* easily *communicated* to us.

> Tolkien communicates all this in poetry rather than prose because with poetry he can foreshadow events and establish ideas that would otherwise be difficult to convey.

The wordiness of this passage results largely from the passive voice. A change to active voice shortens it, clarifies the sense, and produces a crisper style. Begin by making the agent the subject; the rest then follows naturally and logically:

> ✘    Mixing the chemicals, hydrogen sulphide *was formed*.

> By mixing the chemicals, the chemist formed hydrogen sulphide.

In this example, describing the experiment, the passive not only is awkward and weak but it also leads to a dangling modifier (see section 24); there is no subject in the sentence to explain who is doing the mixing. The frequency of such errors is itself a good reason to be sparing with passive voice. The active voice eliminates the grammatical error.

**When to use the passive voice** (see also 18.6)
Use the passive voice when the active voice is impossible or when the passive is for some other reason clearly preferable or demanded by the context. Generally, use passive voice

- when the agent, or doer of the act, is indefinite or not known;
- when the agent is less important than the act itself;
- when you want to emphasize either the agent or the act by putting it at the beginning or end of the sentence.

For example:

> It *was reported* that there were two survivors.

Here the writer doesn't know who did the reporting. To avoid the passive by saying "Someone reported that there were two survivors" would oddly stress the mysterious "someone." And the fact that *someone reported* it is less important than the content of the report.

> The accident *was witnessed* by more than thirty people.

Here the writer emphasizes the large number of witnesses by putting them at the end of the sentence, the most emphatic place.

No doubt you'll want to use passive voice on other sorts of occasions as well, but don't use it unwittingly or uncritically. Remember: a verb in the passive consists of some form of *be* followed by a past participle (*is shown, was accompanied, to be announced, has been decided, are legalized, will be charged, is being removed*). Whenever you find yourself using such verbs, stop to consider whether an active structure would be more effective.

Note: Like mood, voice operates regardless of tense. Don't confuse passive constructions with the past tense just because the past participle is used. Passive constructions can appear in any of the tenses.

# 7. AGREEMENT OF SUBJECT AND VERB

A verb should agree with its subject in number and person. We say *I see*, not *I sees*; *he sees*, not *he see*; and *we see*, not *we sees*. Sometimes people have trouble making verbs agree with subjects in number. Here are the main circumstances to watch out for in your editing:

## 7.1 Words Intervening Between Subject and Verb

When something plural comes between a singular subject and its verb, the verb must still agree with the subject:

> Far below, a *landscape* of rolling brown hills and small trees *lies* among the small cottages.
>
> *Each* of the poems *has* certain striking qualities.
>
> *Neither* of the men *was* willing to compromise.
>
> The whole *experience*—the decision to go, the planning, the journey, and especially all the places we went and things we saw—*was* consistently exciting.

Similarly, don't let an intervening singular noun affect the agreement between a plural subject and its verb.

## 7.2 Compound Subject: Singular Nouns Joined by *and*

A compound subject made up of two or more singular nouns joined by *and* is usually plural:

> Careful thought and attention to detail *are* essential.

> Coffee and tea *were* served in the gazebo.

Occasional exceptions occur. If two nouns identify the same person or thing, or if two nouns taken together are thought of as a unit, the verb is singular:

> A common-law spouse and parent *has* an obligation to share the domestic responsibilities.

> Macaroni and cheese *is* my favourite.

But if you feel an urge to use a singular verb after a two-part subject joined by *and*, make sure you haven't used two nouns that mean the same thing and that are therefore redundant (see 60.3):

> ✗    The strength and power of her argument *is* undeniable.

Remove one or the other, or replace the two nouns with some other single word, such as *force* in this particular example.

## Proofreading Tip

### Agreement When a Subject Is Followed by a Particular Phrase

Phrases such as *in addition to*, *as well as*, and *together with* are prepositions, not conjunctions like *and*. A singular subject followed by one of them still takes a singular verb:

> The cat as well as the dog *comes* when I whistle.

> Ms. Hondiak, along with her daughters, *is* attending law school this year.

Compound subjects preceded by *each* or *every* take a singular verb:

> Each dog and cat *has* its own supper-dish.

## 7.3 Compound Subject: Parts Joined by *or* or a Correlative

When the parts of a subject are joined by the coordinating conjunction *or* (see 12.1) or by the correlative conjunctions *either . . . or, neither . . . nor, not . . . but, not only . . . but also, whether . . . or* (see 12.2), the part nearest the verb determines whether the verb is singular or plural:

> One or the other of you *has* the winning ticket. (both parts singular: verb singular; note that the subject is *one or the other*, not *you*)

> Neither the artists nor the politicians *feel* the arts funding is adequate. (both parts plural: verb plural)

> Neither the mainland nor the islands *are* interested in building the bridge. (first part singular, second part plural: verb plural)

> Neither my parents nor I *was* to blame. (first part plural, second part singular: verb singular)

Try to avoid the construction in the last example, since it usually sounds incorrect (see also 4.2). It's easy to rephrase:

> Neither I nor my parents *were* to blame.

> My parents *were* not to blame, nor *was* I.

## 7.4 Agreement with Indefinite Pronouns (see also 3.7, 4.3)

Most indefinite pronouns are singular: *another, anybody, anyone, anything, each, either, everybody, everyone, everything, much, neither, nobody, no one, nothing, one, other, somebody, someone, something*. A few (namely *all, any, more, most, none, some*) can be either singular or plural, depending on whether they refer to a single quantity or to a number of individual units within a group:

> *Some* of the pasta *is* eaten. (a single amount; *pasta* is singular, a mass noun)

> *Some* of the cookies *are* missing. (a number of cookies; *cookies* is plural)

> *All* of this novel *is* good. (a whole novel; *novel* is singular)

> *All* of his novels *are* well written. (a number of novels; *novels* is plural)

*Most* of the champagne *was* drunk. (a single mass; *champagne* is singular)

*Most* of the cases of champagne *have* been exported. (a number of cases; *cases* is plural)

*None* of the work *is* finished. (a single unit; *work* is singular)

*None* of the reports *are* ready. (a number of reports; *reports* is plural)

## 7.5 Subject Following Verb

When the normal subject–verb order is reversed, the verb still must agree with the real subject, not some word that happens to precede it:

There *is* only one *answer* to this question.

There *are* several possible *solutions* to the problem.

Here *comes* the judge.

Here *come* the clowns.

Thirty days *has September.*

Sitting in the coffee shop *were my archenemy* and *his pet turtle.*

When compounded singular nouns follow an opening *there* or *here*, most writers make the verb agree with the first noun:

There *was a computer* and *a copier* in the next room.

There *was* still *an essay* to be revised and *a play* to be studied before he could think about sleep.

There *was* still *the play* to be read and *his lines* to be memorized.

But others find this wrong or awkward sounding. By rephrasing the sentence you can easily avoid the issue and save a few words as well:

A computer and a copier were in the next room.

He still had an essay to revise and a play to study before he could think about sleep.

He still had to read the play and memorize his lines.

In expletive patterns, *it* takes a singular verb—usually a linking verb (see 6.1):

> It *is* questions like these that give the most trouble.

For more on the expletives *it* and *there*, see 1.11 and 60.1.

## Proofreading Tip

### Agreement and Predicate Nouns

Don't let a predicate noun determine a verb's number; the verb must agree with the subject of the sentence, not the complement (see 1.8 and 6.1):

> The last *word* in style that year *was* platform shoes and bell bottoms.

### 7.6 Agreement with Collective Nouns

Collective nouns (see section 2) are collections or groups that are considered as units and therefore usually take singular verbs:

> The government *has* passed the legislation.
>
> The company *is* planning several events to celebrate *its* centennial.

But when such a noun denotes the individual members of a group, the verb must be plural:

> His family *comes* from Korea. (singular)
>
> His family *come* from Jamaica, India, and Southern Europe. (plural)
>
> The audience *was* composed and attentive. (singular)
>
> The audience *were* sneezing, coughing, blowing their noses, and chatting with one another. (plural)

Such words as *number*, *half*, and *majority* can also be considered collective nouns and either singular and plural. In the following examples, notice how the article—*a* or *the*—changes the verb agreement:

*A number* of optimistic skiers *are* heading to the slopes. (*a number of*: plural)

*The number of* skiers here *is* quite large. (*The number of*: singular)

See also section 61 (amount, number).

## 7.7 Nouns that Are Always Singular or Always Plural

Some nouns, because of their meanings, cannot be inflected for number and will always be either singular or plural. Do not be fooled by some singular nouns that look plural because they end in *s*. Some examples are:

The *gold comes* from the Yukon. (always singular)

*Oxygen is* essential to human life. (always singular)

*Economics is* difficult for some people. (always singular)

Good *news is* always welcome. (always singular)

The *scissors are* in the kitchen. (always plural)

His *glasses are* fogged up. (always plural)

Her *clothes are* very stylish. (always plural)

For more on mass and countable nouns, see 2.1 and 8.3 #6.

## 7.8 Plurals: *criteria, data, media,* etc.

Be especially careful with words of Greek and Latin origin ending in *a*, which look like singular words but are in fact plural. The following words are plural; don't use singular verbs with them (see 51.20 [Borrowed words]):

criteria (singular is *criterion*)

phenomena (singular is *phenomenon*)

strata (singular is *stratum*)

While *criteria, phenomena,* and *strata* should always be treated as plural forms, some similar nouns may take either a singular or plural verb depending on the context. For instance, *data* should be treated as a plural noun in scientific contexts (the singular form is *datum*); in non-scientific practice, it may take a singular verb:

> Vertical meteorological data *are* collected using a parachute-borne sensor. (plural)

> Data from the poll *has been* tabulated and entered in the system. (singular)

It was once considered incorrect to use *media* as anything but a plural noun. But some dictionaries and usage guides have weakened their opposition to its use as a singular noun, arguing that it can be regarded in some contexts as a collective noun and thus followed by either a plural or singular verb, depending on whether it's being used to mean TV, print, and radio journalists collectively or individually.

> Some argue that the media *is* responsible for making health care the number-one concern among voters. (singular)

> A local newspaper broke the story, but other media *were* quick to report it. (plural)

Finally, the noun *trivia*, though it is derived from a Latin plural noun, may be treated as either singular or plural, depending on the writer's preference:

> I love Beatles trivia! If you know any Beatles trivia, please pass *it* on to me. (singular)

> I had hoped to have more information before making the decision, but *these* trivia *are* all I had to go on. (plural)

## 7.9 Agreement with Relative Pronouns

Whether a relative pronoun is singular or plural depends on its antecedent (see section 4). Therefore when a relative clause has *who*, *which*, or *that* as its subject, the verb must agree in number with the pronoun's antecedent:

> Her success is due to her intelligence and perseverance, which *have* overcome all obstacles. (The antecedent of *which* is *intelligence and perseverance*.)

Errors most often occur with the phrases *one of those . . . who* and *one of the . . . who*:

> He is one of those people who *have* difficulty reading aloud.

> He is one of the few people I know who *have* difficulty reading aloud.

*Have* is correct, since the antecedent of *who* is the plural *people*, not the singular *one*. The only time this construction takes a singular verb is when *one* is preceded by *the only*; *one* is then the antecedent of *who*:

> He is the only one of those attending who *has* difficulty reading aloud.

You can avoid the problem by simplifying:

> He has difficulty reading aloud.

> Of those attending, he alone has difficulty reading aloud.

## 7.10 Titles of Works: Words Referred to as Words

Titles of literary and other works and words referred to as words should be treated as singular even if they are plural in themselves:

> *The Two Gentlemen of Verona is* one of Shakespeare's lesser-known comedies.

> *The Four Seasons is* probably Vivaldi's best-known work.

> *Nervous Nellies is* an out-of-date slang term.

# 8. ADJECTIVES

An adjective modifies—limits, qualifies, or particularizes—a noun or pronoun. Adjectives generally answer the questions *Which? What kind of? How many? How much?*

> The *black* cat was *hungry*; he ate *five* sardines and drank some milk.

## 8.1 Kinds of Adjectives

Adjectives fall into two major classes: non-descriptive and descriptive.

### Non-descriptive adjectives

The several kinds of non-descriptive adjectives include some that are basically structure words (see 1.12):

- **articles** (see 8.3):

  *a* cat     *an* article     *the* report

- **demonstrative adjectives** (see 3.6):

  *this* hat     *that* problem     *these* women     *those* books

- **interrogative and relative adjectives** (see 3.4–3.5):

  *Which* book is best?          *What* time is it?

  *Whose* opinion do you trust?     She is the one *whose* opinion I trust.

- **possessive adjectives**—the possessive forms of personal and impersonal pronouns (see 3.1–3.2) and of nouns (see 2.2):

  | | | | |
  |---|---|---|---|
  | *my* book | *her* car | *its* colour | *their* luck |
  | *one's* beliefs | a *man's* coat | the *river's* mouth | |
  | *Hamlet's* ego | *Shirley's* job | the *car's* engine | |

  (Note: People who think of *form* rather than *function* prefer to call these "possessive pronouns" and "possessive nouns.")

- **indefinite and numerical adjectives** (see 3.7):

  | | | | |
  |---|---|---|---|
  | *some* money | *any* time | *more* fuel | *several* keys |
  | *three* ducks | *thirty* ships | the *fourth* act | |

### Descriptive adjectives

Descriptive adjectives give information about such matters as the size, shape, colour, nature, and quality of whatever a noun or pronoun names:

| | |
|---|---|
| a *fast* car | a *delicate* balance |
| a *beautiful* painting | a *brave* man |
| a *tempting* dessert | a *well-done* steak |
| a *once-in-a-lifetime* chance | *Canadian* literature |
| a *Shavian* play | *composted* leaves |
| a *fascinating* place to visit | *kitchen* towels |

a *dictionary* definition                    looking *refreshed*, he . . .

the book *to beat all other*s                the woman *of the hour*

the rabbits *who caused all the trouble*

a *large, impressive, three-storey, grey Victorian* house

As these examples illustrate, adjectival modifiers can be single (*fast, delicate, beautiful,* etc.), in groups or series (*large, impressive, three-storey, grey, Victorian*), or in compounds (*three-storey, well-done, once-in-a-lifetime*); they can be proper adjectives, formed from proper nouns (*Victorian, Canadian, Shavian*); they can be words that are adjectives only (*delicate, beautiful*) or words that can also function as other parts of speech (*fast, brave, tempting,* etc.), including nouns functioning as adjectives (*kitchen, dictionary*); they can be present participles (*tempting, fascinating*), past participles (*composted*), or infinitives (*to visit*); they can be participial phrases (*looking refreshed*), infinitive phrases (*to beat all other books*), or prepositional phrases (*of the hour);* or they can be relative clauses (*who caused all the trouble*).

For more examples see 15.1. On the punctuation of nouns in series, see section 38; on the overuse of nouns as modifiers, see 60.7; on infinitives and participles, see 10.1 and 10.4; on prepositions, see section 11; on relative clauses, see 3.4, 19.3 [Complex sentences], and 37.1.

## 8.2 Comparison of Descriptive Adjectives

Most descriptive adjectives can be inflected or supplemented for degree in order to make comparisons. The basic or dictionary form of an adjective is called its positive form: *high, difficult, calm.* Use it to compare two things that are equal or similar, or with qualifiers such as *not* and *almost* that are dissimilar:

This assignment is *as difficult as* last week's.

It is *not nearly so difficult as* I expected.

To make the comparative form, add *er* or put *more* (or *less*) in front of it: *higher, calmer, more difficult, less difficult.* Use it to compare two unequal things:

My grades are *higher* now than they were last year.

Your part is *more difficult* than mine.

For the superlative form, add *est* or put *most* (or *least*) in front of it: *highest, calmest, most difficult, least difficult.* Generally, use it to compare three or more unequal things:

> Whose blood pressure is the *highest*?

> He is the *calmest* and *least pretentious* person I know.

It is difficult to set rules for when to add *er* and *est* and when to use *more* and *most.* Some dictionaries tell you when *er* and *est* may be added to an adjective; if you have such a dictionary, and it doesn't give those forms for a particular adjective, use *more* and *most.* Otherwise, you can usually follow these guidelines:

- For adjectives of one syllable, usually add *er* and *est*:

| positive | comparative | superlative |
|----------|-------------|-------------|
| short | shorter | shortest |
| low | lower | lowest |
| rough | rougher | roughest |
| dry | drier | driest |
| grim | grimmer | grimmest |
| brave | braver | bravest |

You can also use *more* and *most, less* and *least* with many of these positive forms. (And note the spelling changes for *dry* and *grim*; see 51.4–51.6.)

- For adjectives of three or more syllables, usually use *more* and *most* (or *less* and *least*):

| beautiful | more beautiful | most beautiful |
|-----------|----------------|----------------|
| tiresome | more tiresome | most tiresome |
| sarcastic | more sarcastic | most sarcastic |
| fabulous | more fabulous | most fabulous |

- For most adjectives of two syllables ending in *al, ect, ed, ent, ful, ic, id, ing, ish, ive, less,* and *ous* (and any others where an added *er* or *est* would simply sound wrong), generally use *more* and *most* (or *less* and *least*):

| | | |
|---|---|---|
| formal | more formal | most formal |
| direct | more direct | most direct |
| polished | more polished | most polished |
| potent | more potent | most potent |
| tactful | more tactful | most tactful |
| manic | more manic | most manic |
| soothing | more soothing | most soothing |
| childish | more childish | most childish |
| restive | more restive | most restive |
| reckless | more reckless | most reckless |

- For other adjectives of two syllables, you usually have a choice; for example:

| | | |
|---|---|---|
| gentle | gentler, more gentle | gentlest, most gentle |
| bitter | bitterer, more bitter | bitterest, most bitter |
| lively | livelier, more lively | liveliest, most lively |
| silly | sillier, more silly | silliest, most silly |

When there is a choice, the forms with *more* and *most* will usually sound more formal and more emphatic than those with *er* and *est*. In fact, you can use *more* and *most* with almost any descriptive adjective, even one-syllable ones, if you want a little extra emphasis or a different rhythm:

> Of all my sister's friends, she is by far the *most brave*.

But the converse isn't true: adjectives of three or more syllables, and even shorter ones ending in *ous* and *ful* and so on, almost always require *more* and *most* unless you want to use very informal dialogue, or to create a humorous effect, as when Alice finds things in Wonderland to be growing "curiouser and curiouser."

Because of their meanings, some adjectives should not be compared: see section 61 (unique). See also sections 29 and 30, on faulty comparison.

# Proofreading Tip

## Avoiding "Doubling-Up" Errors in Adjective Forms

Don't double up a comparative or superlative form and write something like *more better* or *most prettiest*. If you want emphasis, use the adverbial intensifiers *much* or *far* or *by far*:

| | |
|---|---|
| much livelier | much more lively |
| far livelier | far more lively |
| livelier by far | by far the liveliest |
| much the liveliest | much the livelier of the two |

# Proofreading Tip

## Irregular Comparative and Superlative Adjective Forms

A few common adjectives form their comparative and superlative degrees irregularly:

| | | |
|---|---|---|
| good | better | best |
| bad | worse | worst |
| far | farther, further | farthest, furthest |
| little | littler, less, lesser | littlest, least |
| much, many | more | most |

(And see section 61 [farther, further].)

Good dictionaries list all irregular forms after the basic entry, including those in which a spelling change occurs.

## 8.3 Articles: *a*, *an*, and *the*

Articles—sometimes considered separately from parts of speech—can conveniently be thought of as kinds of adjectives. Like adjectives, they modify nouns. Like demonstrative and possessive adjectives, they are also sometimes called markers or determiners because an article indicates that a noun will soon follow.

The definite article *the* and the indefinite articles *a* or *an* are used idiomatically (see section 59).They often challenge people whose first language doesn't include articles, and no wonder, for it is almost impossible to set down all the rules for their use. Nevertheless, here are a few principles for your guidance.

1.  The form *a* of the indefinite article is used before words beginning with a consonant (*a dog, a building, a computer, a yellow orchid*), including words beginning with a pronounced *h* (*a horse, a historical event, a hotel, a hypothesis*) and words beginning with a *u* or *o* whose initial sound is that of *y* or *w* (*a useful book, a one-sided contest*). The form *an* is used before words beginning with a vowel sound (*an opinion, an underdog, an ugly duckling, an honour*). Similarly, the pronunciation of *the* changes from "thuh" to "thee" before a word beginning with a vowel sound.

2.  Generally, the definite article designates one or more particular persons or things whose identity is established by context or a modifier:

    *The* black stallion is in *the* barn.

    *The* shoe store is on *the* corner.

    *The* projector faces *the* front of *the* class.

    *The* skaters are at *the* starting line.

    whereas generally a person or thing designated by the indefinite article is not specific:

    He wants to buy *a* stallion.

    This town needs *a* new shoe store.

    Each class has *a* projector.

    The indefinite article is like *one*: it can be used only before singular countable nouns. Sometimes it even means *one*:

    I thought I would like the job, but I lasted only *a* week.

    This will take *an* hour or two.

Here are some further illustrations comparing *a* and *the*:

He gave me *a* gift. (unspecified)

He gave me *the* gift I had hoped for. (particularized by the modifying clause *I had hoped for*)

Give me *a* book. (any book that's handy)

Give me *the* book. (a particular book, one already identified or otherwise clear from the context)

Look up *paradigm* in *a* dictionary. (any dictionary)

Look up *paradigm* in *the* dictionary. (also meaning *any*, but considering all dictionaries as a class; or implying "the particular dictionary you customarily use")

3.   Articles can also be used generically. The horse is a beautiful animal: this emphasizes the class "horse" (and is not, here, equivalent to *That horse, standing over there by the fence, is a beautiful animal*). *A horse is a beautiful animal*: this means the same thing, but using the indefinite article emphasizes an individual member of the class. If no article is used—*Horses are beautiful animals*—the plural *Horses* causes the emphasis to fall on all the individual horses. Compare: *The computer is a prominent feature of our lives. A computer is almost a necessity in our society. Computers dominate our lives.*

4.   Definite articles go with some proper nouns but not with others:

| we say | but also |
| --- | --- |
| Canada | the Dominion of Canada |
| Great Britain | the United Kingdom |
| Gabriola Island | the Thousand Islands |
| Mount Baker | the Rocky Mountains, the Rockies |
| Queen's University | the University of Saskatchewan |

Note that *the* usually goes with plurals, names containing *of-* phrases, and names consisting of a modified common noun (the United *Kingdom*) as opposed to a modified proper noun (Great *Britain*).

5.   The definite article can also be used to indicate exclusiveness; *the* is then equivalent to *the only* or *the best* (in both speech and writing, such a *the* is sometimes emphasized):

He was *the* man we needed to organize us.

But if such exclusiveness is not intended, *the* is wrong:

✘   She soon becomes *the* good friend of the main character.

Change *good* to the superlative *best* (there can be only one *best*) and the definite article is correct; otherwise, *a* is correct:

She soon becomes *the* best friend of the main character.

6.   Uncountable nouns, whether mass nouns (see 2.1) or abstract nouns (see section 2), take no article if the mass or abstract sense governs:

✘   The poem features *a* direct, simple *praise* of nature.

Here the *a* must be removed. But notice the difference if a concrete noun is inserted; then the article is correct:

The poem features *a* direct, simple *hymn* of praise to nature.

If such a noun specifies a particular part of the whole, the definite article is correct:

*The praise* that she bestowed upon him made him blush.

Look at *the snow* I shovelled.

Compare:

He lacks humility.

He lacks *the* humility necessary for that position.

Orange juice is good for you.

Drink *the* orange juice I gave you. ("I gave you" or a similar phrase like "sitting in front of you" could be omitted as understood.)

It sometimes helps to think of each *the* in such instances as similar to a demonstrative or possessive adjective:

*Her* praise was generous.

Look at *that* snow I shovelled.

Drink *your* orange juice.

Drink *that* orange juice sitting in front of you.

If a usually abstract noun is used in a countable but not particularized sense, the indefinite article precedes it; if in a particularized way, the definite article:

This is *an* honour.
He did me *the* honour of inviting me.

Hers is *a* very special honesty.
She has *the* honesty of a saint.

7.    The definite article usually precedes an adjective functioning as a noun that represents a group (see 8.6):

*The* young should heed the advice of *the* elderly.

*The* poor will always have an advocate on city council.

8.    Titles of artistic works are not usually preceded by articles; but usage is inconsistent, and some idiomatically take the definite article. It would be incorrect to say:

✗    Donne's poetic power is evident in *the* "Sonnet X."

Either omit *the* or change it to *his*. And one wouldn't say "the *Alice in Wonderland*" or "the *Paradise Lost*." But it would be natural to refer to "the *Wind in the Willows*" and "the *Adventures of Huckleberry Finn*." (Of course if *A* or *The* is part of a title, it should be included: *A Midsummer Night's Dream*, *The Voyage Out*.) If a possessive (or pronominal) adjective or a possessive form of the author's name precedes, no article is needed: "Milton in his *Areopagitica*," "in Milton's *Areopagitica*."

9.  With names of academic fields and courses, whether proper nouns or abstract common nouns, no article is used:

    She is enrolled in Psychology 301.

    He reads books on psychology.

    He is majoring in communications.

    But if such terms are particularized common nouns or used adjectivally, the definite article is used:

    She studies *the* psychology of animal behaviour.

    You are learning more than you want about *the* English language.

    Yet it would be incorrect to speak of "*the* English literature," unless particularized as *the* English literature of, say, Nigeria, India, or the Philippines.

10. The definite article is used before the names of ships and trains:

    | | | |
    |---|---|---|
    | the *Beagle* | the *Titanic* | the *Mary Ellen Carter* |
    | the *St Roch* | the *Super Chief* | the *Orient Express* |

11. Sometimes the indefinite article is used to identify something in a general sense, but once the context has been clearly established, the definite article takes over:

    Tonight I wish to discuss a proposal that has been put forth recently, for I think it is *an* important one. *The* proposal to which I refer is that of . . .

## 8.4 Placement of Adjectives

Adjectival modifiers usually come just before or just after what they modify. Articles always, and other determiners almost always, precede the nouns they modify, usually with either no intervening words or only one or two other adjectives:

Trying to save *some* money, *the* manager decided to close *his* store early.

*The wise* manager decided not to hire *his scatterbrained* nephew.

Predicate adjectives (see 1.7) almost always follow the subject and linking verb:

> The forest is *cool* and *green* and *full of mushrooms.*

> Shortly after his operation he again became *healthy.*

Adjectives serving as objective complements usually follow the subject–verb–direct object (see 1.9):

> I thought the suggestion *preposterous.*

Most other single-word adjectives, and many compound adjectives, precede the nouns they modify:

> The *tall, dark,* and *handsome* hero lives on only in romantic fiction.

> The *weather* map shows a *cold* front moving into the *northern* prairies.

Phrases like "the map weather" or "a front cold" or "the prairies northern" are unidiomatic in English. (Note that order can determine meaning; for example, a *cold head is* not the same thing as a *head cold*: here, adjective and noun exchange functions as they exchange positions.)

But deviations are possible. Poetry, for example, often uses inversions for purposes of emphasis and rhyme:

> *Red* as a rose is she . . .

> And he called for his fiddlers *three.*

Such inversions also occur outside of poetry, but don't use them often, for when the unusual ceases to be unusual it loses much of its power. But if you want a certain emphasis or rhythm, you can put a predicate adjective before a noun (see 6.1):

> *Frustrated* I may have been, but I hadn't lost my wits or my passport.

or a regular adjective after a noun:

> She did the only thing *possible.*

> There was food *enough* for everyone.

(And note such standard terms as *Governor General* and *court-martial.*)

Compound adjectives and adjectives in phrases are often comfortable after a noun:

His friend, always *faithful and kind*, came at once.

Elfrida, *radiant and delighted*, left the room, *secure* in her victory.

Relative clauses and various kinds of phrases customarily follow the nouns they modify:

He is one detective *who believes in being thorough.*

The president *of the company* will retire next month.

The time *to vote* is now!

The only adjectival modifier not generally restricted in its position is the participial phrase (see 10.4):

*Having had abundant experience*, Kenneth applied for the job.

Kenneth, *having had abundant experience*, applied for the job.

Kenneth applied for the job, *having had abundant experience.*

This movability makes the participial phrase a popular way to introduce variety and to control emphasis (see 18.5). But be careful: writers sometimes lean too heavily on *ing*-phrases to begin sentences; and such phrases can be awkward or ambiguous, especially in the form of a dangling modifier:

✘  Having had abundant experience, the job seemed just right for Kenneth. (This sentence implies it is the job, not Kenneth, that has the abundant experience.)

See section 24; see also section 23, on misplaced modifiers.

## 8.5 Order of Adjectives

Adjectives usually follow an idiomatic order: an article or possessive or demonstrative comes first; then numbers, if any; then descriptive adjectives, usually in an order moving toward the more specific.

Adjectives indicating size, age, and colour usually come in that order. For example:

> the three big old black bears
>
> my two favourite canine hiking companions
>
> that well-known Canadian freestyle swimming champion

## 8.6 Adjectives Functioning as Nouns

If preceded by *the* or a possessive, many words normally thought of as adjectives can function as nouns, usually referring to people, and usually in a plural sense (see 8.3 #7); for example:

| | | | |
|---|---|---|---|
| the Swedish (but Canadians, not *the* Canadians) | the British | the Chinese | the Lebanese |
| the free | the brave | the poor | the sick and dying |
| the powerful | the wealthy | the uneducated | the unemployed |
| the starving | the enslaved | the deceased | the badly injured |
| the abstract | the metaphysical | the good | the true |
| the underprivileged the more fortunate | | the high and the mighty the big and the small | |

# 9. ADVERBS

Adverbs are often thought of as especially tricky. This part of speech is sometimes called the "catch-all" category, since any word that doesn't seem to fit elsewhere is usually assumed to be an adverb. Adverbs, therefore, are a little more complicated than adjectives.

## 9.1 Kinds and Functions of Adverbs

Whereas adjectives can modify only nouns and pronouns, adverbs can modify verbs (and verbals; see section 10), adjectives, other adverbs, and independent clauses or whole sentences. Adverbial modifiers generally answer such questions as *How? When? Where? Why?* and *To what degree?* That is, they indicate such things as manner (*How?*); time (*When? How often? How long?*); place and direction (*Where? In what direction?*); cause, result, and purpose (*Why?*

*To what effect?*); and degree (*To what degree? To what extent?*).
They also express affirmation and negation, conditions, concessions,
and comparisons. Here are some examples:

> *Fully* expecting to get the job, he sat *confidently in his seat* and began
> the interview.

To what degree? *Fully*: the adverb of degree modifies the participial
(verbal) phrase *expecting to get the job*. How? *Confidently*: the adverb
of manner modifies the verb *sat*. Where? *In his seat*: the prepositional
phrase functions as an adverb of place modifying the verb *sat*.

> *For many years* they lived *very happily together in Australia*.

How? *Happily* and *together*: the adverbs of manner modify the verb
*lived*. To what degree? *Very*: the intensifying adverb modifies the
adverb *happily*. Where? *In Australia*: the adverbial prepositional
phrase modifies the verb *lived*. How long? *For many years*: the prepositional phrase functions as an adverb of time or duration modifying the verb—or it can be thought of as modifying the whole clause
*they lived very happily together in Australia*.

> *Fortunately*, the cut was *not* deep.

To what effect? *Fortunately*: a sentence modifier. To what degree?
*Not*: the negating adverb modifies the adjective *deep*.

> *Because their budget was tight*, they *eventually* decided not to buy a car.

Why? *Because their budget was tight*: the adverbial clause of cause
modifies the verb *decided* or, in a way, all the rest of the sentence.
When? *Eventually*: the adverb of time modifies the verb *decided*. The
negating *not* modifies the infinitive (verbal) *to buy*.

> *Last November* it *seldom* snowed.

When? *Last November*: the noun phrase functions as an adverb of
time modifying the verb *snowed*. How often? *Seldom*: the adverb
of time or frequency modifies the verb *snowed*.

> Driving *fast* is *often* dangerous.

How? *Fast*: the adverb of manner modifies the gerund (verbal) *driving*. When? *Often*: the adverb of time or frequency modifies the adjective *dangerous*.

> *If you're tired*, I will walk the dog.

The conditional clause modifies the verb (*will walk*).

> *Although she dislikes the city intensely*, she agreed to go *there in order to keep peace in the family*.

*Intensely* (degree) modifies the verb *dislikes*. *There* (place) modifies the infinitive *to go*. *Although she dislikes the city intensely* is an adverbial clause of concession. The prepositional phrase *in order to keep peace in the family* is an adverb of purpose modifying the verb *agreed*. The smaller adverbial prepositional phrase *in the family* modifies the infinitive phrase *to keep peace*, answering the question *Where?*

> Meredith was *better* prepared *than I was*.

The adverb *better* modifies the adjective *prepared*; it and the clause *than I was* express comparison or contrast.

### Adverbs as condensed clauses

Some single-word adverbs and adverbial phrases, especially sentence modifiers, can be thought of as reduced clauses:

> *Fortunately* [It is fortunate that], the cut was not deep.

> *When possible* [When it is possible], let your writing sit *before proofreading it* [before you proofread it].

### Other kinds of adverbs: relative, interrogative, conjunctive

1.  The relative adverbs *where* and *when* are used to introduce relative (adjective) clauses (see 3.4):

    > She returned to the town *where she had grown up*.

    > Adam looked forward to the moment *when it would be his turn*.

2.  The interrogative adverbs (*where*, *when*, *why*, and *how*) are used in questions:

    > *Where* are you going? *Why? How* soon? *How* will you get there? *When* will you return?

3.   Conjunctive adverbs usually join whole clauses or sentences to each other and indicate the nature of the connection:

> It was an important question; *therefore* they took their time over it.

> Only fifteen people showed up. *Nevertheless*, the promoter didn't let his disappointment show.

> The tornado almost flattened the town; *however*, no one, except Dorothy and her dog, was reported missing.

For more on conjunctive adverbs, see 33.8.

## 9.2 Forms of Adverbs

### Adverbs ending in *ly*

Many adverbs are formed by adding *ly* to descriptive adjectives, for example *roughly, happily, fundamentally, curiously*. Don't use an adjectival form where an adverbial form is needed:

> She is a *careful* driver. (adjective modifying *driver*)

> She drives *carefully*. (adverb modifying *drives*)

### Adverbs not ending in *ly*

Some adverbs don't end in *ly*, for example *ahead, almost, alone, down, however, long, now, often, quite, since, soon, then, there, therefore, when, where*. Others without the *ly* are identical to adjectives, for example *far, fast, little, low, more, much, well*:

> He owns a *fast* car. (adjective)
> He likes to drive *fast*. (adverb)

> They have a *low* opinion of him. (adjective)
> They flew *low* over the coast. (adverb)

*Well* as an adjective means *healthy* (I am quite *well*, thank you) or sometimes *satisfactory, right*, or *advisable* (all is *well*; it is *well* you came when you did; it is *well* to prepare carefully). When someone asks you about your health, don't say you are *good* (unless you want to imply you are the opposite of *bad* or *evil*). You should say "I am well." Otherwise *well* is an adverb and should be used instead of the frequently misused *good*, which is an adjective. Similarly, *bad* is an adjective, *badly* an adverb. Be careful with these often misused forms:

> She did a *good* coaching job. The team played *well.*

> They felt *bad* for the child, who had played *badly* in the game. (*Felt* is a linking verb here and requires a predicate adjective—*bad*—as its subjective complement.)

See also section 61 (good, bad, badly, well).

### Adverbs with short and long forms

Some common adverbs have two forms, one with *ly* and one without. The form without *ly* is identical to the adjective, but the two do not mean the same thing. Check a dictionary if you aren't sure of the meanings of such pairs as these:

| | | | |
|---|---|---|---|
| even, evenly | fair, fairly | hard, hardly | high, highly |
| just, justly | late, lately | near, nearly | right, rightly |

With some of the others, the short form, although informal, is equivalent, sometimes even preferable, to the longer form; for example:

> Don't talk so *loud.*

> Look *deep* into my eyes.

> Come *straight* home.

As for the rest, words such as *cheap, clear, close, direct, loose, quick, quiet, sharp, smooth, strong, tight,* and *wrong* are often used as adverbs, but in formal contexts you should use the *ly* form.

But if you're writing instructions, avoid the opposite error, one found in many cookbooks. It's right to tell readers to "stir the sauce *slowly*," but wrong to tell them to "slice the onion *thinly*." You wouldn't tell someone to "sand the wood *smoothly*," but *smooth*—that is, until it is smooth; so slice the onion [so that it is] *thin*, and chop the nuts [until they are] *fine*, and so on. In such phrases, the modifier goes with the noun, not the verb.

### *Real* and *really, sure* and *surely*

Don't use the adjectival form where the adverbial is needed:

> Her suggestion was *really* [not *real*] different.

> He *surely* [not *sure*] was right about the weather.

But the second example may sound odd. Most people would stick with *sure* in a colloquial context and use *certainly* in a formal one. And *really* is seldom needed at all (see section 61 [very]).

### Adjectives ending in *ly*

Some common adjectives end in *ly*, among them *burly, curly, early, friendly, holy, homely, leisurely, likely, lively, lovely, lowly, orderly, silly, surly, ugly*. Adding another *ly* to these inevitably sounds awkward. And though some dictionaries label such adjectives as adverbs as well (he walked *leisurely* toward the door; she behaved *friendly* toward the strangers), that usage also often sounds awkward. You can avoid the problem by adding a few words or rephrasing:

> He walked toward the door in a leisurely manner.
>
> She behaved in a friendly way toward the strangers.
>
> She was friendly toward the strangers.

In a few instances, however, the *ly* adjectives do also serve idiomatically as adverbs; for example:

> He spoke *kindly* of you.
>
> She rises *early*.
>
> He exercises *daily*.
>
> The tour leaves *hourly*.
>
> Most magazines are published *weekly* or *monthly*.

## 9.3 Comparison of Adverbs

Like descriptive adjectives, most adverbs that are similarly descriptive can be inflected or supplemented for degree (see 8.2). The following are some guidelines on how adverbs are inflected:

- Some short adverbs without *ly* form their comparative and superlative degrees with *er* and *est*; for example:

| positive | comparative | superlative |
| --- | --- | --- |
| fast | faster | fastest |
| hard | harder | hardest |
| high | higher | highest |
| late | later | latest |
| low | lower | lowest |
| soon | sooner | soonest |

*Less* and *least* also sometimes go with these; for example:

Employees work *least hard* on the days following a holiday.

They still ran fast, but *less fast* than they had the day before.

(Note, however, that the second example would be more effective if *less fast* were replaced with *slower*.)

- Adverbs of three or more syllables ending in *ly* use *more* and *most*, *less* and *least*; for example:

| | | |
|---|---|---|
| happily | more happily | most happily |
| stridently | less stridently | least stridently |
| disconsolately | more disconsolately | most disconsolately |

- Most two-syllable adverbs, whether or not they end in *ly*, also use *more* and *most*, *less* and *least*, though a few can also be inflected with *er* and *est*; for example:

| | | |
|---|---|---|
| slowly | more slowly | most slowly |
| grimly | less grimly | least grimly |
| fully | more fully | most fully |
| alone | more alone | most alone |
| kindly | kindlier, more kindly | kindliest, most kindly |
| often | more often | most often |

- Some adverbs form their comparative and superlative degrees irregularly:

| | | |
|---|---|---|
| badly | worse | worst |
| well | better | best |
| much | more | most |
| little | less | least |
| far | farther, further | farthest, furthest |

- A few adverbs of place use *farther* and *farthest* (or *further* and *furthest*; see section 61 [farther, further]); for example:

| | | |
|---|---|---|
| down | farther down | farthest down |
| north | farther north | farthest north |

- As with adjectives, the adverbs *much*, *far*, and *by far* serve as intensifiers in comparisons:

  Bob and Louise live *much* more comfortably than they used to.

  They flew *far* lower than they should have.

  He practises harder *by far* than anyone else in the orchestra.

## 9.4 Placement of Adverbs

### Adverbs modifying adjectives or other adverbs

An intensifying or qualifying adverb almost always goes just before the adjective or adverb it modifies:

*almost* always    *strongly* confident    *very* hot

*only* two    *most* surely

### Modifiers of verbs

Whether single words, phrases, or clauses, most modifiers of verbs are more flexible in their position than any other part of speech. Often they can go almost anywhere in a sentence and still function clearly:

*Proudly*, he pointed to his photo in the paper.

He *proudly* pointed to his photo in the paper.

He pointed *proudly* to his photo in the paper.

He pointed to his photo in the paper *proudly*.

But notice that the emphasis (and therefore the overall effect and meaning) changes slightly. Here is another example; note how much you can control the emphasis:

*Because she likes movies*, Sue *often* goes to the cineplex.

Sue, *because she likes movies*, *often* goes to the cineplex.

Sue *often* goes to the cineplex *because she likes movies*.

And in each version, the adverb *often* could come after *goes* or after *cineplex*.

### Adverbs of place

The preceding example also illustrates the only major restriction on adverbial modifiers of the verb. A phrase like *to the cineplex*, like a direct object, almost has to follow the verb immediately or with no more than an *often* or other such word intervening. But sometimes an adverb of place or direction can come first if a sentence's usual word order is reversed to emphasize place or direction:

> *Off to market* we shall go.

> *There* she stood, staring out to sea.

> *Where* are you going? (but: Are you going *there*?)

> *Downward* he plummeted, waiting until the last moment to pull the ripcord.

### Sentence modifiers

Sentence modifiers usually come at the beginning, but they, too, can be placed elsewhere for purposes of emphasis or rhythm:

> *Fortunately*, the groom was able to stand.

> The groom, *fortunately*, was able to stand.

> The groom was, *fortunately*, able to stand.

> The groom was able to stand, *fortunately*.

With longer or more involved sentences, however, a sentence modifier at the end loses much of its force and point, obviously; obviously it works better if placed earlier. See also 33.8, on the placement and punctuation of conjunctive adverbs, and section 23, on misplaced modifiers.

## 10. VERBALS

Infinitives, participles, and gerunds are called verbals, forms that are derived from verbs but that cannot function as main or finite verbs. Verbals are non-finite forms unfinished, not restricted by person and number as finite verbs are (see 6.4, and the note at the end of 6.2). They function as other parts of speech yet retain some characteristics of verbs: they can have objects, they can be modified by adverbs, and they can express tense and voice. Verbals often introduce verbal phrases, groups of words that themselves function as other parts of speech (see 1.16). Verbals enable you to inject much of the strength and liveliness of verbs into your writing even though the words are functioning as adjectives, adverbs, and nouns.

## 10.1 Infinitives

We sometimes use a form called the infinitive to identify particular verbs. We may speak of "the verb *to be*" or "the verb *to live*." (In this book, however, we usually use just the basic or dictionary form: *be, live*; see note in 6.2.) An infinitive usually consists of the word *to* (often called "the sign of the infinitive") followed by the basic form: *to be, to live*. Infinitives can function as nouns, adjectives, and adverbs.

### Infinitives as nouns

> *To save* the wolves was Farley Mowat's primary intention.

The infinitive phrase *To save the wolves* is the subject of the verb *was*. The noun *wolves* is the direct object of the infinitive *To save*.

> She wanted *to end* the game quickly.

The infinitive phrase *to end the game quickly* is the direct object of the verb *wanted*. The infinitive *to end* is modified by the adverb *quickly* and has the noun *game* as its own direct object.

> She wanted me *to stop* the game.

Here *me to stop the game* is the object of the verb *wanted*.

### Infinitives as adjectives

> His strong desire *to be* a doctor made him studious.

The infinitive phrase *to be a doctor* modifies the noun *desire*. Since *be* is a linking verb, the infinitive is here followed by the predicate noun *doctor*.

> The cappuccino coupons are the ones *to save*.

The infinitive *to save* modifies the pronoun *ones*.

### Infinitives as adverbs

> She was lucky *to have* such a friend.

The infinitive phrase *to have such a friend* modifies the predicate adjective *lucky*. The noun phrase *such a friend* is the direct object of the infinitive *to have*.

> He went to Calgary to experience the Stampede.

The infinitive phrase *to experience the Stampede* is an adverb of purpose modifying the verb *went*; *the Stampede* is the direct object of the infinitive *to experience*.

## 10.2 Tense and Voice of Infinitives (see 6.7–6.8, 6.15–6.16)

Infinitives may be either present (to indicate a time the same as or later than that of the main verb):

> She wants me *to go* to Egypt with her.

> I was pleased *to meet* you.

or present perfect (to indicate a time before that of the main verb); the *to* then goes with the auxiliary *have*, followed by the verb's past participle:

> I was lucky *to have met* the manager before the interview.

Each of these may also take the progressive form, using the auxiliaries *be* and *have*:

> I expect *to be travelling* in Europe this summer.

> He was said *to have been* planning the takeover for months.

> I look forward *to meeting* you.

Infinitives may also be in the passive voice, again putting *to* with the appropriate auxiliaries, then adding a past participle:

> The children wanted *to be taken* to see Cirque du Soleil.

> He was thought *to have been motivated* by sheer ambition.

# Proofreading Tip

## Verb Idioms that Omit *to* Before the Infinitive Verb Form

After some verbs, an infinitive can occur without the customary *to*; for example:

*Let* sleeping dogs *lie.*     It *made* me *cry.*

We *saw* the horse *jump.*     He *felt* the house *shake.*

I *helped* her (to) *decide.*

The *to* in the last example is optional.

## 10.3 Split Infinitives

Since an infinitive is a unit, separating its parts can weaken it and often results in lack of clarity.

✘    He wanted *to* quickly *conclude* the business of the meeting.

✘    She claimed that it was too difficult *to* very accurately or confidently *solve* such a problem in the time allowed.

You can usually avoid or repair such splits by rephrasing or rearranging so the adverbs don't interrupt the infinitive:

He wanted *to conclude* the business of the meeting quickly.

She claimed that it was too difficult, in the time allowed, *to solve* such a problem with any degree of accuracy or confidence.

Occasionally, it is better to split an infinitive than to sound overly formal.

The space crew vowed *to* boldly *go* where no one has gone before.

This split sounds more natural than the formal *boldly to go*, and *boldly* can't be moved to the end of the sentence (see section 23).

If the infinitive includes a form of *be* or *have* as an auxiliary, an adverb before the last part is less likely to sound out of place:

The demonstration was thought *to have been* carefully *planned.*

We seem *to have* finally *found* the right road.

## 10.4 Participles

The past participle and present participle work with various auxiliaries to form a finite verb's perfect and progressive tenses (see 6.7–6.8). But without the auxiliaries to indicate person and number, the participles are non-finite and cannot function as verbs. Instead they function as adjectives, modifying nouns and pronouns:

> *Beaming* happily, Josef received his well-deserved and hard-won promotion.

Present participles always end in *ing*, regular past participles in *ed* or *d*. Irregular past participles end variously: *made, mown, broken*, etc. (see 6.2–6.3). A regular past participle is identical to the past-tense form of a verb, but you can easily check a given word's function in a sentence. In the example above, the past-tense form *received* clearly has *Josef* as it subject; the past participle *well-deserved*, with no subject, is an adjective modifying *promotion*. More examples:

> *Painted* houses require more care than brick ones.

The past participle *painted* modifies the noun *houses*.

> *Impressed*, she recounted the film's more *thrilling* episodes.

The past participle *impressed* modifies the subject, *she*; the present participle *thrilling* modifies the noun *episodes* and is itself modified by the adverb *more*.

> The subject *discussed* most often was the message behind the song.

The past participle *discussed* modifies the noun *subject* and is itself modified by the adverbial *most often*.

> Suddenly *finding* himself alone, he became very *flustered*.

The present participle *finding* introduces the participial phrase *finding himself alone*, which modifies the subject, *he*; *finding*, as a verbal, has *himself* as a direct object and is modified by the adverb *suddenly*. The past participle *flustered* functions as a predicate adjective after the linking verb *became*; it modifies *he* and is itself modified by the adverb *very*.

## 10.5 Tense and Voice of Participles (see 6.7–6.8, 6.15–6.16)

The standard present or past participle indicates a time the same as that of the main verb:

*Being* the tallest, Luzia played centre.

Strictly speaking, a past participle by itself amounts to passive voice:

*Worried* by what he'd heard, Joe picked up the phone.

With *ing* attached to an auxiliary, participles can also be in the perfect or perfect progressive tense, indicating a time earlier than that of the main verb:

*Having painted* himself into a corner, George climbed out the window.

*Having been painting* for over two hours, Leah decided to take a break.

Participles in the present progressive and the perfect tenses can also be in the passive voice:

The subject *being discussed* was the environment.

*Having been warned*, she knew better than to accept the offer.

## Proofreading Tip

### Present Participles and Sentence Fragments

It is particularly important that you know a present participle when you write one. If you use a present participle and think it's functioning as a finite verb, you may well produce a fragment (see 1.24).

## 10.6 Gerunds

When the *ing* form of a verb functions as a noun, it is called a gerund:

Josef gave himself a good *talking* to.

*Moving* offices can be hard work.

Sylvester has a profound fear of *flying*.

Careful preparation—*brainstorming*, *organizing*, and *outlining*—helps produce good writing.

The gerund *talking* is a direct object and is itself modified by the adjective *good*. The gerund *Moving* is the subject of the sentence, and has *offices* as a direct object. The gerund *flying* is the object of the preposition *of*. In the final example, the three gerunds constitute an appositive or definition of the subject noun, *preparation* (see 1.17).

## 10.7 Tense and Voice of Gerunds (see 6.7–6.8 and 6.15–6.16)

As with infinitives and participles, the perfect form of a gerund indicates a time earlier than that of the main verb:

> My *having answered* the phone myself may have secured the contract.

And a gerund can be in the passive voice:

> His *being praised* by the supervisor gave him a big lift.

Be aware, though, that using either the perfect or the passive gerund can produce awkward results:

> The misunderstanding resulted from *our not having received* the latest information.

> He was proud of *her being awarded* the gold star for excellence.

Rephrasing such examples to avoid the gerund will produce clearer sentences:

> The misunderstanding resulted because we didn't receive the latest information.

> He was proud of her for receiving the gold star of excellence.

## 10.8 Possessives with Gerunds

In formal usage, a noun or a personal pronoun preceding a gerund will usually be in the possessive case:

> *His* cooking left much to be desired.

> She approved of *Bob's* cleaning the house.

> Can you explain the *engine's* not starting?

If the gerund is the subject, as in the first example, the possessive is essential. Otherwise, if you are writing informally, and especially if you want to emphasize the noun or pronoun, you don't need to use the possessive:

> She approved of *Bob* cooking the dinner rather than Jim.

> Can you explain the *engine* not starting?

Further, in order to avoid awkward-sounding constructions, you usually won't use a possessive form when the noun preceding a gerund is (a) abstract, (b) plural, (c) multiple, or (d) separated from the gerund by modifiers (other than adverbs like *not* or *always* when they sound almost like part of the verbal):

(a)  He couldn't bear the thought of *love striking* again.

(b)  The possibility of the *thieves returning* to their hideout was slim.

(c)  There is a good chance of *Alberto and Maria agreeing* to your proposal.

(d)  One might well wonder at a *man* with such expertise *claiming* to be ignorant.

## Proofreading Tip

### The Gerund Followed Immediately by Another Noun

A gerund followed immediately by another noun will sometimes sound awkward or ambiguous unless you interpose *of* or *the* or some similar term to keep the gerund from sounding like a participle:

| | |
|---|---|
| his building (of) boats | your organizing (of the) material |
| my practising (the) piano | his revealing (of, the, of the) sources |

## 10.9 Verbals in Absolute Phrases

Infinitives and participles (but not gerunds) can function in absolute phrases (see 1.18):

> *To say the least*, the day was memorable.

> *Strictly speaking*, their actions were not legal.

> *All things considered*, the meeting was a success.

# 11. PREPOSITIONS

Prepositions are structure words or function words (see 1.12); they do not change their form. A preposition is part of a prepositional phrase, and it usually precedes the rest of the phrase, which includes a noun or pronoun as the object of the preposition:

> This is a book *about flirting.*

> She sent an email *to her spouse.*

Make a question of the preposition and ask *what* or *whom* and the answer will always be the object: *About* what? Flirting. *To* whom? Her spouse.

## 11.1 Functions of Prepositions and Prepositional Phrases

A preposition links its object to some other word in the sentence; the prepositional phrase then functions as either an adjectival or an adverbial modifier:

> He laid the digital camera *on the table.*

Here, *on* links *table* to the verb *laid*; the phrase *on the table* therefore functions as an adverb describing *where* the digital camera was laid.

> It was a time *for celebration.*

Here, *for* links *celebration* to the noun *time*; the phrase therefore functions as an adjective indicating *what kind of* time.

## 11.2 Placement of Prepositions

Usually, like articles, prepositions signal that a noun or pronoun soon follows. But prepositions can also come at the ends of clauses or sentences, for example in a question, for emphasis, or to avoid stiffness:

> Which handbag do you want to look *at?*

> Whom are you buying the handbag *for?*

> She is the one I want to give the handbag *to.*

> They had several issues to contend *with.*

> This is the restaurant I was telling you *about.*

> The problem he was dealing *with* seemed insurmountable.

Some would prefer "with which he was dealing," especially in a formal context. But it isn't wrong to end a sentence or clause with a preposition, in spite of what many people have been taught; just don't do it so often that it calls attention to itself. Remember that Sir Winston Churchill is supposed to have said that repeated use of the preposition in this way was the sort of usage "up with which I will not put."

## 11.3 Common Prepositions

Most prepositions indicate a spatial or temporal relation, or such things as purpose, concession, comparison, manner, and agency. Here is a list of common prepositions; note that several consist of more than one word:

| | | | |
|---|---|---|---|
| about | beneath | in front of | past |
| above | beside | in order to | regarding |
| according to | besides | in place of | regardless of |
| across | between | in relation to | round |
| across from | beyond | inside | since |
| after | but | in spite of | such as |
| against | by | into | through |
| ahead of | by way of | like | throughout |
| along | concerning | near | till |
| alongside | considering | next to | to |
| among | contrary to | notwithstanding | toward(s) |
| apart from | despite | of | under |
| around | down | off | underneath |
| as | during | on | unlike |
| as for | except | on account of | until |
| at | except for | onto | up |
| away from | excepting | on top of | upon |
| because of | for | opposite | with |
| before | from | out | within |
| behind | in | outside | without |
| below | in addition to | over | |

## 11.4 Two-part Verbs

English has many two-part and even three-part verbs consisting of a simple verb in combination with another word or words, for example *cool off, act up, blow up, find out, hold up, carry on, get on with, stick up for.* It doesn't matter whether you think of the added words as prepositions, adverbs, or some sort of "particle." Indeed, sometimes it is difficult to say whether a word like *down* in *sit down* is functioning as part of the verb or as an adverb describing how one can sit; but the *down* and *up* in "sit down to a good meal" and "sit up in your chair" seem more like parts of the verbs than, say, the preposition *at* in "He sat at his desk." Usually you can sense a difference in sound: in "He *took over* the operation" both parts are stressed when said aloud, whereas in "He *took* over three hours to get here" only the *took* is stressed; *over* functions separately. Often, too, the parts of a verb can be separated and still mean the same, whereas the verb and preposition or adverb cannot:

> The children were *won over* by the actor's exuberance.
>
> The actor's exuberance *won* the children *over.*
>
> He *won* over his nearest opponent by three points.

> They *blew up* the remains of the old factory.
>
> They *blew* the remains of the old factory *up.*
>
> The wind *blew* up the chimney.

Some two-part verbs cannot be separated, for example *see to, look after, run across, sit up, turn in.* Some simple verbs can take two or more different words to form new verbs; for example:

| | | | |
|---|---|---|---|
| fall in | fill in | think out | try on |
| fall out | fill out | think up | try out |
| | fill up | | |

Some verbs can use several different words to form idiomatic expressions:

| | | |
|---|---|---|
| bring about | let alone | turn down |
| bring around | let down | turn in |
| bring down | let go | turn loose |

| | | |
|---|---|---|
| bring forward | let loose | turn off |
| bring in | let off | turn on |
| bring off | let on | turn out |
| bring on | let up | turn over |
| bring out | | turn to |
| bring over | | turn up |
| bring to | | |
| bring up | | |

See 51.18 on the spelling of two-part verbs.

## 11.5 Using Two-part Verbs: Informality and Formality

By consciously using or avoiding these verbs in a piece of writing, you can help control tone. Most of these verbs are standard and idiomatic, but some are informal or colloquial or even slangy, for example *let up, mess up, shake up, trip up* (see section 53). Even the standard ones are often relatively informal; that is, they have more formal equivalents; for example:

| informal | formal |
|---|---|
| give away | bestow; reveal, betray |
| give back | return |
| give in | yield, concede |
| give off | discharge, emit |
| give out | emit; distribute; become exhausted |
| give over | relinquish, abandon; cease |
| give up | despair; stop, renounce; surrender, cede |
| give way | withdraw, retreat; make room for; collapse |

If you choose *buy* as more appropriate to your context than *purchase*, you'll probably also want to use some two-part verbs rather than their more formal, often Latinate, equivalents; for example you'd probably say *buy up* rather than *acquire*. But if you're writing a strictly formal piece, you may want to avoid the informal terms, or limit yourself to just a couple for contrast or spice.

# 12. CONJUNCTIONS

Conjunctions are another kind of structure word or function word (see 1.12). As their name indicates, conjunctions are words that "join together." There are three kinds of conjunctions: coordinating, correlative, and subordinating.

## 12.1 Coordinating Conjunctions

There are only seven coordinating conjunctions, so they are easy to remember:

and    but    for    nor    or    so    yet

When you use a coordinating conjunction, choose the appropriate one. *And* indicates addition, *nor* indicates negative addition (equivalent to *also not*), *but* and *yet* indicate contrast or opposition, *or* indicates choice, *for* indicates cause or reason, and *so* indicates effect or result. (See also section 28, on faulty coordination.)

Bear in mind that some coordinating conjunctions can also be other parts of speech: *yet* can be an adverb (It's not *yet* ten o'clock); *so* can be an adverb (It was *so* dark that . . .), an adjective (Is that *so?*), a demonstrative pronoun (I liked him, and I told him *so*), and an interjection (*So!*); *for* is also a common preposition (*for* a while, *for* me); and *but* can be a preposition, meaning *except* (all *but* two).

Coordinating conjunctions have three main functions, which are discussed below.

### Joining words, phrases, and subordinate clauses

*And, but, or,* and *yet* join coordinate elements within sentences. The elements joined should be of equal importance and of similar grammatical structure and function. When joined, they are sometimes called compounds of various kinds (see 1.25). Here are examples of how various kinds of sentence elements may be compounded:

I saw *Jean* and *Ralph.* (two direct objects)

*Jean* and *Ralph* saw me. (two subjects)

They *whooped* and *hollered.* (two verbs)

The gnome was *short*, *fat*, and *melancholic*. (three predicate adjectives)

He ate *fast* and *noisily*. (two adverbs)

The bird flew *in the door* and *out the window*. (two adverbial prepositional phrases)

*Tired* but *determined*, the teacher plodded on. (two past participles)

The lovely children *cooked the dinner* and *washed the dishes*. (two verbs with direct objects)

People *who invest wisely* and *who spend carefully* often have boring lives. (two adjective clauses)

I travel *when I have the time and money* and *when I can find someone rich to accompany me*. (two adverbial clauses)

The career coach told him *what he should wear* and *how he should speak*. (two noun clauses)

Obviously the elements being joined won't always have identical structures, but don't disappoint readers' natural expectations that compound elements will be parallel. For example it would be weaker to write the last example with one direct object as a clause and the other as an infinitive phrase (see section 27, on faulty parallelism):

✗    The career coach told him *what he should wear* and *how to speak*.

When three or more elements are compounded, the conjunction usually appears only between the last two, though *and* and *or* can appear throughout for purposes of rhythm or emphasis:

There was a tug-of-war *and* a sack race *and* an egg race *and* a three-legged race *and* . . . well, there was just about any kind of game anyone could want at a picnic.

And occasionally *and* can be omitted entirely also for emphasis (see also 38.3):

There were flowers galore—fuchsias, snap-dragons, jonquils, dahlias, azaleas, tulips, roses, lilacs, camellias—more kinds of flowers than I wanted to see on any one day.

### Joining independent clauses

All seven coordinating conjunctions can join independent clauses to make compound (or compound-complex) sentences (see 1.25). The clauses will be grammatically equivalent, since they are independent; but they needn't be grammatically parallel or even of similar length, though they often are both, for parallelism is a strong stylistic force. Here are some examples:

> The players fought, the umpires shouted, *and* the fans booed.

> The kestrel flew higher and higher, in ever-wider circles, *and* soon it was but a speck in the sky overhead.

> Jean saw me, *but* Ralph didn't.

> I won't do it, *nor* will she. (With *nor* there must be some sort of negative in the first clause. Note that after *nor* the normal subject–verb order is reversed.)

> There was no way to avoid it, *so* I decided to get as much out of the experience as I could.

## Proofreading Tip

### On Using the Conjunction *so*

The conjunction *so* is informal; in formal writing, you can almost always indicate cause-effect relations with a *because* or *since* clause instead:

> *Since* there was no way to avoid it, I decided to get as much out of the experience as I could.

*And so*, however, is acceptable, but don't use it often because it is a weak transition:

> We overslept, *and so* we missed the keynote address.

### Joining sentences

In spite of what many of us have been taught, it isn't wrong to begin a sentence with *And* or *But*, or for that matter any of the other coordinating conjunctions. Be advised, however, that *For*, since it is so similar in meaning to *because*, often sounds strange at the start of a sentence, as if introducing a fragmentary subordinate clause (see 12.3). Another coordinating conjunction, *And so*, often sounds too colloquial. But the rest, especially *And* and *But*, make good openers—as long as you don't overuse them. An opening *But* or *Yet* can nicely emphasize a contrast or other turn of thought (as in the preceding sentence). An opening *And* can also be emphatic:

> He told the people of the province he was sorry. *And* he meant it.

Both *And* and *But* as sentence openers contribute to paragraph coherence (see 66.4). And, especially in a narrative, a succession of opening *Ands* can impart a feeling of rapid pace, even breathless excitement. Used too often, they can become tedious, but used carefully and when they feel natural, they can be effective. For punctuation with coordinating conjunctions, see chapter IV, especially 33.1–33.3 and 44.4.

## 12.2 Correlative Conjunctions

Correlative conjunctions come in pairs. They correlate ("relate together") two parallel parts of a sentence. The following are the principal ones:

| | |
|---|---|
| either . . . or | neither . . . nor |
| whether . . . or | both . . . and |
| not . . . but | not only . . . but also |

Correlative conjunctions enable you to write sentences containing forcefully balanced elements, but don't overdo them. They are also more at home in formal than in informal writing. Some examples:

> *Either* Rodney *or* Elliott is going to drive.

> She accepted *neither* the first *nor* the second job offer.

> *Whether* by accident *or* by design, the number turned out to be exactly right.

> *Both* the administration *and* the employees are pleased with the new plan.

> She *not only* plays well *but also* sings well.

> *Not only* does she play well, *but* she *also* sings well.

Notice, in the last two examples, how *also* or its equivalent can be moved away from the *but*. And in the last example, note how *does* is needed as an auxiliary because the clause is in the present tense. Except for these variations, make what follows one term exactly parallel to what follows the other: *by accident* || *by design*; *the first* || *the second*; *plays well* || *sings well*. (See also section 27, on faulty parallelism.)

Further, with the *not only . . . but also* pair, you should usually make the *also* (or some equivalent) explicit. Its omission results in a feeling of incompleteness:

✖    He was not only smart, but charming.

He was not only smart, but also charming.

He was not only smart, but charming as well.

See 7.3 for agreement of verbs with subjects joined by some of the correlatives.

## 12.3 Subordinating Conjunctions

A subordinating conjunction introduces a subordinate (or dependent) clause and links it to the independent (or main or principal) clause to which it is grammatically related:

She writes *because* she has something to say.

The subordinating conjunction *because* introduces the adverbial clause *because she has something to say* and links it to the independent clause whose verb it modifies. The *because*-clause is subordinate because it cannot stand by itself; alone it would be a fragment (see 1.24). Note that a subordinate clause can also come first:

*Because* she has something to say, she writes articles for magazines.

Even though *Because* does not occur between the two unequal clauses, it still links them grammatically.

*That* Raj will win the prize is a foregone conclusion.

Here *That* introduces the noun clause *That Raj will win the prize*, which functions as the subject of the sentence. Note that whereas a coordinating conjunction is like a spot of glue between two structures and not a part of either, a subordinating conjunction is an integral part of its clause. In the following sentence, for example, the subordinating conjunction *whenever* is a part of the adverbial clause that modifies the imperative verb *Leave*:

Leave whenever you feel tired.

Here is a list of the principal subordinating conjunctions:

| | | | |
|---|---|---|---|
| after | however | than | when(ever) |
| although | if | that | where(ever) |
| as | if only | though | whereas |
| as though | in case | till | whether |
| because | lest | unless | which |
| before | once | until | while |
| even though | rather than | what | who |
| ever since | since | whatever | why |

There are also many terms consisting of two or more words ending in *as*, *if*, and *that* that serve as subordinating conjunctions, including *inasmuch as, insofar as, as long as, as soon as, as far as, as if, even if, only if, but that, except that, now that, in that, provided that, in order that.*

Some subordinating conjunctions can also function as adverbs, prepositions, and relative pronouns. But don't worry about parts of speech at this point. It is easier simply to think of all these terms as subordinators, including the relative pronouns and relative adverbs (*who, which, that, when, where*) that introduce adjective clauses. If you understand their subordinating function, you will understand the syntax of complex and compound-complex sentences (see 1.25) and, most important, will be able to avoid fragments (see 1.24).

# 13. INTERJECTIONS

An interjection is a word or group of words interjected or "thrown into" a sentence in order to express emotion. Strictly speaking, interjections have no grammatical function; they are simply thrust into sentences and play no part in their syntax, though sometimes they act like sentence modifiers. They are often used in dialogue and are not that common in formal writing.

>   But—*good heavens!*—what did you expect?

>   *Gosh*, what fun!

>   It was, *well*, a bit of a disappointment.

A mild interjection is usually set off with commas. A strong interjection is sometimes set off with dashes and is often accompanied by an exclamation point (see 39.2 and 42.3). An interjection may also be a minor sentence by itself (see 1.23):

>   *Ouch*! That hurt!

>   *Well*. So much for the warm up. Now comes real aerobic exercise.

# CHAPTER III
# Writing Strong Sentences

Chapter III deals with the way the various elements work together in sentences. It is designed to enable you to understand how sentences work, how to control some of that working, and how to avoid common problems. If you have difficulty understanding any of the terms and concepts discussed in this chapter, you may need to review some parts of the first two chapters (I–II).

# 14–15 BASIC SENTENCE ELEMENTS AND THEIR MODIFIERS

## 14. SUBJECT, VERB, OBJECT, COMPLEMENT

Consider again the bare bones of a sentence. The two essential elements are a subject and a verb (see 1.1).

### 14.1 Subject

The subject is what is talked about. It is the word or phrase answering the question *who?* or *what?* before the verb. More precisely, it is the source of the action indicated by the verb, or the person or thing experiencing or possessing the state of being or the condition indicated by the verb and its complement:

> *Osman* watched the performance. (*Who* watched? Osman. Osman is the source of the action of watching.)

> *We* are happy about the outcome. (*Who* is happy? We are. We are experiencing the state of being happy.)

> *Bernice* is a physician. (*Who* is a physician? Bernice. Bernice is the person in the state or condition of being a physician.)

> *Education* is important. (*What* is important? Education. Education possesses the condition of being important.)

The subject of a sentence will ordinarily be one of the following: a basic noun (see section 2), a pronoun (see section 3), a gerund or gerund phrase (see 10.6), an infinitive or infinitive phrase (see 10.1), or a noun clause (see 1.15):

*British Columbia* joined Confederation on 20 July 1871. (noun)

*He* is a Manitoba historian. (pronoun)

*Speculating* is a risky business. (gerund)

*Reading newspapers* is part of our daily routine. (gerund phrase)

*To travel* is to enjoy life. (infinitive)

*To order tofu* is to make a healthy choice. (infinitive phrase)

*That British Columbia joined Canada because of the railway* is common knowledge. (noun clause)

Rarely, a prepositional phrase serves as subject; see 11.1.

## 14.2 Finite Verb

The finite verb is the focal point of the sentence. It indicates the nature and time of the action (see section 6):

The prime minister *will respond* during Question Period. (action: responding; time: the future)

Lewis Carroll *invented* the adventures of Alice for a child named Alice Liddell. (action: inventing; time: past)

Cape Breton's fiddlers *have* a distinctive musical style. (action: having, possessing; time: present)

Syntax *is* word order. (action: being something; time: present)

## 14.3 Direct Object

If a verb is transitive (see 6.1), it will have a direct object to complete the pattern (see 1.4). Like the subject, the direct object may be a noun, a pronoun, a gerund or gerund phrase, an infinitive or infinitive phrase, or a noun clause:

The CD features *Wynton Marsalis*. (noun)

The increase in sales taxes disappointed *us*. (pronoun)

Our economy needs *logging*. (gerund)

He enjoys *writing reports*. (gerund phrase)

We wanted *to participate*. (infinitive)

You need *to define your terms*. (infinitive phrase)

The reporter *revealed that his source feared retaliation*. (noun clause)

Along with a direct object, there may also be an indirect object or an objective complement (see 1.6, 1.9, and 1.10).

## 14.4 Subjective Complement

Similarly, a linking verb (see 6.1) requires a subjective complement to complete the pattern. This complement will usually be either a predicate noun or a predicate adjective (see 1.7 and 1.8). A predicate noun may be a noun or a pronoun, or (especially after *be*) a gerund or gerund phrase, an infinitive or infinitive phrase, or a noun clause:

We are *friends*. (noun)

Was he the *one*? (pronoun)

His passion is *travelling*. (gerund)

His passion is *travelling the back country*. (gerund phrase)

My first impulse was *to run*. (infinitive)

Our next challenge was *to take action*. (infinitive phrase)

She remains *what she has long been*: a genuine friend. (noun clause)

A predicate adjective will ordinarily be a descriptive adjective, a participle, or an idiomatic prepositional phrase:

His music has become *joyful*. (descriptive adjective)

The novel's plot is *intriguing*. (present participle)

They seem *dedicated*. (past participle)

The class is *out of ideas*. (prepositional phrase)

The linking verb *be* (and sometimes others) can also be followed by an adverbial word or phrase (I am *here*; he is *in his office*).

These elements—subject, finite verb, and object or complement—are the core elements of major sentences. They are closely linked in the ways indicated above, with the verb as the focal and uniting element. (For a discussion of the order in which these elements occur, see 1.19–1.21.)

# 15. MODIFIERS

Modifiers add to the core grammatical elements listed above. They limit or describe other elements so as to modify—that is, to change—a listener's or reader's idea of them. The two principal kinds of modifiers are adjectives (see section 8) and adverbs (see section 9). Also useful, but less frequent, are appositives (see 1.17) and absolute phrases (see 1.18 and 10.9). An adjectival or adverbial modifier may even be part of the core of a sentence if it completes the predicate after a linking verb (Communication is *important*; Peter is *home*). An adverb may also be essential if it modifies an intransitive verb that would otherwise seem incomplete (Peter lives *in a condominium*). But generally modifiers do their work by adding to—enriching—a central core of thought.

## 15.1 Adjectival Modifiers (see 8.1–8.2, 8.5–8.6)

Adjectival modifiers modify nouns, pronouns, and phrases or clauses functioning as nouns. They commonly answer the questions *which? what kind of? how many?* and *how much?* An adjectival modifier may be a single word adjective, a series, a participle or participial phrase, an infinitive or infinitive phrase, a prepositional phrase, or a relative clause:

> *Early* settlers of *western* Canada encountered *sudden* floods, *prolonged* droughts, and *early* frosts. (single words modifying nouns immediately following)
>
> We are *skeptical.* (predicate adjective modifying the pronoun We)
>
> That the author criticizes globalization is *evident* in his first paragraph. (predicate adjective modifying the noun clause *That the author criticizes globalization*)

*Four ambitious young* reporters are competing to work on this front-page story. (series modifying *reporters*)

The *train* station is filled with commuters and tourists. (noun functioning as adjective, modifying *station*)

*Grinning*, he answered her email message. (present participle modifying *he*)

*Brimming with confidence*, they began their performance. (present participial phrase modifying *they*)

They continued the climb toward the summit, *undaunted*. (past participle modifying *they*)

Gisele applied for the position, *having been encouraged to do so by her adviser*. (participial phrase, perfect tense, modifying *Gisele*)

They prepared a meal *to remember*. (infinitive modifying *meal*)

Our tendency *to favour jazz* is evident in our CD collection. (infinitive phrase modifying *tendency*)

The report *on the evening news* focused on forest fires in northern Quebec. (prepositional phrase modifying *report*)

The soccer team, *which was travelling to a tournament in Mexico*, filed slowly through airport security. (relative clause modifying *team*)

## 15.2 Adverbial Modifiers (see 9.1–9.4)

Adverbial modifiers modify verbs, adjectives, other adverbs, and whole clauses or sentences. They commonly answer the questions *how? when? where?* and *to what degree?* An adverbial modifier may be a single word, a series, an infinitive or infinitive phrase, a prepositional phrase, or an adverbial clause:

Mix the chemicals *thoroughly*. (single word modifying the verb *mix*)

As new parents, we are *completely* happy. (single word modifying the adjective *happy*)

They planned their future together *quite* enthusiastically. (single word modifying the adverb *enthusiastically*)

*Apparently*, the cloning experiment is being delayed. (single word modifying the rest of the sentence)

He loves her *truly, madly, deeply*. (series modifying the verb *loves*)

*To succeed* you must work well with others. (infinitive modifying the verb *must work*)

She was lucky *to have been selected* for the exchange program. (infinitive phrase modifying the predicate adjective *lucky*)

The passenger ship arrived *at the port*. (prepositional phrase modifying the verb *arrived*)

We disagreed *because we were taking different theoretical approaches to the text*. (clause modifying the verb *disagreed*)

The election results trickled in slowly because the ballots were being counted by hand. (clause modifying the adverb *slowly*, or the whole preceding clause, *The election results trickled in slowly*.)

Shut off the computer *when you leave on vacation*. (clause modifying the preceding independent clause)

## 15.3 Overlapping Modifiers

The preceding examples are meant to illustrate each kind of adjectival and adverbial modifier separately, in tidy isolation from the other kinds. And such sentences are not uncommon, for relative simplicity of sentence structure can be a stylistic strength. But many sentences are more complicated, largely because modifiers overlap in them. Modifiers occur as parts of other modifiers: single-word modifiers occur as parts of phrases and clauses, phrases occur as parts of other phrases and as parts of clauses, and subordinate clauses occur as parts of phrases and as parts of other clauses. Here are examples illustrating some of the possible structural variety. (You may want to check sections 1.3–1.11 in order to match these sentences and their clauses with the various patterns they include.)

They walked briskly toward the waiting car.

> *briskly* – adverb modifying *walked*
> *toward the waiting car* – adverbial prepositional phrase modifying *walked*
> *waiting* – participial adjective modifying *car*

He purchased a few of the off-the-rack suits.

> *of the off-the-rack suits* – adjectival prepositional phrase modifying a *few*
>
> *off-the-rack* – hyphenated prepositional phrase, adjective modifying *suits*

Hoping to learn to perform brilliantly, the cast rehearsed until dawn.

> *Hoping to learn to perform brilliantly* – participial phrase modifying *cast*
>
> *to learn to perform brilliantly* – infinitive phrase, object of the participle *hoping*
>
> *to perform brilliantly* – infinitive phrase, object of the infinitive *to learn*
>
> *brilliantly* – adverb modifying infinitive *to perform*
>
> *until dawn* – adverbial prepositional phrase modifying *rehearsed*

It was daunting to think of the consequences that might ensue.

> *to think of the consequences that might ensue* – infinitive phrase, delayed subject of sentence
>
> *of the consequences* – adverbial prepositional phrase modifying infinitive *to think*
>
> *that might ensue* – relative clause modifying *consequences*
>
> *daunting* – participle, predicate adjective modifying subject

The students developed the argument, an intriguing one for them, that postmodern architecture might someday become a distant memory.

> *an intriguing one for them* – appositive phrase further defining *argument*
>
> *intriguing* – participle modifying *one*
>
> *for them* – adverbial prepositional phrase modifying *intriguing*
>
> *that postmodern architecture might someday become a distant memory* – relative clause modifying *argument*
>
> *someday* – adverb modifying *might become*

With several generous donations, we purchased what the homeless shelter had needed since October: warm blankets to distribute in cold weather.

> *With several generous donations* – adverbial prepositional phrase modifying *purchased*

*several generous* – adjective series modifying *donations*

*what the homeless shelter had needed since October* – noun clause, direct object of *purchased*

*since October* – adverbial prepositional phrase modifying *had needed*

*warm blankets to distribute in cold weather* – appositive phrase modifying the noun clause *what the homeless shelter had needed since October*

*to distribute* – adjectival infinitive modifying *blankets*

*in cold weather* – adverbial prepositional phrase modifying *distribute*

Because she wanted to become better educated, she enrolled in night school.

*Because she wanted to become better educated* – adverbial clause modifying the independent clause *she enrolled in night school* (or just the verb *enrolled*)

*to become better educated* – infinitive phrase, direct object of *wanted*

*better* – adverb modifying *educated*, the predicate adjective after *become*

*in night school* – adverbial prepositional phrase modifying *enrolled*

*night* – noun functioning as adjective to modify *school*

He was a child who, being quite introverted in large groups of adults, chose a quiet corner where he could read a book.

*who chose a quiet corner where he could read a book* – relative clause modifying the predicate noun *child*

*where he could read a book* – adverbial clause modifying *chose*

*being quite introverted in large groups of adults* – participial phrase modifying the relative pronoun *who*

*introverted* – past participle, predicate adjective after *being*

*quite* – adverb modifying *introverted*

*in large groups of adults* – adverbial prepositional phrase modifying *introverted*

*of adults* – adjectival prepositional phrase modifying *groups*

The book being one of the kind that puts you to sleep, she laid it aside and dozed off.

> *The book being one of the kind that puts you to sleep* – absolute phrase
> *of the kind that puts you to sleep* – adjectival prepositional phrase modifying *one*
> *that puts you to sleep* – relative clause modifying *kind*
> *to sleep* – adverbial prepositional phrase modifying *puts*

I am the only member who knows what must be done when parliament reconvenes.

> *who knows what must be done when parliament reconvenes* – relative clause modifying *member*
> *what must be done when parliament reconvenes* – noun clause, direct object of *knows*
> *when parliament reconvenes* – adverbial clause modifying verb *must be done*

These examples suggest the richness of structure that is possible, the kind you undoubtedly create at times without even thinking about it. But think about it. Try concocting sentences with these sorts of syntactical complexities. Working with sentences in this way will help you to develop greater variety in your writing.

## 15.4 Using Modifiers: A Sample Scenario

Suppose you were asked to write a short report on your reading habits. In getting your ideas together and taking notes, you might draft a bare-bones sentence such as this:

> Recently, I've been reading fiction.

It's a start. But you soon realize that it isn't exactly true to your thoughts. It needs qualification. So you begin modifying its elements:

> Recently, I've been reading *historical* fiction.

The adjective specifies the kind of fiction you've been reading— you're focused on novels and short stories written about the past.

Then you add an adjectival prepositional phrase to further limit the word *fiction*:

> Recently, I've been reading historical fiction *about the First World War.*

Then you realize that while the fiction you've been reading has been primarily historical and about World War I, you haven't read it all; therefore you insert another adjective to further qualify the noun *fiction*:

> Recently, I've been reading *Canadian* historical fiction about the First World War.

Then you realize that *Canadian historical fiction* implies that you are familiar with all such fiction. But you quickly see a way to revise the sentence to convey your thoughts accurately; you put the adjective *much* in front of the verb:

> Recently, I've been reading *much* Canadian historical fiction about the First World War.

So far so good. But you're not entirely satisfied with the sentence; you suspect that a reader might want a little more information about your reference to Canadian fiction about the First World War. You could go on to explain in another sentence or two, but you'd like to get a little more substance into this sentence. Then you have this thought: you can help clarify your point and at the same time inject some rhythm by adding a participial phrase modifying *fiction*:

> Recently, I've been reading much Canadian historical fiction representing our longstanding ambivalence about the First World War.

You rather like it. But working at this one sentence has got you thinking. Before you leave it you consider your reasons for reading such fiction. You decide that you're doing this reading because this fiction focuses on a major event of the twentieth century, and because it tells stories of a time when Canada is said to have earned its national independence but when it also experienced deep political divisions over conscription. You feel the words beginning to come, and you consider your options: you can put the explanation in a separate sentence;

you can join it to your present sentence with a semicolon or a colon or a coordinating conjunction like *for*, creating a compound sentence; or you can integrate it more closely by making it a subordinate clause, turning the whole into a complex sentence. You decide on the third method, and put the new material in a *because*-clause modifying the verb *have been reading*. And while you're thinking about it, you begin to feel that, given the way your sentence has developed, the word *reading* now sounds rather bland, weak because it doesn't quite reveal your seriousness. So you decide to change it to the more precise verb *examining*. Now your sentence is finished, at least for the time being:

> Recently, I've been examining much Canadian historical fiction about the First World War, because this fiction focuses on a major event of the twentieth century and because it tells stories of a time when Canada is said to have earned its national independence but also to have experienced deep political divisions over conscription.

By adding modifiers, a writer can enlarge the reader's knowledge of the material being presented and impart precision and clarity to a sentence, as well as improve its style. Minimal or bare-bones sentences can themselves be effective and emphatic; use them when they are appropriate. But many of your sentences will be longer. And it is in elaborating and enriching your sentences with modifiers that you as author and stylist exercise much of your control: you take charge of what your readers will learn and how they will learn it.

# 16–18 LENGTH, VARIETY, AND EMPHASIS

## 16. SENTENCE LENGTH

How long should a sentence be to achieve its purpose? That depends. A sentence may, in rare cases, consist of one word, or it may go on for a hundred words or more. There are no strict guidelines to tell you how long to make your sentences. If you're curious, do some research to determine the average sentence length in several pieces of writing you have handy—for example this and other reference books, a recent novel, a collection of essays, newspapers and magazines, email messages, websites you visit regularly. You'll probably find that the average is somewhere between fifteen and twenty-five words per sentence, that longer sentences are more common in formal and specialized writing, and that shorter sentences are more at home in informal and popular writing, in email, and in narrative and dialogue. There are, then, some general guidelines, and you'll probably fit your own writing to them. But if you're far off what seems to be the average for the kind of writing you are doing, you may need to make some changes to adapt to the writing situation.

## 16.1 Short Sentences

If you find that you're writing an excessive number of short sentences, try

- building them up by elaborating their elements with modifiers, including various kinds of phrases and clauses;
- combining some of them to form compound subjects, predicates, and objects or complements;
- combining two or more of them—especially if they are simple sentences—into one or another kind of complex sentence. (Since compound sentences are made up of simple sentences joined by punctuation and coordinating conjunctions, they often read like a series of shorter, simple sentences.)

## 16.2 Long Sentences

If you find yourself writing too many long sentences, check them for two possible problems:

1. You may be rambling or trying to pack too much into a single sentence, possibly destroying its unity (see section 28) and certainly making it difficult to read. Try breaking it up into more unified or more easily manageable parts.

2. You may be using too many words to make your point. Try cutting out any deadwood (see section 60).

In either of these kinds of unwieldy sentences, check that you haven't slipped into what is called "excessive subordination"—too many loosely related details obscuring the main idea, or confusing strings of subordinate clauses modifying each other. Try removing some of the clutter, and try reducing clauses to phrases and phrases to single words.

# 17. SENTENCE VARIETY

Both to create emphasis (see section 18) and to avoid monotony you should vary the lengths and kinds of your sentences. Examine some pieces of prose that you particularly enjoy or that you find unusually clear and especially readable: you will likely discover that they contain both a pleasing mixture of short, medium, and long sentences and a similar variety of kinds and structures.

## 17.1 Variety of Lengths

A string of short sentences will sound choppy and fragmented; avoid the staccato effect by interweaving some longer ones. On the other hand, a succession of long sentences may make your ideas hard to follow; give your readers a break—and your prose some sparkle—by using a few short, emphatic sentences to change your pace occasionally. Even a string of medium-length sentences can bore readers into inattention. Impart some rhythm, some shape, to your paragraphs by varying sentence length. Especially consider using a short, emphatic sentence to open or close a paragraph, and occasionally an unusually long sentence to end a paragraph.

## 17.2 Variety of Kinds

A string of simple and compound sentences risks coming across as simplistic. In a narrative, successive simple and compound sentences may be appropriate for recounting a sequence of events, but when you're writing prose in other modes, let some of the complexity of your ideas be reflected in complex and compound-complex sentences. On the other hand, a string of complex and compound-complex sentences may become oppressive. Give your readers a breather now and then by changing pace.

## 17.3 Variety of Structures

Try to avoid an unduly long string of sentences that use the same syntactical structure. For example, though the standard order of elements in declarative sentences is subject–verb–object or –complement, consider varying that order occasionally for the purpose of emphasis (see 1.19 and section 18). Perhaps use an occasional interrogative sentence (see 1.20), whether a rhetorical question (a question that doesn't expect an answer) or a question that you proceed to answer as you develop a paragraph. An occasional expletive pattern or passive voice can be refreshing—if you can justify it on other grounds as well (see 1.5, 1.11, 6.16, and 18.6).

In particular, try not to begin a string of sentences with the same kind of word or phrase or clause—unless you are purposely setting up a controlled succession of parallel structures for emphasis or coherence (see 66.1). Imagine the effect of several sentences beginning with such words as *Similarly* . . . *Especially* . . . *Consequently* . . . *Nevertheless* . . . Whatever else the sentences contained, the sameness would be distracting. Or imagine a series of sentences all starting with a subject-noun, or with a present-participial phrase. To avoid such undesirable sameness, take advantage of the way modifiers of various kinds can be moved around in sentences (see 1.17, 1.18, 8.4, 9.4, 11.2, and 18.5).

# 18. EMPHASIS IN SENTENCES

To communicate effectively, make sure your readers perceive the relative importance of your ideas the same way you do. Learn to control emphasis so that what you want emphasized is what gets emphasized.

You can emphasize whole sentences in several ways:

- Set a sentence off by itself, as a short paragraph.
- Put an important sentence at the beginning of a paragraph or, even better, at the end.
- Put an important point in a short sentence among several long ones, or in a long sentence among several short ones.
- Shift the style or structure of a sentence to make it stand out from those around it (see section 67).

In similar ways you can emphasize important parts of individual sentences. The principal devices for achieving emphasis within sentences are position and word order, repetition, stylistic contrast, syntax, and punctuation.

## 18.1 Endings and Beginnings

The most emphatic position in a sentence is its ending; the second most emphatic position is its beginning. Consider these two sentences:

> Kerr's new play features seven young actors.

> Seven young actors appear in Kerr's new play.

Each sentence emphasizes both *Kerr's new play* and the *seven young actors*, but the first emphasizes the *seven young actors* a little more, whereas the second emphasizes *Kerr's new play* a little more. Further, the longer the sentence, the stronger the effect of emphasis by position. Consider the following:

(a)   The best teacher I've ever had was my high-school chemistry teacher, a brilliant woman in her early fifties.
(b)   A brilliant woman in her early fifties, my high-school chemistry teacher was the best teacher I've ever had.
(c)   My high-school chemistry teacher, a brilliant woman in her early fifties, was the best teacher I've ever had.
(d)   The best teacher I've ever had was a brilliant woman in her early fifties who taught me chemistry in high school.

Each sentence contains the same three ideas, but each distributes the emphasis differently. In each the last part is the most emphatic, the first part next, and the middle part least. Think of them as topic sentences (see 65.1): sentence *a* could introduce a paragraph focusing on the quality of the teacher but emphasizing her intelligence, her age, and her gender; sentence *b* could introduce a paragraph focusing more on the quality of her teaching; sentence *c* could open a paragraph stressing the quality of the teaching and the nature and level of the subject—details of age, gender, and intelligence would be incidental; sentence *d* may seem the flattest, the least emphatic and least likely of the four, but it could effectively introduce a mainly narrative paragraph focusing on the writer's good experience in the class.

Note that in all four versions the part referring to "the best teacher I've ever had" comes either first or last, since the superlative *best* would sound unnatural in the unemphatic middle position—unless one acknowledged its inherent emphasis in some other way, for example by setting off the appositive with a pair of dashes (see 39.2):

> My high-school chemistry teacher—the best teacher I've ever had—was a brilliant woman in her early fifties.

## 18.2 Loose Sentences and Periodic Sentences

*Loose* is not a pejorative term when it describes a sentence. It simply means that the sentence makes its main point in an early independent clause and then adds modifying subordinate elements:

> The concert began modestly, minus special effects and fanfare, with the performers sitting casually onstage and taking up their instruments to play their first song.

Such sentences—also called cumulative or right-branching—are common, for they are "loose" and comfortable, easygoing, natural. In contrast to the loose is the periodic (or "left-branching") sentence, which wholly or partly delays its main point, the independent clause, until the end:

> With the performers sitting casually onstage and taking up their instruments to play their first song, the concert began modestly, minus special effects and fanfare.

Full periodic sentences are almost always the result of careful thought and planning. However, they can sometimes sound contrived, less natural, and therefore should not be used without forethought. But they can also be dramatic and emphatic, creating suspense as the reader waits for the meaning to fall into place. But if you try for such suspense, don't separate subject and predicate too widely:

> ✘    The abrupt change from one moment when the air is alive with laughing and shouting, to the next when the atmosphere resembles that of a morgue, is dramatic.

Many sentences delay completion of the main clause only until somewhere in the middle rather than all the way to the end. To the degree that they do delay it, they are partly periodic.

## 18.3 The Importance of the Final Position

Because the end of a sentence is naturally so emphatic, readers expect something important there; it is best not to disappoint them by letting something incidental or merely qualifying fall at the end, for then the sentence itself will fall: its energy and momentum will be lost, its essential meaning distorted. For example:

> ✘    That was the best job interview I've had, I think.

The uncertain *I think* should go at the beginning or, even less emphatically, after *That* or *was*.

    ✖    Cramming for exams can be counterproductive, sometimes.

The qualifying *sometimes* could go at the beginning, but it would be best after *can*, letting the emphasis fall where it belongs, on *cramming* and *counterproductive*.

## 18.4 Changing Word Order

Earlier sections point out certain standard patterns: for example, subject–verb–object or –complement (1.3–1.10); single-word adjectives preceding nouns—or, if predicate adjectives, following them (8.4); and so on. But variations are possible, and because these patterns are recognized as standard, any departures from them stand out (see 1.19 and 8.4 for examples). But be careful, for if the inverted order calls attention to itself at the expense of meaning, the attempt may backfire. In the following sentence, for example, the writer strained a little too hard for emphasis.

    ✖    It is from imagination that have come all the world's great literature, music, architecture, and works of art.

## 18.5 Movable Modifiers

Many modifiers other than single-word adjectives are movable, enabling you to shift them or other words to where you want them. Appositives, for instance, can sometimes be transposed (see 1.17). And you can move participial phrases, if you do so carefully (see 8.4). Absolute phrases (see 1.18), since they function as sentence modifiers, can usually come at the beginning or the end—or, if syntax permits, in the middle.

But adverbial modifiers are the most movable of all (see 9.4). As you compose, and especially as you revise your drafts, consider the various possible placements of any adverbial modifiers you've used. Take advantage of their flexibility in order to exercise maximum control over the rhythms of your sentences and, most important, to get the emphases that will best serve your purposes. Some examples:

The creature made its way *slowly and stealthily* through the labyrinth.

The adverbs are slightly more emphatic at the end:

> The creature made its way through the labyrinth *slowly and stealthily*.

They could also go at the beginning of the sentence; punctuation emphasizes the slowness instead of *and*:

> *Slowly*, *stealthily*, the creature made its way through the labyrinth.

Another example that could use improvement:

> When I entered the workforce I naturally expected it to be different from university, but I wasn't prepared for the impact it would have on the way I lived my day-to-day life.

Although this sentence is clear, it could have more emphasis by separating the independent clauses and using a conjunctive adverb:

> When I entered the workforce I naturally expected it to be different from university. However, I wasn't prepared for the impact it would have on the way I lived my day-to-day life.

This revised version sounds too stiff (as *However* oftentimes does at the beginning of a sentence). Some further revisions can help with this problem:

> When I entered the workforce I expected it to be different from university—naturally. I was not, however, prepared for the impact it would have on the way I lived my day-to-day life.

Setting *naturally* off with a dash at the end of the first sentence adds a touch of self-mockery. And moving *however* a few words into the second sentence not only gets rid of the stiffness but also, because of the pause produced by its commas, adds a useful emphasis to *not*, now spelled out in full. (For more on *however*, see 33.8.)

## 18.6 Using the Expletive and the Passive Voice for Emphasis

Two of the basic sentence patterns, the expletive (1.11) and the passive voice (1.5, 6.16), can be weak and unemphatic. Used strategically, however, they can enable you to achieve a desired emphasis. For example:

> Passive voice can be used to move a certain word or phrase to an emphatic place in a sentence.

Here, putting the verb in the passive voice (*can be used*) makes *Passive voice* the subject of the sentence and enables this important element to come at the beginning; otherwise, the sentence would have to begin less strongly (for example, with *You can use passive voice*). And consider this next example, which makes strategic use of the expletive pattern:

> There are advantages to using the expletive pattern for a deliberate change of pace in your writing.

In this case, opening the sentence with *There* is preferable to opening with these long and unwieldy alternatives:

> Advantages to using the expletive pattern for a deliberate change of pace in your writing are significant.

> or

> Using the expletive pattern for a deliberate change of pace in your writing can be advantageous.

Use expletives and passive voice when you need to delete or delay mention of the agent or otherwise shift the subject of a sentence. But use these patterns only when you have good reason to do so.

## 18.7 Emphasis by Repetition

You may wish to repeat an important word or idea in order to emphasize it, to make it stay in your readers' minds. Unintentional repetition can be wordy and tedious (see 60.2); but intentional, controlled repetition—used sparingly—can be very effective, especially in sentences with balanced or parallel structures:

> We particularly enjoy his lyrics—his witty, poignant, brilliant lyrics.

> If you have the courage to face adventure, the adventure can sometimes give you courage.

> If it's a challenge they seek, it's a challenge they'll find.

> Many Vancouver shops are filled with souvenirs: souvenir T-shirts, souvenir postcards, souvenir coffee mugs.

## 18.8 Emphasis by Stylistic Contrast

A stylistically enhanced sentence—for example, a periodic sentence (18.2), a sentence with parallel or balanced structure (section 27,

18.7), or a richly metaphorical or allusive sentence (section 54)—stands out beside plainer sentences. For that reason, such a sentence may be most effective at the end of a paragraph (see 65.3). In the same way, a word or phrase that differs in style or tone from those that surround it may stand out (and note that such terms often gravitate toward that position of natural emphasis, the end of the sentence):

> When the judge chastised the attorney for her sarcasm, her client went ballistic.

> The chef—conservative as her behaviour sometimes appears—dazzles the kitchen staff with her gutsy culinary experiments.

> My grandmother may be almost ninety years old, but she approaches each day with a child's *joie de vivre*.

Terms from other languages naturally stand out, but don't make the mistake of using them pretentiously, for some readers are unimpressed by them or even resent them; use one only after due thought, and preferably when there is no satisfactory English equivalent. And be careful not to overshoot: too strong a contrast may jar; the first example above works only because the emphasis deriving from the shift to colloquialism is deliberate.

## 18.9 Emphasis by Syntax

Put your most important claims in independent clauses; put lesser claims in subordinate clauses and in phrases. Sometimes you have more than one option, depending on what you want to emphasize:

> Reading the menu, she frowned at the high prices.

> Frowning at the high prices, she read the menu.

But more often the choice is determined by the content. Notice how changing the subordinate clause can improve weak emphasis:

> ✘    I strolled into the laboratory, when my attention was attracted by the pitter-pattering of a little white rat in a cage at the back.

> When I strolled into the laboratory, my attention was attracted by the pitter-pattering of a little white rat in a cage at the back.

✖    Choosing my ingredients carefully, I tried to plan a healthy meal
     that everyone would enjoy.

     Because I was trying to plan a healthy meal that everyone would
     enjoy, I chose my ingredients carefully.

✖    I had almost finished the last chapter of my novel when the power
     failed and the computer screen went blank.

     When I had almost finished the last chapter of my novel, the
     power failed and the computer screen went blank.

Granted, the original version of the last example could be appropriate in a particular context; but unless you have a good reason, don't
distort apparently logical emphasis by subordinating main ideas. See
also section 28 and 12.3.

### 18.10 Emphasis by Punctuation

An exclamation point (!) denotes emphasis. But using exclamation points is not the only way, and usually not the best way, to
achieve emphasis with punctuation. Try to make your sentences
appropriately emphatic without resorting to this sometimes artificial device. Arrange your words so that commas and other marks
fall where you want a pause for emphasis (see 18.5). Use dashes,
colons, and even parentheses judiciously to set off important ideas
(see 18.1). Occasionally use a semicolon instead of a comma in
order to get a more emphatic pause (but only in a series or between
independent clauses).

## Proofreading Tip

### Avoiding Artificial Emphasis

As much as possible, avoid emphasizing your own words and sentences with such mechanical devices as underlining, italics, quotation
marks, and capitalization. See 47.18 and 49.4

# 19. ANALYZING SENTENCES

Practise analyzing your own and others' sentences. The better you understand how sentences work, the better able you will be to write effective and correct sentences.

You should be able to account for each word in a sentence: no essential element should be missing, nothing should be left over, and the grammatical relations among all the parts should be clear. If these conditions aren't met, the sentence in question is likely to be misleading or ambiguous. If words, phrases, and clauses fit the roles they are being asked to play, the sentence should work.

The first step in analyzing a sentence is to identify the main parts of its basic structure: the subject, the finite verb, and the object or complement, if any. (If the sentence is other than a simple sentence, there will be more than one set of these essential parts.) Then determine the modifiers of these elements, and then the modifiers of modifiers.

## 19.1 The Chart Method

Here is a convenient arrangement for analyzing the structure of relatively uncomplicated sentences:

The veteran coach warmly praised the young goalie.

| subject | finite verb | object or complement | adjectival modifier | adverbial modifier |
|---------|-------------|---------------------|---------------------|-------------------|
| coach | praised | goalie (direct object of verb *praised*) | The (modifies *coach*) veteran (modifies *coach*) the (modifies *goalie*) young (modifies *goalie*) | warmly (modifies verb *praised*) |

This most beautiful summer is now almost gone.

| subject | finite verb | object or complement | adjectival modifier | adverbial modifier |
|---------|-------------|----------------------|---------------------|--------------------|
| summer | is (linking verb) | gone (predicate adj.) | This (demonstrative adj. modifying *summer*) beautiful (modifies *summer*) | most (modifies adj. *beautiful*) now (modifies verb *is*) almost (modifies *gone*) |

The very befuddled Roger realized that learning Sanskrit was not easy.

| subject | finite verb | object or complement | adjectival modifier | adverbial modifier | other |
|---------|-------------|----------------------|---------------------|--------------------|-------|
| Roger | realized | that . . . easy (noun clause as direct object) | The, befuddled (modify *Roger*) | very (modifies *befuddled*) | |
| learning | was (linking verb) | easy (predicate adj.) Sanskrit (obj. of gerund *learning*) | | not (modifies *easy*) | that (sub. conj.) |

In the last example, the items below the dotted line belong to the subordinate clause of this complex sentence.

## 19.2 The Vertical Method

For more complicated sentences, you may find a different method more convenient, for example one in which the sentence is written out vertically:

When the canoe trip ended, Philip finally realized that the end of his happy summer was almost upon him.

| | Word | Part of speech | Function |
|---|---|---|---|
| **sub. cl. (adv.)** | When | conj. | subordinating / intro. sub. cl. |
| | the | art. | mod. *trip* |
| | canoe | adj. | mod. *trip* |
| | trip | noun | subj. of *ended* |
| | ended | verb | finite v. of cl. / intrans. |
| | Philip | noun (proper) | subj. of ind. cl. |
| | finally | adv. | mod. *realized* |
| | realized | verb | finite v. of cl. / trans. |
| | that | conj. | subordinating / intro. noun cl. |
| | the | art. | mod. *end* |
| | end | noun | subj. of *was* |
| **sub. cl. (n.)** | of | prep. | prep. phrase; adj., mod. *end* |
| | his | adj. (pron.) | mod. *summer* |
| **dir. obj. of verb** | happy | adj. | mod. *summer* |
| | summer | noun | obj. of prep. |
| | was | verb (linking) | finite v. of clause |
| | almost | adv. | mod. adj. phr. *upon him* |
| | upon | prep. | prep. phr. / adj. compl. after *linking verb* |
| | him | pron. | obj. of prep |

*(Bracketed at left: complex sentence → ind. cl.)*

As you can see, this method challenges you to account for the grammatical function of every word in the sentence.

## 19.3 The Diagramming Method

The old but still serviceable diagramming method has its drawbacks: there is no way to distinguish between adjective and adverb, for example, unless you label each one; and it also requires learning a rather complicated system. Nevertheless, it can prove useful by revealing the workings of a sentence. For visual learners—those who learn and understand best when presented with visual representations of abstract or complex verbal patterns—diagrams can make clearer the relationships of modifiers to the main elements (subjects, verbs, and objects) of a clause. They can also demonstrate visually the relationships between and among types of clauses in compound, complex, and compound-complex sentences. If you are taking courses in English language studies—for example, in traditional grammar or syntax—sentence diagrams will be a regular feature of lessons and exercises in sentence analysis. Here are sample diagrams of the most common kinds of sentences:

## Simple sentences

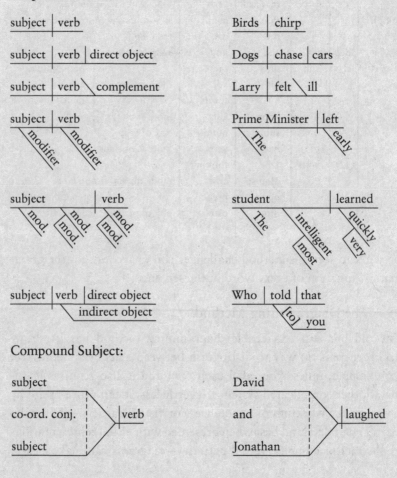

## Compound Subject:

## Compound Verb:

## Compound Object:

## Prepositional Phrases:

## Participial Phrase:

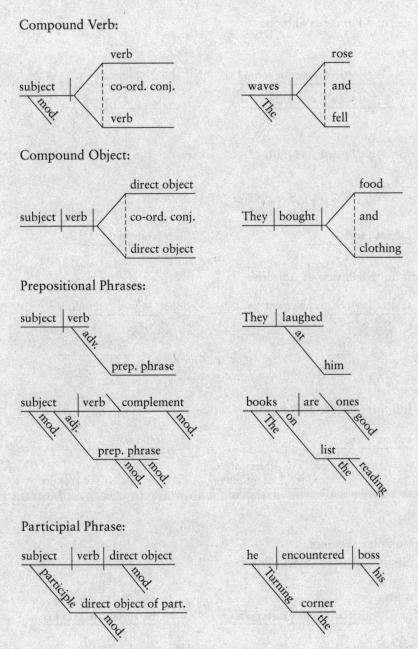

Gerund Phrase as Subject:

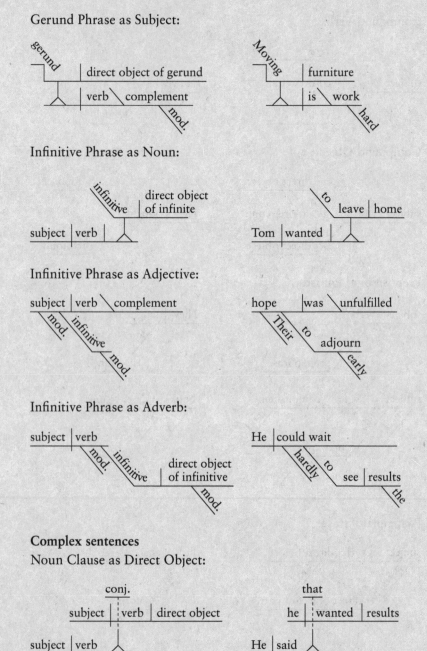

Infinitive Phrase as Noun:

Infinitive Phrase as Adjective:

Infinitive Phrase as Adverb:

**Complex sentences**

Noun Clause as Direct Object:

## Noun Clause as Object of Preposition:

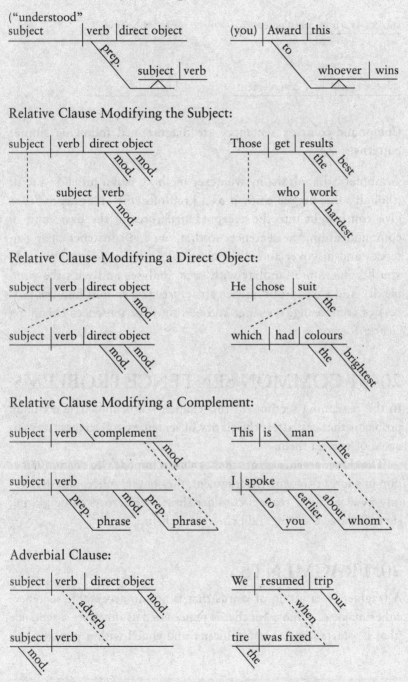

## Relative Clause Modifying the Subject:

## Relative Clause Modifying a Direct Object:

## Relative Clause Modifying a Complement:

## Adverbial Clause:

**Compound sentences**

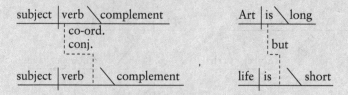

**Compound-complex sentences are diagrammed following similar patterns.**

Grammatical analysis, by whatever method, is not an end in itself (though some people enjoy it as a kind of game). Its purpose is to give you insight into the accepted structures of the basic unit of communication, the sentence, so that you can construct clear sentences and discover and eliminate weaknesses in your writing. As you become more familiar with such analyses and with the complexity and variety of sentence structure, you should find the process of composing, revising, and editing your sentences becoming clearer for you.

# 20–31 COMMON SENTENCE PROBLEMS

In the remaining sections of this chapter we define some common problems that can affect the clarity of sentences and suggest ways to avoid or correct them.

The three sentence errors that can most impede clear communication in your writing are the fragment, the comma splice, and the run-on sentence. Some readers consider these three errors to be glaring signs of flawed writing. Edit closely for them.

# 20. FRAGMENTS

A fragment is a group of words that is not an acceptable sentence, either major or minor, but that is punctuated as if it were a sentence (that is, started with a capital letter and ended with a period). The fragment is discussed along with the minor sentence, which it sometimes resembles: see 1.23 and 1.24.

# 21. COMMA SPLICES

A comma splice occurs when two independent clauses are joined with only a comma, rather than with a semicolon. Although the error usually stems from a misunderstanding of sentence structure, it is discussed under punctuation, since it requires attention to punctuation marks: see 33.5–33.8.

# 22. RUN-ON (FUSED) SENTENCES

A run-on sentence, sometimes called a fused sentence, is in fact not a single sentence but two sentences run together with neither a period to mark the end of the first nor a capital letter to mark the beginning of the second. An error most likely to occur when a writer is rushed, it can sometimes, like the comma splice, result from a problem in understanding how sentences work. And since a run-on sentence occurs with the same kind of sentence structure as does the comma splice, and like it requires attention to punctuation, we discuss it alongside the other error: see 33.10.

# 23. MISPLACED MODIFIERS

## 23.1 Movability and Poor Placement

As we point out in the introduction to chapter II, part of the meaning in English sentences is conveyed by the position of words in relation to each other. And though there are certain standard or conventional arrangements, a good deal of flexibility is possible (see 1.19, 1.20, 8.4, 11.2, and section 15). Adverbial modifiers are especially movable (see 9.4 and 18.5). Because of this flexibility, writers sometimes put a modifier where it conveys an unintended or ambiguous meaning, or where it is linked by juxtaposition to a word it can't logically modify.

To say precisely what you mean, you have to be careful in placing your modifiers—especially adverbs. Note the changes in meaning that result from the different placement of the word *only* in the following sentences:

> *Only* her daughter works in Halifax. (No other member of her family works there.)

> Her *only* daughter works in Halifax. (She has no other daughters.)

> Her daughter *only* works in Halifax. (She doesn't live in Halifax, but commutes.)

> Her daughter works *only* in Halifax. (She works in no other place.)

The following sentence demonstrates how a misplaced modifier can produce absurdity:

> ✘  While testifying before the Transport Committee, the minister denied allegations heatedly concerning inadequate passenger screening reported recently in a CBC documentary at Calgary airport.

The adverb *heatedly* belongs before *denied*, the verb it modifies. The adjective phrase *reported in a recent CBC documentary* belongs after *allegations*, the noun it modifies. And the adverbial phrase *at Calgary airport* belongs after the phrase *concerning inadequate passenger screening.*

Usually it is best to keep modifiers and the words they modify as close together as possible. Here is an example of an adjective out of place:

> ✘  Love is a *difficult* emotion to express in words.

> Love is an emotion (that is) difficult to express in words.

and an example of a misplaced relative clause:

> ✘  Every year the Royal St John's Regatta is held on Quidi Vidi Lake, which has been called "the world's largest garden party."

Is it the lake that has been called "the world's largest garden party"? The writer likely meant something else:

Every year the Royal St John's Regatta, which has been called "the world's largest garden party," is held on Quidi Vidi Lake.

## 23.2 *Only, almost,* etc.

Pay particular attention (as illustrated in the preceding section) to such adverbs as *only, almost, just, merely,* and *even.* In speech, we often place these words casually, but in writing we should put them where they clearly mean what we want them to:

✘  Hardy *only* wrote novels as a sideline; his main interest was poetry.
   Hardy wrote novels *only* as a sideline; his main interest was poetry.

✘  The teenagers *almost* washed fifty cars last Saturday.
   The teenagers washed *almost* fifty cars last Saturday.

## 23.3 Squinting Modifiers

A squinting modifier is a word or phrase put between two elements either of which it could modify. That is, a modifier "squints" so that a reader can't tell which way it is looking; the result is ambiguity:

✘  It was so warm *for a week* we did hardly any skiing at all.

Which clause does the adverbial phrase modify? It is ambiguous, even though the meaning would be about the same either way. A speaking voice could impart clarifying emphasis to such a sentence, but a writer must substitute words or structures for the missing vocal emphasis. Here, adding a simple *that* removes the ambiguity:

It was so warm that for a week we did hardly any skiing at all.

It was so warm for a week that we did hardly any skiing at all.

Another example:

✘  My sister advised me *now and then* to travel in the Rockies.

This time, rearrangement is necessary:

My sister now and then advised me to travel in the Rockies.

My sister advised me to travel now and then in the Rockies.

Even a modifier at the end of a sentence can, in effect, squint. When rearrangement doesn't work, further revision may be necessary:

✘ He was overjoyed when she agreed for more reasons than one.

He was overjoyed for more reasons than one when she agreed.

He had more than one reason to be overjoyed when she agreed.

He was overjoyed because, she had more than one reason for agreeing.

## Proofreading Tip

### On Split Infinitives

An awkwardly split infinitive is also caused by a kind of misplaced modifier; see 10.3.

# 24. DANGLING MODIFIERS

Like a pronoun without an antecedent, a dangling modifier has no word in the rest of the sentence to attach to; instead it is left dangling, grammatically unattached, and so it often tries to attach itself, illogically, to some other word. Most dangling modifiers are verbal phrases; be watchful for them in editing drafts of your work.

## 24.1 Dangling Participial Phrases (see 10.4)

✘ *Strolling casually beside the lagoon*, my eyes fell upon two children chasing a pair of geese.

Since the adjectival phrase wants to modify a noun, it tries to link with the subject of the adjacent clause, *eyes*. One's eyes may be said, figuratively, to "fall" on something, but they can scarcely be said to "stroll." To avoid the unintentionally humorous dangler, simply change the participial phrase to a subordinate clause:

*As I strolled casually beside the lagoon*, my eyes fell upon two children chasing a pair of geese.

Or, if you want to keep the effect of the opening participial phrase, rework the clause so that its subject is the logical word to be modified:

> Strolling casually beside the lagoon, I let my gaze fall upon two children chasing a pair of geese.

Here is another example, one with no built-in absurdity:

> ✗ *Living in a small town,* there was a strong sense of community among us.

To correct the dangling participle, you need to provide something for the phrase to modify, or revise the sentence in some other way:

> Living in a small town, *we* had a strong sense of community among us.

> Since we lived in a small town, there was a strong sense of community among us.

In the next example, passive voice causes the trouble (see 6.16):

> ✗ *Looking up to the open sky,* not a cloud could be seen.

> Looking up to the open sky, I could not see a cloud.

> There wasn't a cloud to be seen in the open sky.

## 24.2 Dangling Gerund Phrases (see 10.6)

When a gerund phrase is the object of a preposition, it can dangle much like a participial phrase:

> ✗ *After being informed of the correct procedure,* our attention was directed to the next steps.

It isn't "our attention" that was "informed." The use of the passive voice contributes to the confusion here.

> After being informed of the correct procedure, we were directed to attend to the next steps.

But this revision is still passive and somewhat awkward. Such a sentence can be better revised another way:

> After informing us of the correct procedure, the instructor directed our attention to the next steps.

## 24.3 Dangling Infinitive Phrases (see 10.1)

> ✗ *To follow Freud's procedure,* the speaker's thoughts must be fully explored.

Ineffective passive voice is again the issue, depriving the infinitive phrase of a logical word to modify.

> To follow Freud's procedure, *one* must explore the speaker's thoughts fully.

The next example is more complicated:

> ✘   *To make the instructor's lab successful*, it requires the students' co-operation.

Here the infinitive phrase seems to be the antecedent of *it*. Dropping the *it* lets the phrase act as a noun; or the sentence can be revised in some other way:

> To make the instructor's lab successful will require the students' co-operation.

> If the instructor's lab is to succeed, the students will have to co-operate.

## 24.4 Dangling Elliptical Clauses

An elliptical clause is an adverbial clause that has been abridged so that its subject and verb are only understood, or implied rather than stated; the subject of the independent clause then automatically serves also as the implied subject of the elliptical clause. If the implied subject is different from the subject of the independent clause, the subordinate element will dangle, sometimes illogically.

> ✘   Once in disguise, the hero's conflict emerges.

It isn't "the hero's *conflict*" that is in disguise, but the *hero*. Either supply a logical subject and verb for the elliptical clause, or retain the elliptical clause and make the other subject logically agree with it:

> Once *the hero* is in disguise, *his conflict* emerges.

> *Once in disguise, the hero* begins to reveal his conflicts.

Another example:

> ✘   When well marinated, put the pieces of chicken on the barbecue.

Here the understood subject is *the pieces*, but the subject of the independent clause of this imperative sentence is an understood *you*. Give the elliptical clause a subject and verb:

When the pieces of chicken are well marinated, put them on the barbecue.

## 24.5 Dangling Prepositional Phrases and Appositives
(see section 11 and 1.17)

A prepositional phrase can also dangle. In this example, an indefinite *it* (see 5.5) is the issue:

> ✗ *Like a child in a toy shop*, it is all she can bear not to touch everything.

> Like a child in a toy shop, *she* can hardly bear not to touch everything.

And so can an appositive prove to be problematic:

> ✗ *A superb racing car*, a Ferrari's engine is a masterpiece of engineering.

The phrase seems to be in apposition with the noun *engine*, but it is illogical to equate an engine with an entire car (the possessive *Ferrari's* is adjectival). Revise it:

> A superb racing car, *a Ferrari* has an engine that is a masterpiece of engineering.

# 25. MIXED CONSTRUCTIONS

To begin a sentence with one construction and then inadvertently shift to another can create confusion for one's readers:

> ✗ Eagle Creek is a small BC community is located near Wells Gray Provincial Park.

The writer here sets up two clauses beginning with *is* but then omits a subject for the second occurrence of *is*. Either drop the first *is* and add commas around the resulting appositive phrase ("a small BC community"), or add *that* or *which* before the second *is*.

> ✗ Since Spain was a devoutly Catholic country, therefore most of its pre-twentieth century art was on religious themes.

Here the writer begins with a subordinating *Since* but then uses *therefore* to introduce the second clause, which would be correct only if the first clause were independent. Fix this by dropping either the *Since* or the *therefore* (if you drop *Since*, change the comma to a semicolon to avoid a comma splice: see 33.5).

# 26. INCONSISTENT POINT OF VIEW

Be consistent in your point of view within a sentence and, except in special cases, from one sentence to the next. Avoid illogical shifts in the tense, mood, and voice of verbs, and in the person and number of pronouns.

## 26.1 Shifts in Tense (see 6.7–6.8)

✗   The professor *explained* what she expected of us and then she *sits* in her chair and *tells* us to begin.

All of the events described in this sentence occurred at a particular time in the past. So, change *sits* and *tells* to the past tense to coincide with *explained*.

## 26.2 Shifts in Mood (see 6.12–6.13)

✗   If it *were* Sunday and I *was* feeling more energized, I would go skiing with you.

This sentence begins and ends in the subjunctive, but *was* is indicative. Correct this by changing indicative *was* to subjunctive *were*.

✗   First *put* tab A in slot B; next *you will put* tab C in slot D.

Omit *you will* to correct the shift from imperative to indicative.

## 26.3 Shifts in Voice (see 6.15–6.16)

The following examples illustrate the shift between active and passive voice and how to avoid this common error:

✗   Readers should not ordinarily have to read instructions a second time before some sense *can be made* of the details.

Readers should not ordinarily have to read instructions a second time before they can make sense of the details.

✘  We drove thirty kilometres to the end of the road, after which five
more kilometres *were covered* on foot.

We drove thirty kilometres to the end of the road and then covered
another five kilometres on foot.

## 26.4 Shifts in Person of Pronoun (see 3.1–3.2)

Shifts in person from words such as *one*, *a person*, *somebody*, or
*someone* to the second-person *you*, while common in informal conversation, are likely to be questioned in print, and particularly in
formal writing. Edit to produce consistency in person.

✘  If *one* wants to be a cautious investor, *you* should not invest in the
stock market.

If *you* want to be a cautious investor, *you* should not invest in the
stock market.

If *one* wants to be a cautious investor, *he or she* should not invest
in the stock market.

While *you* is an ineffective replacement for *someone*, it can be used
effectively in the first revision suggested above. To avoid gender bias
in references to *one* of unspecified gender, use *he or she* as in the
second revision above.

## 26.5 Shifts in Number of Pronoun (see 3.1)

✘  *If* the committee wants *its* recommendations followed, *they*
should have written *their* report more carefully.

The committee changed from a collective unit (*it*) to a collection of
individuals (*they*, *their*); the committee should be either singular or
plural throughout. See also 4.5 and 7.6.

# 27. FAULTY PARALLELISM

Parallelism, the balanced and deliberate repetition of identical grammatical structures (words, phrases, clauses) within a single sentence,
can be a strong stylistic technique. Not only does it make for vigorous, balanced, and rhythmical sentences, but it can also help develop

and tie together paragraphs (see 66.1). Like any other device, parallelism can be overdone, but more commonly writers underuse it. Of course, if you're writing an especially sober piece, like a letter of condolence, you probably won't want to use lively devices like parallelism and metaphor. But in most writing some parallel structure is appropriate. Build parallel elements into your sentences, and now and then make two or three successive sentences parallel with each other. Here is a sentence about computer crime. Note how parallelism (along with alliteration) strengthens the first part, thereby helping to set up the second part:

> Although one can distinguish *the malicious from the mischievous or the harmless hacker from the more dangerous computer criminal*, security officials take a dim view of anyone who romps through company files.

But be careful, for it is easy to slip, to set up a parallel structure and then lose track of it. Study the following examples of faulty parallelism. (See also 12.1–12.2.)

## 27.1 With Coordinate Elements

Coordinate elements in a sentence should have the same grammatical form. If they don't, the sentence will lack parallelism and therefore be ineffective.

> ✗    Reading should be engrossing, active, and a challenge.

The first two complements are predicate adjectives, the third a predicate noun. Change *a challenge* to the adjective *challenging* so that it will be parallel.

The coordinate parts of compound subjects, verbs, objects, and modifiers should be parallel in form.

> ✗    *Eating* huge meals, *too many sweets*, and *snacking* between meals can lead to obesity.

This sentence can be corrected either by making all three parts of the subject into gerunds:

> *Eating* huge meals, *eating* too many sweets, and *snacking* between meals can lead to obesity.

or by using only the first gerund and following it with three parallel objects:

> Eating *huge meals*, *too many sweets*, and *between-meal snacks* can lead to obesity.

Another example:

> ✘ He talks about his computer in terms *suggesting a deep affection for it* and *that also demonstrate a thorough knowledge of it.*

Simply change the participial phrase (*suggesting . . .*) to a relative clause (*that suggests . . .*) so that it will be parallel with the second part.

It is particularly easy for a writer to produce faulty parallelism by omitting a second *that*:

> ✘ Marvin was convinced *that the argument was unsound* and *he could profitably spend some time analyzing it.*

A second *that*, before *he*, corrects the error and clarifies the meaning, for this slip is not only a breakdown of parallelism but also an implied shift in point of view (see section 26). The omission of a second *that* invites a reader to take *he could profitably spend some time analyzing it* as an independent clause (expressing the writer's own opinion about what Marvin should do) rather than a second subordinate clause expressing a part of Marvin's opinion, which is what the writer intended.

## 27.2 With Correlative Conjunctions (see 12.2)

Check for parallel structure when using correlative conjunctions:

> ✘ Whether *for teaching a young child the alphabet* or *in educating an adult about the latest political controversy*, television is probably the best device we have.

The constructions following the *whether* and the *or* should be parallel: change *in* to *for*.

The correlative pair *not only . . . but also* can be particularly troublesome:

> ✘ She not only *corrected my grammar* but also *my spelling*.

The error can be corrected either by repeating the verb *corrected* (or using some other appropriate verb, such as *criticized* or *repaired*) after *but also*:

> She not only *corrected my grammar* but also *corrected my spelling*.

or by moving *corrected* so that it occurs before *not only* rather than after it:

> She corrected not only *my grammar* but also *my spelling*.

Either method makes what follows *not only* parallel in form to what follows *but also*. The second version is more economical.

### 27.3 In a Series

In any series of three or more parallel elements, make sure that little beginning words like prepositions, pronouns, and the *to* of infinitives precede either the first element alone or each of the elements. And don't omit needed articles:

> ✘ The new library is noted for *a large auditorium, state-of-the-art computer lab, an impressive collection of journals*, and *brilliant, hard-working staff*.

The article *a* is missing before the second and fourth items and should be added to make the items parallel. Another way to fix this would be to remove the articles and insert the possessive pronoun *its* before the first item.

> ✘ She exhorted her teammates to obey the rules, *to think positively*, and *ignore criticism*.

Since *to* occurs in the first two phrases, it should lead off the third phrase as well—or else be omitted from the second one. If necessary, jot down the items in such a series in a vertical list after the word that introduces them: any slips in parallelism should then be clearer to you.

## 28. FAULTY COORDINATION

If unrelated or unequal elements—usually clauses—are presented as coordinate, the result is faulty coordination.

> ✘ Watches are usually water-resistant *and* some have the ability to glow in the dark.

There is no logical connection between the two clauses—other than that they both say something about watches. The ideas would be better expressed in separate sentences. Coordinating two such clauses produces a sentence that also lacks unity. Here is another example, from a description of a simple object; the lack of unity is even more glaring:

> ✘　One might find this kind of a jar in a small junk shop *and* it can
> be used for anything from cotton balls to rings and things, or just
> to stand as a decoration.

The suggestion about the junk shop should either be in a separate sentence or be subordinated.

Similarly, if two elements are joined by an inappropriate coordinating conjunction, the result is again faulty coordination—sometimes referred to as "loose" coordination. Here is an example of this more common weakness:

> ✘　Nationalism can affect the relations between nations by creating
> a distrustful atmosphere, *and* an ambassador's innocent remark
> can be turned into an insult by a suspicious listener.

The *and* misrepresents the relation between the two clauses; the second is not an additional fact but rather an example or result of the fact stated in the first. It would be better either to join the two clauses with a semicolon or colon, or to change *and* to *in which*, and to drop the comma, thereby subordinating the second clause. (The first clause could be made subordinate by adding an opening *Because*, but this would distort emphasis, since the first clause appears more important; see 18.9). Here is another example, from a description of how a particular scene in *Hamlet* should be staged:

> ✘　In this scene Rosencrantz is the main speaker of the two courtiers;
> therefore he should stand closer to Hamlet.

This sentence could be sharpened. The first clause would be better subordinated:

> Because in this scene Rosencrantz is the main speaker of the two
> courtiers, he should stand closer to Hamlet.

The original *therefore* does express this relation, but the sentence was nonetheless a compound one, tacitly equating the two clauses.

Emphasis and clarity are better served by letting the syntax acknowledge the logically subordinate nature of the first clause.

Sometimes faulty coordination produces a sentence that lacks not just clarity but also logic:

> ✗    Alliteration is a very effective poetic device when used sparingly but appropriately.

The meaning expressed by *but* here is entirely illogical. *But* implies opposition, yet it is likely that a poet who uses alliteration sparingly would also use it appropriately. *And* would be a better coordinator here.

A particularly weak form of loose coordination overlaps with the overuse of *this* (see 5.3):

> ✗    The poem's tone is light and cheery, *and this* is reinforced by the mainly one-syllable words and the regular rhythm and rhyme.

If you ever find such an *and this* in your writing, try to revise it, for not only is the coordination weak, but the demonstrative *this* is weak as well, since it has no antecedent:

> The poem's light and cheery tone is reinforced by the mainly one-syllable words and the regular rhythm and rhyme.

Another kind of faulty coordination links several short independent clauses with coordinating conjunctions, mostly *and*'s; the result is a loose string of seemingly unrelated parts. Such sentences tend to ramble on and on, emphasizing very little.

> ✗    The ferry rates were increased and the bigger commercial vehicles had to pay more to use the ferry service and so the cost of transporting goods rose and the consumers who bought those goods had to pay more for them but they had to pay higher fares on the ferries as well and naturally most people were unhappy about it.

The information needed to make the point is here, but ineffective syntax leaves the reader floundering, trying to decipher the connections and the thoughts behind the whole utterance. The *but* seems to be used less for logic than for variety, and the vague *it* at the end effectively dissipates any emphasis the sentence might have had. A little tinkering sorts out the facts, shortens the sentence by almost half, reduces the five coordinating conjunctions to a pair of correlative conjunctions, reduces the six independent clauses to two independent and one subordinate, and achieves some emphasis at the end:

> Not only did the increased ferry rates cost travellers more, but, since the operators of commercial vehicles also had to pay more, the cost of transported goods rose as well, affecting all consumers.

See also 18.9 and 16.2.

# 29. FAULTY LOGIC

Clear and logical thinking is essential to clear and effective writing. For example, avoid sweeping statements: over-generalization is one of the most common weaknesses in writing. Precise claims and statements of fact will make your writing clearer. Make sure that the evidence you use is sound and that the authorities you cite are credible, current, and reliable. Such matters are particularly important in argumentative writing. Weak reasoning will hurt your attempt to convince the reader of the point you're trying to argue. You will want to avoid such logical missteps as begging the question, reasoning in a circle, jumping to conclusions, and leaning on false analogies, which can seriously decrease the effectiveness of your writing (see 71.5–71.8).

There are many ways in which logic is important even in something so small as a sentence. The problems discussed in sections 23–28 are in many instances problems in logic. Following are some examples of other ways in which sentences can be illogical. Unsound reasoning leads to sentences like this:

> ✗ You could tell that James's father was proud of him, for he had the boy's picture on his desk.

The conclusion may seem reasonable, but it should at least be qualified with a *probably*, or more evidence should be provided; for there are other possible reasons for the picture's being on the desk. James's mother could have put it there, and the father not bothered to remove it; perhaps he's afraid to. Or he could feel love for his son, but not pride. Or he could be feigning love and pride for appearances' sake, knowing inside that he doesn't feel either. Here's another example:

> ✗   Wordsworth is *perhaps* the first English Romantic poet, *for* his major themes—nature and human life—are characteristic of the Romantic style of poetry.

To begin with, the word *perhaps* is ineffective: either the writer is making a point of Wordsworth's primacy and there is no "perhaps" about it, or there is no point to be made and the whole clause is superfluous. Even more serious is the way evidence is given to substantiate the statement: if the mere presence in his poetry of themes common to Romanticism makes him first, then all Romantic poets are first. The writer probably meant something like "Wordsworth is the first English Romantic poet to develop the major themes of the Romantic movement." As for these "major themes," just how valid is the implication that "human life" is especially characteristic of Romantic writers? No amount of revision can repair this muddy thinking.

Even if writers know clearly what they want to say, they have to choose and use words thoughtfully:

> ✗   The town is *surrounded* on one side by the ocean.

If the town were indeed *surrounded* by the ocean, it would be an island. The correct word here is *bounded*. This error might equally well be designated an error in diction: see section 58.

Faulty logic can also affect the way writers put sentences together:

> ✗   Having a car with bad spark plugs or points or a dirty carburetor causes it to run poorly and to use too much gas.

The intention in the above example is clear, but the verb, *causes*, has as its subject the gerund *having*; consequently the sentence says that the mere possession of the afflicted car is what causes it to run poorly—as if one could borrow a similar car and it would run well. A logical revision:

> Bad spark plugs or bad points or a dirty carburetor cause a car to run poorly and to use too much gas.

Faulty comparisons are another cause of illogicality:

> ✘    French painting did not follow the wild and exciting forms of
> Baroque art as closely as most European countries.

Again the meaning is apparent, but the syntax faulty; readers would
be annoyed at having to revise the sentence themselves in order to
understand it. The sentence says either that "European countries followed the wild and exciting forms of Baroque art" to some degree
or that "French painting followed most European countries more
closely than it followed the wild and exciting forms of Baroque art,"
neither of which makes sense. Simply completing the comparison
straightens out the syntax and permits the intended meaning to come
through unambiguously:

> French painting did not follow the wild and exciting forms of Baroque
> art as closely as did *that* of most European countries.

Another kind of ambiguity appears in this sentence:

> ✘    Numerous scientific societies were founded in every developed
> country.

The intended meaning is probably that every developed country had
at least one scientific society—but it could just as well mean that
there were numerous such societies in each country.

Here's another kind of illogical sentence:

> ✘    His lack of cynicism was visible in every paragraph of his book.

The meaning is clear, but a reader might find it odd to think of a *lack*
being *visible*. Put it more logically:

> Every paragraph of his book revealed his idealism.

Make sure that nouns are inflected to agree logically with the context:

> ✘    All the legislators appeared at the committee to express their view
> on health care reforms.

Clearly the legislators expressed their *views*, not just one *view*.

Sometimes an extra word creeps in and weakens an otherwise logical sentence:

✘  Alexander Graham Bell is known as the modern inventor of the telephone.

The writer was probably thinking subconsciously of the telephone as a *modern* invention, and the word just popped into the sentence. Thinking critically, one sees that the word *modern* implies that there have been one or more earlier, perhaps even ancient, inventors of the telephone.

Finally, make sure your sentences actually say something worth saying. Here's one that doesn't:

✘  The mood and theme play a very significant part in this poem.

This could be called an "empty" sentence (the weak intensifier *very* suggests that the writer subconsciously felt the need to prop it up). It would be illogical for the *theme* of a poem to play other than a significant part in it.

# 30. FAULTY ALIGNMENT

Poor alignment results when two or more elements in a sentence are illogically or incongruously aligned with each other. Such errors often take the form of a verb saying something illogical about its subject—an error sometimes called faulty predication; that is, what is predicated about the subject is an impossibility. For example:

✘  Many new inventions and techniques occurred during this period.

An invention could, with some strain, be said to *occur*, but *techniques* do not *occur*. Revision is necessary; one possibility is to use an expletive and the passive voice:

During this period there were many new inventions, and many new techniques were developed.

In the next example the verb repeats the meaning of the subject:

✘    The setting of the play takes place in Verona.

The play takes place in Verona.

The play is set in Verona.

Errors in predication often occur with a form of *be* and a complement:

✘    The amount of gear to take along is the first step to consider when planning a long hike.

But an *amount* cannot be a *step*; revision is needed:

The first step in planning a hike is to decide how much gear to take along.

Note that this also removes the other illogicality: one does not *consider* a *step*; rather the considering, or deciding, is itself the step. Another example:

✘    The value of good literature is priceless.

It is not the *value* that is priceless, but the *literature* itself. Here is a similar error, of a common kind:

✘    The cost of my used car was relatively inexpensive.

The cost of my used car was relatively low.

My used car was relatively inexpensive.

Other errors in alignment aren't errors in predication, but are similar to them in using words illogically:

✘    In narrative, the author describes the occurrences, environment, and thoughts of the characters.

It is logical to speak of characters having thoughts and an environment, but not *occurrences*; substitute *experiences*.

✘    Its fine texture was as smooth and hard as a water-worn rock.

This, which illogically equates texture and rock, is also a form of incomplete comparison. Insert *that of* after *hard as*. (See also section 29.)

> ✘   Professions such as a doctor, a lawyer, or an engineer require
>     extensive post-secondary education.

But *being* a doctor, a lawyer, or an engineer is not a *profession*. Change *profession* to *professional*:

> Professionals such as doctors, lawyers, and engineers require extensive
> post-secondary education.

Or recast the sentence completely:

> Professions such as medicine, law, or engineering require extensive
> post-secondary education.

# 31. SENTENCE COHERENCE

Although the word *coherence* usually refers to the connection between sentences and between paragraphs (see sections 64–66 and 69.2), the parts of a sentence must also cohere. Each sentence fault discussed in the preceding sections is capable of making a sentence incoherent. If a sentence lacks coherence, the fault probably lies in one or more of the following: faulty arrangement (faulty word order, misplaced modifier), unclear or missing or illogical connections and relations between parts (faulty reference, lack of agreement, dangling modifier, faulty coordination, faulty logic, incongruous alignment), syntactic shift from one part to another (mixed construction, shift in point of view, faulty parallelism); or the weakness may be due to something that can only be labelled unclear. Consult these specific sections as necessary to ensure that your sentences are coherent within themselves.

# CHAPTER IV
# Punctuation

There are two common misconceptions about punctuation: first, punctuation is of no importance—it has little to do with the effectiveness of written English—and second, good punctuation is a mystery whose secrets are available only to those with a special instinct. Those who believe one or both of these misconceptions may punctuate poorly, whether through fear or lack of concern or both.

First, good punctuation is essential to clear and effective writing. It helps writers clarify meaning and tone and, therefore, helps readers understand what writers communicate: try removing the punctuation marks from a piece of prose, and then see how difficult it is to read it. Punctuation points to meaning that in spoken language would be indicated by pauses, pitch, tone, and stress. In effect, punctuation helps readers hear a sentence the way a writer intends. Commas, semicolons, colons, and dashes help to clarify the internal structure of sentences; often the very meaning or beauty of a sentence depends on how it is punctuated.

Second, the principles of good punctuation are not mysterious; mastering them shouldn't be difficult. Even the most inexperienced writers depend on punctuation to help them understand what they read; becoming more aware of the way punctuation operates in the writing of others will help them control punctuation in their own writing.

And here yet another misconception needs to be examined: what are often called the "rules" aren't rules but conventions. For example, English-speakers agree that the word for a small domestic feline animal is *cat*. If you wrote about a *kat*, your readers would probably understand you, but they would wonder why you had strayed from the conventional spelling, and to that extent you would have lost touch with them. But if you chose to call the animal a *zyb*, you would have departed completely from the convention, and you would have lost your readers entirely. The "rule" that *cat* is spelled *c-a-t* is not a moral or legal restraint; no one is going to sue you for spelling it *z-y-b*. But in exercising your freedom of choice you would only be defeating your purpose: clear and effective communication.

Similarly, the conventions of punctuation have come to be agreed upon by writers and readers of English for the purpose of clear and effective communication. Although good writers do sometimes stray from these conventions, they usually do so because they have a suf-ficient command of them to break a "rule" in order to achieve a desired effect.

A good way to improve your sense of punctuation is to become more aware of others' punctuation. Look not only for weaknesses but strengths as well. If you do this consciously as you read, you will soon acquire a better sense of what punctuation does and how it does it.

The following discussions cover the common circumstances and even some relatively uncommon ones. If you find it hard to grasp the principles, you may need to review the appropriate sections on gram-mar and sentence structure in the preceding chapters. Note further that many of the principles not only allow but even invite you to exercise a good deal of choice.

Note that hyphens and apostrophes are dealt with in the discus-sion of spelling in chapter V: see 51.15–51.19 and 51.22, respectively.

# 32. INTERNAL PUNCTUATION

## 32.1 Comma ,

The comma is a light or mild separator. It is the most neutral punctu-ation mark and the most used mark. A comma makes a reader pause slightly. Use it to separate words, phrases, and clauses from each other when no heavier or more expressive mark is required or desired.

### Main functions of commas

Basically, commas are used in three ways; if you know these conven-tions, you should have little trouble with commas:

1.  Generally, use a comma between independent clauses joined by a coordinating conjunction (*and, but, or, nor, for, yet, so*; see 12.1; see also 33.1 and 33.5–33.7):

    We went to the National Gallery, and then we walked to the Parliament Buildings.

    Most of us went back to work after the holidays, but Dorothy Wang was tempted by an opportunity to extend her vacation, so she took off an extra week.

2.   Generally, use commas to separate items in a series of three or more (see 38.1–38.2):

> It is said that early to bed and early to rise will make one healthy, wealthy, and wise.

> Robert Bateman, Emily Carr, and Mary Pratt are three Canadian painters.

See 44.3 on a common error with such constructions.

3.   Generally, use commas to set off parenthetical elements, such as interruptive or introductory words, phrases, and clauses and nonrestrictive appositives or nonrestrictive relative clauses (see sections 34–37 and 39.1):

> There are, however, some exceptions.

> Grasping the remote control firmly, she walked away.

> E.M. Forster's last novel, *A Passage to India*, is both serious and humorous.

> Caffè latte, which has always been a popular drink in Europe, is now popular in North America.

### Other conventional uses of the comma

1.   Use a comma between elements of an emphatic contrast:

> This is a practical lesson, not a theoretical one.

2.   Use a comma to indicate a pause where a word has been acceptably omitted:

> Ron is a conservative; Sally, a radical.

> To err is human; to forgive, divine.

3.   Use commas to set off a noun of address (see 2.2):

> Simon, please write a thank-you note to your grandparents.

> Tell me, my darling, how you think I should handle this.

4.   Generally, use commas with a verb of speaking before or after a quotation (see also 43.4–43.5):

Then Dora remarked, "That book gave me nightmares."

"It doesn't matter to me," said Alain laughingly.

5. Use commas after the salutation of informal letters (Dear Gail,) and after the complimentary close of all letters (Yours truly,). In formal letters, a colon is conventional after the salutation (Dear Mr. Eng:).

6. Use commas with dates. Different forms are possible:

> She left on January 11, 1991, and was gone a month. (Note the comma *after* the year.)

You may also place the date before the month—a style preferred by some writers in Canada and Britain—in which case no comma is required:

> She left on 11 January 1991 and was gone a month.

Whichever style you choose, make sure you use it consistently. When referring only to month and year, you may use a comma or not, but again, be consistent:

> The book was published in March, 2003, in Canada.

> It was published here in March 2003.

7. Use commas to set off geographical names and addresses:

> She left Fredericton, New Brunswick, and moved to Hamilton, Ontario, in hopes of finding a better-paying job. (Note the commas *after* the names of the provinces.)

> Their summer address will be 11 Bishop's Place, Lewes, Sussex, England.

For some common errors with commas, see 44.1–44.8.

## 32.2 Semicolon ;

The semicolon is a heavy separator, often almost equivalent to a period or "full stop." It forces a much longer pause than a comma does. And compared with the comma, it is used sparingly. Basically, semicolons have only two functions:

1.  Generally, use a semicolon between closely related independent clauses that are not joined by one of the coordinating conjunctions (see 12.1 [Joining words ...] and 33.4):

> Tap water often tastes of chemicals; spring water imported from France usually does not.

> The office had twenty new laptop computers; however, there were twenty-five employees in the company.

See 44.10 on common misuses of the semicolon.

2.  Use a semicolon instead of a comma if a comma would not be heavy enough; for example, if the clauses or the elements in a series have internal commas of their own (see 33.2 and 38.3).

## 32.3 Colon :

Colons are commonly used to introduce lists, examples, and long or formal quotations, but their possibilities in more everyday sentences are often overlooked. The reason a colon is useful is that it looks forward or anticipates: it gives readers a push toward the next part of the sentence. In the preceding sentence, for example, the colon sets up a sense of expectation about what is coming. It points out, even emphasizes, the relation between the two parts of the sentence (here, a relation in which the second part clarifies what the first part says). A semicolon in the same spot would bring readers to an abrupt halt, leaving it up to them to make the necessary connection between the two parts. Here are more examples; in some, the anticipatory function of the colon is perhaps less obvious, but it is there:

> Vita's garden contained only white flowers: roses, primulas, and primroses.

> Let me add just this: anyone who expects to lose weight must be prepared to exercise.

> It was an unexpectedly lovely time of year: trees were in blossom, garden flowers bloomed all around, the sky was clear and bright, and the temperature was just right.

> The rain came down during the race: we soon started slipping on the slick pavement.

Nevertheless, don't get carried away and overuse the colon: its effectiveness would wear off if it appeared more than once or twice a page. And see 44.11 on how to avoid a common misuse of the colon.

## Proofreading Tip

### Spacing after a Colon

One space after a colon is the norm. And only one space follows colons setting off subtitles or in footnotes or bibliographical entries.

## 32.4 Dash —

The dash is a popular punctuation mark, especially in email. Hasty writers often use it as a substitute for a comma, or where a colon would be more emphatic. Use a dash only when you have a definite reason for doing so. Like the colon, the dash sets up expectations in a reader's mind. But whereas the colon sets up an expectation that what follows will somehow explain, summarize, define, or otherwise comment on what has gone before, a dash suggests that what follows will be somehow surprising, involving some sort of twist, or at least a contrary idea. Consider the following sentence:

> My boss praised my wit, my intelligence, my organization, and my findings—and criticized the report for its poor spelling and punctuation.

Here the dash adds to the punch of what follows it. A comma there would deprive the sentence of much of its force; it would even sound odd, since the resulting matter-of-fact tone would not be in harmony with what the sentence was saying. Only a dash can convey the appropriate tone (see the introduction to chapter VI). Another example:

> What he wanted—and he wanted it very badly indeed—was the last piece of chocolate cake.

To set off the interrupting clause with commas instead of dashes wouldn't be "incorrect," but the result would be weaker, for the content of the clause is clearly meant to be emphatic. Only dashes have the power to signal that emphasis; commas would diminish the force of the clause. (See the Proofreading Tip in 39.3).

The dash is also handy in some long and involved sentences, for example after a long series before a summarizing clause:

> Our longing for the past, our hopes for the future and our neglect of the present moment—all these and more go to shape our everyday lives, often in ways unseen or little understood.

Even here, the emphatic quality of the dash serves the meaning, though its principal function in such a sentence is to mark the abrupt break.

As with colons, don't overuse dashes. They are even stronger marks, but they lose effectiveness if used often.

# 33–38 HOW TO USE COMMAS, SEMICOLONS, COLONS, AND DASHES

# 33. BETWEEN INDEPENDENT CLAUSES

## 33.1 Comma and Coordinating Conjunction

Generally, use a comma between independent clauses joined by one of the coordinating conjunctions (*and*, *but*, *or*, *nor*, *for*, *yet*, and sometimes *so*; see 12.1 [Joining sentences]):

> The revision of the report proved difficult, and she found herself burning the midnight oil.

> It was a serious speech, but Gordon included many jokes along the way, and the audience loved it.

> Naieli could go into debt for the sports car, or she could go on driving her old jalopy.

> Ira knew he shouldn't do it, yet he couldn't stop himself.

If the clauses are short, or if only one of a pair of clauses is short, the comma or commas may be omitted:

> The road was smooth and the car was running well and the weather was perfect.

> We practised all day so we were ready.

But sometimes even with a short clause the natural pause of a comma may make the sentence read more smoothly and clearly:

> The building was respectably old, for the ivy had climbed nearly to the top of its three storeys.

When the clauses are parallel in structure the comma may often be omitted:

> Art is long and life is short.

> He smirked and she simpered.

When two clauses have the same subject, a comma is less likely to be needed between them:

> It was windy and it was wet. (A comma here would detract from the effect produced by the parallel structure and alliteration of these two short clauses.)

> The play was well produced and it impressed everyone who saw it.

When the subject is omitted from the second clause, a comma should not be used (see 44.4):

> It was windy and wet.

## Proofreading Tip

### Using Commas between Independent Clauses of Contrast and Before *For* and *So*

Independent clauses joined by *but* and *yet*, which explicitly mark a contrast, will almost always need a comma, even if they are short or parallel, or have the same subject:

> It was windy, yet it was warm.

And when you join two clauses with the coordinating conjunction *for*, always put a comma in front of it to prevent its being misread as a preposition:

> Amanda was eager to leave early, for the restaurant was sure to be crowded.

The conjunction *so* almost always needs a comma, but remember that *so* is considered informal (see 12.1 [Joining sentences]).

## 33.2 Semicolon and Coordinating Conjunction

You will sometimes want to use a semicolon between independent clauses even though they are joined by a coordinating conjunction. A semicolon is appropriate when at least one of the clauses contains other punctuation:

> Distracted as he was, the English professor, Herbert, the best cryptic crossword player in the district, easily won the contest; and no one who knew him—or even had only heard of him—was in the least surprised.

## 33.3 Dash and Coordinating Conjunction

When you want a longer pause to create extra emphasis, a dash placed before a coordinating conjunction would produce a stronger effect than either a comma or a semicolon:

> Sameer protested that he was sorry for all his mistakes—but he went right on making them.

For a different rhetorical effect, change *but* to the more neutral *and*; a dash then takes over the contrasting function:

> Sameer protested that he was sorry for all his mistakes—and he went right on making them.

Similarly, consider the different effects of these two versions of the same basic sentence:

> It may not be the easiest way, but it's the only way we know.

> It may not be the easiest way—but it's the only way we know.

Even a period could be used between such clauses, since there is nothing inherently wrong with beginning a sentence with *And* or *But*. Even as sentence openers, they are still doing their job of coordinating. See 12.1 (Joining sentences).

## 33.4 Semicolon Without Coordinating Conjunction

To avoid a comma splice (see the next section), generally use a semicolon between independent clauses that are not joined with one of the coordinating conjunctions (*and, but, or, nor, for, yet, so*):

> The actual prize is not important; it is the honour connected with it that matters.

> Leanna was exhausted and obviously not going to win; nevertheless, she persevered and finished the race.

## 33.5 Comma Splice

Using only a comma between independent clauses not joined with a coordinating conjunction results in a comma splice:

   ✖    The actual prize is not important, it is the honour connected with it that matters.

   ✖    Being a mere child I didn't fully understand what I had witnessed, I just knew it was wrong.

   ✖    He desperately wanted to eat, however he was too weak to get out of bed.

A semicolon signals that an independent clause comes next. But a comma tells readers that something subordinate comes next; an independent clause coming instead would derail their train of thought. A comma with a coordinating conjunction is enough to prevent the derailment of thought:

> The prime minister is elected, but the senate members are not.

With few exceptions (see below), a comma without a coordinating conjunction is not enough. In most such sentences, then, in order to avoid seriously distracting your readers, use semicolons:

> Being a mere child I didn't fully understand what I had witnessed; I just knew it was wrong.

> Adverbs can usually move around in a sentence; conjunctions are not as flexible.

> Vancouver, the largest city in British Columbia, is not the capital; Victoria has that distinction.

# 33.6–33.7 Exceptions: Commas Alone Between Independent Clauses

## 33.6 Commas with Short and Parallel Clauses

If the clauses are short enough that a reader can take them both in with a single glance, and especially if they are also parallel in structure, a comma rather than a semicolon may be enough:

> He cooked, she ate.

> Lightning flashed, thunder roared.

## 33.7 Commas with Series of Clauses

Relatively short independent clauses in a series of three or more, especially if they are grammatically parallel, may be separated by commas rather than semicolons:

> I saw, I shopped, I bought.

> He cooked, she ate, they fell in love.

> If you want to do well, you must read carefully, you must write thoughtfully, and you must be passionate.

## 33.8 Semicolons with Conjunctive Adverbs and Transitions

Be sure to use a semicolon and not just a comma between independent clauses that you join with a conjunctive adverb, including *however* and *therefore*. Here is a list of most of the common ones:

| | | | |
|---|---|---|---|
| accordingly | finally | likewise | similarly |
| afterward | further | meanwhile | still |
| also | furthermore | moreover | subsequently |
| anyway | hence | namely | then |
| besides | however | nevertheless | thereafter |
| certainly | indeed | next | therefore |
| consequently | instead | nonetheless | thus |
| conversely | later | otherwise | undoubtedly |

The same caution applies to common transitional phrases such as these:

| | | |
|---|---|---|
| after this | if not | in the meantime |
| as a result | in addition | on the contrary |
| for example | in fact | on the other hand |
| for this reason | in short | that is |

Conjunctive adverbs often have the feel of subordinating conjunctions, but they are not conjunctions, although some dictionaries label them as conjunctions for these meanings. Think of them as adverbs doing a joining or "conjunctive" job:

> The text was turgid; therefore, she got a headache as she read it.

Here *therefore* works very much like *so*; nevertheless, *therefore* is a conjunctive adverb and requires the semicolon.

> He felt well enough to go; however, his doctor ordered him to stay in bed.

Here *however* works very much like *but*; nevertheless, *however* is a conjunctive adverb and requires the semicolon.

## Proofreading Tip

### On the Comma Following *However*

Note that whereas other conjunctive adverbs will often, but not always, be followed by commas, *however* as a conjunctive adverb (unless it ends a sentence) is followed by a comma to prevent its being misread as a regular adverb meaning "in whatever way" or "to whatever degree," as in "However you go, just make sure you get there on time."

*However* sometimes sounds overly formal at the beginning of a sentence or clause. Unless you want special emphasis on it, put it at some other appropriate place in the clause. Often, delaying it just one or two words works best:

> His doctor, however, ordered him to stay in bed.

Since conjunctive adverbs can easily be shifted around within a clause, you may find it helpful to apply this test if you aren't sure whether a particular word is a conjunctive adverb or a conjunction. Just remember that adverbs can move around in the sentence; conjunctions cannot.

> His doctor ordered him, however, to stay in bed.

### 33.9 Dashes and Colons Without Coordinating Conjunctions

Dashes and colons may also be used between independent clauses not joined by coordinating conjunctions. Use a dash when you want stronger emphasis on the second clause; use a colon when the second clause explains or enlarges upon the first (see 32.3 and 32.4). In many sentences, either a dash or a colon would work; the choice depends on the desired tone or emphasis:

> The film was dreadful from beginning to end: a plausible plot must have been the last thing on the director's mind.

> The proposal horrified Jon—it was ludicrous.

> Derek took the evolutionary way out: he turned and ran.

> It was a unique occasion—everyone at the meeting agreed on what should be done.

Note that a comma would not be correct in any of these examples. A semicolon would work, but it would be weak and usually inappropriate (except perhaps in the first example). But note that a period, especially in the second and third examples, would achieve a crisp and emphatic effect by turning each into two separate sentences.

## 33.10 Run-on (Fused) Sentences

Failure to put any punctuation between independent clauses where there is also no coordinating conjunction results in a run-on or fused sentence:

> ✘ Philosophers' views did not always meet with the approval of the authorities therefore there was constant conflict between writers and the church or state.

A semicolon after *authorities* corrects this serious error. See section 22.

> Philosophers' views did not always meet with the approval of the authorities; therefore, there was constant conflict between writers and the church or state.

# 34. TO SET OFF ADVERBIAL CLAUSES

## 34.1 Commas with Introductory Clauses

Generally, use a comma between an introductory adverbial clause and an independent (main) clause:

> After I had selected all the items I wanted, I discovered that I had left my wallet at home.

> Since she was elected by a large majority, she felt that she had a strong mandate for her policies.

> When the party was over, I went straight home.

When the introductory clause is short and when there would be no pause if the sentence were spoken aloud, you may often omit the comma. But if omitting the comma could cause misreading, retain it:

> Whenever I wanted, someone would bring me something to eat.

> After the sun had set, high above the mountains came the fighter jets.

Whenever you're not sure the meaning will be clear without it, use a comma.

## 34.2 Commas with Concluding Clauses

A comma may or may not be needed between an independent clause and a following adverbial clause. If the subordinate clause is essential to the meaning of the sentence, it is in effect restrictive and should not be set off with a comma; if it is not essential but contains only additional information or comment, it is nonrestrictive and should be set off with a comma (see section 37). Consider the following examples:

> I went straight home when the party was over.

> She did an excellent job in her first interview, although the second one was a disaster.

In most cases final clauses such as these will be necessary and won't require a comma. When in doubt, try omitting the clause to see if the sentence still says essentially what you want it to. See also 37.3.

# 35. TO SET OFF INTRODUCTORY AND CONCLUDING WORDS AND PHRASES

## 35.1 Adverbs and Adverbial Phrases

Generally, set off a long introductory adverbial phrase with a comma:

> After many years as leader of the party, Jean retired gracefully.

> In order to get the best results from your computer, you must follow the instruction manual carefully.

> Just like all the other long-time employees, Radha felt loyal to the company.

Generally, set off a word or short phrase if you want a distinct pause, for example, for emphasis or qualification or to prevent misreading:

> Unfortunately, Mother Nature didn't co-operate.

> Generally, follow my advice about punctuation.

> Usually, quiet people are difficult to work with.

Of the conjunctive adverbs, *however* is most often set off, though the others frequently are as well (see 33.8 and 44.6).

When such words and phrases follow the independent clause, most will be restrictive and therefore not set off with commas:

> Jean retired gracefully after many years as leader of the party.

> You must follow the instruction manual carefully in order to get the best results from your computer.

> Aarti moved to Calgary in 1983.

If you intend the concluding element to complete the sense of the main clause, don't set it off; if it merely provides additional information or comment, set it off. The presence or absence of punctuation tells your readers how you want the sentence to be read.

## 35.2 Participles and Participial Phrases

Always set off an introductory participle or participial phrase with a comma (see 10.4):

> Finding golf unexpectedly difficult, Kevin sought extra help.

> Feeling victorious, Shirin left the room.

> Having been in the darkroom so long, Jason scarcely recognized the world when he emerged.

> Puzzled, Karen turned back to the beginning of the novel.

Closing participles and participial phrases almost always need to be set off as well. Read the sentence aloud; if you feel a distinct pause, use a comma:

> Kevin sought extra help, finding golf unexpectedly difficult.

> Higher prices result in increased wage demands, contributing to the inflationary spiral.

Occasionally such a sentence will flow clearly and smoothly without a comma, especially if the modifier is essential to the meaning:

> Shirin left the room feeling victorious.

> She sat there looking puzzled.

If the closing participle modifies a predicate noun or a direct object, there usually should not be a comma:

> He was a man lacking in courage.

> I left him feeling bewildered. (He was bewildered.)

But if the participle in such a sentence modifies the subject, if it could also conceivably modify the object, then a comma is necessary:

> I left him, feeling bewildered. (I was bewildered.)

Only the presence or absence of the comma tells a reader how to understand such a sentence.

## Proofreading Tip

### Commas and Gerunds; Commas and Participial Phrases

Don't mistake a gerund for a participle (see 10.4 and 10.6). A gerund or gerund phrase functioning as the subject should not be followed by a comma (see 44.1):

> Dancing in the street, we celebrated the arrival of summer. (participle)

> Dancing in the street is a wonderful release of energy. (gerund)

## Proofreading Tip

### Commas and Infinitive Phrases

Don't mistake a long infinitive phrase functioning as a subject noun for one functioning as an adverb (see 10.1):

> To put together a meal for six without help is a remarkable feat. (noun)

> To put together a meal for six without help, you need to be very organized or a professional chef. (adverb)

### 35.3 Absolute Phrases

Always set off absolute phrases with commas (see 1.18 and 10.9):

> The doors locked and bolted, they went to bed feeling secure.

> Timmy went on stage, head held high, a grin spreading across his face.

# 36. TO SET OFF CONCLUDING SUMMARIES AND APPOSITIVES

Both dashes and colons can set off concluding summaries and appositives. Some writers think dashes are best for short concluding elements and colons for longer ones; but what matters isn't their length but their relation to the rest of the sentence. Use colons for straightforward conclusions, dashes for emphatic or unexpected ones. For example, the following sentences express a conventional idea, with the colon straightforwardly, with the dash somewhat emphatically:

> He wanted only one thing from life: happiness.

> He wanted only one thing from life—happiness.

But with a less expected final word the tone changes:

> He wanted only one thing from life—money.

Here a colon would do, since a colon followed by a single word automatically conveys some emphasis, but the strength of the idea would not be as well served by the quietness of a colon as it is by the dash. The same principles apply to setting off longer concluding appositives and summaries, though colons are more common; use a dash only when you want to take advantage of its special emphasis.

# 37. TO SET OFF NONRESTRICTIVE ELEMENTS

Words, phrases, and clauses are nonrestrictive when they are not essential to the principal meaning of a sentence; they should be set off from the rest of the sentence, usually with commas, though dashes and parentheses can also be used (see section 39). A restrictive modifier is essential to the meaning and should not be set off:

> Anyone wanting a refund should see the manager. (restrictive)

> Alex, wanting a refund, asked to see the manager. (nonrestrictive)

The participial phrase explains why Alex asked to see the manager, but the sentence is clear without it: "Alex asked to see the manager"; the phrase *wanting a refund* is therefore not essential and is set off with commas. But without the phrase the first sentence wouldn't make sense: "Anyone should see the manager"; the phrase *wanting a refund* is essential and is not set off. The question most often arises with relative clauses (see 1.15 and 3.4); appositives, though usually nonrestrictive, can also be restrictive, and some other elements can also be either restrictive or nonrestrictive (see 34.2 and 35.1–35.2).

## 37.1 Restrictive and Nonrestrictive Relative Clauses

Always set off a nonrestrictive relative clause; do not set off restrictive relative clauses:

> She is a woman who likes to travel.

The relative clause is essential and is not set off.

> Carol, who likes to travel, is going to Greece this summer.

Now the relative clause is merely additional—though explanatory—information: it is not essential to the identification of Carol, who has been explicitly named, nor is it essential to the meaning of the main clause. Being nonrestrictive, then, it should be set off. Consider the following pair of sentences:

> ✘ *Employees*, who are hard-working, should expect an annual raise.

> *Employees* who are hard-working should expect an annual raise.

Set off as nonrestrictive, the relative clause applies to all employees, which makes the sentence inaccurate. Left unpunctuated, the relative clause is restrictive, making the sentence correctly apply only to employees who are in fact hard-working.

> The book, which I so badly wanted to read, was not in the library.

> The book which I so badly wanted to read was not in the library.

With the clause set off as nonrestrictive, we must assume that the book has been clearly identified in an earlier sentence. Left unpunctuated, the clause identifies "The book" as the particular one the speaker wanted to read but which the library didn't have.

## Proofreading Tip

### Determining Whether a Clause Is Restrictive

If you can use the relative pronoun *that*, you know the clause is restrictive; *that* cannot begin a nonrestrictive clause:

> The book *that* I wanted to read was not in the library.

Further, if the pronoun can be omitted (see 3.4) altogether, the clause is restrictive, as with *that* in the preceding example and *whom* in the following:

> The person [whom] I most admire is the one who works hard and plays hard.

Don't omit *that* when it is necessary to prevent misreading:

> ✗    Examples of the quality of art advertisements contain can be found in almost any magazine.

A *that* after *art* prevents misreading the phrase as "art advertisements":

> Examples of the quality of art that advertisements contain can be found in almost any magazine.

# Proofreading Tip

## Using *that* and *which* in Relative Clauses

*That* is much more common than *which* in restrictive clauses. Indeed, some writers prefer to use *which* only in nonrestrictive clauses. But the use of *which* in both nonrestrictive and restrictive clauses is becoming the norm.

## 37.2 Restrictive and Nonrestrictive Appositives

Always set off a nonrestrictive appositive:

> Jan, *our youngest daughter*, keeps the lawn mowed all summer.

> Karl—*my current accountant*—is very imaginative.

> *King Lear* is a noble work of literature, *one that will live in human minds for all time.*

> Virginia is going to bring her sister, *Vanessa*.

In the last example, the comma indicates that Virginia has only the one sister. Left unpunctuated, the appositive would be restrictive, meaning that Virginia has more than one sister and that the particular one she is going to bring is the one named Vanessa.

Don't mistake a restrictive appositive for a nonrestrictive one:

> ✘ The proceedings were opened by union leader, *Peter Smith*, with remarks attacking the government.

The commas are wrong, since it is only his name, Peter Smith, that clearly identifies him; the appositive is therefore restrictive. But alter the sentence slightly:

> The proceedings were opened by *the* union's leader, Peter Smith, with remarks attacking the government.

Now the phrase *the union's leader*, with its definite article, identifies the person; the name itself, *Peter Smith*, is only incidental information and is therefore nonrestrictive. This example works only if the union has been introduced in an earlier sentence.

> ✘ According to spokesperson, Janina Fraser, the economy is improving daily.
>
> According to spokesperson Janina Fraser, the economy is improving daily.
>
> According to *the* spokesperson, Janina Fraser, the economy is improving daily.

The definite article makes all the difference. But even the presence or absence of the definite article is not always a sure test:

> ✘ One of the best-known mysteries of the sea is that of the ship, *Mary Celeste*, the disappearance of whose entire crew has never been satisfactorily explained.
>
> One of the best-known mysteries of the sea is that of the ship *Mary Celeste*, the disappearance of whose entire crew has never been satisfactorily explained.

The phrase *the ship* is insufficient identification; the proper name is needed and is therefore restrictive. This error most often occurs when a proper name follows a defining or characterizing word or phrase. In the reverse order, such a phrase is set off as a nonrestrictive appositive:

> Janina Fraser, the spokesperson, said the economy is improving daily.

See 44.7 for more on restrictive appositives.

## 37.3 *Because*-Clauses and Phrases

Adverbial clauses or phrases beginning with *because* (or otherwise conveying that sense) can be a problem when they follow an explicit negative. When *because* follows a negative, punctuate the sentence so that it means what you want it to:

> Mary wasn't late for work, because her husband drove her: he was always very punctual in the morning. (She wasn't late for work).
>
> Mary wasn't late for work just because her husband drove her. He was often slow in the morning, but she had also forgotten to make her lunch the night before, which caused further delay. (She was late for work.)

Often you can best avoid the possible awkwardness or ambiguity by simply rephrasing a sentence in which *because* follows a negative.

## 37.4 Modifiers with *such as*

Nonrestrictive modifiers beginning with *such as* should be set off with commas:

> Johan played all kinds of sports, such as hockey, baseball, and lacrosse.

But be careful not to mistake a nonrestrictive *such as* modifier for a restrictive one. Consider the following example:

> Antibiotics, *such as penicillin*, are ineffective against the disease.

Because the modifier *such as penicillin* is set off, the sentence implies that *all* antibiotics (of which penicillin is an example) are ineffective against the disease. If the commas were removed, the modifier would become restrictive, and the meaning would change: the sentence would imply that only those antibiotics that are like penicillin are ineffective, though other antibiotics might not be.

# 38. BETWEEN ITEMS IN A SERIES

## 38.1 Commas

Generally, use commas between words, phrases, or clauses in a series of three or more:

> He sells books, magazines, candy, and life insurance.

> She promised the voters to cut taxes, to limit government spending, and to improve transportation.

> Carmen explained that she had visited the art gallery, that she had walked in the park, and that eventually she had gone to a movie.

> He stirred the sauce frequently, carefully, and hungrily.

## 38.2 Comma Before Final Item in a Series

The common practice of omitting the final comma (known as the serial comma or Oxford comma—found before the conjunction) can be misleading. That final pause will give your sentences a better rhythm, and you will avoid the kind of possible confusion apparent in sentences like these (try adding the final comma and then reading them again):

> The manufacturers sent us shirts, wash-and-wear slacks and shoes. (The shoes were wash-and-wear?)

> They prided themselves on having a large and bright kitchen, a productive vegetable garden, a large recreation room with a huge fireplace and two fifty-foot cedar trees. (The trees were in the recreation room?)

> The Speech from the Throne discussed international trade, improvements in transportation, slowing down inflation and the postal service. (Do we need to slow down the postal service?)

## 38.3 Semicolons

If the phrases or clauses in a series are unusually long or contain other internal punctuation, you might want to separate them with semicolons rather than commas:

> How wonderful it is to awaken in the morning when the birds are clamouring in the trees; to see the bright light of a summer morning streaming into the room; to realize, with a sudden flash of joy, that it is Sunday and that this perfect morning is completely yours; and then to loaf in a deckchair without a thought of tomorrow.

> Saint John, New Brunswick; Victoria, British Columbia; and Kingston, Ontario, are all about the same size.

## 38.4 Dashes

You can also emphasize items in a series by putting dashes between them—but don't do it often. The sharpness of the breaks greatly heightens the effect of a series:

> Rising taxes—rising insurance rates—rising gas costs—skyrocketing food prices: it is becoming more and more difficult to live decently and still keep within a budget.

Here the omission of *and* before the final item, together with the repetition and parallel structure, heightens the stylistic effect by adding to the stridency; even the colon adds its touch. But dashes can also be effective in a quieter context:

> Upon rounding the bend we were confronted with a breathtaking panorama of lush valleys with meandering streams—flower-covered slopes—great rocks and trees—and, overtopping all, the mighty peaks with their hoods of snow.

## 38.5 Colons

Colons, too, can be used in a series but even more rarely than dashes. Colons add emphasis because they are unusual, but mainly their anticipatory nature produces a cumulative effect suitable when successive items in a series build to a climax:

> He held on: he persevered: he fought back: and eventually he won out, regardless of the punishing obstacles.

> It blew: it rained: it hailed: it sleeted: it even snowed—it was a most unusual June even for Calgary.

(Note how the dash in the last example prepares for the final clause.)

## 38.6 Series of Adjectives

Use commas between two or more adjectives preceding a noun if they are parallel, each modifying the noun itself; do not put commas between adjectives that are not parallel:

> He is an intelligent, efficient, ambitious officer.

> She is a tall young woman.

> She wore a new black felt hat, a long red coat, and a woollen scarf with red, white, and black stripes.

In the first sentence, each adjective modifies *officer*. In the second, *tall* modifies *young woman*; it is a *young woman* who is *tall*, not a *woman* who is *tall* and *young*. In the third, *new* modifies *black felt hat*, *black* modifies *felt hat*, and *long* modifies *red coat*; *red, white*, and *black* all separately modify *stripes*.

But it isn't always easy to tell whether or not such adjectives are parallel. It often helps to think of each comma as substituting for *and*: try putting *and* between the adjectives. If it sounds logical there, the adjectives are probably parallel and should be separated by a comma; if *and* doesn't seem to work, a comma won't either. For example, you wouldn't say *a black and felt hat* or *a long and red coat*, whereas *red and white and black stripes* is natural. Another test is to change the order of the adjectives. If it sounds odd to say *a felt black hat* instead of *a black felt hat*, then the adjectives probably aren't parallel. A final aid to remember: usually no comma is needed after a number (*three blind mice*) or after common adjectives for size or age (*tall young woman*; *long red coat*; *new brick house*). But sometimes you'll have to rely on instinct or common sense. For example, the following sentences seem fine without commas:

> There was an ominous wry tone in her voice.

> What caught our eye in the antique shop was a comfortable-looking tattered old upholstered leather chair.

See also 44.3.

# 39–41 PUNCTUATION MARKS IN PAIRS

# 39. SENTENCE INTERRUPTERS

Sentence interrupters are parenthetical elements—words, phrases, or clauses—that interrupt the syntax of a sentence. Although we discuss some of these under other headings, here we stress two points: (1) interrupters are set off at both ends; (2) you can choose from among three kinds of punctuation marks to set them off: a pair of commas, a pair of dashes, or a pair of parentheses.

### 39.1 Interrupters Set Off with Commas

Set off light, ordinary interrupters with a pair of commas:

> Robert Munsch, *a children's book author*, is a favourite with young readers. (nonrestrictive appositive phrase)

> This document, *the lawyer says*, will complete the contract. (explanatory clause)

> Thank you, *David*, for this much needed advice and the martini. (noun of address)

Mr. Hao, *feeling elated*, left the judge's office. (participial phrase)

At least one science course, *such as botany or astronomy*, is required of all students. (prepositional phrase of example)

You may, *on the other hand*, wish to read only for pleasure. (transitional prepositional phrase)

Could you be persuaded to consider this money as, *well*, a loan? (mild interjection)

Grandparents, *who are wise and loving*, should be allowed to spend a lot of time with their grandchildren. (nonrestrictive relative clause)

Jet lag, *it now occurs to me*, may after all be responsible for our falling asleep at dinner. (clause expressing afterthought)

It was, *all things considered*, a successful concert. (absolute phrase)

## 39.2 Interrupters Set Off with Dashes

Use a pair of dashes to set off abrupt interrupters or other interrupters that you wish to emphasize. An interrupter that sharply breaks the syntax of a sentence will often be emphatic for that very reason, and dashes will be appropriate to set it off:

The increase in enrolment—over fifty per cent—demonstrates the success of our program.

The stockholders who voted for him—quite a sizable group—were obviously dissatisfied with our recent conduct of the business.

He told me—believe this or not!—that he would never drink beer again.

Stephen J. Gould—the well-known scientist—began his career by studying snails.

In the last example, commas would suffice, but dashes work well because of both the length and the content of the appositive. Wherever you want emphasis or a different tone, you can use dashes where commas would ordinarily serve:

The employee of the year—Denise Dione—was delighted to receive the prize.

The modern age—as we all know—is a noisy age.

Dashes are also useful to set off an interrupter consisting of a series with its own internal commas, such as our first sentence in this section; set off with commas, such a structure can be confusing:

> ✘ Sentence interrupters are parenthetical elements, words, phrases, or clauses, that interrupt the syntax of a sentence.

> Sentence interrupters are parenthetical elements—words, phrases, or clauses—that interrupt the syntax of a sentence.

### 39.3 Interrupters Set Off with Parentheses

Use parentheses to set off abrupt interrupters or other interrupters that you wish to de-emphasize; often interrupters that could be emphatic can be played down in order to emphasize the other parts of a sentence:

> The stockholders who voted for him (quite a sizable group) were obviously dissatisfied with our recent conduct of the business.

> It is not possible at this time (it is far too early in the growing season) to predict with any confidence just what the crop yield will be.

> Speculation (I mean this in its pejorative sense) is not a safe foundation for a business enterprise.

> Some modern sports activities (hang-gliding for example) involve unusually high insurance claims.

By de-emphasizing something striking, parentheses can also achieve an effect similar to that of dashes, though by an ironic tone rather than an insistent one.

## Proofreading Tip

### Punctuation Marks that Occur in Pairs

Remember, punctuation marks that set off sentence interrupters come in pairs. If you put down an opening parenthesis you shouldn't omit the closing one. But sometimes writers accidentally omit the second dash or—especially—the second comma. Reading aloud, perhaps with exaggerated pauses, can help you spot that a mark is missing.

# 40. PARENTHESES ( )

Parentheses have three principal functions in non-technical writing: (1) to set off certain kinds of interrupters (see 39.3 above), (2) to enclose cross-reference information within a sentence, as we just did and as we do throughout this book, and (3) to enclose numerals or letters setting up a list or series, as we do in this sentence. Note that if a complete sentence is enclosed in parentheses within another sentence (here is an example of such an insertion), it needs neither an opening capital letter nor a closing period. Note also that if a comma or other mark is called for by the sentence (as in the preceding sentence, and in this one), it comes *after* the closing parenthesis, not before the opening one. Exclamation points and question marks go inside the parentheses only if they are a part of what is enclosed. (When an entire sentence or more is enclosed, the terminal mark comes inside the parentheses—as does this period.)

# 41. BRACKETS [ ]

Brackets (often referred to as "square brackets," since some people use the term *brackets* also to refer to parentheses) are used primarily to enclose something inserted in a direct quotation: see 43.10. And if you have to put parentheses inside parentheses—as in a footnote or a bibliographical entry—change the inner ones to brackets.

# 42. END PUNCTUATION

The end of every sentence must be marked with a period, a question mark, or an exclamation point (but see the Proofreading Tip at the end of 42.1). The period is the most common terminal punctuation; it ends the vast majority of sentences. The question mark is used to end direct questions or statements that are intended as questions. The exclamation point is used to end sentences that express strong emotion, emphatic surprise, or even emphatic query. Sometimes you will need to consider just what effect you want to achieve. Note for example the different effects of the following; in each instance, the end punctuation would dictate the necessary tone of voice and distribution of emphasis and pitch with which the sentence would be said aloud:

We won. (matter-of-fact)

We won! (surprised or emphatic)

We won? (skeptical or surprised)

## 42.1 Period .

Use a period to mark the end of statements and neutral commands:

Canadians use the telephone more than any other people in the world.

Ezra Pound, the author of *The Cantos*, died in 1972.

Don't let yourself be fooled by cheap imitations.

Use a period after most abbreviations:

| | | | | |
|---|---|---|---|---|
| abbr. | Mr. | Ms. | Dr. | Jr. |
| Ph.D. | B.A. | St. | Mt. | etc. |

Generally use a period in abbreviated place names:

B.C.     P.E.I.     Nfld.     N.Y.     MASS.

But note that two-letter postal abbreviations do not require periods:

BC     PE     NF     NY     MA

Periods are not used after metric and other symbols (unless they occur at the end of a sentence):

| | | | | |
|---|---|---|---|---|
| km | cm | kg | mc$^2$ | ml |
| kJ | C | Hz | Au | Zr |

Periods are often omitted with initials, especially of groups or organizations, and especially if the initials are acronyms—that is, words or names made up of initials (AIDS, NATO, CEGEP):

| | | | | |
|---|---|---|---|---|
| UN | UNICEF | WHO | RCMP | RAF |
| CBC | TV | APA | MLA | MP |

When in doubt, consult a good dictionary. If there is more than one acceptable usage, be consistent: stick with the one you choose.

## Proofreading Tip

### On Abbreviations and Periods

1. Although *Ms.* is not a true abbreviation, it is usually followed by a period.
2. Some Canadian writers and publishers follow the British convention of omitting the period after abbreviations that include the first and last letter of the abbreviated word: Mr, Mrs, Dr, Jr, St, etc. (And note in the preceding sentence that a period after an abbreviation at the end of a sentence serves as the sentence's period.)

## 42.2 Question Mark ?

Use a question mark at the end of direct questions:

Who is the greatest poet of all time?

When will the lease expire?

Do not use a question mark at the end of an indirect question: see 44.9.

Note that a question mark is necessary after questions that aren't phrased in the usual interrogative way (as might occur if you were writing dialogue):

You're leaving so early? (Are you leaving so early?)

You want him to accompany you? (Do you want him to accompany you?)

A question appearing as a sentence interrupter still needs a question mark at its end:

I went back to the beginning—what else could I do?—and tried to get it right the second time.

The man in the scuba outfit (what was his name again?) took a rear seat.

Since such interrupters are necessarily abrupt, dashes or parentheses are the appropriate marks to set them off. See also 1.20.

### 42.3 Exclamation Point !

Use an exclamation point after an emphatic statement or after an expression of emphatic surprise, emphatic query, and strong emotion:

> He came in first, yet it was only his second time in professional competition!
>
> What a loser!
>
> You don't say so!
>
> Isn't it beautiful today!
>
> Not again!
>
> Gosh!

Occasionally an exclamation point may be doubled or tripled for emphasis. It may even follow a question mark, to emphasize the writer's or speaker's disbelief:

> She said what?!
>
> You bought what?! A giraffe?! What were you thinking?!

This device should not be used in formal writing.

## Proofreading Tip

### On Using Exclamation Points

Use exclamation points sparingly, if at all, in formal writing. Achieve your desired emphasis by other means: see 18.10.

## Proofreading Tip

### Ending a Sentence with a Dash or Ellipsis

The dash and the three dots of an ellipsis (see 43.9) are sometimes used at the end of a sentence, especially in dialogue or at the end of a paragraph or a chapter in order to indicate a pause, a fading away, or an interruption, or to create mild suspense.

# 43. QUOTATION MARKS " "

There are two kinds of quotation: dialogue or direct speech (such as you might find in a story, novel, or nonfiction narrative) and verbatim quotation from a published work or other source. For the use of quotation marks around titles, see 48.1 and 48.3.

## 43.1 Direct Speech

Enclose all direct speech in quotation marks:

> I remember hearing my mother say to my absentminded father, "Henry, why is the newspaper in the fridge?"

In written dialogue, it is conventional to begin a new paragraph each time the speaker changes:

> "Henry," she said, a note of exasperation in her voice, "why is the newspaper in the fridge?"
>     "Oh, yes," he replied. "The fish is wrapped in it."
>     She examined it. "Well, there may have been a fish in it once, but there is no fish in it now."

Even when passages of direct speech are incomplete, the part that is verbatim should be enclosed in quotation marks:

> After only two weeks, he said he was "fed up" and that he was "going to look for a more interesting job."

## 43.2 Direct Quotation from a Source

Enclose in quotation marks any direct quotation from another source that you run into your own text:

> According to Anthony Powell, "Books do furnish a room."

### Prose

Prose quotations of no more than four lines are normally run into the text. Quotations of more than four lines should be treated as block quotations: they should be indented and generally follow the same spacing as the rest of the text.

When asked why she writes about food, M.F.K. Fisher answers directly:

> It seems to me that our three basic needs, for food and security and love, are so mixed and mingled and entwined that we cannot straightly think of one without the others. So it happens that when I write of hunger, I am really writing about love and the hunger for it, and warmth and the love of it and the hunger for it . . . and then the warmth and richness and fine reality of hunger satisfied . . . and it is all one.

Do not place quotation marks around a block quotation, but do reproduce any quotation marks that appear in the original:

> Budgets can be important. As Dickens has Mr. Micawber say in *David Copperfield*,
>
> > "Annual income twenty pounds, annual expenditure nineteen nineteen six, result happiness. Annual income twenty pounds, annual expenditure twenty pounds ought and six, result misery."

If you're quoting only a single paragraph or part of a paragraph, do not include the paragraph indentation. If you are quoting a passage that is longer than one paragraph, include additional indentations for the second and subsequent paragraphs. If you are quoting a passage of multiple paragraphs that are in quotation marks in the original, include the quotation marks at the beginning of each paragraph, but at the end only of the last one.

### Poetry
Set off quotations of four or more lines of poetry in the same way. A quotation of one, two, or three lines of poetry may be set off if you want to give it special emphasis; otherwise, run such a quotation into your text. When you run in more than one line of poetry, indicate the line-breaks with a slash mark or virgule—with a space on each side:

> Dante's spiritual journey begins in the woods: "Midway this way of life, we're bound upon / I woke to find myself in a dark wood / Where the right road was wholly lost and gone."

### 43.3 Single Quotation Marks: Quotation Within Quotation ' '

Put single quotation marks around a quotation that occurs within another quotation; this is the only standard use for single quotation marks:

> In Joseph Conrad's *Heart of Darkness*, after a leisurely setting of the scene by the unnamed narrator, the drama begins when the character who is to be the principal narrator first speaks: "'And this also,' said Marlow suddenly, 'has been one of the dark places of the earth.'"

### 43.4 With Verbs of Speaking Before Quotations

When verbs of speaking precede a quotation, they are usually followed by commas:

> Helen said, "There is something nasty growing in my fridge."

> Adriana fumbled around in the dark and asked, "Now where are the matches?"

(Note that when a quotation ends a sentence, its own terminal punctuation serves also as that of the sentence.)

With short or emphatic quotations, commas often aren't necessary:

> He said "Hold your horses," so we waited a little longer.

> Someone shouted "Fire!" and we all headed for the exits.

Again, punctuate a sentence the way you want it to be heard; your sense of its rhythm should help you decide. On the other hand, if the quotation is long, especially if it consists of more than one sentence, or if the context is formal, a colon will probably be more appropriate than a comma to introduce it:

> When the movie was over, Joanna turned to her companion and said: "We have wasted ninety minutes of our lives. The movie lacked an intelligent plot, sympathetic characters, and an interesting setting. Even the soundtrack was pathetic."

If the introductory element is itself an independent clause, then a colon or period must be used:

> Joanna turned to her and spoke: "What a waste of time."

*Spoke*, unlike *said*, is here an intransitive verb.

If you work a quotation into your own syntax, don't use even a comma to introduce it; for example, when the word *that* follows a verb of speaking:

> It is often said that "Sticks and stones may break my bones, but words will never hurt me"—a singularly inaccurate notion.

## 43.5 With Verbs of Speaking after Quotations

If a verb of speaking or a subject–verb combination follows a quotation, it is usually set off by a comma placed inside the closing quotation mark:

> "You attract what you manifest in your personality," said the speaker.

> "I think there's a fly in my soup," she muttered.

But if the quotation ends with a question mark or an exclamation point, no other punctuation is added:

> "What time is it?" asked Francis, looking up.

> "I insist that I be heard!" he shouted.

If the clause containing the verb of speaking interrupts the quotation, it should be preceded by a comma and followed by whatever mark is called for by the syntax and the sense. For example,

> "Since it's such a long drive," he said, "we'd better get an early start."

> "It's a long drive," he argued; "therefore I think we should start early."

> "It's a very long way," he insisted. "We should start as early as possible."

## 43.6 With Quotations Set Off by Indention

Colons are conventionally used to introduce block quotations:

> Jane Austen begins her novel *Pride and Prejudice* with the observation:
>
> > It is a truth universally acknowledged, that a single man in possession of a good fortune must be in want of a wife. However little known the feelings or views of such a man may be on his first entering a neighbourhood, this truth is so well fixed in the minds of the surrounding families, that he is considered as the rightful property of some one or other of their daughters.

## 43.7 Words Used in a Special Sense

As we do with block quotations in 43.6 above, put quotation marks around words used in a special sense or words for which you wish to indicate some qualification:

> What she calls a "ramble" I would call a twenty-mile hike.

> He had been up in the woods so long he was "bushed," as Canadians put it.

## Proofreading Tip

### On the Use of Quotation Marks to Call Attention to Words

Some writers put quotation marks around words referred to as words, but it is sometimes better practice to italicize them (see 49.3):

> The word *toboggan* comes from a Mi'kmaq word for sled.

Don't put quotation marks around slang terms, clichés, and the like. If a word or phrase is so weak or inappropriate that you have to apologize for it, you shouldn't be using it in the first place. And the last thing such a term needs is to have attention called to it. Even if a slang term is appropriate, putting quotation marks around it implicitly insults readers by presuming that they won't recognize slang when they see it. And avoid using quotation marks for emphasis; they don't work that way.

## 43.8 Other Marks with Quotation Marks

Put periods and commas inside closing quotation marks; put semicolons and colons outside them:

> "Knowing how to write well," he said, "can be a source of great pleasure"; and then he added that it had "one other important quality": he identified it simply as "hard work."

We recommend this standard North American practice.

In British usage, periods and commas also are put outside quotation marks unless they are part of what is being quoted, and single rather than double quotation marks are conventional. Some

Canadian writers and publishers follow British practice, putting periods and commas inside closing quotation marks only when they are actually in the material being quoted, as for example with a period at the end of a sentence. Question marks and exclamation points go either outside or inside, depending on whether they apply to the quotation or to the whole sentence:

'Knowing how to write well', he said, 'can be a source of great pleasure.'

'What smells so good?' she asked.

Who said, 'Change is inevitable except from a pop machine'?

Did you find out who shouted 'See you in court, toad breath!'?

## 43.9 Ellipses for Omissions . . .

If when quoting from a written source you decide to omit one or more words from the middle of the passage you are quoting, indicate the omission with an ellipsis. For example, if you wanted to quote only part of the passage from Austen quoted at length earlier (43.6), you might do it like this:

As Jane Austen wryly observes, "a single man in possession of a . . . fortune must be in want of a wife."

Note that you need not indicate an ellipsis at the beginning of a quotation unless the quotation could be mistaken for a complete sentence—for example, if it began with *I* or some other capital letter.

When the ellipsis is preceded by a complete sentence, include the period (or other terminal punctuation) of the original before the ellipsis points. Similarly, if when you omit something from the end of a sentence, what remains is grammatically complete, a period (or question mark or exclamation point, if either of these is more appropriate) goes before the ellipsis. In either case, the terminal punctuation marking the end of the sentence is close up:

As Jane Austen wryly observes, "a single man in possession of a good fortune must be in want of a wife. . . . this truth is so well fixed in the minds of surrounding families, that he is considered the rightful property of some one or other. . . ."

Other punctuation may also be included before or after the ellipsis if it makes the quoted material clearer:

> However little known the feelings or views of such a man may be . . .,
> this truth is so well fixed in the minds of the surrounding families.

Three periods can indicate the omission of one or more entire sentences, or even whole paragraphs. Again, if the sentence preceding the omitted material is grammatically complete, it should end with a period preceding the ellipsis.

An ellipsis should also be used to indicate that material from a quoted line of poetry has been omitted. When quoting four or more lines of poetry, use a row of spaced dots to indicate that one or more entire lines have been omitted:

> E.J. Pratt's epic "Towards the Last Spike" begins:
>
>> It was the same world then as now—the same,
>> Except for little differences of speed
>> And power, and means to treat myopia.
>> . . . . . . . . . . . . . . . . . . . . . . . . . . . . . . . . . . . . . .
>> The same, but for new particles of speech. . . .

Note that sometimes ellipses added to quotations are enclosed in square brackets, but this is not a standard practice in formal writing.

## Proofreading Tip

### On Ineffective Omission of Material from a Quotation

Don't omit material from a quotation in such a way that you distort what the author is saying or destroy the integrity of the syntax. Similarly, don't quote unfairly "out of context"; for example, if an author qualifies a statement in some way, don't quote the statement as if it were unqualified.

## 43.10 Brackets for Additions, Changes, and Comments [ ]

Keep such changes to a minimum, but enclose in square brackets any editorial addition or change you find it necessary to make within a quotation, for example, a clarifying fact or a change in tense to make the quoted material fit the syntax of your sentence:

> The author states that "the following year [1990] marked a turning point in [his] life."

> One of my friends wrote me that her "feelings about the subject [were] similar to" mine.

Use the word *sic* (Latin for "thus") in brackets to indicate that an error in the quotation occurs in the original:

> One of my friends wrote me: "My feelings about the subject are similiar [sic] to yours."

# 44. COMMON ERRORS IN PUNCTUATION

## 44.1 Unwanted Comma Between Subject and Verb

Generally, do not put a comma between a subject and its verb unless some intervening element calls for punctuation:

> ✘    His enthusiasm for the project and his desire to be of help, led him to add his name to the list of volunteers.

Don't be misled by the length of a compound subject. The comma after *help* in the above example is just as wrong as the comma in the following sentence:

> ✘    Edna, addressed the audience.

But if some intervening element, for example an appositive or a participial phrase, requires setting off, use a pair of marks (see section 39):

> His enthusiasm for the project and his desire to be of help, both strongly felt, led him to add his name to the list of volunteers.

> Edna—the star performer—addressed the audience.

## 44.2 Unwanted Comma Between Verb and Object or Complement

Although in Jane Austen's time it was conventional to place a comma before a clause beginning with *that*, today this practice is considered an error. Do not put a comma between a verb and its object or complement unless some intervening element calls for punctuation.

Especially, don't mistakenly assume that a clause opening with *that* always needs a comma before it:

> ✗ Jeremy realized, that he could no longer keep his eyes open.

The noun clause beginning with *that* is the direct object of the verb *realized* and should not be separated from it. Only if an interrupter requires setting off should there be any punctuation:

> Jeremy realized, moreover, that he could no longer keep his eyes open.
>
> Jeremy realized, as he tried once again to read the paragraph, that he could no longer keep his eyes open.

Another example:

> ✗ Ottawa's principal claim to fame is, that it has the world's longest skating rink.

Here the comma intrudes between the linking verb *is* and its complement, the predicate noun consisting of a *that*-clause.

## 44.3 Unwanted Comma after Last Adjective of a Series

Do not put a comma between the last adjective of a series and the noun it modifies:

> ✗ How could anyone fail to be impressed by such an intelligent, outspoken, resourceful, fellow as Jonathan is?

The comma after *resourceful* is wrong, though it may briefly feel right because a certain rhythm has been established and because there is no *and* before the last of the three adjectives.

## 44.4 Unwanted Comma Between Coordinated Words and Phrases

Generally, don't put a comma between words and phrases joined by a coordinating conjunction; use a comma only when the coordinate elements are clauses (see 33.1):

> ✗ The dog and cat circled each other warily, and then went off in opposite directions.
>
> ✗ I was a long way from home, and didn't know how to get there.
>
> ✗ She was not only intelligent, but also very kind.

The commas in these three sentences are all unnecessary. Sometimes a writer uses such a comma for a mild emphasis, but if you want an emphatic pause a dash will probably work better:

> The dog and cat circled each other warily—and then went off in opposite directions.

Or the sentence can be slightly revised in order to gain the emphasis:

> She was not only intelligent; she was also very kind.

> I was a long way from home, and I had no idea how to get there.

## 44.5 Commas with Emphatic Repetition

If the two elements joined by a conjunction constitute an emphatic repetition, a comma is sometimes optional:

> I wanted not only to win, but to win overwhelmingly.

This sentence would be equally correct and effective without the comma. But in the following sentence the comma is necessary:

> It was an object of beauty, and of beauty most spectacular.

Again, sounding a sentence over to yourself will sometimes help you decide.

## 44.6 Unwanted Comma with Short Introductory or Parenthetical Element

Generally, do not set off introductory elements or interrupters that are very short, that are not really parenthetical, or that are so slightly parenthetical that you feel no pause when reading them:

> ✗ Perhaps, she was trying to tell us something.

> ✗ But, it was not a case of mistaken identity.

> ✗ Therefore, he put on his toque.

> ✗ We asked if we could try it out, for a week, to see if we really liked it.

When the pause is strong, however, be sure to set it off:

> It was only then, after the very formal dinner, that we were all able to relax.

Often such commas are optional, depending on the pattern of intonation the writer wants:

> In Canada(,) the change of the seasons is sharply evident.
>
> In Canada(,) as elsewhere, money talks.
>
> Last year(,) we went to Quebec City.
>
> The committee(,) therefore(,) decided to table the motion.
>
> After dinner(,) we all went for a walk.
>
> As she walked(,) she thought of her childhood in Cabbagetown.

Sometimes such a comma is necessary to prevent misreading:

> ✗    After eating the cat Irene gave me jumped out the window.
>
> After eating, the cat Irene gave me jumped out the window.

See also 35.1.

## 44.7 Unwanted Comma with Restrictive Appositive

Don't incorrectly set off proper nouns and titles of literary works as non-restrictive appositives (see 37.2). For instance, it's "Dickens's novel *Great Expectations*," not "Dickens's novel, *Great Expectations*." Dickens, after all, wrote more than one novel.

> ✗    In her poem, "Daddy," Sylvia Plath explores her complicated relationship with her father.
>
> ✗    The home port of the Canadian Coast Guard icebreaker, *Terry Fox* is Dartmouth, Nova Scotia.

The punctuation makes it sound as though Plath wrote only this one poem and that the *Terry Fox* is the only icebreaker in the Canadian Coast Guard's fleet. The titles are restrictive: if they were removed, the sentences would not be clear. If the context is clear, the explanatory words often aren't needed at all:

> In "Daddy" Plath explores . . .
>
> The home port of the *Terry Fox* is . . .

If Sylvia Plath had in fact written only one poem, or if the Canadian Coast Guard had only one icebreaker, it would be correct to set off its title. Similarly, it would be correct to set off a title after referring to an author's "first novel" or the like, since an author, regardless of how many novels she or he has written, can have only one first novel. The urge to punctuate before titles of literary works sometimes leads to the error of putting a comma between a possessive and the title.

    ✘    I remember enjoying Anne Carson's, "Father's Old Blue Cardigan."

## 44.8 Unwanted Comma with Indirect Quotation

Do not set off indirect quotations as if they were direct quotations:

    ✘    In his last chapter the author says, that civilization as we have come to it is in jeopardy.

    ✘    If you ask Tomiko she's sure to say, she doesn't want to go.

In an indirect quotation, what was said is being reported, not quoted. If Tomiko is quoted directly, a comma is correct:

If you ask Tomiko she's sure to say, "I don't want to go."

See also 43.1 and 43.4.

## 44.9 Unwanted Question Mark after Indirect Question

Don't put a question mark at the end of indirect questions—questions that are only being reported, not asked directly:

I asked what we were doing here.

She wanted to find out what had happened in the parking lot.

What he asked himself then was how he was going to explain it to the shareholders.

## 44.10 Unwanted Semicolon with Subordinate Element

Do not put a semicolon in front of a mere phrase or subordinate clause. Use such a semicolon only where you could, if you chose to, put a period instead:

    ✘    They cancelled the meeting; being disappointed at the low turnout.

    ✘    Only about a dozen people showed up; partly because there had been too little publicity and no free muffins.

Those semicolons should be commas. Periods in those spots would turn what follows them into fragments (see 1.24); in effect, so do semicolons. Since a semicolon signals that an independent clause is coming, readers are distracted when only a phrase or subordinate clause arrives. If you find yourself trying to avoid comma splices and overshooting in this way, devote some further study to the comma splice (33.5) and to learning how to recognize an independent clause (see 1.13–1.14 and 1.16). Similarly, don't put a semicolon between a subordinate clause and an independent clause:

> ✘    After the show, when they got home, tired and with their eardrums ringing; Sheila said she was never going to another musical again.

> After the show, when they got home, tired and with their eardrums ringing, Sheila said she was never going to another musical again.

Change the semicolon after *ringing* to a comma. The presence of earlier commas in the sentence doesn't mean that the later one needs promoting to semicolon; there is no danger here of confusing the reader as there sometimes is when a coordinating conjunction without a preceding comma is used to join two independent clauses (see 33.2).

## 44.11 Unwanted Colon after Incomplete Construction

Do not use a colon after an incomplete construction; a colon is appropriate only after an independent clause:

> ✘    She preferred comfort foods such as: potatoes, bread, and pasta.

The prepositional *such as* needs an object to be complete. Had the phrase been extended to "She preferred such foods as these" or ". . . as the following," it would have been complete and an independent clause; a colon would have been correct.

> She preferred comfort foods such as the following: potatoes, bread, and pasta.

Here is another example of this common error:

> ✘    His favourite pastimes are: swimming, hiking, and sipping fine cognac by the fire.

> His favourite pastimes are swimming, hiking, and sipping fine cognac by the fire.

Since the linking verb *are* is incomplete without a complement, the colon is incorrect. Remember in most formal writing not to use a colon after a preposition or after a form of the verb *be*. Scientific and business writing does allow for the use of a colon after the verb *be* or a preposition if the colon introduces a list that begins on a separate line.

### 44.12 Unwanted Double Punctuation: Comma or Semicolon with a Dash

Avoid putting a comma or a semicolon together with a dash. Use whichever mark is appropriate.

# CHAPTER V
# Mechanics and Spelling

# 45. FORMATTING A DOCUMENT

## 45.1 Format

Unless directed otherwise, follow these conventions when you are preparing a document to give it a professional, polished look:

1. Prepare your document at 8½ by 11 inches (or 21 by 28 cm). Print only one side of each page.

2. Choose a plain, readable typeface (12-point Times New Roman or 10-point Arial). Do not try to spruce up your document with coloured paper or fancy fonts: these will only detract from the professional appearance of your work.

3. Leave margins of about 1 inch (2.5 cm) on all four sides of the page. The document may be either fully justified or justified flush left with a ragged (i.e. unjustified) right-hand margin. Full justification may cause such typesetting problems as inconsistent spacing, gappy or loose lines, and ineffective word breaks. For these reasons, it is preferable to use only flush-left justification.

4. Indent each paragraph 1 inch (2.5 cm) from the margin. Do not leave extra space between indented paragraphs. Indent long block quotations 2 inches (5 cm) from the left margin. Do not leave any additional space before or after a double-spaced block quotation.

5. Leave only one space after any terminal punctuation, and remember to leave spaces before and after each of the three dots of an ellipsis (see 43.9). If you are typing, use two unspaced hyphens to make an em-dash, with no space before or after them; most word-processing software will automatically convert two hyphens to an em-dash.

6. Never begin a line with a comma, semicolon, period, question mark, exclamation point, or hyphen. On rare occasions, a dash or the dots of an ellipsis may have to come at the beginning of a line, but if possible place them at the end of the preceding line.

7.  Save your work frequently—every five minutes or so. Create a back-up folder, and save all drafts in that folder. Always keep a copy of the final draft and be sure to clearly label it as "Final."

8.  Fasten the pages of your printed document together with a paper clip or staple. Long reports are sometimes submitted in folders.

## 45.2 Syllabication and Word Division

Generally, do not divide words at the end of a line. Inserting word breaks manually can be time-consuming, and relying on your computer to insert word breaks automatically can result in too many hyphens. Although you can control the guidelines to a certain extent, computer-generated hyphenation can produce undesirable word breaks that you will need to correct before printing the final copy of your document. It is better to rely on the word-wrap feature of your word-processing software to shorten a line and to move a word that might otherwise be divided to the beginning of the next line.

One circumstance in which you may need to insert a word break is in a reference to an electronic source identified by its website or network address. When this address (also known as a URL, or uniform resource locator) is a long one, then it may need to be spread over two lines. The *MLA Handbook* and the *Chicago Manual of Style* recommend that the URL be broken after a punctuation mark (colon or slash). Introducing a hyphen or other punctuation, such as a period, into a URL is not recommended, for it will introduce an ambiguity into the data and make the website difficult for your reader to locate and access:

> To learn more about André Alexis, one of Canada's most lively young writers and broadcasters, consult the entry for his program, "Radio Normand," at <http://www.cbc.ca/ programguide/program/index.jsp? program=Radio+Normand>.

> David Mamet has written an essay sure to provoke debate. It is entitled "Why Can't I Show a Woman Telling Lies?," and it is located online at <http://www.guardian.co.uk/ arts/features/story/0,11710,117963,00. html>.

On the rare occasions when you need to divide a word in a handwritten document, insert a hyphen at the end of a line, after the first part of the word, and begin the next line with the rest of the word. You should not begin a new line with a hyphen. Nor should you divide a word at the end of a page or at the end of a paragraph. Divide words only between syllables, and if you are uncertain, check your dictionary for a word's syllabication.

# 46. ABBREVIATIONS

Abbreviations are expected in technical and scientific writing, legal writing, business writing, memos, reports, reference works, bibliographies and works cited lists, footnotes, tables and charts, and sometimes in journalism. The following relatively few kinds are in common use. (See also 75.5.)

## 46.1 Titles before Proper Names

The following abbreviations can be used with or without initials or given names:

| | |
|---|---|
| Mr. | (Mr. Eng, Mr. Marc Ramsay) |
| Mrs. | (Mrs. L.W. Smith, Mrs. Tazim Khan) |
| M. | (M. André Joubert; M. J.-F. Sauvé) |
| Mme. | (Mme. Girard; Mme. Nathalie Gagnon) |
| Mlle. | (Mlle. Stephanie Sevigny; Mlle. R. Pelletier) |
| Dr. | (Dr. Paula Grewal; Dr. P. Francis Fairchild) |
| St. | (St. John; St. Beatrice) |

## 46.2 Titles before Proper Names with Initials or Given Names

In informal writing, abbreviations of professional or honorific titles can be used before proper names only with initials or given names:

Prof. Reah Jamalali (*but* Professor Jamalali)

Sen. H.C. Tsui (*but* Senator Tsui)

Gov. Gen. David Lloyd Johnston (*but* Governor General Johnston) the Rev. Lois Wilson (*or, more formally*, the Reverend Lois Wilson)

the Hon. Maurice Desjardins (*more formally*, the Honourable Maurice Desjardins, the Honourable Mr. Desjardins)

In formal writing, spell out these and similar titles.

## 46.3 Titles and Degrees after Proper Names

David Adams, M.D. (*but not* Dr. David Adams, M.D.)

Claire T. McFadden, D.D.S.

Paul Martin, Jr.

Laurel McGregor, Ph.D., F.R.S.C.

Academic degrees not following a name may also be abbreviated:

Shirley is working toward her B.A.

Amir is working on his M.A. thesis.

## 46.4 Standard Words Used with Dates and Numerals

720 B.C.

A.D. 231, the second century A.D.

7 a.m. (*or* 7 A.M.), 8:30 p.m. (*or* 8:30 P.M.)

no. 17 (*or* No. 17)

Note that *A.D.* precedes a date whereas *B.C.* follows one. Note also that some people now use *B.P.* ("before the present") or *B.C.E.* ("before the common era") and *C.E.* ("of the common era"), both following the date, instead of *B.C.* and *A.D.*

## 46.5 Agencies and Organizations Known by Their Initials
(see also 42.1)

Capitalize names of agencies and organizations commonly known by their initials:

UNICEF    CAW    CBC    CNN    RCMP    NATO

## 46.6 Scientific and Technical Terms Known by Their Initials

Some scientific, technical, or other terms (usually of considerable length) are commonly known by their initials (see also 42.1):

| BTU | URL | DDT | DNA | ESP | FM |
|------|------|------|-----|-----|-----|
| SARS | ISBN | HTML | MP | GST | TNT |

## 46.7 Latin Expressions Commonly Used in English

i.e. (that is)              etc. (and so forth)

e.g. (for example)      vs. (versus)

cf. (compare)            et al. (and others)

Note that in formal writing, it is better to spell out the English equivalent.

# Proofreading Tip

### On Punctuating Latin Expressions and Abbreviations

(a) If you use e.g., use it only to introduce the example or list of examples; following the example or list, write out *for example*:

> Some provinces—e.g., Manitoba, Saskatchewan, and New Brunswick—supported a single national standard for homecare programs.

> Some provinces—Manitoba, Saskatchewan, and New Brunswick, for example—supported a single national standard for homecare programs.

Note also that if you introduce a list with *e.g.* or *for example* or even *such as*, it is illogical to follow it with *etc.* or *and so forth*.

(b) Generally use a comma after *i.e.*, just as you would if you wrote out *that is*. And usually use one after *e.g.* as well (test for the pause by reading it aloud as *for example*).

(c) The abbreviation *cf.* stands for Latin *confer*, meaning "compare." Do not use it to mean simply "see"; for that, the Latin *vide* (*v.*) would be correct.

(d) Use *etc.* carefully. Use it only when there are at least several more items to follow and when they are reasonably obvious:

> Evergreen trees—cedars, pines, etc.—are common in northern latitudes.
>
> Learning the Greek alphabet—alpha, beta, gamma, delta, etc.—isn't really difficult.
>
> ✘ He considered several possible occupations: accounting, teaching, nursing, etc.

In the case of the last example, a reader can have no idea of what the other possible occupations might be. Further, don't write *and etc.*: *and* is redundant, since *etc.* (*et cetera*) means "*and* so forth."

## 46.8 Terms in Official Titles

Capitalize terms used in official titles being copied exactly:

| | |
|---|---|
| Johnson Bros., Ltd. | Ibbetson & Co. |
| Smith & Sons, Inc. | *Quill & Quire* |

## Proofreading Tip

### Limiting the Use of the Ampersand (&)

Don't use the ampersand (&) as a substitute for *and*; use it only when presenting the title of a company or a publication exactly, as above.

# 47. CAPITALIZATION

Generally, capitalize proper nouns, abbreviations of proper nouns, and words derived from proper nouns, as follows:

## 47.1 Names and Nicknames

Capitalize names and nicknames of real and fictional people and individual animals:

| | | |
|---|---|---|
| Nelson Mandela | Margaret MacMillan | Tiger Woods |
| Kenneth Branagh | Clarissa Dalloway | Rumpelstiltskin |
| Cinderella | Lassie | King Kong |

## 47.2 Professional and Honorific Titles

Capitalize professional and honorific titles when they directly precede and thus are parts of names:

Professor Tamara Jones (*but* Tamara Jones, professor at Mount Allison)

Captain Janna Ting (*but* Janna Ting is a captain in the police force.)

Rabbi Samuel Small (*but* Mr. Small was rabbi of our synagogue.)

## Proofreading Tip

### On Capitalizing Titles after Names

Normally titles that follow names aren't capitalized unless they have become part of the name:

Bernard Lord, premier of New Brunswick

Stephen Harper, prime minister of Canada

Beverly McLachlin, justice of the Supreme Court

Romeo Dallaire, the general

*but*

Catherine the Great

Peter the Hermit

Smokey the Bear

Some titles of particular distinction are customarily capitalized even if the person isn't named:

> The Queen toured Canada to celebrate her fifty years on the Throne.

> On Easter Sunday, the Pope will address the crowd gathered in St. Peter's Square.

> The university was honoured with a visit by the Dalai Lama.

Opinion is divided on the question of whether "prime minister" and "president" are titles in the same category of distinction as "the Queen," "the Pope," and "the Dalai Lama." Some writers and news outlets make it a policy always to capitalize these titles. In your own writing, you should aim for consistency in whatever practices you adopt.

> Prime Minister Harper met with President Obama at the White House. (In each case, the title is capitalized as part of the leader's name.)

> The Prime Minister met with the President at the White House.

> *Or*

> The prime minister met with the president at the White House.

Whichever practice you follow, be consistent in your choice.

## 47.3 Words Designating Family Relationships

Capitalize words designating family relationships when they are used as parts of proper names and also when they are used in place of proper names, except following a possessive:

> Uncle Peter (*but* I have an uncle named Peter.)

> There's my uncle, Peter. (*but* There's my Uncle Peter.)

> I told Father about it. (*but* My father knows about it.)

> I have always respected Grandmother. (*but* Diana's grandmother is a splendid old woman.)

## 47.4 Place Names

Capitalize place names—including common nouns (*river*, *street*, *park*, etc.) when they are parts of proper nouns (see section 2):

| | | | |
|---|---|---|---|
| Active Pass | Alberta | the Amazon | the Andes |
| Asia | Banff | Buenos Aires | Mt. Etna |
| Hudson Bay | Japan | Lake Ladoga | Moose Jaw |
| Niagara Falls | Québec | Rivière-du-Loup | Yonge Street |
| the Gobi Desert | Vancouver Island | the Miramichi River | |
| the Suez Canal | Trafalgar Square | Kootenay National Park | |

# Usage Note

## On Capitalizing North, South, East, West

As a rule, don't capitalize north, south, east, and west unless they are part of specific place names (North Battleford, West Vancouver, the South Shore) or designate specific geographical areas (the frozen North, the East Coast, the Deep South, the Northwest, the Wild West, the Far East).

Since writers in Canada usually capitalize East, West, North (and sometimes South) to refer to parts of the country (the peoples of the North, the settlement of the West), it makes sense to capitalize Eastern, Western, Northern, and Southern when they refer to ideas attached to parts of the country (Northern peoples, Western settlement). Otherwise, except for cases when they appear as parts of specific place names (the Eastern Townships), these adjectives should not be capitalized. This practice applies even to cases such as northern Canada, eastern Canada, western Canada, which are not specific place names but descriptions of geographic regions.

## 47.5 Months, Days, Holidays

Capitalize the names of the months (January, February, etc.) and the days of the week (Monday, Tuesday, etc.), but not the seasons (spring, summer, autumn, fall, winter). Also capitalize holidays, holy days, and festivals (Christmas, Canada Day, Remembrance Day, Hanukkah, Ramadan).

## 47.6 Religious Names

Capitalize names of deities and other religious names and terms:

| | | | |
|---|---|---|---|
| God | the Holy Ghost | the Virgin Mary | the Bible |
| the Torah | the Talmud | the Dead Sea Scrolls | Islam |
| Allah | the Prophet | the Quran | Apollo |
| Jupiter | Vishnu | Taoism | |

Note: Some people capitalize pronouns referring to a deity; others prefer not to. Either practice is acceptable as long as you are consistent.

## 47.7 Names of Nationalities and Organizations

Capitalize names of nationalities and other groups and organizations and of their members:

Canadian, Australian, Malaysian, Scandinavian, South American, Irish, Somalian, Texan

New Democrats, the New Democratic Party

Liberals, the Liberal Party

Conservatives, the Conservative Party

Bloquistes, the Bloc Québécois, the Bloc

Roman Catholics, the Roman Catholic Church

Lions, Kiwanis

Teamsters

the Vancouver Canucks, the Montreal Expos

the Taliban

## 47.8 Names of Institutions and Sections of Government, Historical Events, and Buildings

Capitalize names of institutions, sections of government, historical events and documents, and specific buildings:

> McGill University, The Hospital for Sick Children
>
> the Ministry of Health, Parliament, the Senate, the Cabinet, the Opposition
>
> the French Revolution, the Great War, World War I, the Gulf War, the Cretaceous period, the Renaissance; the Magna Carta, the Treaty of Versailles, the Charter of Rights and Freedoms
>
> the British Museum, the Museum of Civilization, Westminster Abbey

## 47.9 Academic Courses and Languages

Capitalize specific academic courses, but not the subjects themselves, except for languages:

> Philosophy 101, Fine Arts 300, Mathematics 204, English 112, Food Writing
>
> an English course, a major in French (*but* a history course, an economics major, a degree in psychology)

## 47.10 Derivatives of Proper Nouns

Capitalize derivatives of proper nouns:

> French Canadian, Haligonian, Celtic, Québécoise, Ethiopian, Kuwaiti
>
> Confucianism, Christian
>
> Shakespearean, Keynesian, Edwardian, Miltonic

## 47.11 Abbreviations of Proper Nouns

Capitalize abbreviations of proper nouns:

> PMO    TVA    CUPE    CUSO    P.E.I    B.C.    the BNA Act

Note that abbreviations of agencies and organizations commonly known by their initials do not need periods (see 46.5), but that non-postal abbreviations of geographical entities such as provinces usually do. When in doubt, consult your dictionary. See also 42.1.

# Proofreading Tip

## On Words Once but No Longer Capitalized

Some words derived from proper nouns—and some proper nouns themselves—are so much a part of everyday usage or refer to such common things that they were never or are no longer capitalized; some examples:

bible (in secular contexts), biblical

herculean, raglan, martial, quixotic, erotic, jeremiad, bloomers, gerrymander

hamburger, frankfurter, french fries, champagne, burgundy,

roman and italic, denim, china, japanned

vulcanized, macadamized, galvanized, pasteurized, volt, ampere

## 47.12 *I* and *O*

Capitalize the pronoun *I* and the vocative interjection *O*:

O my people, what have I done unto thee? (Micah 6: 3)

Do not capitalize the interjection *oh* unless it begins a sentence.

## 47.13 Titles of Written and Other Works

In the titles of written and other works, use a capital letter to begin the first word, the last word, and all other important words; leave uncapitalized only articles (*a*, *an*, *the*) and any conjunctions and prepositions less than five letters long (unless one of these is the first or last word):

| | |
|---|---|
| *The Blind Assassin* | "The Dead" |
| *The Pianist* | "O Canada" |
| "The Metamorphosis" | "Amazing Grace" |
| *The Disappearance of Childhood* | *As for Me and My House* |
| *Paris 1919* | "Shooting an Elephant" |
| *Roughing It in the Bush* | *In the Skin of a Lion* |

But there can be exceptions; for example the conjunctions *Nor* and *So* are usually capitalized, the relative pronoun *that* is sometimes not capitalized (*All's Well that Ends Well*), and in Ralph Ellison's "Tell It Like It Is, Baby" the preposition-cum-conjunction *Like* demands capitalization. (See section 48 for more on titles.)

If a title includes a hyphenated word, capitalize the part after the hyphen only if it is a noun or adjective or is otherwise an important word:

> *Self-Portrait*
>
> *The Scorched-Wood People*
>
> *Murder Among the Well-to-do*

Capitalize the first word of a subtitle, even if it is an article:

> *Beyond Remembering: The Collected Poems of Al Purdy*

See 48.2 for the use of italics in titles.

## 47.14 First Words of Sentences

Capitalize the first word of a major or minor sentence—of anything, that is, that concludes with terminal punctuation:

> Racial profiling. Now that's a controversial topic. Right?

## 47.15 First Words of Quotations that Are Sentences

Capitalize the first word of a quotation that is intended as a sentence or that is capitalized in the source, but not fragments from other than the beginning of such a sentence:

> When he said "Let me take the wheel for a while," I shuddered at the memory of what had happened the last time I had let him "take the wheel."

If something interrupts a single quoted sentence, do not begin its second part with a capital:

> "It was all I could do," she said, "to keep from laughing out loud."

## 47.16 First Words of Sentences Within Parentheses

Capitalize the first word of an independent sentence in parentheses only if it stands by itself, apart from other sentences. If it is incorporated within another sentence, it is neither capitalized nor ended with a period (though it could end with a question mark or exclamation point: see sections 40 and 42).

> She did as she was told (there was really nothing else for her to do), and the tension was relieved. (But of course she would never admit to herself that she had been manipulated.)

## 47.17 First Words of Sentences Following Colons

An incorporated sentence following a colon may be capitalized if it seems to stand as a separate statement, for example if it is itself long or requires emphasis; the current trend is away from capitalization.

> There was one thing, she said, which we must never forget: No one has the right to the kind of happiness that deprives someone else of deserved happiness.

> It was a splendid night: the sky was clear except for a few picturesque clouds, the moon was full, and even a few stars shone through. (The first *The* could be capitalized if the writer wanted particular emphasis on the details.)

> It was no time for petty quarrels: everything depended on unanimity.

## 47.18 With Personification and for Emphasis

Although it is risky and should not be done often, writers who have good control of tone can occasionally capitalize a personified abstraction or a word or phrase to which they want to impart a special importance of some kind:

> In his quest to succeed, Greed and Power came to dominate his every waking thought.

> Only when it begins to fade does Youth appear so valuable.

Sometimes the slight emphasis of capitalization can be used for a humorous or ironic effect:

> He insisted on driving His Beautiful Car: everyone else preferred to walk the two blocks without benefit of jerks and jolts and carbon monoxide fumes.

And occasionally, but rarely, you can capitalize whole words and phrases or even sentences for a special sort of graphic emphasis:

> When we reached the excavation site, however, we were confronted by a sign warning us in no uncertain terms to KEEP OUT—TRESPASSERS WILL BE PROSECUTED.

> When she made the suggestion to the group, she was answered with a resounding YES.

Clearly in such instances there is no need for further indications, such as quotation marks or underlining, though the last one could end with an exclamation point.

# 48. TITLES (see also 47.13)

## 48.1 Quotation Marks for Short Works and Parts of Longer Works

Put quotation marks around the titles of short works and of parts of longer works, such as short stories, articles, essays, short poems, chapters of books, songs, and individual episodes of television programs:

> Leonard Cohen's "Joan of Arc" and "Democracy" are songs featured in this documentary about the music of Canada.

> "A Wilderness Station" is an Alice Munro story that begins in Ontario in the 1850s.

> The first chapter of Margaret Atwood's novel is called "The Jagged Edge."

> "Her Gates Both East and West" is the final poem in Al Purdy's last collection of poems.

> I am hoping to watch the rebroadcast of "Oppenheimer Park," a memorable episode of the CBC series *Da Vinci's Inquest*.

There can be exceptions, however. For example, the title of each of the ten plays in volume 1 of *Modern Canadian Plays* deserves italicizing in its own right. And some works, for example Coleridge's *The Rime of the Ancient Mariner*, E.J. Pratt's *Towards the Last Spike*, and Conrad's *Heart of Darkness*, although originally parts of larger collections, are fairly long and have attained a reputation and importance as individual works; most writers feel justified in italicizing their titles.

## 48.2 Italics for Whole or Major Works

Use italics (see section 49) for titles of written works published as units, such as books, magazines, journals, newspapers, and plays; for films and television programs; for paintings and sculptures; and for musical compositions (other than single songs), such as operas and ballets:

*Paradise Lost* is Milton's greatest work.

Have you read Michael Crummey's *River Thieves*?

*The New Yorker* is a weekly magazine.

The scholarly journal *Canadian Literature* is published quarterly.

I prefer *The Globe and Mail* to the *National Post*.

I recommend that you see the Stratford production of *Antony and Cleopatra*.

*The Passionate Eye* is a CBC program featuring the best in current documentaries.

One tires of hearing Ravel's *Bolero* played so often.

Michelangelo's *David* is worth a trip to Florence.

Picasso's *Guernica* is a haunting representation of the Spanish Civil War.

We saw a fine production of Puccini's *La Bohème*.

Every spring, the CBC Radio website features information about *Canada Reads*, a program seeking to select the one book all Canadians should read.

Note that instrumental compositions may be known by name or by technical detail, or both. A title name is italicized (Beethoven's *Pastoral Symphony*); technical identification is usually not (Beethoven's Sixth Symphony, or Symphony no. 6, op. 68, in F).

## 48.3 Titles Within Titles

If part of a book title requires quotation marks, retain the quotation marks and italicize the whole thing:

*From Fiction to Film: D.H. Lawrence's "The Rocking-Horse Winner"*

If a book title includes something that itself would be italicized, such as the name of a ship or the title of another book, either put the secondary item in quotation marks or leave it in roman type (i.e., not italicized):

*The Cruise of the "Nona"*

*D.H. Lawrence and* Sons and Lovers: *Sources and Criticism*

# Proofreading Tip

## On Articles as Parts of Titles

Double check in the titles you cite for the role of the definite article, *the*: italicize and capitalize it only when it is actually a part of the title: Margaret Lawrence's *The Stone Angel*; Yann Martel's *Life of Pi*; Roman Polanski's *The Pianist*; the *Partisan Review*; *The Encyclopaedia Britannica*; the *Atlas of Ancient Archaeology*. Occasionally the indefinite article, *a* or *an*, bears watching as well.

Practice varies with the definite article as part of the name of a newspaper, and sometimes even with its city; try to refer to a newspaper the way it refers to itself—on its front page or masthead: the Victoria *Times Colonist*; the Regina *Leader-Post*; *The Vancouver Sun*; the *Calgary Herald*; *The Globe and Mail*.

# 49. ITALICS

Italics are a special kind of slanting type that contrasts with the surrounding type to draw attention to a word or phrase, such as a title (see 48.2). The other main uses of italics are discussed below. In handwritten work, represent italic type by underlining.

## 49.1 Names of Ships and Planes

Italicize names of individual ships, planes, and the like:

the *Golden Hind*          *The Spirit of St. Louis*

the *St. Bonaventure*      *Mariner IX*

the *Lusitania*            the *Columbia*

the *Erebus* and the *Terror*   the *Orient Express*

## 49.2 Non-English Words and Phrases

Italicize non-English words and phrases that are not yet sufficiently common to be entirely at home in English. English contains many terms that have come from other languages but that are no longer thought of as non-English and are therefore not italicized; for example:

| | | | |
|---|---|---|---|
| moccasin | prairie | genre | tableau |
| bamboo | arroyo | corral | sushi |
| chutzpah | spaghetti | goulash | eureka |
| litotes | hiatus | vacuum | sic |

There are also words that are sufficiently Anglicized not to require italicizing but that usually retain their original accents and diacritical marks; for example:

cliché   naïf   fête   façade   Götterdämmerung

But English also makes use of many terms still felt by many writers to be sufficiently non-English to need italicizing, for example:

*Bildungsroman*   *au courant*   *coup d'état*        *savoir faire*

*Lebensraum*      *outré*        *Weltanschauung*   *carpe diem*

Many such expressions are on their way to full acceptance in English. If you are unsure, consult a good up-to-date dictionary.

## 49.3 Words Referred to as Words

Italicize words, letters, numerals, and the like when you refer to them as such:

> The word *helicopter* is formed from Greek roots.

> There are two *r*'s in *embarrass*. (Note that only the r is italicized; the s making it plural stays roman.)

> The number *13* is considered unlucky by many otherwise rational people.

> Don't use *&* as a substitute for *and*.

See also 43.7. For the matter of apostrophes for plurals of such elements, see 51.22.

## 49.4 For Emphasis

On rare occasions, italicize words or phrases—or even whole sentences—that you want to emphasize, for example, as they might be stressed if spoken aloud:

> One thing he was now sure of: *that* was no way to go about the task.

> Careful thought should lead one to the conclusion that *character*, not wealth or connections, will be most important in the long run.

> If people try to tell you otherwise, *don't listen to them.*

> Try to remember that *Fredericton*, not Saint John, is the capital of New Brunswick.

> He gave up his ideas of fun and decided instead to finish his education. *And it was the most important decision of his life.*

Like other typographical devices for achieving emphasis (boldface, capitalization, underlining), this method is worth avoiding, or at least minimizing, in most writing. No merely mechanical means of emphasis is, ultimately, as effective as punctuation, word order, and syntax. Easy methods often produce only a transitory effect, and repeated use soon saps what effectiveness they have. Consider the following sentences:

> Well, I felt just *terrible* when he told me that!

> I felt terrible, just terrible, when he told me that.

> I can think of only one way to describe how I felt when he told me that: I felt terrible.

# 50. NUMERALS

Numerals are appropriate in technical and scientific writing, and newspapers sometimes use them to save space. But in ordinary writing certain conventions limit their use. Use numerals for the following purposes:

## 50.1 Time of Day

Use numerals for the time of day with *a.m.* or *p.m.* and *midnight* or *noon*, or when minutes are included:

> 3 p.m. (*but* three o'clock, three in the afternoon)

> 12 noon, 12 midnight (these are often better than the equivalents, *12 p.m.* and *12 a.m.*, which may not be understood)

> 4:15, 4:30 (*but* a quarter past four; half past four)

## 50.2 Dates

Use numerals for dates:

> September 11, 2001, *or* 11 September 2001

The year is almost always represented by numerals, and centuries written out:

> 2000 was the last year of the twentieth century, not the first year of the twenty-first century, wasn't it? (See 50.8.)

## Proofreading Tip

### Adding Suffixes to Numerals in Dates

The suffixes *st*, *nd*, *rd*, and *th* go with numerals in dates only if the year is not given, or the number may be written out:

| | |
|---|---|
| May 12, 1955 | May 12th |
| the twelfth of May | May twelfth |

## 50.3 Addresses

Use numerals for addresses:

| | |
|---|---|
| 2132 Fourth Avenue | P.O. Box 91 |
| 4771 128th Street | Apartment 8 |

## 50.4 Technical and Mathematical Numbers

Use numerals for technical and mathematical numbers, such as percentages and decimals:

| | |
|---|---|
| 31 per cent | 31% |
| 37 degrees Celsius | 37 °C |
| 2.54 centimetres | 2.54 cm |

## 50.5 Pages and Chapters

Use numerals for page numbers and other divisions of a written work, especially in documentation (see sections 72, 73, and 74):

| | |
|---|---|
| page 27, p. 27, pp. 33–38 | line 13, lines 3 and 5, ll. 7–9 |
| Chapter 4, Ch. 4, chapter IV | section 3, section III |
| Part 2 | Book IX, canto 120 (IX, 120) |
| 2 Samuel 22: 3, II Samuel 19: 1 | |

(Note that books of the Bible are not italicized.)

## 50.6 Parts of a Play

Use numerals for acts, scenes, and line numbers of plays (some readers may prefer that you use roman numerals for acts and scenes):

In act 4, scene 2, . . .

See act IV, scene ii, line 77.

Remember Hamlet's "To be, or not to be" (3. 1. 56). (*or* III. i. 56)

## 50.7 Statistics and Numbers of More than Two Words

Generally, spell out numbers that can be expressed in one or two words; use numerals for numbers that would take more than two words:

four; thirty; eighty-three; two hundred; seven thousand; 115; 385; 2120

one-third; one-half; five thirty-seconds

three dollars, $3.48; five hundred dollars, $517

If you are writing about more than one number, say for purposes of comparison or giving statistics, numerals are usually preferable:

> Enrolment dropped from 250 two years ago, to 200 last year, to only 90 this year.

Don't mix numerals and words in such a context. On the other hand, if in your writing you refer alternately to two sets of figures, it may be better to use numerals for one and words for the other:

> We're building a 60-foot border; we can use either five 12-foot timbers or six 10-foot timbers.

## 50.8 Avoiding Numerals at the Beginning of a Sentence

Don't begin a sentence with a numeral. Either spell out the number or rewrite the sentence so that the number doesn't come first:

> ✘    30–40% goes for taxes.
>
> Thirty to forty per cent goes for taxes.
>
> Taxes consume from 30 to 40 per cent.

> ✘    750 people showed up to watch the chess tournament.
>
> As many as 750 people came to watch the chess tournament.
>
> The chess tournament drew 750 interested spectators.

Dates are sometimes considered acceptable at the beginning of a sentence, but since some people object to the practice it is worth avoiding. In 50.2 above we could easily have rewritten the example:

> Wasn't 2000 the last year of the twentieth century, and not the first year of the twentieth-first century?

## 50.9 Commas with Numerals

Commas have long been conventional to separate groups of three figures in long numbers:

> 3,172,450    17,920

In the metric system, however, along with the rest of SI (Système Internationale, or International System of Units), groups of three digits on either side of a decimal point are separated by spaces; with four-digit numbers a space is optional:

| 7723 | *or* | 7 723 |

3 172 450

| 3.1416 | *or* | 3.141 6 (*but* 3.141 59) |

There are two exceptions to this convention: amounts of money and addresses. Use commas to separate dollar figures preceding a decimal into units of three:

$3,500    £27,998.06

Street addresses of four or more figures are usually not separated by commas or spaces:

18885 Bay Mills Avenue

For further information about SI consult the *Canadian Metric Practice Guide,* published by the Canadian Standards Association.

# 51. SPELLING

Some writers have little trouble with spelling; others have a lot—or is that *alot*? Even confident writers must consult a dictionary or spell checker occasionally; poor spellers need to do this all the time. The good news is that good spelling comes with practice; taking the time to look up a word now will help you remember its proper spelling the next time you need to use it.

English spelling isn't as bizarre as some people think, but there are oddities. Sometimes the same sound can be spelled in several ways (*fine, offer, phone, cough; or so, soap, sow, sew, beau, dough*), or a single element can be pronounced in several ways (*cough, tough, dough, through, bough, fought*). When such inconsistencies occur in longer and less familiar words, sometimes only a dictionary can help us. And remember, a dictionary isn't prescribing but describing: it isn't commanding us to be correct but simply recording the currently accepted conventions.

English has changed a great deal over the centuries, and it is still changing. Old words pass out of use, new words are added, conventions of grammar evolve, pronunciations and spelling change. Words in transition may have more than one acceptable meaning or pronunciation or spelling. The word *pejorative*, for example, has several acceptable pronunciations (dictionaries usually record them in what they consider the order of preference, with the most acceptable or most common first). The past tense of *dream* can be either *dreamed* or *dreamt*. The past tense of *slide* changed from *slided* to *slid* a century or so ago; will the past tense of *glide* someday be *glid*? Just a few years ago *dove* was considered unacceptable as the past tense of *dive*; now, it is at least as acceptable as *dived*. And so on. Dictionaries can tell you what is preferred or accepted right now—just make sure you're using an up-to-date dictionary and not an old one.

In Canada, we also have to contend with the influence of British and American spelling. Broadly speaking, Canadian conventions—whether of spelling, punctuation, usage, or pronunciation—are closer to American than to British, and where they are changing they are changing in the direction of American conventions. Many of us, when we see the word *lieutenant*, still say "leftenant" instead of "lootenant," but we say and spell *aluminum* rather than *aluminium*. The alphabet still ends in *zed* rather than *zee* for most of us, though the distinction may be fading. Most Canadians write *centre* and *theatre* rather than *center* and *theater*; but we write *curb* rather than *kerb*, and "skedule" is replacing "shedule" as the pronunciation of *schedule*. Endings in *our* (*colour, honour, labour,* etc.) are preferred over those in *or*. Similarly, endings in *ize* are generally preferred over those in *ise*. We have the useful alternatives *cheque* (bank), *racquet* (tennis), and *storey* (floor); Americans have only *check, racket,* and *story* for both meanings. But *draught* is losing ground to *draft,* and *program* and *judgment* are rapidly replacing *programme* and *judgement*.

Where alternatives exist, either is correct. But be consistent. If you choose *analyze*, write *paralyze* and *modernize*; if you choose *centre*, write *lustre* and *fibre*; if you spell *honour*, then write *humour, colour, labour*. But if you do choose the *our* endings, watch out for the trap: when you add the suffixes *ous, ious, ate* or *ation*, and *ize* (or *ise*), you must drop the *u* and write *humorous, coloration, vaporize, laborious*, and there is no *u* in *honorary*.

The point is, there is choice. In this book, for example, we use the *our* ending because we think it is still considered standard outside the popular media. And we use the *ize* ending (where the alternatives exist) because we believe it to be the dominant form. If a particular form is clearly dominant or an acknowledged standard, we think it should be used. (The Spelling List at the end of the chapter includes some words with alternative spellings that might occasionally be troublesome; the word listed first is preferred.)

But such dilemmas, if they are dilemmas, are infrequent. The real spelling difficulties, those shared by all writers of English, are of a different sort.

Many spelling errors can be prevented only with the help of a good dictionary. Many others, however, fall into clear categories. Familiarizing yourself with the main rules and the main sources of confusion will help you avoid these errors.

### 51.1 *ie* or *ei*

The old jingle should help: use *i* before *e* except after *c*, or when sounded like *a* as in *neighbour* and *weigh*.

> achieve, believe, chief, field, fiend, shriek, siege, wield
>
> ceiling, conceive, deceive, perceive, receive
>
> eight, neighbour, sleigh, veil, weigh

When the sound is neither long *e* nor long *a*, the spelling *ei* is usually right:

> counterfeit, foreign, forfeit, height, heir, their

But there are several exceptions; memorize them by writing a sentence using all the words:

> either, neither; leisure; seize; weird
>
> financier; friend; mischief; sieve

When in doubt, consult your dictionary.

## 51.2–51.9 Prefixes and Suffixes

The more you know about how words are put together, the less trouble you will have spelling them. Many of the words that give writers difficulty are those with prefixes and suffixes. Understanding how these elements operate will help you avoid errors.

## 51.2 Prefixes

A prefix is one or more syllables added to the beginning of a root word to form a new word. Many common spelling mistakes could be avoided by recognizing that a word consists of a prefix joined to a root word. For example, *pre* is from a Latin word meaning "before"; *fix* is a root, meaning "fasten" or "place": the new word, *prefix*, is then literally something fastened before. *Prefix* is not a difficult word for most writers to spell, but recognizing its prefix and root will ensure that it is spelled correctly.

One mistake writers often make is omitting the last letter of a prefix when it is the same as the first letter of the root. When a prefix ends with the same letter that the root begins with, the result is a double letter; don't omit one of them:

> ad + dress = address          mis + spell = misspell
>
> com + motion = commotion     un + necessary = unnecessary

(Similarly, don't omit one of the doubled letters in compounds such as *beachhead*, *bookkeeping*, and *roommate*.)

In some cases the first letter of a root has "pulled" the last letter of a prefix over. In other words, the first letter of the root is doubled to replace the last letter of a prefix in order to make the resulting word less difficult to pronounce. Writers unaware of the prefix sometimes forget to double the consonant. The Latin prefix *ad* (meaning "to," "toward," "near") is commonly affected this way. For example, it became *af* in front of *facere* (a Latin verb meaning "to do"); hence our word *affect* has two *f*'s. Here are some other examples:

| ad | > | ac | in | *access, accept, accommodate* |
|----|---|-----|-----|-------------------------------|
|    |   | al | in | *alliance, allusion* |
|    |   | an | in | *annul, annihilate* |
|    |   | ap | in | *apprehend, apparatus, application* |
| com | > | col | in | *collide, colloquial, collusion* |
|    |   | con | in | *connect, connote* |
|    |   | cor | in | *correct, correspond* |
| ob | > | op | in | *oppose, oppress* |
| sub | > | suc | in | *success, succumb* |
|    |   | sup | in | *suppress, supply, support* |

Note the structure of the frequently misspelled *accommodate:* both *ac* and *com* are prefixes, so the word must have both a double *cc* and a double *mm*. It may help to think of the meaning of the word: *to make room for.* Be sure to *make room for* the double *cc* and the double *mm.*

Errors can also be prevented by correctly identifying a word's prefix. A writer who knows that the prefix of *arouse* is *a* and not *ar* will not be tempted to spell the word with a double *rr.* Knowing that the prefix of *apology* is *apo,* not *ap,* will curb the temptation to spell the word with a double *pp.* (Knowing that the root is from the Greek *logos* would also help.) Familiarize yourself with prefixes. The following are some of the more common prefixes, along with their meanings:

**a**      not, without (*amoral*); onward, away, from (*arise, awake*); to, at, or into a particular state (*agree*); utterly (*abash*)
           variant:   **an** before a vowel (*anaemia*)

**ab**     off, away, from (*abduct, abnormal, abuse*)
           variant:   **abs** before *c, t* (*abscess, abstain*)

**ad**     denoting motion towards (*advance*), change into (*adapt*), or addition (*adjunct*)
           variants: **ac** before *c, k, q* (*accept, accede; acknowledge; acquire*)
                        **af** before *f* (*affirm*)
                        **ag** before *g* (*aggravate*)
                        **al** before *l* (*allocate*)
                        **an** before *n* (*annotate*)
                        **ap** before *p* (*apprehend*)
                        **ar** before *r* (*arrive*)
                        **as** before *s* (*assemble*)
                        **at** before *t* (*attend*)

**ante**   before (*antecedent*)

**anti**   opposed to, against (*anti-hero, antibacterial*)

**bi**     two, twice (*bicoloured, biennial*)
           variant:   **bin** before a vowel (*binoculars*)

by      subordinate, secondary (*by-election, by-product*)

com     with, together (*combine, command*)
        variants: **col** before *l* (*collocate, collude*)
                **con** before *c, d, f, g, j, n, q, s, t, v,* and sometimes
                    before vowels (*concord, condescend, confide*)
                **cor** before *r* (*correct*)

de      down, away, from (*descend, de-ice*); completely (*denude*)

di      twice, two (*dichromatic, dilemma*)

dis     not (*disadvantage*); denoting reversal (*disappear*), removal
        (*dismember*), or separation (*disjoin, dispel, dissect*)
        variant:  **dif** before *f* (*diffuse*)

dys     bad, difficult (*dysfunctional*)

e       electronic (*email, e-zine*)

ef      before *f* (*efface*)

en      in, into (*ensnare, engulf; encrust; energy*); used in verbs
        ending in *en* (*enliven*)
        variant:  **em** before *b, p* (*embed, embolden*)

epi     upon, above (*epidemic, epicentre*); in addition (*epilogue*)

ex      out (*exclude; exodus*); upward (*extol*); thoroughly (*excruci-
        ate*); into the state of (*exasperate*)
        variant:  **e** (*elect, emit*)

for     denoting prohibition (*forbid*), neglect (*forget*), or absten-
        tion (*forbear, forgo*)

fore    in front, beforehand (*forebear; foreshadow; forecourt*)

hyper   over, beyond, excessively (*hypersensitive*); relating to
        hypertext (*hyperlink*)

hypo    under, below normal (*hypotension*)

in      not, without (*infertile*); in, towards (*influx, inbounds*)
        variants: **il** before *l* (*illegal, illegible*)
                **im** before *b, m, p* (*immature, imbibe*)
                **ir** before *r* (*irrelevant, irradiate*)

| | |
|---|---|
| inter | between, among (*interactive*) |
| intra | on the inside (*intravenous, intramural*) |
| intro | in, inwards (*introvert*) |
| mis | wrongly, badly (*misapply, mismanage*); expressing negativity (*misadventure; mischief*) |
| multi | more than one, many (*multicoloured, multiple*) |
| ob | blocking, opposing, against (*obstacle, object*); to, towards (*oblige*) |
| | variants:  oc before *c* (*occasion*) |
| | of before *f* (*offend*) |
| | op before *p* (*oppose*) |
| para | beyond or distinct from but analogous to (*paranormal, paramilitary*); protecting from (*parachute*) |
| | variant:  par before a vowel (*parody*) |
| per | through, all over, completely (*pervade, perforate, perfect*) |
| peri | around, about (*perimeter*) |
| pre | before (*precaution, precede*) |
| pro | supporting (*pro-industry*); forwards or away (*proceed*); before (*proactive*) |
| | variant:  pur (*pursue*) |
| re | once more, afresh (*reactivate, restore, revert*); mutually (*resemble*); in opposition (*repel*); behind, back (*remain, recluse*) |
| se | apart, without (*separate, secure*) |
| sub | denoting subsequent or secondary action (*subdivision*); lower, less, below (*subalpine, subculture*) |
| | variants:  suc before *c* (*succeed*) |
| | suf before *f* (*suffix*) |
| | sug before *g* (*suggest*) |
| | sup before *p* (*support*) |
| syn | united, acting together (*synchronize*) |
| | variant:  sym before *b, m, p* (*symbiosis, symmetry*) |
| uni | one (*unicorn, unicycle*) |

# Proofreading Tip

## Recognizing Prefixes

The following are some words with their prefixes in italics; after each is a common misspelling that knowing the prefix would have prevented:

| | | |
|---|---|---|
| *afore*mentioned | ✘ | aformentioned |
| *by*-product | ✘ | biproduct |
| *contro*versial | ✘ | conterversial |
| *de*scribe | ✘ | discribe |
| *dia*logue | ✘ | diologue |
| *dis*appointed | ✘ | dissappointed |
| *milli*metre | ✘ | milimetre |
| *mini*ature | ✘ | minature |
| *pen*insula | ✘ | penninsula |
| *per*suade | ✘ | pursuade |
| *por*traying | ✘ | protraying |
| *pro*fessor | ✘ | proffessor |

## 51.3 Suffixes

A suffix is one or more syllables added to the end of a root word to form a new word, usually changing its part of speech. For example:

| root | suffix | new word |
|---|---|---|
| appear (**v.**) | ance | appearance (**n.**) |
| content (**adj.**) | ment | contentment (**n.**) |
| occasion (**n.**) | al | occasional (**adj.**) |
| occasional (**adj.**) | ly | occasionally (**adv.**) |

Suffixes, like prefixes, can give writers difficulty. For example, if you add *ness* to a word ending in *n*, the result is a double *nn*: *barrenness, openness, stubbornness*. And remember that the correct suffix is *ful*, not *full*: *spoonful, cupful, shovelful, bucketful, roomful, successful.* The following sections should help you avoid the common spelling mistakes that writers make when adding suffixes.

## 51.4 Final *e* Before a Suffix

When a suffix is added to a root word that ends in a silent *e*, certain rules generally apply. If the suffix begins with a vowel (*a, e, i, o, u*), the *e* is usually dropped:

| | |
|---|---|
| desire + able = desirable | forgive + able = forgivable |
| sphere + ical = spherical | argue + ing = arguing |
| come + ing = coming | allure + ing = alluring |
| continue + ous = continuous | desire + ous = desirous |
| sense + ual = sensual | rogue + ish = roguish |

(*Dyeing* retains the *e* to distinguish it from *dying.* If a word ends with two *e*'s, both are pronounced and therefore not dropped: *agreeing, fleeing.*)

If the suffix begins with *a* or *o*, most words ending in *ce* or *ge* retain the *e* in order to preserve the soft sound of the *c* (like *s* rather than *k*) or the *g* (like *j* rather than hard as in *gum*):

| | |
|---|---|
| notice + able = noticeable | outrage + ous = outrageous |

(Note that *vengeance* and *gorgeous* also have such a silent *e*.) Similarly, words like *picnic* and *frolic* require an added *k* to preserve the hard sound before suffixes beginning with *e* or *i*: *picknicked, picknicking, frolicked, frolicking, politicking.* (An exception to this rule is *arc*: *arced, arcing.*) When the suffix does not begin with *e* or *i*, these words do not add a *k*: *tactical, frolicsome.*

If the suffix begins with a consonant, the silent *e* of the root word is usually not dropped:

| | |
|---|---|
| awe + some = awesome | effective + ness = effectiveness |
| definite + ly = definitely | hoarse + ly = hoarsely |
| immediate + ly = immediately | mere + ly = merely |
| immense + ly = immensely | separate + ly = separately |
| involve + ment = involvement | woe + ful = woeful |

(But note a common exception: awe + ful = awful.)

And there is a subgroup of words whose final *e*'s are sometimes wrongly omitted. The *e*, though silent, is essential to keep the sound of the preceding vowel long:

completely    extremely    hopelessness    livelihood
loneliness    remoteness    severely    tasteless

But such an *e* is sometimes dropped when no consonant intervenes between it and the long vowel:

due + ly = duly    true + ly = truly    argue + ment = argument

## 51.5 Final *y* after a Consonant and Before a Suffix

When the suffix begins with *i*, keep the *y*:

baby + ish = babyish    carry + ing = carrying
try + ing = trying    worry + ing = worrying

(Note: Words ending in *ie* change to *y* before adding *ing*: die + ing = dying; lie + ing = lying.)

When the suffix begins with something other than *i*, change *y* to *i*:

happy + er = happier    duty + ful = dutiful
happy + ness = happiness    silly + est = silliest
harmony + ous = harmonious    angry + ly = angrily

Some exceptions: *shyly*, *shyness*; *slyer*, *slyly*; *flyer* (though *flier* is sometimes used); *dryer* (as a noun—for the comparative adjective use *drier*).

## 51.6 Doubling of a Final Consonant Before a Suffix

When adding a suffix, double the final consonant of the root if:

(a)  that consonant is preceded by a single vowel,

(b)  the root is a one-syllable word or a word accented on its last syllable, and

(c)  the suffix begins with a vowel.

One-syllable words:

| | | |
|---|---|---|
| bar + ed = barred | bar + ing = barring | |
| fit + ed = fitted | fit + ing =fitting | fit + er = fitter |
| hot + er = hotter | hot + est = hottest | |
| shop + ed =shopped | shop + ing =shopping | shop +er = shopper |

Words accented on last syllable:

| | |
|---|---|
| allot + ed = allotted | allot + ing = allotting |
| commit + ed = committed | commit + ing = committing |
| occur + ed = occurred | occur + ing = occurring |
| occur + ence = occurrence | |
| propel + ed = propelled | propel + ing = propelling |
| propel + er = propeller | |

But when the addition of the suffix shifts the accent of the root word away from the last syllable, do not double the final consonant:

| | | |
|---|---|---|
| infer + ed = inferred | infer + ing = inferring | (*but* inference) |
| prefer + ed = preferred | prefer + ing = preferring | (*but* preference) |
| refer + ed = referred | refer + ing = referring | (*but* reference) |

Do not double the final consonant if it is preceded by a single consonant (sharp + er = sharper) or if the final consonant is preceded by two vowels (fail + ed = failed, stoop + ing = stooping) or if the root word is more than one syllable and not accented on its last syllable (benefit + ed = benefited, parallel + ing = paralleling) or if the suffix begins with a consonant (commit + ment = commitment).

## 51.7 The Suffix *ly*

When *ly* is added to an adjective already ending in a single *l*, that final *l* is retained, resulting in an adverb ending in *lly*. If you pronounce such words carefully you will be less likely to misspell them:

| | |
|---|---|
| accidental + ly = accidentally | cool + ly = coolly |
| incidental + ly = incidentally | mental + ly = mentally |
| natural + ly = naturally | political + ly = politically |

If the root ends in a double *ll*, one *l* is dropped: full + ly = fully, chill + ly = chilly, droll + ly = drolly.

# Proofreading Tip

## On Doubling the Final Consonant *l* or *p*

Unlike *parallel*, other words often double a final *l*, even when they are of two or more syllables and not accented on the final syllable; for example, *labelled* or *labeled*, *traveller* or *traveler*. Either form is correct, though the Canadian preference is for the doubled *l*. (Some even double the *l* at the end of *parallel*, in spite of the present double *ll* preceding it.)

The word *kidnap* is a similar exception, for the obvious reason of pronunciation: either *kidnapped* or *kidnaped* is correct (and *kidnapping* or *kidnaping*). Another is *worship*: either *worshipped* or *worshiped*, *worshipping* or *worshiping*. In both instances, the double final consonant is preferred in Canada.

# Proofreading Tip

## On Adding the Suffix *ally*

Many adjectives ending in *ic* have alternative forms ending in *ical*. But even if they don't, nearly all add *ally*, not just *ly*, to become adverbs—as do nouns like *music* and *stoic*. Again, careful pronunciation will help you avoid error:

| | |
|---|---|
| alphabetic, alphabetical, alphabetically | drastic, drastically |
| basic, basically | scientific, scientifically |
| cyclic, cyclical, cyclically | symbolic, symbolical, symbolically |

An exception: *publicly*.

## 51.8 Troublesome Word Endings

Several groups of suffixes, or word endings, consistently plague weak spellers and sometimes trip even good spellers. There are no rules governing them, and pronunciation is seldom any help; one either knows them or does not. Whenever you aren't certain of the correct spelling, check your dictionary. The following examples will at least alert you to the potential trouble spots:

### able, ably, ability; ible, ibly, ibility

It should be helpful to remember that many more words end in *able* than in *ible*; yet it is the *ible* endings that cause the most trouble:

| able | | ible | |
|------|------|------|------|
| advisable | inevitable | audible | inexpressible |
| comparable | laudable | contemptible | irresistible |
| debatable | noticeable | deductible | negligible |
| desirable | quotable | eligible | plausible |
| immeasurable | respectable | flexible | responsible |
| indispensable | syllable | forcible | tangible |
| indubitable | veritable | incredible | visible |

### ent, ently, ence, ency; ant, antly, ance, ancy

| en | | an | |
|------|------|------|------|
| apparent | independent | appearance | flamboyant |
| coherent | permanent | blatant | irrelevant |
| confidence | inherent | attendance | hindrance |
| consistent | persistence | brilliant | maintenance |
| excellent | resilient | concomitant | resistance |
| existence | tendency | extravagant | warrant |

### tial, tian; cial, cian, ciate

| tia | | cia | |
|------|------|------|------|
| confidential | influential | beneficial | mathematician |
| dietitian | martial | crucial | mortician |
| existential | spatial | emaciated | physician |
| expatiate | substantial | enunciate | politician |

*ce; se*

| ce | | se | |
|---|---|---|---|
| choice | defence | course | expense |
| evidence | presence | dense | phrase |
| fence | voice | dispense | sparse |

# Proofreading Tip

*practice, practise; licence, license*

Canadian writers tend to follow the British practice of using the *ce* forms of *practice* and *licence* as nouns and the *se* forms *practise* and *license* as verbs:

> We will *practise* our fielding at today's slo-pitch *practice*.
>
> Are you *licensed* to drive?
>
> Yes, I've had my driver's *licence* since I was sixteen.

American writers tend to favour the *ce* spelling of *practice* and *se* spelling of *license* regardless of whether each is being used as a noun or a verb.

Note also that Canadian as well as British writers generally prefer the *ce* spelling for *offence* and *defence*, while American writers tend to use the *se* spellings of these words.

*ative; itive*

| ative | | itive | |
|---|---|---|---|
| affirmative | informative | additive | positive |
| comparative | negative | competitive | repetitive |
| imaginative | restorative | genitive | sensitive |

## 51.9 *cede, ceed,* or *sede*

Memorize if necessary: the *sede* ending occurs only in *supersede.* The *ceed* ending occurs only in *exceed, proceed,* and *succeed.* All other words ending in this sound use *cede: accede, concede, intercede, precede, recede, secede.*

## 51.10 Changes in Spelling of Roots

Be careful with words whose roots change spelling, often because of a change in stress, when they are inflected for a different part of speech, for example:

| | |
|---|---|
| clear, clarity | maintain, maintenance |
| curious, curiosity | prevail, prevalent |
| despair, desperate | pronounce, pronunciation |
| exclaim, exclamatory | repair, reparable |
| generous, generosity | repeat, repetition |
| inherit, heritage, *but* heredity, hereditary | |

## 51.11 Faulty Pronunciation

Acquire the habit of correct pronunciation; sound words to yourself, exaggeratedly if necessary, even at the expense of temporarily slowing your reading speed. Here is a list of words some of whose common misspellings could be prevented by careful pronunciation:

| | | | |
|---|---|---|---|
| academic | disgust | insurgence | prevalent |
| accelerate | disillusioned | interpretation | pronunciation |
| accidentally | elaborate | intimacy | quantity |
| amphitheatre | emperor | inviting | repetitive |
| analogy | environment | irrelevant | reservoir |
| approximately | epitomize | itinerary | sacrilegious |
| architectural | escape | larynx | separate |
| athlete | especially | lightning | significant |
| authoritative | etcetera | limpidly | similar |

| | | | |
|---|---|---|---|
| biathlon | evident | lustrous | strength |
| camaraderie | excerpt | mathematics | subsidiary |
| candidate | February | negative | suffocate |
| celebration | film | nuclear | surprise |
| conference | foliage | optimism | temporarily |
| congratulate | further | original | triathlon |
| controversial | government | particular | ultimatum |
| definitely | governor | peculiar | village |
| deteriorating | gravitation | permanently | villain |
| detrimental | hereditary | phenomenon | visible |
| dilapidated | hurriedly | philosophical | vulnerable |
| disgruntled | immersing | predilection | wondrous |

## Proofreading Tip

### Spelling Unpronounced Sounds; Telescoping

Don't omit the *d* or *ed* from such words as *used* and *supposed*, *old-fashioned* and *prejudiced*, which are often pronounced without the *d* sound. And be careful not to omit whole syllables that are near-duplications in sound. Write carefully, run a spell-check when possible, and proofread, sounding the words to yourself. Here are some examples of "telescoped" words that occur frequently:

| | | |
|---|---|---|
| convenience | ✘ | convience |
| criticize | ✘ | critize |
| examining | ✘ | examing |
| inappropriate | ✘ | inappriate |
| institution | ✘ | instution |
| politician | ✘ | politian |
| remembrance | ✘ | rembrance |
| repetition | ✘ | repition |

## 51.12 Confusion with Other Words

Don't let false analogies and similarities of sound lead you astray.

| A writer who thinks of a word like ... | ... may spell another word wrong ... | ... instead of right. |
|---|---|---|
| young | ✗ amoung | among |
| breeze | ✗ cheeze | cheese |
| conform | ✗ conformation | confirmation |
| diet | ✗ diety | deity |
| desolate | ✗ desolute | dissolute |
| exalt | ✗ exaltant | exultant |
| democracy | ✗ hypocracy | hypocrisy |
| ideal | ✗ idealic | idyllic |
| restaurant | ✗ restauranteur | restaurateur |
| comrade | ✗ comraderie | camaraderie |
| air | ✗ ordinairy | ordinary |
| knowledge | ✗ priviledge | privilege |
| size | ✗ rize | rise |
| religious | ✗ sacreligious | sacrilegious |
| familiar | ✗ similiar | similar |
| summer | ✗ grammer | grammar |
| prize | ✗ surprize | surprise |
| sink | ✗ zink | zinc |

# Proofreading Tip

## On the Limitations of Spell-Checking

Your word-processing program's spell-check feature will help you catch spelling mistakes like "grammer" and "surprize", but it will *not* help you when you've used *principle* when you meant to use *principal*, or *birth* instead of *berth*. *You* will need to catch such slips in your own close checking of your documents.

## 51.13 Homophones and Other Words Sometimes Confused

Be careful to distinguish between homophones (or homonyms)—words pronounced alike but spelled differently. Here are some that can be troublesome; consult a dictionary for any whose meanings you aren't sure of; this is a matter of meaning as well as of spelling (see also section 58):

| | |
|---|---|
| aisle, isle | its, it's |
| alter, altar | led, lead |
| assent, ascent | manner, manor |
| bear, bare | meat, meet |
| birth, berth | past, passed |
| board, bored | patience, patients |
| boarder, border | piece, peace |
| born, borne | plain, plane |
| break, brake | pore, pour |
| by, buy, bye | pray, prey |
| capital, capitol | presence, presents |
| complement, compliment | principle, principal |
| council, counsel | rain, rein, reign |
| course, coarse | right, rite, write |
| desert, dessert | road, rode, rowed |
| die, dye, dying, dyeing | sight, site, cite |
| discreet, discrete | stationary, stationery |
| forth, fourth | there, their, they're |
| hear, here | to, too, two |
| heard, herd | whose, who's |
| hole, whole | your, you're |

There are also words that are not pronounced exactly alike but that are similar enough to be confused. Again, look up any whose meanings you aren't sure of:

| | |
|---|---|
| accept, except | diary, dairy |
| access, excess | emigrate, immigrate |
| adopt, adapt, adept | eminent, imminent, immanent |
| adverse, averse | ensure, insure, assure |
| advice, advise | enquire, inquire, acquire |

| | |
|---|---|
| affect, effect | envelop, envelope |
| afflicted, inflicted | evoke, invoke |
| allude, elude | illusion, allusion |
| angle, angel | incident, incidence, instant, instance |
| appraise, apprise | incredulous, incredible |
| assume, presume | ingenious, ingenuous |
| bizarre, bazaar | insight, incite |
| breath, breathe | later, latter |
| choose, chose | loose, lose |
| cloth, clothe | moral, morale |
| conscious, conscience | practice, practise |
| custom, costume | tack, tact |
| decent, descent, dissent | than, then |
| decimate, disseminate | whether, weather |
| device, devise | while, wile |

Be careful also to distinguish between such terms as the following, for although they sound the same, they function differently depending on whether they are spelled as one word or two:

| | |
|---|---|
| already, all ready | awhile, a while |
| altogether, all together | everybody, every body |
| anybody, any body | everyday, every day |
| anymore, any more | everyone, every one |
| anyone, any one | maybe, may be |
| anytime, any time | someday, some day |
| anyway, any way | sometime, some time |

## 51.14 One Word or Two?

Do not spell the following words as two or three separate or hyphenated words; each is one unhyphenated word:

| | | | |
|---|---|---|---|
| alongside | lifetime | outshine | sunrise |
| background | nevertheless | setback | sunset |
| countryside | nonetheless | spotlight | throughout |
| easygoing | nowadays | straightforward | wrongdoing |

The following, on the other hand, should always be spelled as two unhyphenated words:

| | | |
|---|---|---|
| a bit | at least | in order (to) |
| a few | close by | in spite (of) |
| after all | even though | no longer |
| all right (*alright* is informal) | every time | (on the) other hand |
| a lot | in between | (in) other words |
| as though | in fact | up to |

## Proofreading Tip

### On *cannot* and *can not*

The word *cannot* should usually be written as one word; write *can not* only when you want special emphasis on the *not*.

### 51.15 Hyphenation

To hyphenate or not to hyphenate? That is often the question. There are some firm rules; there are some sound guidelines; and there is a large territory where only common sense and a good dictionary can help you find your way. Since the conventions are constantly changing, sometimes rapidly, make a habit of checking your dictionary for current usage. (For hyphens to divide a word at the end of a line, see 45.2.) Here are the main points to remember:

1. Use hyphens in compound numbers from twenty-one to ninety-nine.

2. Use hyphens with fractions used as adjectives:

   A two-thirds majority is required to defeat the amendment.

   When a fraction is used as a noun, you may use a hyphen, though many writers do not:

   One quarter of the audience was asleep.

3. Use hyphens with compounds indicating time, when these are written out: seven-thirty, nine-fifteen.

4. Use an en-dash (–) between a pair of numbers (including hours and dates) indicating a range. The en-dash is slightly longer than a regular hyphen.

> pages 73–78

> June 20–26

The en-dash is equivalent to the word *to*. If you introduce the range with *from,* write out the word *to*: from June 20 to June 26. If you use *between,* write out the word *and*: between June 20 and June 26.

5. Use hyphens with prefixes before proper nouns:

| | | |
|---|---|---|
| all-Canadian | pan-Asian | pseudo-Modern |
| anti-Fascist | post-Victorian | semi-Gothic |
| ex-Prime Minister | pre-Babylonian | trans-Siberian |
| non-Communist | pro-Liberal | un-American |

But there are long-established exceptions, for example:

antichrist    transatlantic    transpacific

6. Use hyphens with compounds beginning with the prefix *self*: *self-assured, self-confidence, self-deluded, self-esteem, self-made, self-pity,* etc. (The words *selfhood, selfish, selfless,* and *selfsame* are not hyphenated, since *self* is the root, not a prefix.) Hyphens are conventionally used with certain other prefixes: *all-important, ex-premier, quasi-religious.* Hyphens are conventionally used with most, but not all, compounds beginning with *vice* and *by*: *vice-chancellor, vice-consul, vice-president, vice-regent,* etc. (but *viceregal, viceroy; by-election, by-product,* etc.; and *bygone, bylaw, byroad, bystander, byword*). Check your dictionary.

7. Use hyphens with the suffixes *elect* and *designate*: *mayor-elect, ambassador-designate.*

8.  Use hyphens with *great* and *in-law* in compounds designating family relationships: *mother-in-law, son-in-law, great-grandfather, great-aunt*.

9.  Use hyphens to prevent a word's being mistaken for an entirely different word:

    He recounted what had happened after the ballots had been re-counted.

    If you're going to re-strain the juice, I'll restrain myself from drinking it now, seeds and all.

    Once at the resort after the bumpy ride, we sat down to re-sort our jumbled fishing gear.

    Check out the great sale prices of the goods at the check-out counter.

10. Use hyphens to prevent awkward or confusing combinations of letters and sounds: *anti-intellectual, doll-like, photo-offset, re-echo, set-to*.

11. Hyphens are sometimes necessary to prevent ambiguity:

    ✘   The ad offered six week old kittens for sale.

    The ad offered six week-old kittens for sale.

    The ad offered six-week-old kittens for sale.

Note the difference a hyphen makes to the meaning of the last two examples.

In the following, hyphenating *levelling out* removes the possibility of misreading the sentence:

To maintain social equality, we need a levelling-out of benefits.

## 51.16 Compound Nouns

Some nouns composed of two or more words are conventionally hyphenated, for example:

| | | | |
|---|---|---|---|
| free-for-all | half-and-half | jack-o-lantern | runner-up |
| merry-go-round | rabble-rouser | shut-in | trade-in |
| paper-pusher | two-timer | | |

But many that one might think should be hyphenated are not, and others that may once have been hyphenated, or even two separate words, have become so familiar that they are now one unhyphenated word. Usage is constantly and rapidly changing, and even dictionaries don't always agree on what is standard at a given time. Some dictionaries still record such old-fashioned forms as *to-night* and *to-morrow* as alternatives; use *tonight* and *tomorrow*. Clearly it is best to consult a dictionary that is both comprehensive and up-to-date and use the form it lists first.

## 51.17 Compound Modifiers

When two or more words occur together in such a way that they act as a single adjective before a noun, they are usually hyphenated in order to prevent a momentary misreading of the first part:

| | |
|---|---|
| a well-dressed man | greenish-grey eyes |
| middle-class values | computer-ready forms |
| a once-in-a-lifetime chance | a three-day-old strike |

When they occur after a noun, misreading is unlikely and no hyphen is needed:

The man was *well dressed*.

Her eyes are *greenish grey*.

But many compound modifiers are already listed as hyphenated words; for example, the *Canadian Oxford Dictionary* lists these, among others:

| | | | |
|---|---|---|---|
| first-class | fly-by-night | good-looking | habit-forming |
| open-minded | right-hand | short-lived | tongue-tied |
| warm-blooded | wide-eyed | | |

Such modifiers retain their hyphens even when they follow the nouns they modify:

The tone of the speech was quite *matter-of-fact*.

## Proofreading Tip

### On Hyphens and Adverbs Ending in *ly*

Since one cannot mistake the first part of a compound modifier when it is an adverb ending in *ly*, even in front of a noun, do not use a hyphen:

He is a *happily married* man.

The *superbly wrought* sculpture was the centre of attention.

## 51.18 Hyphenated Verbs

Verbs, too, are sometimes hyphenated. A dictionary will list most of the ones you might want to use; for example:

double-click    pan-broil    pole-vault    re-educate

second-guess    sight-read    soft-pedal    two-time

But be aware that some two-part verbs can never be hyphenated. Resist the temptation to put a hyphen in two-part verbs that consist of a verb followed by a preposition (see 11.4). Be particularly careful with those that are hyphenated when they serve as other parts of speech:

I was asked to *set up* the display. (*but* Many customers admired the set-up.)

*Call up* the next group of trainees. (*but* The rookie awaited a *call-up* to the big leagues.)

## Proofreading Tip

### Compounds that Change Their Spelling with the Part of Speech

Note that some expressions can be spelled either as two separate words or as compounds, depending on what part of speech they are functioning as; for example:

He works *full time*. (*but* He has a *full-time* job.)

If you get too dizzy you may *black out*. You will then suffer a *blackout*.

## 51.19 Suspension Hyphens

If you use two prefixes with one root, use what is called a "suspension" hyphen after the first prefix, even if it would not normally be hyphenated:

> The audience was about equally divided between *pro-* and *anti-Liberals*.

> You may choose between the *three-* and the *five-day* excursions.

> You may either *pre-* or *postdate* the cheque.

## 51.20 Plurals (See also 51.22 [For plurals].)

### Regular nouns

For most nouns, add *s* or *es* to the singular form to indicate plural number:

| | |
|---|---|
| one building, two buildings | one box, two boxes |
| one cat, two cats | one church, two churches |
| one girl, two girls | one wish, two wishes |

### Nouns ending in *o*

Some nouns ending in *o* preceded by a consonant form their plurals with *s*, while some use *es*. For some either form is correct—but use the one listed first in your dictionary. Here are a few examples:

| | | |
|---|---|---|
| altos | echoes | cargoes *or* cargos |
| pianos | heroes | mottoes *or* mottos |
| solos | potatoes | zeroes *or* zeros |

If the final *o* is preceded by a vowel, usually only an *s* is added: *arpeggios*, *cameos*, *ratios*, *cuckoos*, *embryos*.

### Nouns ending in *f* or *fe*

For some nouns ending in a single *f* or an *fe*, change the ending to *ve* before adding *s*, for example:

| | | |
|---|---|---|
| knife, knives | life, lives | shelf, shelves |
| leaf, leaves | loaf, loaves | thief, thieves |

But for some simply add *s*:

| | | |
|---|---|---|
| beliefs | gulfs | safes |
| griefs | proofs | still lifes |

Some words ending in *f* have alternative plurals:

dwarfs *or* dwarves    scarves *or* scarfs
hoofs *or* hooves    wharves *or* wharfs

The well-known hockey team called the Maple Leafs is a special case, a proper noun that doesn't follow the rules governing common nouns.

### Nouns ending in *y*
For nouns ending in *y* preceded by a vowel, add *s*:

bays    buoys    guys
keys    toys    valleys

For nouns ending in *y* preceded by a consonant, change the *y* to *i* and add *es*:

city, cities    cry, cries    kitty, kitties
country, countries    family, families    trophy, trophies

Exception: Most proper nouns ending in *y* simply add *s*:

There are two *Marys* and three *Henrys* in my daughter's class.

From 1949 to 1990 there were two *Germanys*.

But note that we refer to the Rocky Mountains as the Rockies and to the Canary Islands as the Canaries.

### Compounds
Generally, form the plurals of compounds simply by adding *s*:

major generals    lieutenant-governors    forget-me-nots
backbenchers    second cousins    great-grandmothers
merry-go-rounds    prizewinners    privy counsellors
shut-ins    webmasters    best-sellers

But if the first part is a noun and the rest is not, or if the first part is the more important of two nouns, that one is made plural:

governors general    daughters-in-law    passersby
mayors elect    jacks-of-all-trades
poets laureate    holes-in-one

But there are exceptions, and usage is changing. Note for example *spoonfuls* (this is the form for all nouns ending in *ful*). And a few compounds conventionally pluralize both nouns, for example, *men-servants*, *ups and downs*. And a few are the same in both singular and plural, for example, *crossroads*, *daddy-long-legs*, *underpants*.

### Irregular plurals

Some nouns are irregular in the way they form their plurals, but these are common and generally well known, for example:

child, children     foot, feet     mouse, mice     woman, women

Some plural forms are the same as the singular, for example:

one deer, two deer          one series, two series

one moose, two moose     one sheep, two sheep

### Borrowed words

The plurals of words borrowed from other languages (mostly Latin and Greek) can pose a problem. Words used formally or technically tend to retain their original plurals; words used more commonly tend to form their plurals according to English rules. Since many such words are in transition, you will probably encounter both plural forms. When in doubt, use the preferred form listed in your dictionary. Here are some examples of words that have tended to retain their original plurals:

| | |
|---|---|
| alumna, alumnae | larva, larvae |
| alumnus, alumni | madame, mesdames |
| analysis, analyses | nucleus, nuclei |
| basis, bases | parenthesis, parentheses |
| crisis, crises | phenomenon, phenomena |
| criterion, criteria | stimulus, stimuli |
| hypothesis, hypotheses | synthesis, syntheses |
| kibbutz, kibbutzim | thesis, theses |

Here are some with both forms, the choice often depending on the formality or technicality of the context:

| | |
|---|---|
| antenna | antennae (insects) *or* antennas (radios, etc.) |
| apparatus | apparatus *or* apparatuses |
| appendix | appendices *or* appendixes |
| beau | beaux *or* beaus |
| cactus | cacti *or* cactuses |
| château | châteaux *or* châteaus |
| curriculum | curricula *or* curriculums |
| focus | foci *or* focuses (focusses) |
| formula | formulae *or* formulas |
| index | indices *or* indexes |
| lacuna | lacunae *or* lacunas |
| matrix | matrices *or* matrixes |
| memorandum | memoranda *or* memorandums |
| referendum | referenda *or* referendums |
| stratum | strata *or* stratums |
| syllabus | syllabi *or* syllabuses |
| symposium | symposia *or* symposiums |
| terminus | termini *or* terminuses |
| ultimatum | ultimata *or* ultimatums |

And here are a few that now tend to follow regular English patterns:

| | |
|---|---|
| bureau, bureaus | sanctum, sanctums |
| campus, campuses | stadium, stadiums |

genius, geniuses (*genii* for mythological creatures)

Opinion, as well as usage, is divided on the spelling of the plurals of these and similar words. Most writers, for example, find *criterions* and *phenomenons* odd, preferring the original *criteria* and *phenomena*. On the other hand, some don't object to *data* and *media* as singular nouns. And *agenda*, originally the plural of *agendum*, is now simply a singular noun with its own plural, *agendas*. Your dictionary should indicate any irregular plurals; if you aren't sure of a word, look it up.

# Proofreading Tip

## Spelling Irregular Plural Nouns

When writing and speaking be mindful of the following usages:

- *Data* is the plural of *datum*, but it has become acceptable in informal and non-scientific cases to treat it as if it were singular.
- *Strata* is plural; the singular is *stratum*.
- *Kudos* is singular; don't use it as if it were plural.
- *Bacteria* is plural; don't use it as if it were singular.
- *Media* is the plural of *medium*, but it has become acceptable to treat it as if it were singular in fields outside of science. (*Mediums* is the correct plural for *medium* when it refers to spiritualists who claim to communicate with the dead.)

# Proofreading Tip

## Spelling Accented Words from Other Languages

If you use or quote words from other languages that have such diacritical marks as the cedilla(¸), the circumflex(ˆ), the tilde(˜), the umlaut(¨), or acute(´) or grave(`) accents, write them accurately. For example:

| | | | |
|---|---|---|---|
| façade | fête | cañon | Götterdämmerung |
| passé | à la mode | cliché | résumé |

See also 49.2.

## 51.21 Third-Person-Singular Verbs in the Present Tense

The third-person-singular inflection of verbs in the present tense is usually formed by following the same rules that govern the formation of plurals of nouns. For example:

| | |
|---|---|
| I brief him. She briefs me. | I lurch. It lurches. |
| I buy. He buys. | I portray. He portrays. |
| I carry. She carries. | I run. He runs. |

I wait. She waits.          I try. She tries.

I lift. The fog lifts.          I wish. He wishes.

But be careful, for there are exceptions; for example:

He loafs on weekends and wolfs his food.

She hoofs it to work every day.

## 51.22 Apostrophes

### For plurals

An apostrophe and an *s* may be used to form the plural, but only of numerals, symbols, letters, and of words referred to as words:

She knew her *ABC*'s at the age of four.

Study the three *r*'s.

It happened in the 1870's.

Indent all ¶'s five spaces.

*Accommodate* is spelled with two *c*'s and two *m*'s.

There are four *t*'s in my password.

There are too many *and*'s in that sentence.

Between them they have three Ph.D.'s.

Note that when a word, letter, or figure is italicized, the apostrophe and the *s* are not.

Many people prefer to form such plurals without the apostrophe: *r*s, *7*s, *1870*s, *and*s. But this practice can be confusing, especially with lowercase letters and words, which may be misread:

✘    How many *ss* are there in Nipissing?

✘    Too many *this*s can spoil a good paragraph.

In cases such as these, it is clearer and easier to use the apostrophe. Keep in mind that it is sometimes better to rephrase instances that are potentially awkward:

*Accommodate* is spelled with a double-*c* and a double-*m*.

*And* is used too many times in that sentence.

# Proofreading Tip

### Apostrophes Misused with Regular Common and Proper Nouns

Beware of the "grocer's apostrophe," so called because of its frequent appearance on signs in store windows:

✘ Escape the winter *blah's* with one of our romantic weekend *getaway's*.

✘ *Banana's* and *tomato's* are sold here.

Use *'s* for the plural form only in cases such as those outlined in 51.22; don't use it to form any other kind of plural—that is, of regular common and proper nouns.

### To indicate omissions

Use apostrophes to indicate omitted letters in contractions and omitted (though obvious) numerals:

| | |
|---|---|
| aren't (are not) | they're (they are) |
| can't (cannot) | won't (will not) |
| doesn't (does not) | wouldn't (would not) |
| don't (do not) | goin' fishin' (going fishing)[informal] |
| isn't (is not) | back in '83 |
| it's (it is) | the crash of '29 |
| she's (she is) | the summer of '96 |

If an apostrophe is already present to indicate a plural, you may omit the apostrophe that indicates omission: the *20's*, the *90's*.

### 51.23 Possessives

1. To form the possessive case of a singular or a plural noun that does not end in *s*, add an apostrophe and *s*:

| | | |
|---|---|---|
| Alberta's capital | a day's work | yesterday's news |
| the car's colour | deer's hide | children's books |
| the girl's teacher | Emil's briefcase | the women's jobs |

2.  To form the possessive of compound nouns, use *'s* after the last noun:

    > The Solicitor General's report is due tomorrow.

    > Sally and Mike's dinner party was a huge success.

    If the nouns don't actually form a compound, each will need the *'s*:

    > Sally's and Mike's versions of the story were markedly different.

3.  You may correctly add an apostrophe and an *s* to form the possessive of singular nouns ending in *s* or an *s*-sound:

    | | |
    |---|---|
    | the class's achievement | an index's usefulness |
    | the cross's meaning | Keats's poems |
    | the congress's debates | a platypus's bill |

    However, some writers prefer to add only an apostrophe if the pronunciation of an extra syllable would sound awkward:

    | | |
    |---|---|
    | Achilles' heel | Moses' miracles |
    | for convenience' sake | Demosthenes' speeches |

    But the *'s* is usually acceptable: *Achilles's heel*; *for convenience's sake*; *Moses's miracles*; *Demosthenes's speeches*. In any event, one can usually avoid possible awkwardness by showing possession with an *of*-phrase instead of *'s* (see #5, below):

    | | |
    |---|---|
    | for the sake of convenience | the poems of Keats |
    | the miracles of Moses | the bill of a platypus |

4.  To indicate the possessive case of plural nouns ending in *s*, add only an apostrophe:

    | | |
    |---|---|
    | the cannons' roar | the girls' sweaters |
    | the Joneses' garden | the Smiths' cottage |

5.  Possessive with *'s* or with *of*: Especially in formal writing, the *'s* form is more common with the names of living creatures, the *of* form with the names of inanimate things:

    | | |
    |---|---|
    | the cat's tail | the leg of the chair |
    | the girl's coat | the contents of the report |
    | Sheldon's home town | the surface of the desk |

## Proofreading Tip

### On Forming/Spelling Possessive Pronouns

Do not use apostrophes in possessive pronouns:

hers (*not* her's)            its (*not* it's)

ours (*not* our's)            theirs (*not* their's)

yours (*not* your's)          whose (*not* who's)

See also 3.1.

But both are acceptable with either category. The *'s* form, for example, is common with nouns that refer to things thought of as made up of people or animals or as extensions of them:

the team's strategy              the committee's decision

the company's representative     the government's policy

the city's bylaws                Canada's climate

the factory's output             the heart's affections

the law's delay

or things that are "animate" in the sense that they are part of nature:

the dawn's early light           the wind's velocity

the comet's tail                 the sea's surface

the plant's roots                the sky's colour

or periods of time:

today's paper                    a day's work

a month's wages                  winter's storms

Even beyond such uses the *'s* is not uncommon; sometimes there is a sense of personification, but not always:

beauty's ensign                  at death's door

freedom's light                  *Love's Labour's Lost*

time's fool                      the razor's edge

the ship's helm

If it seems natural and appropriate to you, go ahead and speak or write of a car's engine, a book's contents, a rocket's trajectory, a poem's imagery, and the like.

Conversely, for the sake of emphasis or rhythm you will occasionally want to use an *of*-phrase where *'s* would be normal; for example *the jury's verdict* lacks the punch of *the verdict of the jury*. You can also use an *of*-phrase to avoid awkward pronunciations (see above: those who don't like the sound of *Dickens's novels* can refer to *the novels of Dickens*) and unwieldy constructions (*the opinion of the minister of finance* is preferable to *the minister of finance's opinion*). Further, whether you use *'s* or just *s* to form the plural of letters, figures, and the like (see 51.22 [For plurals]), it is probably best, in order to avoid ambiguity, to form possessives of abbreviations with *of* rather than with apostrophes: *the opinion of the MLA, the opinion of the MLA's, the opinion of the MLAs*.

6. Double Possessives: There is nothing wrong with double possessive, showing possession with both an *of*-phrase and a possessive inflection. They are standard with possessive pronouns and can be used similarly with common and proper nouns:

| | |
|---|---|
| a favourite *of* mine | a friend *of* the family *or of* the family's |
| a friend *of* hers | a contemporary *of* Shakespeare *or of* Shakespeare's |

And a sentence like *The story was based on an idea of Shakespeare* is at least potentially ambiguous, whereas *The story was based on an idea of Shakespeare's* is clear. But if you feel that this sort of construction is unpleasant to the ear, you can usually manage to revise it to something like *on one of Shakespeare's ideas*. And avoid such double possessives with a *that* construction: *His hat was just like that of Arthur's*.

## 51.24 Spelling List

In addition to the words listed and discussed in the preceding pages, other words often cause spelling problems. Following is a list of frequently misspelled words. If you are at all weak in spelling, you should test yourself on these words, as well as those discussed earlier.

But you should also keep your own spelling list: whenever you mis-spell a word, add it to your list, and try to decide which rule the error violates or which category of error it falls into. Write only the correct spelling of the word: never write a misspelled word—even deliberately—when making your list, since this may reinforce the incorrect spelling in your mind when your goal should be to forget it. If a word continues to give you trouble, it can help to concentrate not on the rules that govern its spelling but on how the word looks, by taking a mental "photo" of it. Practise spelling the words on your list until you have mastered them.

| | | |
|---|---|---|
| absence | burglar | curiosity |
| absorption | buried | cylinder |
| accessible | cafeteria | decorative |
| acclaim | calendar | decrepit |
| accumulate | calvinist | defence (*or* defense) |
| acknowledgement | camaraderie | defensive |
| acquaintance | candidate | delusion |
| acquire | cannibal | desperate |
| additional | captain | develop |
| advertise | careful | devastation |
| adviser (*or* advisor) | carnival | diameter |
| aesthetic (*or* esthetic) | cartilage | dilemma |
| affection | catalogue | diminution |
| affidavit | category | dining |
| aging | cemetery | diphtheria |
| allege | chagrin | dispatch |
| alternately | challenge | dissatisfied |
| always | champion | dissipate |
| amateur | changeable | divide |
| amour | chocolate | doctor |
| analyze (*or* analyse) | cinnamon | drunkenness |
| analogy | clamour (*or* clamor) | eclectic |
| anonymous | clothed | ecstasy |
| anticipated | coincide | efficient |
| apartment | colossal | elegiac |

appall (*or* appal)

approach

architect

arctic

arithmetic

article

atmosphere

audience

automatically

auxiliary

axe (*or* ax)

background

beggar

beneficent

benefit

botany

bullet

buoyant

bureau

exaggerate

excel

exercise

exhausted

exhilarating

exorbitant

exuberant

facilities

fallacy

fascination

feasible

fervour (*or* fervor)

filter

flippant

flourish

flyer (*or* flier)

committee

complexion

comprise

comrade

concomitant

conqueror

conscious

consensus

conservative

consider

consumer

control

controlled

convenient

court

courteous

create

criticism

criticize (*or* criticise)

illegitimate

illiterate

imagery

imagination

imitate

immediate

impious

implementation

importance

imposter

improvise

inadequacy

incidentally

incompatible

indefinite

industrialization

eligible

embarrassment

emancipation

emphasize (*or* emphasise)

employee

emulate

encompass

encyclopedia

endeavour (*or* endeavor)

enforced

engraver

enterprise

epilogue

equip

equipment

equipped

erupt

euphonious

exalt

marriage

marshal

mattress

meant

medieval

melancholy

menace

metaphor

mineralogy

minuscule

mischievous

molester

monologue

monotonous

mould (*or* mold)

museum

focuses (*or* focusses)

foreign

foresee

forty

fulfill

fundamentally

furor

gaiety

gauge

genealogy

gleam

goddess

grammar

grey (*or* gray)

grievous

guarantee

guard

harass

harmonious

height

heinous

heroin

heroine

hesitancy

hindrance

homogeneous

horseshoe

household

humorous

hygienist

hypocrisy

hypocrite

illegal

plough (*or* plow)

poem

inevitable

influence

injuries

innocent

inoculate

inquire (*or* enquire)

integrated

interrupt

intimate

intriguing

jealousy

jeweller (*or* jeweler)

jewellery (*or* jewelry)

judgment (*or* judgement)

knowledge

knowledgeable

laboratory

leeches

library

licence (*or* license) (n.)

license (*or* licence) (v.)

lieutenant

likelihood

lineage

liquefy

liqueur

liquor

luxury

magnificent

mammoth

manoeuvre (*or* maneuver)

manual

manufactured

restaurant

rhythm

moustache (*or* mustache)

naive, naïveté

necessary

ninety

nosy (*or* nosey)

nostrils

numerous

obstacle

occurred

occurrence

offence (*or* offense)

omniscient

oneself

operator

opulent

ostracize (*or* ostracise)

paralleled (*or* parallelled)

paralyze (*or* paralyse)

paraphernalia

parliament

partner

peculiar

peddler

perfectible

perseverance

personality

personify

personnel

persuade

pharaoh

phony (*or* phoney)

plagiarism

playwright

superintendent

susceptible

pollution

porous

positioning

possession

practicality

practice

practise (v.), practice (n.)

predecessors

prejudice

prestige

pretense (or pretence)

primitive

procedure

proletariat

prominent

proscenium

psychiatry

psychology

pursue

putrefy

puzzled

quandary

quantity

quatrain

quizzically

rarefied

reality

recognize

recommend

reflection

registration

reminisce

repel

repetition

ridiculous

sacrifice

safety

scandal

skeptic (or sceptic)

sentence

separate

sheik

shepherd

sheriff

shining

shiny

signifies

simile

sincerity

siphon (or syphon)

simultaneous

skiing

skilful (or skillful)

smoulder (or smolder)

solely

soliloquy

species

spectators

speech

sponsor

storey (or story) (floor)

straddle

strategy

stretched

styrofoam

subconsciously

subsequent

subtly

suspense

symbolic

symbolize (or symbolise)

symmetry

synonymous

syrup

tariff

temperament

temperature

territory

theory

therein

threshold

tragedy

trailed

tranquility (or tranquillity)

transferred

troubadour

tyranny

unavailing

undoubtedly

unmistakable

until

usefulness

vehicle

veterinarian

weary

whisky (or whiskey)

wilful (or willful)

wintry

wistfulness

withdrawal

writing

written

# CHAPTER VI
# Diction

# INTRODUCTION

## Style and the Larger Elements of Composition

Jonathan Swift's definition of style may be the best, at least for simplicity and directness: "Proper words in proper places make the true definition of a style." In its broadest sense, style consists of everything that is not the content of what is being expressed. It is the manner more than the matter: everything that is a part of the way something is said constitutes its style.

But though many of us distinguish between style and content to facilitate discussion and analysis, the distinction is in some ways arbitrary, for the two are inseparable. Since the way in which something is expressed inevitably influences the effect, it is necessarily part of what is being expressed. "I have a hangover" may say essentially the same thing as "I'm feeling a bit fragile this morning," but the different styles of the statements create different effects, different meanings. The medium, then, if it is not the entire message, is a substantial part of it.

An important attribute of style is tone, usually defined as a writer's attitude toward both subject matter and audience. Tone in writing is analogous to tone in speech. We hear or describe someone as speaking in a sarcastic tone of voice, or as sounding jolly, or angry, or matter-of-fact. Writing, like speech, can "sound" ironic, conversational, intimate, morbid, tragic, frivolous, cold, impassioned, comic, coy, energetic, phlegmatic, detached, sneering, contemptuous, laudatory, condescending, and so forth. The tone of a piece of writing— whether an entire book or only a sentence—largely determines the feeling or impression that writing creates.

The style of a piece of writing, including its tone, arises from such features as syntax, point of view, and even punctuation. But it is largely determined by diction: by choice of words, figurative language, and sounds. Diction, then, is near the heart of effective writing and style. No amount of correct grammar or rhetorical skill can compensate for poor diction. This chapter isolates the principal difficulties writers encounter in choosing and using words, and offers some suggestions for overcoming them.

# 52. DICTIONARIES

The first suggestion is the simplest one: when you think "diction," think "dictionary." Make sure you have a good dictionary, and use it to full advantage. Become familiar with it: find out how it works, and discover the variety of information it offers. A good dictionary doesn't merely give you the spelling, pronunciation, and meaning of words; it also offers advice on such matters as usage and idioms to help you decide on the best word for a particular context; it lists irregularities in the principal parts of verbs, in the inflection of adjectives and adverbs, and in the formation of plurals; it supplies etymologies (or word histories); it tells you if a word or phrase is considered formal, informal, slang, or archaic. And it usually has an interesting and useful introductory essay and relevant appendices. Take advantage of the many resources of your dictionary.

Whether you're browsing through the reference section of your library or considering the vast selection of dictionaries at your local bookstore, you may feel overwhelmed by the number of dictionaries available to you. The following sections offer some advice on how to find the dictionary that's most appropriate for your needs.

## 52.1 Kinds of Dictionaries

Dictionaries range in scope and function from multi-volume works offering detailed word histories to tiny word books designed to fit in your pocket for quick reference. Most of the information you will require will be contained in one of three kinds of dictionary: an unabridged dictionary, an abridged dictionary, or a learners' dictionary for students of English as an additional language.

### Unabridged dictionaries

Unabridged dictionaries, in one or more volumes, offer the most comprehensive view of English as it is now and has been used. The twenty-volume *Oxford English Dictionary* (2nd edn, 1989), the most famous of unabridged dictionaries, is based on historical principles, which means that it presents definitions for each word, accompanied by historical quotations, in the order of their first recorded use. The *OED* is most useful when you want to see how the meaning of a word has changed over time. For example, a look at the *OED*'s entry for *silly* will enable you to trace the word to its Old English roots, when it meant "fortunate; blessed by God," to Middle English, when it meant "deserving of compassion," to the sixteenth century, when it came to be used to mean "showing a lack of judgment or common sense." The *OED* is available on CD-ROM, and most libraries subscribe to the *OED Online*, which is updated quarterly and offers a convenient way to search for the information you might need.

Not all unabridged dictionaries are based on historical principles, nor do they all comprise multiple volumes. *Webster's Third New International Dictionary* and the *Random House Webster's Unabridged Dictionary* are excellent single-volume unabridged dictionaries. Though the former is rather out of date, an updated version is available online for a monthly or annual fee. The latter is available on CD-ROM. (Be aware that there is no copyright on the name *Webster's*, so many American dictionary publishers use the name in their titles hoping that the good reputation of the famous American lexicographer Noah Webster will rub off on their own products.)

### Abridged dictionaries

Although some questions will demand online research or a trip to the library to consult an unabridged dictionary, an abridged dictionary is the most useful for the everyday needs of most writers. An abridged dictionary may be as large as the two-volume *Shorter Oxford English Dictionary* or as small as a mini-dictionary, but the most practical is a "college" or "desk dictionary" that includes words and senses in current use, along with some historical senses, pronunciations, illustrative examples, etymologies, usage notes, and "encyclopedic" entries that provide information on people and places.

For years Canadians had to choose from among British and American dictionaries such as the *Concise Oxford Dictionary*, *Collins English Dictionary*, *Random House Webster's College Dictionary*, and *Merriam Webster's Collegiate Dictionary*. Today there are some very good desk dictionaries produced in Canada, including the *Canadian Oxford Dictionary* and the *Collins Canadian Dictionary*, which offer a more accurate reflection of the language as it is spoken, written, and used by Canadians.

### Learners' dictionaries

Although learners' dictionaries are designed especially for people whose first language is not English, the advice on usage and grammar and the simplified defining style of several excellent learners' dictionaries make them enormously helpful even to native speakers of English. Some learner's dictionaries use a limited defining vocabulary of a few thousand words likely to be understood, or at least recognized, by readers of English as an additional language. This reduces the chances that a definition will contain words the user will have to look up.

A good learners' dictionary features numerous notes and examples to illustrate the idiomatic use of words. It may contain additional pages of information on such matters as understanding English grammar and spelling, and writing tests, essays, and letters. Some excellent learners' dictionaries include the *Oxford ESL Dictionary*, the *Oxford Advanced Learner's Dictionary*, the *Collins Cobuild*

## Research Tip

### Assessing the Size of a Dictionary

The standard way to gauge a dictionary's size is to count its entries. An entry is any word, form of a word, component of a word, or phrase that is presented explicitly as a distinct element of the English language. These elements are usually set in bold type. When a dictionary presents itself as having a certain number of entries, then, it is in fact giving a total of all the words and phrases in bold type in the text.

Some dictionaries advertise themselves as including a certain number of definitions. Since there are usually several definitions for any defined word, a dictionary's definition count will be greater than its entry count: don't compare one dictionary's entries with another's definitions.

*English Dictionary for Advanced Learners*, and the *Longman Dictionary of Contemporary English*.

Some learners of English find it useful to keep a dictionary on hand for troublesome words that occur in conversation or during reading. In this situation, a desk dictionary is unwieldy, and a compact or paperback learners' dictionary is more appropriate. Bear in mind, however, that although dictionary makers have certain methods of shrinking dictionaries without removing content—for example, by using more abbreviations or by reducing the type size—a smaller dictionary usually means some loss of useful material, and so some archaic or less common words may be removed, or etymologies may be truncated.

## 52.2 Features of Dictionaries

Most people who consult a dictionary are looking for one of two things: the meaning of a word, or the spelling of a word. When assessing a dictionary, it is helpful to know how its editors made their decisions about meaning and spelling. Was their research based on analysis of a large corpus of English texts? An extensive reading program designed to capture new words and usages? If it is a Canadian dictionary, what kind of research was used to determine preferred Canadian spellings? All of this sort of information can usually be found on the inside dust jacket.

You will also want to make sure that the dictionary you're using is up to date and not just a recent reissue of an older work. When comparing dictionaries, have a list of newer words and see how many of them are included in each of the dictionaries you're considering. This should give you a good indication of whether or not a dictionary is sufficiently up to date.

Beyond meaning and spelling, a dictionary entry includes several features that may be useful. Deciding how important each of the following is to you will help you decide which dictionary is most appropriate for your needs.

### Word breaks

Most North American dictionaries and some learner's dictionaries indicate syllable breaks or word breaks in headwords and other bold forms by means of points ( · ), pipes ( | ), or other symbols. Knowing an unfamiliar word's syllabication can make it easier to pronounce.

It can also help if you need to hyphenate a long word at the end of a line. Remember, though, that not all syllable breaks are good places to insert a hyphen; in some multisyllabic words there is no desirable place to insert a hyphen, and these words should not be broken at all (see 45.2, 51.15).

## Pronunciations

All dictionaries contain pronunciations, though some may not provide pronunciations for all words. A dictionary may transcribe a word's pronunciation using the International Phonetic Alphabet, or IPA, so that various sounds are represented by specific symbols that are usually displayed across the bottom of the page. Or a dictionary may "respell" the word using a combination of letters and diacritical marks to indicate long and short vowels.

|               | IPA          | respelling  |
|---------------|--------------|-------------|
| curtains      | 'kɜrtənz     | kûr´tnz     |
| eavestroughing | 'iːvzˌtrɒfiŋ | ēvz´trôfiŋ  |
| shrivel       | 'ʃrɪvəl      | shriv´əl    |
| cookie        | 'kʊki        | kŏŏk´ē      |

The IPA pronunciations, though they may appear at first confusing, produce the most accurate representations of a word's pronunciation. The respelling method is the easiest way to convey a reasonably accurate pronunciation without the user's having to learn a complicated set of symbols.

## Examples and illustrations

Definitions for technical words can often be enhanced with illustrations. Consider the following definition, from *Webster's New World Dictionary*: "a lamp in which the light is produced by a filament of conducting material contained in a vacuum and heated to incandescence by an electric current." This definition, though accurate, likely will not produce for the reader a perfect idea of "incandescent lamp" the way the accompanying illustration of a standard light bulb does. Not all dictionaries contain illustrations, and of those that do, some provide illustrations to accompany definitions that don't really require them. If you are considering the suitability of a dictionary with illustrations, make sure the illustrations really benefit the definitions they accompany, bearing in mind that illustrations often take space away from definitions. The *Oxford Picture Dictionary: Canadian Edition* is an excellent illustrated dictionary for Canadians.

Picture dictionaries are often well paired with learners' dictionaries, which will greatly enhance a definition by providing an example that shows the way a word is used in a sentence. This is an important feature of learners' dictionaries, which strive to show their users not just what words mean but how they should be used in natural speech.

## Usage information

An important thing to remember about dictionaries is that they are descriptive, not prescriptive. This means that they record the language as it is actually used, not as some people think it should be used. As a result, a dictionary includes words or senses that may meet with the disapproval of some users. For example, most dictionaries include two nearly opposite definitions for the word *peruse*: "to read thoroughly or carefully" (the original sense), and "to read in a casual manner" (the more common sense). Many critics object to the second use, yet it would be inappropriate for a dictionary to exclude this sense, since it is the one most people have in mind when they use the word. A good dictionary will point out the usage issue in a brief note in the entry.

Most dictionaries also include register labels to indicate whether a word is formal, informal, slang, archaic, and so on.

## Idioms and phrasal verbs

An idiom is an expression whose meaning is not easily deduced from the meanings of the words it comprises, for example *a flash in the pan*, *take one on the chin*, *be run off one's feet*. Idioms and phrasal, or two-part, verbs (see 11.4) are often defined at the end of a word's entry. Bear in mind that an idiom such as *flash in the pan* could be defined at the entry for *flash* or the entry for *pan*.

## Derivatives

A derivative is a word derived from another, such as *quickness* or *quickly* from *quick*. It is common for dictionaries to "nest" undefined derivatives at the main entry for a word if the derivatives' meanings can be easily deduced. For example, a word like *logically* does not require a separate definition as long as *logical* is well defined; the reader can safely assume that *logically* means "in a logical manner." But the word *practically* should not be nested in the entry for *practical*, since it has a sense beyond "in a practical manner." Be aware that some smaller dictionaries, in order to save space, nest derivatives that should be defined separately; this is something you should keep in mind when evaluating the usefulness of a dictionary.

### Etymologies

Knowing a word's etymology, its original form and meaning, can sometimes help you remember or get a clearer idea of its meaning. For example, knowing that the word *recalcitrant* comes from a Latin word meaning "kicking back," from *calx* ("heel"), may help you remember that it means "stubborn, uncooperative." And knowing that *peruse* comes from the prefix *per*, meaning "thoroughly", plus *use* will help you understand why some critics object to its use to mean "read in a casual manner." A word's etymology can be fascinating as well as helpful: *climax* comes from a Greek word for ladder, *vegetable* comes from a Latin verb meaning "to be healthy," *pyjamas* comes from a Persian word meaning "leg clothing." If you find this kind of information interesting, make sure your dictionary goes into detail in its etymologies. Reading that *berserk* comes from an Old Norse compound meaning "bear coat" or that *amethyst* comes from a Greek word meaning "not drunk" without any accompanying explanation can be unsatisfying.

### Canadian content

Because Canada has its own political, cultural, historical, and geographical realities, it has its own words to describe these realities. As a result of Canada's unique history and settlement patterns, Canadian English also includes words borrowed from languages that do not appear in other varieties of English. Since dictionaries inevitably describe and reflect the language and culture of the country in which they are edited, American dictionaries and British dictionaries overlook some words, senses, spellings, and pronunciations that are unique to Canadian English. Good Canadian dictionaries, such as the *Canadian Oxford Dictionary* and the *Collins Canadian*

*Dictionary*, offer a more accurate view of Canadian English than either American or British dictionaries.

### Encyclopedic entries

Some abridged dictionaries include entries for important people, places, and events. These may be quite short, consisting of little more than a person's years of birth and death or a city's population, or they can provide more information about a person's life and work or a city's importance. If you are considering dictionaries with encyclopedic entries, pick a couple of people or places and see how various dictionaries treat them.

## 52.3 Three Sample Dictionary Entries

The following three entries, from an abridged, a compact, and a learners' dictionary, illustrate some of the features just described. Dictionaries follow certain conventions, but each features a unique design. A final consideration when judging the suitability of a dictionary is how easy it is for you to navigate through it.

part of speech

headword

**table ●** *noun* **1 a** a piece of furniture with a flat top and one or more legs, providing a level surface for eating, writing, or working at, playing games on, etc. **b** (*attributive*) designating an object designed to sit or be used on a table (*table clock*). **2** a flat surface serving a specified purpose (*altar table*). **3 a** food provided in a household (*keeps a good table*). **b** a group seated at table for dinner etc. **4 a** a set of facts or figures systematically displayed, esp. in columns (*a table of contents*). **b** matter contained in this. **5** a flat surface for working on or for machinery to operate on. **6 a** a slab of wood or stone etc. for bearing an inscription. **b** matter inscribed on this. **7** = TABLELAND. **8** *Archit.* **a** a flat usu. rectangular vertical surface. **b** a horizontal moulding, esp. a cornice. **9 a** a flat surface of a gem. **b** a cut gem with two flat faces. **10** each half or quarter of a folding board for backgammon. **11** (prec. by *the*) = BARGAINING TABLE (*sought to draw them back to the table*). **12** any plane or level area (*water table*). **●** *transitive verb* **1** *Cdn & Brit.* bring forward for discussion or consideration at a meeting. **2** esp. *US* postpone consideration of (a matter). ¶ Because both of these contradictory meanings are in use in Canada, confusion may arise if the verb *table* is used outside of the strictly parliamentary context, where the first sense should be understood. As a result, it is better to use a different verb altogether, such as *present* or *postpone*, as the context requires. □ **at table** taking a meal at a table. **lay on the table 1** submit for discussion. **2** esp. *US* postpone indefinitely. **on the table** offered for discussion. **turn the tables** (often foll. by *on*) reverse one's relations (with), esp. by turning an inferior into a superior position (originally in backgammon). **under the table** *informal* **1** (of a transaction etc., esp. payment) done surreptitiously esp. to avoid taxes or duties. **2** very drunk after a meal or drinking bout. □ **table‑ful** *noun* (*pl.* **-fuls**). **tabling** *noun* [Old French from Latin *tabula* plank, tablet, list]

grammatical information

cross reference

example

subject label

geographic label

usage note

idioms

register label

derivative

etymology

word break

inflection

From the *Canadian Oxford Dictionary* (2nd edn: 2004).

**WRITING TIP**
**table**

In Canada *to table a bill* usually means "to introduce a bill for discussion," especially in parliamentary contexts, while in the US it means "to set a bill aside indefinitely." Because of these contradictory senses, make sure your meaning is clear if you use the word, or use another word instead, e.g. **introduce** or **set aside**.

*usage box*

*part of speech*
*headword*
*example*
*geographic label*
*idioms (phrases)*
*register label*

**table** • *noun* **1** a piece of furniture with a flat top and one or more legs. **2** a group seated at table for dinner etc. **3** a set of facts or figures systematically displayed, esp. in columns: *a table of contents.* **4** a flat surface for working on or for machinery to operate on. **5** a tableland. **6** (**the table**) = BARGAINING TABLE: *sought to draw them back to the table.* **7** any plane or level area: *water table.* • *verb* (**tables, tabled, tabling**) **1** *Cdn & Brit.* bring forward for discussion or consideration at a meeting. **2** esp. *US* postpone consideration of (a matter). PHRASES **at table** taking a meal at a table. **lay on the table 1** submit for discussion. **2** esp. *US* postpone indefinitely. **on the table** offered for discussion. **turn the tables** (often foll. by *on*) reverse one's relations (with), esp. by turning an inferior into a superior position (originally in backgammon). **under the table** *informal* **1** (of a transaction etc., esp. payment) done surreptitiously esp. to avoid taxes or duties. **2** very drunk after a meal or drinking bout.

*variant*
*cross reference*
*verb forms*
*grammatical information*

From the *Student's Canadian Oxford Dictionary* (2004).

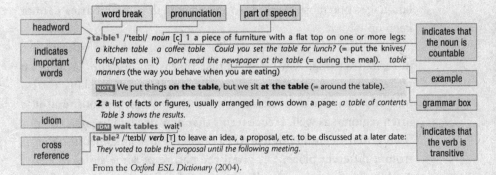

*headword*
*word break*
*pronunciation*
*part of speech*
*indicates important words*

**ta·ble¹** /'teɪbl/ *noun* [C] **1** a piece of furniture with a flat top on one or more legs: *a kitchen table   a coffee table   Could you set the table for lunch?* (= put the knives/forks/plates on it)   *Don't read the newspaper at the table* (= during the meal).   *table manners* (the way you behave when you are eating)

NOTE We put things **on the table**, but we sit **at the table** (= around the table).

**2** a list of facts or figures, usually arranged in rows down a page: *a table of contents   Table 3 shows the results.*
IDM **wait tables** wait¹
**ta·ble²** /'teɪbl/ *verb* [T] to leave an idea, a proposal, etc. to be discussed at a later date: *They voted to table the proposal until the following meeting.*

*indicates that the noun is countable*
*example*
*grammar box*
*indicates that the verb is transitive*

*idiom*
*cross reference*

From the *Oxford ESL Dictionary* (2004).

# 53. LEVEL

In any piece of writing, use words that are appropriate to you, to your topic, and to the circumstances in which you are writing. That is, consider the occasion, the purpose, and the audience. Avoid words and phrases that call attention to themselves rather than to the meaning you want to convey. In formal writing, adopt diction appropriate to the topic on which and the audience for which you are writing. Avoid slang and colloquial or informal terms at one extreme, and pretentious language at the other. Of course there will be times when one or the other, or both, will be useful—for example to make a point in a particularly telling way, to achieve a humorous effect, or to make dialogue sound realistic. But it is usually preferable to adopt a straightforward, moderate style, a medium level of diction that both respects the intelligence of the reader and strives to communicate with the reader as effectively as possible. (See also 11.5.)

## 53.1 Slang

Since slang is diction opposite to formal diction, it is seldom appropriate in a formal context. There is nothing inherently wrong with slang; it is undeniably a colourful part of the language and can help you express complicated ideas with clarity and force. But its very liveliness and vigour make it faddish: some slang terms remain in vogue only for a few weeks, some linger on for a few years, and new ones are constantly popping up to replace those going out of fashion. Some slang terms eventually become part of the standard written language, but most slang is so ephemeral that dictionaries cannot keep up with it.

It is principally slang's transitoriness that makes it risky to use in formal writing. A word or phrase that is *hot* (or *cool*) when you write it may sound stale and dated soon after. Much slang is also limited to particular social groups, classes, or professions, and it is often regional as well. Hence terms that may be vivid to you and your friends may be unintelligible to an outsider, such as someone older or from a different place. Or, given the nature of some slang words, a reader who finds them intelligible may also find them offensive.

If you are considering using slang in your writing, consult not only one or more good dictionaries but also members of your audience: trust your ear, your common sense, and your good taste.

## Proofreading Tip

### On Slang and the Use of Quotation Marks

If you do use a slang term, do not use quotation marks to call attention to it (see 43.7).

## 53.2 Informal, Colloquial

Even dictionaries can't agree on what constitutes slang versus informal or colloquial usage. Slang terms are in one sense simply extreme examples of the colloquial or informal. Nevertheless, there are many words and phrases that may be labelled *inf* or *colloq* in a dictionary, and although not slang, they do not ordinarily belong in formal writing. For example, unless you are aiming for a somewhat informal level, you should avoid such abbreviations as *esp., etc., no., orig.,* and *OK*; and you should also avoid contractions (*can't, don't,* etc.), though they are common in our own discourse in this book and in everyday speech.

Here are more examples of informal or colloquial usages that would be out of place in strictly formal writing:

| informal or colloquial | acceptable equivalents |
| --- | --- |
| absolutely | very, thoroughly |
| a lot of, lots of, lots | much, many, a great deal of |
| anyplace, everyplace, noplace, someplace | anywhere, everywhere, nowhere, somewhere |
| around | approximately |
| awful | bad, ill, ugly, unpleasant, etc. |
| back of, in back of | behind |
| be sure and | be sure to |
| chance of + gerund (e.g., chance of getting) | chance + infinitive (chance to get) |
| expect (as in "I expect you want me here") | suppose, suspect, imagine |
| figure | think, believe, etc. |
| fix (verb) | prepare (food or drink); manipulate fraudulently (an election, a contract, a competition) |
| fix (noun) | predicament |
| funny | odd, peculiar, strange, unusual |
| guess (as in "I guess that. . .") | believe, suppose, think |
| mean | cruel, evil, deceitful, etc. |

| informal or colloquial | acceptable equivalents |
|---|---|
| most (as in "most everyone") | almost, nearly |
| nice | agreeable, attractive, pleasant, etc. |
| nowhere near | not nearly, not at all, not anywhere near |
| out loud | aloud |
| over with | ended, finished, done |
| phone | telephone |
| photo | photograph |
| plan on + gerund (e.g., plan on going) | plan + infinitive (plan to go) |
| quite, quite a bit, quite a few, quite a lot | somewhat, rather, many, a large amount, much |
| real, really (as intensive adverb) | very, greatly, surely |
| right away, right now | immediately, at once |
| shape (good, bad, etc.) | condition |
| show up | appear, arrive; prove better than, best |
| size up | judge, assess |
| sure and (as in "be sure and call") | sure to |
| terrible, terribly (also as vague modifiers) | unpleasant, uncomfortable, very, extremely |
| try and | try to |
| wait on | await, wait for |
| where (as in "I see where we're in for fun") | that |

In addition, many words have been so abused in advertising, used for gushy and exaggerated effect, that they can now seldom be used with precision in formal writing. For example:

|       |       |       |
|-------|-------|-------|
| awesome | fantastic | marvelous |
| stupendous | terrific | tremendous |

## 53.3 "Fine Writing"

Unnecessarily formal or pretentious diction is called "fine writing"—here, an ironic term of disapproval. Efforts to impress with such writing almost always backfire. For example, imagine yourself trying to take seriously someone who wrote "It was felicitous that the canine in question was demonstrably more exuberant in emitting threatening sounds than in attempting to implement said threats by engaging in actual physical assault," instead of simply saying "Luckily, the dog's bark was worse than its bite." This is an exaggerated example, of course; but it illustrates how important it is to be natural (within reason) and straightforward. Writers who overreach themselves often use supposedly elegant terms incorrectly. The individual who wrote "Riding majestically down the street on a magnificent float was the Festival Queen surrounded by all her courtesans" was striving for sophistication, but succeeded only in getting an undesired laugh from the reader who knew the correct meaning of *courtesans*.

# 54. FIGURATIVE LANGUAGE

Strictly speaking, figurative language includes mostly "figures of speech," such as personification, synecdoche, metonymy, hyperbole, litotes, and even paradox, irony, and symbolism. Generally, however, the term *figurative language* refers to metaphoric language, whose most common devices are the metaphor and the simile. A simile is an explicit comparison that is usually marked by *like* or *as*:

> The river *is like* a snake winding across the plain.

> The Internet *is like* a highway without speed limits.

A metaphor, on the other hand, is an implicit comparison; the items being compared are assumed to be identical:

> The river *is* a snake winding its way across the plain.

> The Internet *is* a highway without speed limits.

Often a metaphor is condensed into a verb:

> The river *snakes* its way across the plain.

an adjective:

> The *serpentine* river meanders across the plain.

or an adverb:

> The river winds *snakily* across the plain.

Figurative language is often an important element of good style. Writing that lacks it will be relatively dry, flat, and dull. But remember that a good metaphor doesn't merely enhance style: it also sharpens meaning. Use metaphors not only for their own sake, but to convey meaning more effectively. For example, to say that "the hillside was covered with a profusion of colourful flowers" is clear enough; but if one writes instead that "the hillside was a tapestry of spring blossoms," the metaphor not only enriches the style but also provides readers with something concrete (see 54.1), an image (that of the tapestry) that helps them visualize the scene.

## 54.1 Inappropriate Metaphors

If you force a metaphor into your writing just to embellish style, it will likely be inappropriate and call attention to itself rather than enhance the desired meaning. It will, to use a tired but still expressive simile, stick out like a sore thumb. For example, "the tide of emotion suddenly stopped" doesn't work, since tides don't start and stop; they ebb and flow. And a phrase like "bomb craters blossoming all over the landscape" works only if one intends the inherent discord between bombs and blossoms. And a simile such as "he ran like an ostrich in heat" may confuse the reader with inappropriate associations.

## 54.2 Overextended Metaphors

Extended metaphors can be effective, but don't let yourself become so enamoured with a metaphor that you extend it too far, to the point where it takes control of what is being said:

> When she came out of the surf her hair looked like limp spaghetti. A sauce of seaweed and sand, looking like spinach and grated cheese, had been carelessly applied, the red flower fastened in her tresses looked like a wayward piece of tomato, and globs of mud clung like meatballs to the pasty pasta of her face. The fork of my attention hovered hesitatingly over this odd dish. Clearly I would need more than one glass of the red wine of remembered beauty and affection to wash it all down.

This may all be very clever, but after the first sentence—the spaghetti image itself being somewhat questionable—one quickly loses sight of the original descriptive intention and becomes mired in all the associated metaphors and similes; in short, a reader is likely to feel fed up and turn to something less overdone.

## 54.3 Dead Metaphors

Guard against dead metaphors and clichés (see 60.5). The language contains many dead metaphors like the *"leg* of a table," *"branching* out," and *"flew* to the rescue," which are acceptable since we no longer think of them as metaphors. But many other metaphors, whether altogether dead or only moribund but with little metaphoric force left, can be ineffective. Such overused phrases as *the ladder to success, making mountains out of molehills, nipped in the bud, flogging a dead horse,* and *between the devil and the deep blue sea* are usually muddying and soporific instead of enlivening and clarifying.

Occasionally, however, a dead or trite metaphor can be revivified if consciously used in a fresh way. For example, the hackneyed phrase *bit off more than he could chew* was given new life by the person who, discussing Henry James's writing, said that James "chewed more than he bit off." *Sound as a dollar* would these days be more appropriately rendered as "unpredictable as the loonie." Even a slangy phrase like *chew the fat* might be transformed and updated in a description of people sitting down to "chew the bad cholesterol." But take some care, for such attempts can misfire; like an over-extended metaphor, they sometimes call attention to their own cleverness at the expense of the intended meaning.

## 54.4 Mixed Metaphors

Edit out of your writing incongruously mixed metaphors. The person who wrote, of the Great Depression, that "what began as a zephyr soon blossomed into a giant" had lost control of metaphor. The following paragraph about Shakespeare's *Othello* was written by one who obviously began with the good intention of using metaphors to describe the evil of Iago, but who became lost in a maze of contradictions and incongruities:

> Iago has spun his web and like a spider he waits. His beautiful web of silk is so fragile and yet it captures the souls of its victims by gently

luring them into his womb. Unsuspecting are those unfortunate creatures who sense the poisonous venom oozing through their veins. It has a tranquil effect, for it numbs the mind with its magical potion. The victims are transformed into pawns as they satisfy the queen's appetite and so they serve their purpose.

Here, in contrast, is a paragraph that successfully uses a single extended metaphor to create its effect:

I remember vividly my first days as a teacher. They were the closest I have ever come to knowing what it must feel like to be part of a high-wire act. Walking into that high school classroom for the first time was like taking the first tentative steps onto the wire: the eyes of the audience were upon me, my knees were shaking, and I was struggling to keep my balance. But as that first morning went on and as my students and I moved forward into the lesson, I felt the exhilaration of the high-wire performer as she finds her equilibrium and moves with confidence to the middle and then the end of that tightrope. The only thing missing was the cheering.

Certainly, then, use figurative language. It can lend grace and charm and liveliness and clarity to your writing. But be alert to its potential pitfalls: inappropriate, overextended, and mixed metaphors.

# 55. CONCRETE AND ABSTRACT DICTION; WEAK GENERALIZATIONS

## 55.1 Concreteness and Specificity

Concrete words denote tangible things, capable of being apprehended by our physical senses (*children, skyscraper, flowers, parks, broccoli, ice, fire, walking*). Abstract words denote intangible things, like ideas or qualities (*postmodernism, agriculture, nature, health, creativity, progress*). Much of the writing you do is likely a blend of the abstract and the concrete. The more concrete your writing, the more readily your readers will grasp it, for the concreteness will provide images for their imaginations to respond to. If you write

Transportation is becoming a major problem in our city.

and leave it at that, readers will understand you. But if you write, or add,

> In the downtown core of our city, far too many cars and far too few buses travel the streets.

you know that your readers will see exactly what you mean: in their minds they will see the traffic jams and the overloaded buses.

As your writing moves from generalizations to specifics, it will move from the abstract to the concrete. And the more specific your writing is, the clearer and more effective it will often be. *General* and *specific* are relative terms: a general word designates a class (e.g. *modes of transportation*); a less general or more specific word designates members of that class (*vehicles*, *ships*, *airplanes*); a still more specific word designates members of a still smaller class (*cars*, *trucks*, *bicycles*, *buses*); and so on, getting narrower and narrower, the classes and sub-classes getting smaller and smaller, until—if one wants or needs to go that far—one arrives at a single, unique item, a class of one, such as the particular car sitting in your own parking spot, driveway, or garage.

Of course it is appropriate to write about "plant life," and then to narrow it, say, to "flowers"; and if you can write about "marigolds," "roses," "daffodils," and so on, you'll be more specific. Even the generalization "fire" is unquestionably vivid, but "forest fires" makes it sharper, and mentioning the specific example of "the huge forest fires in the B.C. Interior" will likely enable you to make your point even more sharply. Don't vaguely write "We experienced a warm day" when you could write more clearly, "We stayed outdoors all afternoon in the 25-degree weather," or "We basked in the warm spring sunshine all afternoon." Don't write "I found the city interesting" when you could write "I admired the city's architecture and enjoyed its nightlife," or, better still, "I was fascinated by the architecture in the city's French quarter, and I took delight in the many fine cafés, restaurants, and jazz clubs that I found there."

The following passage makes sense, but its abstractness and generality prevent it from being more memorable or effective:

> If one makes a purchase that a short time later proves to have been ill-advised due to the rapid deterioration of quality, then it is the opinion of this writer that one has every right to seek redress either

by expressing one's displeasure to the individual who conducted the original transaction or, if it should prove necessary, by resorting to litigation.

Writers sometimes assume that this kind of language is good because it sounds formal and sophisticated. But notice how much more vivid a revised version is:

> If you buy a car on Thursday and the engine falls out of it on Saturday, I think you should complain to the dealer who sold it to you, and sue him if necessary to get back the good money you paid for what turned out to be a useless vehicle.

Of course, abstract and general terms are legitimate and often necessary, for one can scarcely present all ideas concretely, and the kind of concrete language illustrated in the above example is hardly appropriate to all situations. Try, though, to be as concrete and specific as your subject and the context will allow.

## 55.2 Weak Generalizations

A common weakness in writing is an overdependence on unsupported generalizations. Consider: "Children today are reluctant readers." Few readers would or should accept such a general assertion, for the statement calls for considerably more illustration, evidence, and qualification. It evokes all kinds of questions: All children? Of all ages? In all countries? What are they reluctant to read? What is the connotation of "reluctant" here? Is such reluctance really something new? Merely stating a generalization or assumption is not enough; to be clear and effective it must be illustrated and supported by specifics.

Here are two sample pieces of writing on the same topic. Read the first one through:

> Travel can be a very broadening experience for people who go with the intention of having their eyes opened, which may often occur by unpleasant means. Culture shock can be a very unpleasant and hurtful experience to people who keep their eyes and minds closed to different attitudes or opinions. This problem of culture shock is an example of why people should prepare for the unexpected and try to learn from difficult experiences, rather than keeping a closed mind, which will cause them to come away with a grudge or hurt feelings.

Besides causing negative attitudes, travel can also confirm the prejudices of people with narrow minds. For example, I once met a man from England who had travelled around the world visiting the last vestiges of the British empire. He had even travelled to South Africa, and still come away with his colonialist attitudes.

Even if one goes to a country with an open mind, one may still come away with a superficial perception of that country. It takes time to get to know a country and understand its people. The time one spends in a country will thus greatly affect one's perception of that country.

Time is also needed before travelling begins, for people to read and learn about the area they will be going to. This background will enable them to look for things they might otherwise never see, and they will appreciate more the things they do discover. For example, if one knows something about the architecture of a country before one visits it, one can plan one's trip to include visits to buildings of special interest.

Thus an open, well-prepared mind will benefit from the experiences of travel, but otherwise travel is likely to have a very negative, narrowing effect on people's minds.

Now, without looking back at the essay, ask yourself what it said. You will probably have a vague sense of its thesis, and chances are you will remember something about a well-travelled but still narrow-minded traveller from England, and perhaps something about the advisability of knowing something in advance about foreign architecture— for those are the only two concrete items in the piece. (Think how much more vivid and therefore meaningful and memorable the point about architecture would have been had it included a reference to a specific landmark, such as the Leaning Tower of Pisa or the Taj Mahal or the Parthenon or St. Paul's Cathedral.)

Now read the second example, noting as you read how much clearer its points are than the relatively unsupported generalizations of the first sample pieces of writing:

Travel can be broadening. The knowledge gained in the areas of historical background, cultural diversity, and the range of personalities encountered in foreign lands gives us a fuller outlook on ourselves, on Canada and Canadian issues, and on our position in the global context.

The impact of history upon visitors to other lands is immense indeed. One cannot help but feel somewhat small when looking across valley upon valley of white crosses in France, coming face to face with the magnitude of death taking place in the World Wars of the last century. Before long, one realizes that many of the events that took place years ago have an effect upon the way in which we live today.

In some areas, scars of the recent past remain. The bits of rubble left from the once formidable Berlin Wall, for example, remind visitors that the way they live is not the same way others live, that, indeed, for decades millions lived grim and limited lives, never dreaming that in their lifetimes revolutionary changes would bring freedom, if not immediate comfort and prosperity.

This is not to say that there are not pleasant aspects of history as well. Sixteenth-century cobblestone lanes, usually less than ten feet wide, still remain in many old English villages, surrounded by Tudor cottages, complete with thatched roofs, oil lamps, and sculpted wrought-iron fences. Standing in such an environment and thinking about the writings of masters like Shakespeare brings out a much deeper and richer taste than merely reading about them at home. And places like this remind us of how our ancestors lived, making it easier to understand the customs and ideas of the past.

In going through different foreign lands, one cannot ignore the great cultural diversity. This is best illustrated by contrasting fiestas in Spain and Oktoberfest in Munich with Canadian celebrations. Many countries, besides having different languages (and dialects of those languages), also have their own dress, holidays, and religious beliefs. This variety is often startling to the tourist, who may take it for granted that what is standard for him or her is also the norm throughout much of the rest of the world.

There is also a wide range of social habits within a country. This is especially true of Britain, which still shows signs of its once all-powerful class system. A visitor from Canada may find it hard to understand such a system, not realizing that it is a centuries-old tradition; a son does the same job as his father, whether knight or knave, and lives in the same place, and often dies there.

Above all, the differences among people from other countries are what leave a visitor with the most lasting impression. From the street person in the slums of Casablanca, to the well-dressed gentleman walking briskly in the streets of Hanover, to the British executive sipping beer in "the local" on Hyde Street, there are myriad personalities as one travels through other lands. When we look at the world from this perspective, realizing that we are *not* all the same, we are better equipped to understand many of the problems throughout the globe.

The first writing sample is not without a message, for unsupported generalizations do have content, do say something; but the message of the second is clearer, more forceful; readers will better understand and remember what it said because their minds have something concrete and specific to hang on to.

## 56. CONNOTATION AND DENOTATION

Keep connotation in mind both to convey the meaning you intend and to enable yourself to convey particular shades of meaning you do intend. A word may denote (literally mean) what you want it to, yet connote (suggest) something you don't intend. For example, if you describe someone as "brash," your reader will understand the denotative meaning of "confident" but will also understand you to feel at least somewhat negative; if you in fact approve of the condition (and the person), you'll use a word like "self-assured," for its connotation is favourable rather than unfavourable.

## Proofreading Tip

### On Using a Thesaurus

It is best not to use an online or book-form thesaurus without using a standard dictionary in conjunction with it. Words listed together in such books are not necessarily identical in meaning; they can be subtly different not only in denotation but, especially, in connotation as well. A thesaurus is a vocabulary-building tool, but it should be used with care, for it can trap unwary writers into saying things they don't mean.

## 57. EUPHEMISM

Euphemisms are substitutes for words whose meanings are felt to be unpleasant and therefore, in certain circumstances, undesirable. In social settings we tend to ask for the location not of the toilet, which is what we want, but of the restroom, the bathroom, the washroom, or the powder room. Interestingly, the word *toilet* was itself once a euphemism.

But the euphemism is sometimes abused. Euphemisms used to gloss over some supposed unpleasantness may actually deceive. Innocent civilians killed in bombing raids are referred to as "collateral damage," and assassination squads are termed "special forces." What was once faced squarely as an economic depression is now, in an attempt to mitigate its negative implications, termed at worst a "recession," or an "economic downturn," or even a mere "growth cycle slowdown." Government officials who have patently lied admit only that they "misspoke" themselves.

Such euphemisms commonly imply a degree of dignity and virtue not justified by the facts. Calling genocide "ethnic cleansing" seriously distorts the meanings of both "ethnic" and "cleansing." Some euphemisms cloud or attempt to hide the facts in other ways. Workers are "laid off" or "declared redundant" or even "downsized" rather than "fired." A man who has died in a hospital is said to have "failed to fulfill his wellness potential" or undergone a "negative patient-care outcome." A spy is directed to "terminate with extreme prejudice" rather than "assassinate" or "murder." George Orwell, in his 1946 essay "Politics and the English Language," referred to such usages as linguistic dishonesty.

Other euphemisms help people avoid the unpleasant reality of death, which is often called "passing away" or "loss"; the lifeless body, the cadaver or corpse, is deemed "the remains." Such usages may be acceptable, even desirable, in certain circumstances, since they may enable one to avoid aggravating the pain and grief of the bereaved. But in other circumstances, direct, more precise diction is preferable.

Euphemisms that deceive are obviously undesirable. Others may be acceptable if circumstances seem to justify them, but one must exercise taste and judgment.

# 58. WRONG WORD

Incorrect word choice is an error in diction. The use of *infer* where the correct word is *imply* is an example. Don't write *effect* when you mean *affect*. Don't write *ex-patriot* when you mean *expatriate*. (See the lists of often-confused words, 51.12 and 51.13, and section 61.) But other kinds of wrong word choices occur as well; here are a few examples:

✘ Late in the summer I met my best friend, *which* I hadn't seen since graduation.

✘ Most men would have remembered spending several days in an open *ship* with little water and under the tropic sun as a terrible hardship, but Marlow recalls only that he felt he could "last forever, outlast the sea, the earth, and all men."

✘ Many miles of beach on the west coast of Vancouver Island are *absent* of rocks.

*Whom*, not *which,* is the correct pronoun for a person (see 3.4). The word *ship* won't do for a small open vessel like a rowboat; *boat* is the appropriate word here. The wrong phrase came to the third writer's mind; *devoid of* was the one wanted (and see section 59, on idiom).

# 59. IDIOM

A particular kind of word choice has to do with idiom. An idiom is an expression peculiar to a given language, one that may not make logical or grammatical sense but that is nevertheless understood because it is customary. The English expression "to sow one's wild oats," for example, if translated into another language would not have its idiomatic meaning; but French has an equivalent expression, *jeter sa gourme,* which would make little sense if translated literally into English. Here are some other peculiarly English turns of phrase: *to have a go at, to be down in the dumps, to be at loose ends.* You will notice that these idioms have a colloquial flavour about them, and may even sound like clichés or euphemisms; but other similar idioms are a part of our everyday language and occur in formal writing as well; for example, to "do justice to" something, to "take after" someone, to "get along with" someone.

Most mistakes in idiom result from using a wrong preposition in combination with certain other words. For example, we get *in* or *into* a car, but *on* or *onto* a bus; one is usually angry *with* a person, but *at* a thing; one is *fond of* something or someone, but one has *a fondness for* something or someone. Here are some examples of errors in idiom:

✖ Her feelings *toward* her new job are mixed.
  Her feelings *about* her new job are mixed.

✖ She took the liberty *to introduce* herself to the group.
  She took the liberty *of introducing* herself to the group.

✖ He plans to get married *with* my youngest sister.
  He plans to get married *to* my youngest sister.

✖ It is pleasant to live in close proximity *of* the ocean.
  It is pleasant to live in close proximity *to* the ocean.

Idiomatic expressions sometimes involve choosing between an infinitive and a prepositional gerund phrase. After some expressions either is acceptable; for example:

> He is afraid *to lose*. He is afraid *of losing*.

> They are hesitant *to attend*. They are hesitant *about attending*.

> They plan *to appeal*. They plan *on appealing*. (informal)

But some terms call for one or the other:

> They propose *to go*. They are prepared *to go*.

> They insist *on going*. They are insistent *on going*.

And sometimes when a word changes to a different part of speech, the kind of phrase that follows must also change:

> It was *possible to complete* the project in three days. We agreed on the *possibility of completing* the project in three days.

> Our tennis coach *emphasized basic skills*. Our tennis coach puts *emphasis* on basic skills.

> It is *pleasant to remember*. She spoke of the *pleasantness of remembering*.

But it isn't always predictable:

> He *intended to go*. He spoke of *his intention to go*. He had every *intention of going*.

And sometimes a *that*-clause is the only idiomatic possibility:

> I asked them *to attend*. I recommended *that they attend*. I requested *that they attend*.

See also section 61 (different from, different than; let, make; recommend; and very).

Idiom is a matter of usage. But a good learner's dictionary such as the *Oxford Advanced Learner's Dictionary* can often help. For example, if you look up *adhere*, you will find that it is to be used with *to*, so you would know not to write "adhere on" or "adhere with." Or, should you be wondering about using the word *oblivious*, your dictionary will inform you that it can be followed by either *of* or *to*. (See also section 61 [agree and differ].)

Other references that help with idiom (and with other matters) are *Fowler's Modern English Usage*, the *Canadian Oxford Dictionary* (and the *Student's Oxford Canadian Dictionary*), and the *Guide to Canadian English Usage*. Students for whom English is an additional language will benefit from using specialized learners' dictionaries, which offer a wealth of information about idiomatic uses of articles and prepositions and examples of idioms used in complete sentences (see 52.1 [Learners' dictionaries]).

# 60. WORDINESS, JARGON, AND ASSOCIATED PROBLEMS

Diction that decreases precision and clarity is worth avoiding. Using too many words, or tired words, or fuzzy words weakens communication. We discuss and illustrate these weaknesses all in one section because they are related and sometimes overlapping. For example, phrases like "on the order of" and "on the part of" could be considered wordy or cliché. Jargonauts are fond of wordy and pretentious phrases like "make a determination" (instead of simply *determine*), or "at this point in time" (instead of *now*), or "due to the fact that" (instead of *because*), or "be of assistance to" (instead of *help*). They refuse to settle for the verb *support* when they can say instead that people "are supportive of" someone or something, and they increasingly use "characterize" rather than *call* or *name*, "necessitate" rather than "need."

Even without such overlapping, there is an inevitable family relationship among the several groupings of weaknesses—if only because one bad habit frequently leads to, or is accompanied by, others. Considering them all together rather than separately should give you a better sense of the kinds of difficulties they may cause. No lists such as those that follow can be exhaustive, because new words and phrases are making their way into these categories every day.

But once you understand the principles, you will get a feeling for the kinds of impediments to good communication such terms represent.

## 60.1 Wordiness

Generally, the fewer words you use to make a point, the better. Useless words—often called *deadwood*—clutter up a sentence; they dissipate its force, cloud its meaning, blunt its effectiveness. The writer of the following sentence, for example, used many words where a few would have done a better job:

> ✗   What a person should try to do when communicating by writing
> is to make sure the meaning of what he is trying to say is clear.

Notice the gain in clarity and force when the sentence is revised:

> A writer should strive to be clear.

### Expletives

When used to excess, expletive constructions can be a source of weakness and wordiness (see 1.11 and 18.6). There is nothing inherently wrong with them (there are many in this book—two already in this sentence), and they are invaluable in enabling us all to form certain kinds of sentences the way we want to. Nevertheless writers sometimes use them when a tighter and more direct form of expression would be preferable. If you can get rid of an expletive without creating awkwardness or losing desired emphasis, do it. Don't write

> ✗   There are several reasons why it is important to revise carefully.

when you can so easily get rid of the excess caused by the *there are* and *it is* structure:

> Careful revision is important for several reasons.
> For several reasons, careful revision is important.

> ✗   It is one of the rules in this house that you make your own bed.
> One rule in this house requires you to make your own bed.
> In this house you must make your own bed.

> ✗   In this small city, there are over a hundred people without housing.
> Over a hundred people in this small city are homeless.

The number of words you save may not always be great, but such changes can help strengthen your style. See also 6.16 and 18.6, on the passive voice.

## 60.2 Repetition

Repetition can be useful for coherence and emphasis (see 65.2, 68.2, 18.7, and section 66). But unnecessary repetition usually produces wordiness, and often awkwardness as well. Consider this sentence:

> ✘ Looking at the general appearance of the buildings, you can see that special consideration was given to the choice of colours for these buildings.

The sentence is wordy in general, but one could begin pruning by cutting out the needless repetition of *buildings*. Another example:

> ✘ She is able to make the decision to leave her job and to abide by her decision.

It might be argued that the repetition of *decision* adds emphasis, but "make the decision" could be shortened to "decide," or the final "her decision" could be simply "it."

## 60.3 Redundancy

Redundancy, another cause of wordiness, is repetition of an idea rather than a word. (The term *redundancy* can mean "excess" in general, but it is also used to designate the particular stylistic weakness known technically as "tautology.") Something is redundant if it has already been expressed earlier in a sentence. In the preceding sentence, for example, the word *earlier* is redundant, since the idea of *earlier* is present in the word *already*: repeating it is illogical and wordy. (Double negatives are a kind of redundancy, and also illogical: *can't never, don't hardly.*) To begin a sentence, "In my opinion, I think . . ." is redundant. The statement, "Tamiko is a personal friend of mine" is redundant, for a friend can scarcely be other than personal. To speak of a "new innovation" is to be redundant. The television writer describing a movie in which "Meryl Streep heads a stellar all-star cast" evidently didn't consider what "stellar" means. And the person who wrote, in a letter to a prospective employer, that "an interview would be mutually helpful to both of us" might not be called in for an interview. Here are some other frequently encountered phrases that are redundant because the idea of one word is present in the other as well:

| | |
|---|---|
| added bonus | erode away |
| advance planning | general consensus |
| basic fundamentals | low ebb |
| but nevertheless | mental attitude |
| character trait | more preferable |
| climb up | necessary prerequisite |
| close scrutiny | new record |
| completely eliminate | past history |
| consensus of opinion | reduce down |
| continue on | refer back |
| enter into | revert back |

One common kind of redundancy is called "doubling"—adding an unnecessary second word (usually an adjective) as if to make sure the meaning of the first is clear:

✘    The report was brief and concise.

Either *brief* or *concise* alone would convey the meaning. Sometimes an insecure writer goes to even greater lengths:

✘    The report was brief, concise, and to the point.

## 60.4 Ready-made Phrases

"Prefabricated" or formulaic phrases that leap to our minds whole are almost always wordy. They are a kind of cliché (see 60.5), and many also sound like jargon (see 60.8). You can often edit them out of a draft altogether, or at least use shorter equivalents:

a person who, one of those who

as of the moment

at that time, at that point in time (use *then*)

at the present time, at this time, at this point in time (use *now*)

at the same time (use *while*)

by and large

by means of (use *by*)

due to the fact that, because of the fact that, on account of the fact that, in view of the fact that, owing to the fact that (use *because*)

during the course of, in the course of (use *during*)

except for the fact that (use *except that*)

for the purpose of (use *for, to*)

for the reason that, for the simple reason that (use *because*)

in all likelihood, in all probability (use *probably*)

in a very real sense

in character, of a . . . character

in colour (as in "was blue in colour")

in fact, in point of fact

in height (use *high*)

in length (use *long*)

in nature

in number

in order to (use *to*)

in reality

in shape

in size

in spite of the fact that (use *although*)

in the case of

in the event that (use *if*)

in the form of

in the light of, in light of (use *considering*)

in the midst of (use *amid*)

in the near future, in the not too distant future (use *soon*) in the neighbourhood of, in the vicinity of (use *about, near*)

in this day and age (use *now, today*)

manner, in manner, in a . . . manner

period of time (use *period, time*)

personal, personally

previous to, prior to (use *before*)

the fact that

up until, up till (use *until, till*)

use of, the use of, by the use of, through the use of

when all is said and done

with the exception of (use *except for*)

with the result that

And the prevalence of such ready-made phrases as *point of view* caused a writer unthinkingly to tack *of view* onto *point* in the following sentence: "My dentist made the point of view that candy is bad for one's teeth." Two-part verbs (see 11.4) sometimes trip up writers in the same way: *fill in* is correct for "*Fill in* this form," but not for "The pharmacist *filled in* the prescription."

## 60.5 Triteness, Clichés

Trite or hackneyed expressions, clichés, are another form of wordiness: they are tired, worn out, all too familiar, and therefore generally contribute little to a sentence. Since they are, by definition, prefabricated phrases, they are another kind of deadwood that can be edited out of a draft. Many trite phrases are metaphors, once clever and fresh, but now so old and weary that the metaphorical sense is weak at best (see 54.3); for some, the metaphor is completely dead, which explains errors such as "tow the line" (for "toe the line") and "the dye is cast" (for "the die is cast"), "dead as a doorknob," and "tarnish everyone with the same brush." "To all intents and purposes" now sometimes comes out "to all intensive purposes"; "taken for granted" becomes "taken for granite"; "by a hair's breadth" turns up as "by a hare's breath"; and so on. A writer aiming for "time immemorial" instead wrote "time in memoriam." Another referred to the joys of "flying off into the wide blue yonder." And another asserted that a particular poet's message was that "we should make hay while the tide's in." A reviewer of a novel imagined angry characters "tearing the author from limb to limb." Even the once-familiar proverb "The proof of the pudding is in the eating" is now often heard as the relatively meaningless "The proof is in the pudding."

Some clichés are redundant as well: *first and foremost, few and far between, over and above, each and every, one and only, to all intents and purposes, ways and means, various and sundry, all and sundry, part and parcel, in this day and age, in our world today, in our modern world today,* and so on.

Of course clichés can be useful, especially in speech; they can help one fill in pauses and gaps in thinking and get on to the next point. Even in writing they can sometimes—simply because they are so familiar—be an effective way of saying something. And they can be used for a humorous effect. But in writing, in all such instances, they should only be used consciously. It isn't so much that clichés are bad in themselves as that the thoughtless use of clichés weakens style. Generally, then, avoid them. No list can be complete, but here are a few more examples to suggest the kinds of expressions to edit from your work:

| | |
|---|---|
| a bolt from the blue | it goes without saying |
| a heart as big as all outdoors | it stands to reason |
| all things being equal | last but not least |
| a matter of course | lock, stock, and barrel |
| as a last resort | love at first sight |
| as a matter of fact | many and diverse |
| as the crow flies | moment of truth |
| beat a hasty retreat | needless to say |
| brown as a berry | nipped in the bud |
| busy as a bee | no way, shape, or form |
| by leaps and bounds | off the beaten path, track |
| by no manner of means | one and the same |

| | |
|---|---|
| by no means | on the right track |
| clear as crystal (or *mud*) | par for the course |
| conspicuous by its absence | pride and joy |
| cool as a cucumber | raining cats and dogs |
| corridors of power | rears its ugly head |
| doomed to disappointment | rude awakening |
| easier said than done | sadder but wiser |
| fast as greased lightning | seeing is believing |
| from dawn till dusk | sharp as a tack |
| gentle as a lamb | slowly but surely |
| good as gold | smart as a whip |
| if and when | strike while the iron is hot |
| in a manner of speaking | strong as an ox |
| in one ear and out the other | the wrong side of the tracks |
| in the long run | when all is said and done |

Edit for the almost automatic couplings that occur between some adjectives and nouns. One seldom hears of a circle that isn't a *vicious* circle, or a fog that isn't a *pea-soup* fog, or a tenement that isn't a *run-down* tenement. Mere insight is seldom enough: it must be labelled *penetrating* insight. A few more examples:

| | | |
|---|---|---|
| acid test | devastating effect | natty dresser |
| ardent admirers | drastic action | proud possessor |
| blushing bride | festive occasion | sacred duty |
| budding genius | hearty breakfast | severe stress |
| bulging biceps | heated opposition | tangible proof |
| consummate artistry | knee-jerk reaction | vital role |

Several of this kind are redundant as well:

| | |
|---|---|
| advance notice | foreseeable future |
| advance warning | just desserts |
| blazing inferno | perfectly clear |
| cozy (little) nook | serious concern |
| end result | serious crisis |

| | |
|---|---|
| final outcome | terrible tragedy |
| final result | total (complete) surprise |

## 60.6 Overuse of Nouns

The over-reliance on nouns is another source of deadwood; it is also a form of jargon. The focus of a sentence or clause is its main verb; the verb activates it, moves it, makes it go. Too many nouns piled on one verb can slow a sentence down, especially if the verb is *be* or some other verb with little or no action in it. Consider the following:

> ✘    The opinion of the judge in this case is of great significance to the outcome of the investigation and its effects upon the behaviour of all the members of our society in the future.

The verb in this sentence must struggle to move the great load of nouns and prepositional phrases along to some kind of finish. One could easily improve the sentence by reducing the proportion of nouns to verbs and making the verbs more vigorous:

> The judge's decision will inevitably influence how people act.

The piling up of nouns ending in *tion* can also weaken style and bury meaning:

> ✘    The depredations of the conflagration resulted in the destruction of many habitations and also of the sanitation organization of the location; hence the necessity of the introduction of activation procedures in relation to the implementation of emergency preparations for the amelioration of the situation.

This example is not so exaggerated as you might think. In any event, here is a simpler version of it:

> Since the fire destroyed not only many houses but also the water-treatment plant for the town, emergency procedures had to be set up quickly.

The verbs in this revised sentence have a third as much noun-baggage to carry as the original verb *resulted* had. There is nothing inherently wrong with nouns ending in *tion*; the damage is done when they come in clusters.

# Proofreading Tip

## Checking on the Sound of Your Prose

Reading your work aloud can help you avoid other unpleasant patterns of sound and rhythm, such as excessive alliteration or too regular a metrical pattern:

✘    At the top of the tree sat a bird on a branch.

or jarring repetitions of sound:

✘    They put strict restrictions on lending, which constricted the flow of funds.

or accidental rhyme:

✘    At that time he was in his prime; the way he later let himself go was a crime.

## 60.7 Nouns Used as Adjectives

Another insidious trend is the unnecessary use of nouns as if they were adjectives. Many nouns have long functioned adjectivally, some even becoming so idiomatic as to form parts of compounds:

school board, school book, schoolteacher
bathing suit, bath towel, bathtub
lunch hour, lunch box, lunchroom
fire alarm, fire engine, firewood
heart attack, heart monitor, heart-smart
business school, business card, businessperson

Such nouns-cum-adjectives are quite acceptable, but the practice can be carried too far. "Lounge chair" is clearly preferable to "chair for lounging," but just as clearly "medicine training" does not conform to the usages of English as well as "medical training" or "training in medicine," nor "poetry skills" as well as "poetic skills" or "skill in poetry." In these last two examples, since there is a standard adjectival form available, the simple nouns need not and should not be so used.

But increasingly in recent years, speakers and writers—especially those in government, business, and the media—have settled for, or even actively chosen, noun combinations that contribute heavily to the jargon cluttering the language, cumbersome phrases such as *learning facilitation*, *resource person*, *demonstration organizer*, *cash flow position*, *opinion sampling*, *consumer confidence number*. Newspapers report that "a weapons of mass destruction update is expected next month," where "an update on weapons of mass destruction" would be better. The piling up of several nouns, as in such phrases as "the labour force participation rate," "the Resource Management Personnel Training and Development Program," and "a city park recreation facility area" can confuse or alienate readers.

Resist this tendency. Do not write of volunteer work taking place "either in a school situation or a community-type situation"; refer not to "emergency situations" or "crisis situations," but to *emergencies* and *crises*. And try to avoid the unnecessary use of the word *situation* altogether.

## Proofreading Tip

### On Nouns Functioning as Verbs

Many nouns also function quite normally as verbs. But some usages have provoked criticism. For example, though it is now commonly accepted, some people once objected to the use of *chair* as a verb, as in "to chair a meeting" (see section 61 [man]); and *contact*, meaning "get in touch with," was once criticized, although it is widely accepted today.

Certain other nouns have not received such widespread acceptance as verbs, and you may be best to avoid them. For instance, some critics accept *critique* as a verb, but some do not; some also continue to object to *parent* as a verb, and to its gerund *parenting*.

Many wince when they hear *dialogue* used as a verb, or of something *transitioning*. And many still deplore referring to someone as having *gifted* another with a present, or *impacted* a process, or *authored* a piece of writing, or *suicided*. And unless you're writing specifically about using computers, it's probably wise not to refer to *accessing* and *networking*. See also section 61 (-ize).

## 60.8 Jargon

The word *jargon*, in a narrow sense, refers to terms peculiar to a specific discipline, such as psychology, chemistry, literary theory, or computer science, terms unlikely to be fully understood by an outsider. Here we use it in a different sense, to refer to all the incoherent, unintelligible phraseology that clutters contemporary expression. The private languages of particular disciplines or special groups are quite legitimately used in writing for members of those communities. Much less legitimate are the gobbledygook and bafflegab that so easily find their way into the speech and writing of most of us. As potential jargonauts, we should all be on guard against creeping bureaucratese and the like, baffling terms from other disciplines and from business and government that infiltrate everyday language. Bombarded by such words and phrases, we may uncritically use them in our own speech and writing, often assuming that automatic prestige attaches to such language. If you write to communicate rather than to impress, you will edit to avoid the pitfalls discussed and illustrated here and in the rest of section 60; you will then impress your readers in the best way.

The following list is a sampling of words and phrases that are virtually guaranteed to decrease the quality of expression, whether spoken or written. Some of the terms sound pretentious and technical, imported from specialized fields; others are fuzzy, imprecise, unnecessarily abstract; and still others are objectionable mainly because they are overused, whether as true clichés or merely popular jargon, or "buzz words" (which is itself a buzz word). If you are thinking of using these words or phrases in your writing, consider the context in which you are writing. Are you addressing readers who will be familiar and comfortable with such language? Ask yourself whether another word or words would communicate your thoughts more effectively. If you don't come up with a more suitable alternative, then you are likely choosing well.

Terms discussed further in section 61 are marked with an asterisk (*):

access (as a verb)

affirmative, negative

along the lines of, along that line, in the line of

angle

area*

aspect

at that point in time (*then*)

at this point in time (*now*)

background (as a verb)

basis, on the basis of, on a . . . basis*

bottom line

case

concept, conception

concerning, concerned

connection, in connection with, in this (that) connection

considering, consideration, in consideration of

definitely

dialogue (especially as a verb)

escalate

eventuate

evidenced by

expertise

facet

factor

feedback

hopefully*

identify with

image

impact (especially as verb)

implemented, implementation

importantly

indicated to (for *told*)

infrastructure

input, output

in regard to, with regard to, regarding, as regards

in relation to

in respect to, with respect to, respecting

interface

in terms of*

in the final analysis

-ize (-ise) verbs*

| | |
|---|---|
| lifestyle | relate to |
| marginal | relevant |
| meaningful, meaningful dialogue | replicate |
| mega- | scenario, worst-case scenario |
| motivation | sector |
| ongoing | self-identity |
| on stream | situation |
| parameters | standpoint, vantage point, |
| personage |     viewpoint |
| phase | type, -type* |
| picture, in the picture | viable |
| posture | -wise* |
| profile, low profile | worthwhile* |
| realm | |

Of course, many of these words can be used in normal and accept-able ways. But even such acceptable words can be used as jargon, and those in this list are among the most likely offenders. For example, *angle* is a good and useful word, but in such expressions as "look-ing at the problem from a different angle" it begins to become jar-gon. *Aspect* has precise meanings, but they are seldom honoured; the writer of the following sentence didn't know them, but just grabbed at an all too familiar word: "Due to money aspects, many high-school graduates would rather work than enter university." Here *aspects* has no real meaning at all (see also section 61 [due to]). A phrase like "For financial reasons" or "Because of a need for money" would be far better. The sentence "The third quatrain develops the aspect of time" is as ineffective as "The third quatrain brings in the factor of time." Unless you use *case* to mean a box or container, a medical case, a legal case, or a grammatical case, or in phrases like "in case of fire," you are likely to create wordy jargon with it: "In most cases, employees who worked hard got bonuses." Why not "Most employ-ees who worked hard got bonuses"? And why say "He replied in the affirmative" when "He said yes" would do? *Interface*, as a noun, has a precise technical meaning; but after some writers adopted it for their purposes, it began surfacing as jargon, used—even as a verb—by many who are evidently unaware of its meaning. *Realm* means a kingdom, and it can—or once could—be useful metaphorically in phrases like "the realm of poetry" or "the realm of ideas"; but it has long been so loosely and widely applied that most careful writers will avoid it except in its meaning of kingdom. Only as jargon does the verb *relate to* mean "understand" or "empathize" or "interact meaningfully with." And so on. If you read and listen carefully you will often find the listed terms, and others like them, being used in ways that impede clear, concise, and precise expression.

## Proofreading Tip

### On Using Short Rather Than Long Word Forms

Writers addicted to wordiness and jargon will prefer long words to short ones, and pretentious-sounding words to relatively simple ones. Generally, choose the shorter and simpler form. For example, the shorter word in each of the following pairs is preferable:

| | |
|---|---|
| analysis, analyzation | (re)orient, (re)orientate |
| connote, connotate | preventive, preventative |
| consultative, consultitative | remedy (vb.), remediate |
| courage, courageousness | symbolic, symbolical |
| disoriented, disorientated | use (n. & vb.), utilize, utilization |
| existential, existentialistic | |

## 61. USAGE: TROUBLESOME WORDS AND PHRASES

This section features words and phrases that have a history of being especially confusing or otherwise troublesome. Study the whole list carefully, perhaps marking for frequent review any entries you recognize as personal problem spots. Like any such list, this one is selective rather than exhaustive; we have tried to keep it short enough to be manageable. (Even whole books on usage invariably leave out matters someone else would think important.) As with the list of frequently misspelled words, then, you should keep a list of your own for special study. You can often supplement the information and advice provided here by consulting a good dictionary—especially one that includes notes on usage. See also the index and the following lists and discussions: Words Sometimes Confused (51.12–51.13), Slang (53.1), Informal, Colloquial (53.2), Wordiness (60.1), Triteness, Clichés (60.5), Overuse of Nouns (60.6), Nouns Used as Adjectives (60.7), and Jargon (60.8).

**about** (See **on.**)

**above, below**
Avoid stiff references to discussions that precede or follow. Rather than "for the *above* reasons," write "for *these* (or *those*, or *the foregoing*, or *the preceding*) reasons"; instead of "for the reasons given *below*," write "for the *following* reasons." If you find yourself writing "as I said above" or "as I will explain below" and the like, the organization of your writing may need work; try revising your plan or outline.

**absolute** (See **unique, etc.**)

**actually** (See **very.**)

**affect, effect**
Avoid the common confusion of these two words. *Affect* is a transitive verb meaning "to act upon" or "to influence"; *effect* is a noun meaning "result, consequence":

> He tried to *affect* the outcome, but his efforts had no *effect*.

Proofread carefully, since this error often appears in writing done under time pressures. (Note: *Effect* can also be a verb, meaning "to bring about, to cause"; see your dictionary for two other meanings of *affect*, one a verb and one a noun.)

**afterward, afterwards** (See **toward, towards.**)

## aggravate

The verb *aggravate* is often colloquially or informally used to mean "annoy, irritate, anger, vex." But properly speaking, only a condition, not a person, can be *aggravated*, and only if it is already bad: *aggravate* means "make worse":

> Standing in the hot sun will *aggravate* your headache.

> The unexpectedly high tax bill *aggravated* the small company's already serious financial condition.

## agree to, agree with, agree on

Use the correct preposition with *agree*. One agrees *to* a proposal or request, or agrees *to* do something; one agrees *with* someone about a question or opinion, and certain climates or foods agree *with* a person; one agrees *on* (or *about*) the terms or details of something settled after negotiation, or agrees *on* a course of action.

## ain't

A nonstandard contraction, *ain't* is primarily equivalent to *aren't* and *isn't*. Avoid it in all writing unless for deliberate colloquial or humorous effect, as in "If it ain't broke, don't fix it."

## all, all of (See of.)

## along the lines of (See in terms of.)

## alternate, alternative; alternately, alternatively

*Alternate* (adjective) means "by turns" or "every other one." *Alternative* (adjective or noun) refers to one of a number of possible choices (usually two). Don't use *alternate* or *alternately* when the sense has something to do with choice:

> In summer they could water their lawns only on *alternate* days.

> The squares on the board are *alternately* red and black.

> The judge had no *alternative*: he had to dismiss the charges.

> There is an *alternative* method, much simpler than the one you are using.

> She could meekly resign or, *alternatively*, she could take her case to the grievance committee.

*Alternate* is used legitimately to refer to a substitute or standby: "Each delegate to the convention had a designated *alternate*. She served as an *alternate* delegate."

## although, though

These conjunctions introduce adverbial phrases or clauses of concession. They mean the same, but *although* with its two syllables usually sounds smoother, less abrupt, at the beginning of a sentence; *though* is more commonly used to begin a subordinate clause following an independent clause, though it can be slightly emphatic at the start of a sentence. But the two words are not always interchangeable: in *even though* and *as though* one cannot substitute *although*, and *although* cannot serve as an adverb at the end of a sentence or clause. (See also **despite that** and **while**.)

## among (See **between, among**.)

## amount, number

Use *number* only with countable things (i.e. with nouns that have both singular and plural forms), *amount* only with mass, uncountable nouns: a *number* of coins, an *amount* of change; a large *number* of cars, a large *amount* of traffic. *Number* usually takes a singular verb after the definite article, and a plural verb after the indefinite article (see 7.6).

> *The number* of participants taking the workshop *is* encouraging.

> *A number* of participants *are* planning to take the workshop.

(See also **less, fewer**.)

## and (See **while**.)

## and/or

This is worth avoiding, unless you're writing legal phraseology. Write "We'll get there on foot or horseback, or both," rather than "We'll get there on foot and/or horseback." And with more than two items, *and/or* muddies meaning: "This bread can be made with wheat, barley, *and/or* rye."

**angry** (See **mad**.)

**anxious**
*Anxious* means much more than just "eager": use it only when there is at least some degree of real anxiety or angst.

**any more, anymore**
For the adverb meaning "now" or "nowadays," both spellings are common (though some dictionaries still don't recognize one or the other). Whichever spelling you use, use it only in negative statements (or positive statements with a negative implication) and in questions ("I don't get around much any more"; "I seldom attend sports events any more"; "Do you lie in the sun anymore?").

**anyplace, someplace**
These colloquial synonyms for *anywhere* and *somewhere* should be avoided in formal writing.

**anyways, anywheres, everywheres, nowheres, somewheres**
These are nonstandard forms. Use *anyway*, *anywhere*, etc.

**approach** (See **in terms of**.)

**apt** (See **likely, liable, apt**.)

**area**
The word *area* refers strictly to a physical division of space on a surface. Avoid using it as an unnecessarily vague term to refer to some abstract division, such as a field of study, a problem, or an activity (the *area* of the social sciences, the *area* of finance, the *area* of biblical interpretation). Weather forecasters and others are also fond of *area* as a substitute for *region, district, neighbourhood* (the eastern Alberta *area*, the Ottawa *area*). And journalists sometimes use it

awkwardly as an adjective, e.g. in headlines ("Area man attacked by rabid dog"; "Area teenagers march in protest"). These usages, too, are worth avoiding.

**as**
To avoid ambiguity, don't use *as* in such a way that it can mean either "while" or "because":

✘    *As* I was walking after dark I tripped over a tree root.

✘    *As* I added the brandy, the cherries jubilee caught fire.

✘    The car gathered speed quickly *as* I pressed harder on the accelerator.

Because of such potential ambiguity, some writers have banished *as* in the sense of *because* from their vocabularies. Another awkward use of *as* occurs in sentences like

✘    The book was considered as a threat to the state.

Here, *as* is unnecessary—or else needs something like "as a possible threat" to be clear. (See also **like, as, as if, as though,** and **so . . . as.**)

**as . . . as** (See **equally as** and **so . . . as.**)

**as being**
Don't follow with *being* when *as* alone is enough:

He always thinks of himself *as* [not *as being*] the life of the party.

She sees the deputy premier *as* [not *as being*] an incompetent legislator.

**as far as . . . is (are) concerned, as far as . . . goes (go)**
This construction has a wordy, jargon-like air about it, but if you feel that you need to use it anyway, don't leave it unfinished, as in this example:

✘    *As far as* financing my house, I'm going to have to get a mortgage.

The error may stem from a confusion of *as far as* with *as for*.

**as regards** (See **in terms of.**)

**as such**

This phrase shouldn't be used as if it were equivalent to *thus* or *therefore*:

> ✘ My uncle wants to be well liked. *As such*, he always gives expensive gifts.

In this phrase, *as* is a preposition and *such* is a pronoun that requires a clear noun antecedent:

> My uncle is a generous man. *As such*, he always give me expensive gifts.

**as though** (See **like, as, as if, as though.**)

**as to**

This is a stiff jargon phrase worth avoiding; substitution or rephrasing will usually improve expression:

> ✘ He made several recommendations *as to* the best method of proceeding.
>
> He made several recommendations with respect to the best method of proceeding.
>
> He recommended several methods of proceeding.

> ✘ I was in doubt *as to* which road to take.
>
> I was in doubt about which road to take.
>
> I was not sure which road to take.
>
> I did not know which road to take.

*As to* at the beginning of a sentence may seem more tolerable, but even there it usually sounds out of place; try changing it to *as for*. (See also **in terms of.**)

**awaiting for**

*Awaiting* is not followed by the preposition *for*; *waiting* is:

> I was *awaiting* the train's arrival.
>
> I was *waiting for* the light to change.

**awful, awfully**

When used as intensifiers ("They were *awfully* kind to us") *awful* and *awfully* are colloquialisms that should be avoided in formal writing. (See also **very** and 53.2.)

**a while, awhile**

Most authorities object to the adverb *awhile* instead of the noun phrase *a while* in some positions, for example after a preposition such as *for*: sleep *awhile*; sleep for *a while*. Others contend that either form is acceptable.

**backward, backwards** (See **toward, towards**.)

**bad, badly** (See **good, bad, badly, well**.)

**barely** (See **can't hardly, etc**.)

**basis, on the basis of, on a . . . basis**

*Basis* is a perfectly good noun, but some prepositional phrases using it are worth avoiding when possible, for outside of technical contexts they usually amount to wordy jargon.

> ✘   She made her decision *on the basis* of the committee's report.

This can easily be improved:

> She based her decision on the committee's report.

Again:

> ✘   He selected the furniture *on the basis* of its shape and colour.  (by? for? according to? because of?)

The phrase *on a . . . basis* is sometimes useful, but more often than not it can profitably be edited out: *on a daily basis* is usually jargon for *daily*; *on a yearly basis* or *on an annualized basis*, for *annually*; *on a temporary basis*, for *temporarily*; *on a regular basis*, for *regularly*; *on a voluntary basis*, for *voluntarily*; *on a political basis*, for *politically* or *for political reasons*; *We'll do this for a week on a trial basis* is jargon for *We'll try this for a week*; and so on. (See also **in terms of**.)

**because** (See **reason . . . is because;** see also 37.3.)

**because of** (See **due to.**)

**being that, being as, being as how**
These are colloquial or dialectal substitutes for *because* or *since* to introduce a subordinate clause, as is *seeing as (how)*, though *seeing that* is acceptable.

**believe** (See **feel[s].**)

**below** (See **above, below.**)

**beside, besides**
*Beside,* a preposition, means "next to, in comparison with"; *besides* as an adverb means "in addition, also, too, as well"; as a preposition, *besides* means "in addition to, except for, other than":

> She stood *beside* her car.

> Her objections were minuscule *beside* those of her brother.

> She knew she would have to pay the cost of repairs and the towing charges *besides*.

> *Besides* the cost of repairs, she knew she would have to pay towing charges.

> There was no one on the beach *besides* the three of us.

> *Besides* this, what am I expected to do?

**between, among**
Generally, use *between* when there are two persons or things, and *among* when there are more than two:

> There is ill feeling *between* the two national leaders.

> There were predictable differences *between* the Liberal and Conservative leaders during the debate.

> They divided the cost equally *among* the three of them.

On occasion *between* is appropriate for groups of three or more, for example if the emphasis is on the individual persons or groups as overlapping pairs, or on the relation of one particular person to each of several others:

> It seems impossible to keep the peace *between* the nations of the world.

> One expects there to be good relations *between* a prime minister and the members of the caucus.

*Between* is also commonly used informally or colloquially to refer to more than two, as in the idiom "between you and me and the lamppost."

## bi-

*Bimonthly* and *biweekly* usually mean "every two months" and "every two weeks." But since the prefix *bi* is sometimes also used to mean "twice," *bimonthly* and *biweekly* could mean the same as *semimonthly* and *semiweekly*, i.e. "twice a month" and "twice a week." In order to be clear, therefore, you may want to avoid *bi-* and spell out "every two months," "twice a month," etc. *Semiannually* clearly means "twice a year," and *biannual* ("twice a year") is distinguished from *biennial* ("every two years," "lasting two years")—but again you may want to use *semiannually* or the equivalent phrases, just to be sure.

## but (See can't hardly, etc., and while.)

## can, may (could, might)

Opinion and usage are divided, but in formal contexts it is still advisable to use *can* to denote ability, *may* to denote permission:

> *May* I have your attention, please?

> He *can* walk and chew gum at the same time.

> He knew that he *might* leave if he wished, but he *could* not make himself rise from his chair.

But both *may* and *can* are commonly used to denote possibility: "Things *may* (*can*) turn out worse than you expect. Anything *can* (*may*) happen." And *can* is often used in the sense of permission, especially in informal contexts and with questions and negatives ("*Can* I go?" "No, you *cannot!*") or where the distinction between ability (or possibility) and permission is blurred ("Anyone with an invitation *can* get in")—a blurring which, inherent in the concepts, is making the two increasingly interchangeable. (See also **may, might.**)

### can't hardly, etc.
*Barely*, *hardly*, *never*, *only*, and *scarcely* are regarded as negatives or as having a negative force. Therefore don't use words like *can't*, *don't*, *couldn't*, and *without* with them, for the result is an ungrammatical double negative. Use instead the positive forms: "I *can* hardly believe it. He *could* scarcely finish on time. He emerged from the ordeal *with* hardly a scratch." (Some writers also consider *but* a word not to be preceded by negatives, especially *can't* or *cannot*; others object only to *cannot but* or *can't help but* as redundant; but many consider both usages acceptable.)

### centre around, centre about
This is an illogical phrase. The meaning of the word *centre* (or *focus*) calls for a different preposition:

> The discussion *centred on* the proposed amendment.

Or something can centre *upon*, *in*, or *at*. One can say *revolved around*, *circled around*, and be quite logical.

### compare to, compare with
In formal contexts, use *compare to* to liken one thing to another, to express similarity:

> Shall I *compare* thee *to* a summer's day?

> He *compared* his work *to* flying a kite.

and *compare with* to measure or evaluate one thing against another:

> She *compared* the sports car *with* the SUV to see which would be best for her.

> He *compared* favourably *with* the assistant she had had the previous year.

> *Compared with* a desk job, farm work is more healthful by far.

**complete** (See **unique, etc.**)

**comprise, compose**
Distinguish carefully between these words. Strictly, *comprise* means "consist of, contain, take in, include":

> The municipal region *comprises* several cities and towns.

> His duties *comprise* opening and shutting the shop, keeping the shelves stocked at all times, and making daily bank deposits.

*Compose* means "constitute, form, make up":

> The seven cities and towns *compose* the municipal region.

Don't use *comprise* in the passive voice—saying for example that some whole "is comprised of" several parts; use *is composed of*:

> The municipal region *is composed* of seven cities and towns.

**continual, continuous**
These words are sometimes considered interchangeable, but *continual* more often refers to something that happens frequently or even regularly but with interruptions, and *continuous* to something that occurs constantly, without interruptions:

> The speaker's voice went on in a *continuous* drone, in spite of the heckler's *continual* attempts to interrupt.

For something that continues in space rather than time, *continuous* is the correct adjective:

> The bookshelf was *continuous* for the entire length of the hallway.

**convince, persuade**
These words are often used interchangeably; both mean "to cause someone to believe or do something." But for many writers there is still a useful distinction between them: with *convince* the emphasis is more likely to be on the belief, with *persuade* on the action. You either *convince* or *persuade* someone *of* something or *that* something is so, but you *persuade* someone *to do* something. Further, *convince* implies appeal to reason, logic, hard facts; *persuade* implies appeal both to reason and to emotion. *Convince* also connotes an overcoming of

objections, a change of mind. (The distinction is perhaps blurred by the fact that changing one's mind is itself a sort of action.)

**could** (See **can, may.**)

**culminate**
Many writers find this verb awkward when used with a direct object or in the passive voice:

✗   He *culminated* his remarks with strong support for the health care legislation.

✗   The building *was culminated* by a revolving restaurant and an observation deck.

It is better to use it only intransitively, usually with the preposition *in*:

Our search *culminates* here.

His speech *culminated in* strong support for the healthcare legislation.

The building *culminated in* a revolving restaurant and an observation deck.

**despite that**
The phrase *despite that* is similar in meaning to *but, nevertheless, however*:

The weather was cold. *Despite that*, we enjoyed our hike.

Don't use the phrase as if it were equivalent to *though* or *although*:

✗   *Despite that* the weather was cold, we enjoyed our hike.

To be used this way *Despite that* would have to be expanded to the wordy *Despite the fact that* (or *In spite of the fact that*); use the simpler alternatives *Although* or *Though* or *Even though*, or rephrase using *Despite* on its own:

Despite the cold weather, we enjoyed the hike.

**different from, different than**
*From* is the idiomatic preposition after *different*:

Your car is noticeably *different from* mine.

*Than*, however, is becoming increasingly common, especially when followed by a clause and when it results in fewer words:

> The finished sketch looks far *different than* I expected it to.

But to avoid the label "colloquial," use the construction with *from:*

> The finished sketch looks far *different from* what I intended.

### differ from, differ with

To *differ from* something or someone is to be unlike in some way; to *differ with* someone is to disagree, to quarrel:

> She *differed from* her colleague in that she was less prone than he to *differ with* everyone on every issue.

### disinterested

A much misused word, the adjective *disinterested* means "impartial, objective, free from personal bias." Although it is often used as a synonym for *uninterested, not interested* (no doubt partly because of increasing use of the noun *disinterest* to mean "lack of interest" as well as "impartiality"), in formal contexts retain the distinction between the two:

> It is necessary to find a judge who is *disinterested* in the case, for she will then try it fairly; we assume that she will not also be *uninterested* in it, for then she would be bored by it, and not pay careful attention.

### due to

Use *due to* only as a predicate adjective + preposition after a form of the verb *be:*

> The accident was *due to* bad weather.

Many writers object to it as a preposition to introduce an adverbial phrase, especially at the beginning of a sentence; use *Because of* or *On account of* instead:

> *Because of* the bad weather, we had an accident.

As a substitute, *Owing to* is little if any better.

### each other, one another

These are interchangeable, though *each other* more often refers to two, *one another* to more than two (see also **between, among**):

The bride and groom kissed *each other*.

The five boys traded hockey cards with *one another*.

**effect, affect** (See **affect, effect.**)

**either, neither**
As indefinite pronouns or adjectives, these usually refer to one or the other of two things, not more than two; for three or more, use *any* or *any (one)* or *none*:

Either of these two advisers can answer your questions.

Neither of the two answers is correct.

Any (one) of the four proposals is acceptable.

None of the four of us drove in today.

If *either* or *neither* is part of a correlative conjunction (see 12.2), it can refer to more than two:

Either Howard, Kiu, or Peter will act as referee.

**empty** (See **unique, etc.**)

**enormity**
This noun does not mean "immensity, great size, enormousness," but rather "outrageousness, heinousness, atrocity," or at least "immoderateness, immorality."

In pronouncing sentence, the judge emphasized the *enormity* of the arsonist's crime.

**equal** (See **unique, etc.**)

**equally as**
Avoid this redundancy by dropping one word or the other or by substituting *just as*. In expressions like the following, *as* is unnecessary:

Her first novel was highly praised, and her second is *equally* good.

He may be a good high jumper, but she can jump *equally* high, if not higher.

In expressions like the following, *equally* is unnecessary:

> In a storm, one port is *as* good as another.
>
> His meat pies were *as* tasty as hers.

### especially, specially

*Especially* means "particularly, unusually"; *specially* means "specifically, for a certain or special purpose":

> We *especially* want our parents to come; we planned the party *specially* for their wedding anniversary.
>
> It's *especially* cold today; I'm going to wear my *specially* made jacket.

### -ess (See man, woman, lady, etc.)

### essential (See unique, etc.)

### ever

*Ever* is not needed after *seldom* and *rarely*. Instead of *rarely ever*, you may say *hardly ever*.

### farther, further

Although the distinction between these is often overlooked, use *farther* and *farthest* to refer to physical distance and *further* and *furthest* everywhere else, such as when referring to time and degree, and when used to mean something like "more" or "in addition":

> To go any *farther* down the road is the *furthest* thing from my mind.
>
> Rather than delay any *further*, he began his research, beginning with the book *farthest* from him.
>
> Without *further* delay, she began her speech.

Further, only *Further* can function as a sentence adverb, as in this sentence.

### fatal (See unique, etc.)

### fatal, fatalistic (See simple, simplistic.)

**feel(s)**

Don't loosely use the word *feel* when what you really mean is *think* or *believe*. *Feel* is more appropriate to emotional or physical attitudes and responses, *think* and *believe* to those dependent on reasoning:

> The defendant *felt* cheated by the decision; she *believed* that her case had not been judged impartially.

> I *feel* the need of sustenance; I *think* I had better have something to eat.

> I *feel* good about starting my new job; given my previous experience, I *think* I will fit in well.

**fewer** (See **less, fewer.**)

**figuratively** (See **literally, virtually, figuratively.**)

**firstly, secondly, etc.**

Since some find the *ly* ending old-fashioned and unnecessary in enumerations, just say *first, second, third*, etc. Many object only to the word *firstly*, so even if you decide to use *secondly, thirdly*, etc., begin with *first*, not *firstly*.

**focus** (See **centre around.**)

**following**

If you avoid using *following* as a preposition meaning simply "after," you'll avoid both the criticism of those who object to it as pretentious and the possibility of its being momentarily misread as a participle or a gerund:

> ✘    *Following* the incident, she interviewed those involved to gain further details.

**former, latter**

Use these only when referring to the first or second of two things, not three or more (when *first* or *last* would be appropriate), and only when the reference is clear and unambiguous—i.e. when it is to something immediately preceding. Like *above* and *below*, they are worth avoiding if possible.

**forward, forwards** (See **toward, towards.**)

**from the standpoint (viewpoint) of** (See **in terms of.**)

**frontward, frontwards** (See **toward, towards.**)

**full** (See **unique, etc.**)

**fulsome**
Although frequently used as if it meant "full, copious, abundant," especially in the phrase "fulsome praise," the word actually means "overfull, excessive" because insincere, and therefore "disgusting, offensive to good taste," and even "nauseating."

**further** (See **farther, further.**)

**good, bad, badly, well**
To avoid confusion and error with these words, remember that *good* and *bad* are adjectives, *badly* and *well* adverbs (except when *well* is an adjective meaning "healthy"). (See also 9.2 [Adverbs not ending in *ly*].)

> The model looks *good* in that business suit. (He is attractive.)

> That suit looks *bad* on you because it fits *badly*.

> Nathan acted *bad*. (He was naughty.)

> Nathan acted *badly*. (His performance as Hamlet was terrible.)

> I feel *good*. (I am happy, in good spirits.)

> I feel *bad*. (I have a splitting headache.)

> She feels *bad* about what happened. (She broke her mother's vase.)

> Sophia looks *well*. (She looks healthy, not sick.)

> This wine travels *well*. (It wasn't harmed by the long train journey.)

> The infielders played especially *well* today; they are all *good* players.

> The steak smells *good*. (My mouth is watering.)

> Your dog doesn't smell *well*. (He's too old to hunt.)

## half a(n), a half

Both are correct; use whichever sounds smoother or more logical. (Is *half a* loaf better than *a half* loaf? Is *a half* hour more formal than *half an* hour?) But don't use *a half a(n)*; one article is enough.

## hanged, hung

In formal writing, use the past-tense form *hanged* only when referring to a death by hanging. For all other uses of the verb *hang*, the correct past form is *hung*.

## happen, occur

These verbs sometimes pose a problem for students with English as an additional language. Both verbs are intransitive and cannot take the passive voice form in any tense.

> ✘  The revolution *was happened* in 1917.
> The revolution *happened* in 1917.

> ✘  My parents' wedding *was occurred* in September 1970.
> My parents' wedding *occurred* in September 1970.

## hardly (See can't hardly, etc.)

## have, of (See of.)

## healthy, healthful

Although *healthy* is common in both senses, in formal writing it may be useful to preserve the distinction, using *healthy* to mean "in good health" and *healthful* to mean "contributing to good health":

> To stay *healthy*, one should participate in a *healthful* sport like swimming.

## he or she, his or her, he/she, s/he (See 4.4.)

## herself, himself, myself, etc. (See 3.8.)

## hopefully

In formal writing, use this adverb, meaning "full of hope," only to modify a verb or a verbal adjective:

> "Will you lend me ten dollars?" I asked *hopefully*.

> Smiling *hopefully*, she began to untie the package.

To avoid potential ambiguity, don't use it as a sentence adverb (in spite of its similarity to such acceptable sentence adverbs as *Happily* and *Fortunately*):

> ✘  *Hopefully*, the sun will shine tomorrow
>
> ✘  *Hopefully*, many people will come to the prize drawing.

Instead use *I hope* or *We hope* or *One hopes*.

**hung** (See **hanged, hung.**)

**imply** (See **infer, imply.**)

**impossible** (See **unique, etc.**)

**in, into**
These are often interchangeable, but usually you will want to use *in* to indicate location inside of, or a state or condition, and *into* to indicate movement toward the inside of, or a change of state or condition; in other words, generally use *into* with verbs of motion and the like:

> He went *into* the kitchen, but she was *in* the den.
>
> We moved *into* our new home *in* the suburbs.
>
> After getting *into* trouble, he was understandably *in* a bad temper.
>
> I assured her I would look *into* the matter.

**in connection with** (See **in terms of.**)

**individual**
This is not simply a synonym for *person*. Reserve the word *individual* for times when the meaning "distinct from others" is present, or when certain people are being distinguished from a different kind of body or institution:

> The person [not *individual*] you are referring to is my aunt.
>
> Elsa is very much an *individual* in her behaviour. (i.e. she behaves like no one else.)
>
> The legal restrictions apply to the company itself, but not to the *individuals* within it.

It is often best to use *individual* as an adjective rather than as a noun. But see also **person, persons, people.**

**infer, imply**
Use *imply* to mean "suggest, hint at, indicate indirectly" and *infer* to mean "conclude by reasoning, deduce." A listener or reader can *infer* from a statement something that its speaker or writer *implies* in it:

> Her speech strongly *implied* that we could trust her.

> I *inferred* from her speech that she was trustworthy.

The word *inference*, then, means "something inferred, a conclusion"; it does not mean *implication* or *innuendo*.

**infinite** (See **unique, etc.**)

**in regard to** (See **in terms of.**)

**in relation to** (See **in terms of.**)

**in respect to** (See **in terms of.**)

**inside, inside of** (See **of.**)

**in terms of**
This phrase is another example of contemporary clutter. Note that it is similar, sometimes even equivalent, to those other wordy expressions, *on the basis of* (see **basis**) and **-wise.** Although it is common in speech, and though occasionally it is the precisely appropriate phrase, it is more often vague, worse, it is capable of leading to such inane utterances as this (by a governor of a drought-stricken state): "We're very scarce in terms of water." If you can avoid it, especially in writing, do so; don't write sentences like these:

> ✘ He tried to justify the price increase *in terms of* [or *on the basis of*] the company's increased operating costs.

> ✘ *In terms of* experience [or *Experience-wise*], she was as qualified for the post as anyone else applying for it.

> ✘ *In terms of* fuel economy, this car is better than any other in its class.

> ✘ She first considered the problem *in terms of* the length of time it would take her to solve it.

Opt instead for sentences such as these:

> He tried to justify the increase in price by citing the company's increased operating costs.

> She was as experienced as anyone else applying for the post.

> This car has the best fuel economy of any in its class.

> First she thought about how long it would take her to solve the problem.

And note the further family resemblance of this phrase to others like *along the lines of, in connection with, in relation to, in [with] regard to, as regards, regarding, in [with] respect to,* and *from the standpoint [viewpoint] of. Perspective* and *approach* are two more words often used in a similar way. (See also 60.4 and 60.8.)

**in (with) regards to**
Drop the *s: in (with) regard to. As regards* is acceptable. But see 60.8 and **in terms of.**

**into** (See **in, into.**)

**irregardless**
This is nonstandard, as your dictionary should tell you. The prefix *ir* (= not) is redundant with *less,* forming a double negative (see **can't hardly**). The correct word is *regardless.*

**is because** (See **reason . . . is because.**)

**is when, is where**
Although often standard ("Early morning is when the cocks crow," "Home is where the heart is"), avoid these phrases in statements of definition, where adverbial clauses following linking verbs are considered ungrammatical:

> ✘ A double play *is when* two base runners are put out during one play.

> In a double play, two base runners are put out during one play.

> A double play occurs when two base runners are put out during one play.

Since *occurs* is not a linking verb, the adverbial clause beginning with *when* is acceptable. Compare **reason . . . is because.**

## its, it's

*Its*—without the apostrophe—is the possessive form of *it*; *it's*—with the apostrophe—is the contracted form of *it is*, or occasionally of *it has* (as in "*It's* been a long day"). It's easy to slip when writing at speed, so proofread carefully for these usages.

## -ize

The suffix *ize* (or *ise*) has long been used to turn nouns and adjectives into verbs (e.g. *democratize, galvanize, generalize, harmonize, idolize, modernize, satirize, theorize*). But like **-wise**, it is now sometimes overused, especially in business and other jargon (*finalize, concretize, prioritize*), leading even to such absurdities as this: "Let us not forget that the minister voluntarily resigned; had he not, he would surely have been *pressurized* to go." The *ize* ending remains acceptable in established words, but avoid using it to make new ones. (See **-wise**, and see also the Proofreading Tip in 60.7.)

## kind of, sort of

Used adverbially, as in "*kind of* tired" or "*sort of* strange," these terms are colloquial—as they are when followed by an article: "I had a bad *kind of an* afternoon"; "She was a rather peculiar *sort of a* guide." More formally, say "I had a bad afternoon" and "She was a rather peculiar guide." (See also **type**, and 4.6.)

## lack, lack of, lacking, lacking in

*Lack* in its various forms and parts of speech can sometimes pose problems for students with English as an additional language. Note the following standard usages:

This manual *lacks* clear instructions. (*lack* as a transitive verb)

A major weakness of his argument was its *lack* of evidence. (*lack* as a noun followed by the preposition *of*)

*Lacking* confidence, she gave up on her research. (*lacking* as a present participle followed by a direct object)

*Lacking* in experience, they had difficulty in job interviews. (*lacking* as a present participle in combination with the preposition *in*)

**lady** (See **man, woman, lady, etc.**)

**latter** (See **former, latter**.)

**lay** (See **lie, lay.**)

**lend** (See **loan.**)

**less, fewer**
*Fewer* refers to things that are countable (i.e. that appear as plural nouns); *less* is sometimes used the same way (e.g. on the signs at the express checkout lanes in supermarkets—"9 items or less"), but usually it is preferable to use it for things that are measured rather than counted or considered as units (i.e. with uncountable nouns):

> *fewer* dollars, *less* money
>
> *fewer* hours, *less* time
>
> *fewer* shouts, *less* noise
>
> *fewer* cars, *less* traffic
>
> *fewer* bottles of wine, *less* wine

(See also **amount, number.**)

**less, least; more, most** (See 8.2 and 9.3.)

**let, make**
The verbs *let* and *make* are parts of an idiom that causes problems, especially for those with English as an additional language. When *let* or *make* is followed by a direct object and an infinitive, the infinitive does not include the customary *to*:

> ✘ They *let* me *to borrow* their new car.
> They *let* me *borrow* their new car.

> ✘ Our professor *made us to participate* in the experiment.
> Our professor *made us participate* in the experiment.

(See also the note in 10.2.)

**liable** (See **likely, liable, apt.**)

**lie, lay**
Since *lay* is both the past tense of *lie* and the present tense of the verb *lay*, some writers habitually confuse these two verbs. If necessary, memorize their principal parts: *lie, lay, lain; lay, laid, laid.* The verb

*lie* means "recline" or "be situated"; *lay* means "put" or "place." *Lie* is intransitive; *lay* is transitive:

> I *lie* down now; I *lay* down yesterday; I *have lain* down several times today.

> I *lay* the book on the desk now; I *laid* the book on the desk yesterday; I *have laid* the book on the desk every morning for a week.

> The book *lies* on the desk now; the book lay on the desk yesterday; the book *has lain* on the desk for an hour.

However common it may be colloquially, don't use *lay* for *lie*, or *laying* for *lying*. (See also **set, sit.**)

**like, as, as if, as though**
*Like* is a preposition:

> Roger is dressed exactly *like* Ray.

But if Ray is given a verb, then he becomes the subject of a clause, forcing *like* to serve incorrectly as a conjunction; use the conjunction *as* when a clause follows:

> ✗ Roger is dressed exactly *like* Ray is.

> Roger is dressed exactly *as* Ray is.

In slightly different constructions, use *as if* or *as though* to introduce clauses:

> It looks *like* rain.

> It looks *as if* [or *as though*] it will rain.

> He stood there *like* a statue.

> He stood there *as though* [or *as if*] he were a statue.

> She spent money *as if* [or *as though*] there were no tomorrow.

But don't hypercorrect: don't shun *like* for *as* when what follows it is not a clause:

> ✗ Rover stood stiffly alert, pointing, head and tail down, *as* any well-trained dog. (like)

> ✗ Tiger Woods, just *as* last year's winner, sank a stunning birdie putt on the final hole. (like)

### likely, liable, apt

Although often used interchangeably, especially in informal contexts, in formal writing use *likely* to mean "probable, probably, showing a tendency, suitable"; *liable* to mean "legally obligated, responsible, susceptible to (usually something undesirable)"; and *apt* to refer to probability based on habitual tendency or inclination:

> A storm seems *likely*. He is *likely* to succeed. This is a *likely* spot.

> She is *liable* for damages. Tom is *liable* to headaches. He is *liable* to hurt himself.

> Damon is *apt* to trip over his own feet.

*Apt* can also mean "exactly suitable" (It was an *apt* remark) and "quick to learn" (Maki is an *apt* pupil).

### literally, virtually, figuratively

*Literally* means "actually, really." *Virtually* means "in effect, practically." *Figuratively* means "metaphorically, not literally." All too often the first two are used to mean their opposites, or as weak intensifiers:

> ✗  She was *literally* swept off her feet. (i.e. *figuratively*)

> ✗  They were caught in a *virtual* downpour. (It *was* a downpour; drop *virtual*)

### loan, lend

Although some people restrict *loan* to being a noun, it is generally acceptable as a verb equivalent to *lend*—except in such figurative uses as "Metaphors *lend* colour to one's style" and "*lend* a hand."

### mad

Although common in informal contexts to mean "angry," *mad* in formal contexts is usually restricted to the meaning "insane, crazy."

### make (See let, make.)

### man, woman, lady, -ess, Ms., etc.

Like the use of *he* as a generic pronoun (see 4.4), the general or generic use of the word *man* causes difficulties. To avoid biased language, most writers now try to avoid the term *man* where it could include the meaning *woman* or *women*. If you're referring to a single individual, often simply substituting the word *person* will do, or in some contexts *human being*. If you're referring to the race, instead of *man* or *mankind*, use *human beings, humanity, people, humankind,* or *the human race*. Instead of *manmade*, use *synthetic* or *artificial* or *manufactured*. (Note that several words beginning with *man-*, such as *manufacture, manuscript, manoeuvre,* come not from the English word *man* but from the Latin *manus,* "hand.") Similarly, in compounds designating various occupations and positions, try to avoid the suffix *man* by using gender-neutral terms such as *fire-fighter, police officer, letter carrier, worker* or *labourer* (instead of *workman*), *supervisor* or *manager* (instead of *foreman*); and though some people object to it, the suffix *person* is becoming more and more common: *spokesperson, chairperson* (or just *chair*), *anchorperson* (or just *anchor*), *businessperson, salesperson* (but see section 56). (See also **person, persons, people.**)

Another concern is the suffix *-ess*. Usefully gender-specific (and power-designating) terms like *princess, empress, duchess,* and *goddess* are firmly established, but there is seldom if ever any need to refer to an *authoress* or *poetess* when simply *author* or *poet* will serve; many now eschew *actress,* finding *actor* more suitable for both sexes. *Stewardess* has given way to *flight attendant*; and *waitress* and *waiter* have been replaced by *server*. The suffix *-ette*, as in *usherette*, is similarly demeaning; use *usher*. And don't use *lady* as a substitute for *woman*.

Further, don't thoughtlessly gender-stereotype occupations and other activities that are engaged in by both men and women; think about doctors, lawyers, business executives, secretaries, nurses, construction workers, cabdrivers, truck drivers, family cooks, food-shoppers, fishing enthusiasts, and so on. And don't, for example, highlight gender (as in *female athlete, female doctor*) unless it is somehow relevant to the context, in which case you would also refer to a *male athlete* or a *male doctor*. Similarly, if you're writing about English novelists and refer to Charles Dickens, refer also to Jane Austen, not "Miss Austen"; if you subsequently refer to him as simply *Dickens*, refer to her as *Austen*. Finally, use the title *Ms.* for a woman unless you know that a specific woman prefers *Miss* or *Mrs.*

Sources focused on issues of gender and English usage differ on the use of the word *woman* in phrases such as *woman doctor, woman judge, woman premier.* These sources suggest that it is only appropriate to use *woman* adjectivally if one would also use *man* in the same manner. And one would rarely, if ever, use *man* in this way. Instead, *male* would be the obvious choice. It follows, then, that *female* is preferable to *woman* in specific contexts calling attention to gender.

> The accident victim asked to be examined by a *female doctor.*

> The prime minister set a precedent by appointing the first *female judge* to the Supreme Court.

> She has been featured in a magazine story as the longest serving *female premier* in Canada.

**material, materialistic**
Don't use *materialistic* when all you need is the adjective *material.* *Material* means "physical, composed of matter," or "concerned with physical rather than spiritual or intellectual things"; it is often the sufficient word:

> Her life is founded almost entirely on *material* values.

*Materialistic* is the adjectival form of the noun *materialist*, which in turn denotes one who believes in materialism, a philosophical doctrine holding that everything can be explained in terms of matter and physical laws. A *materialist* can also be one who is notably or questionably concerned with material as opposed to spiritual or intellectual things and values:

> She is very *materialistic* in her outlook on life.

Unless you intend the philosophical overtones, use the simpler *material.* There is an analogous tendency to use *relativistic* rather than *relative* and *moralistic* rather than *moral.* Consult your dictionary. (See also **simple, simplistic,** and **real, realism, realist, realistic.**)

**may** (See **can, may.**)

**may, might**
Don't confuse your reader by using *may* where *might* is required:

(a)  after another verb in the past tense:

> ✖  She thought she *may* get a raise. (use *might*)

In the present tense, either *may* or *might* would be possible:

She thinks she *may* get a raise. (It's quite likely that she will.)

She thinks she *might* get a raise. (It's less likely, but possible.)

(b)  for something hypothetical rather than factual:

> ✖  This imaginative software program *may* have helped Beethoven, but it wouldn't have changed the way Mozart composed.

The word *may* makes it sound as if it is possible that the program *did* help Beethoven, which is of course absurd. Use *might*. (For other examples, see 6.5.)

**media** (See 7.8 and 51.20 [Borrowed words].)

**might** (See **may, might** and **can, may**.)

**momentarily**
Though often used to mean "in a moment, soon" ("We'll be eating *momentarily*"), many prefer to restrict it to meaning "for a moment" ("Her attention wandered *momentarily*"). Since the word is therefore sometimes capable of being misunderstood, some writers avoid it altogether. (See also **presently**.)

**moral, moralistic** (See **material, materialistic**.)

**more, most; less, least** (See 8.2 and 9.3.)

**more important, more importantly**
Although *more importantly* is widely used as a kind of sentence adverb, many writers object to it on grammatical grounds, preferring *more important* (as if it were a shorter version of "what is more important").

**Ms.** (See **man, woman, lady, etc.**, and 42.1.)

**muchly**
This is an unnecessary non-word, acceptable only colloquially and facetiously, like *muchness*. (See also **thusly.**)

**myself, herself, himself, etc.** (See 3.8.)

**necessary** (See **unique, etc.**)

**neither** (See **either, neither.**)

**never** (See **can't hardly, etc.**)

**nowheres** (See **anyways, etc.**)

**number** (See **amount, number.**)

**occur** (See **happen, occur.**)

**of**
*Of* is usually unnecessary, though not considered incorrect, after the prepositions *off*, *inside*, and *outside*, and is often unnecessary after the pronoun *all*, especially when countable items are not involved:

> She fell *off* the fence.

> He awoke to find himself *inside* a large crate.

> As requested, she remained in the hall *outside* the room for five minutes.

> We had *all* the time in the world.

> All [or *All of*] the members were present.

*Of* is needed with *all* before some pronouns, and usually helps before proper nouns:

> Bring *all of* them.

> We travelled across *all of* Canada.

And because of the way we speak, such phrases as "would have," "could have," and "might have" often come out as contractions ("would've," "could've," "might've"); and because of the way they hear such words, some people mistakenly think the *'ve* is *of* and proceed to write, incorrectly, "would *of*," "could *of*," "might *of*," and so on. (See also **on**.)

**off, off of** (See **of**.)

**on**
This preposition is sometimes unidiomatic when used as a substitute for *about* or *of*:

   ✘   She had no doubts *on* what to do next. (*about*)

   ✘   I am calling my book "A Study *on* the Effects of Globalization." (*of*)

**on account of** (See **due to**.)

**one another** (See **each other, one another**.)

**only** (See **can't hardly, etc.**)

**oral, verbal** (See **verbal, oral**.)

**outside, outside of** (See **of**.)

**owing to** (See **due to**.)

**people** (See **person, persons, people**.)

**per**
Although useful and at home in technical and business writing, the Latin *per* is usually out of its element in other writing, except when part of a Latin phrase (*per capita*, *per cent*); especially do not use it to mean simply "by, by means of, through" (as in business contexts: "per bearer") or "according to" ("per your instructions").

**perfect** (See **unique, etc.**)

**person, persons, people**
Partly to avoid gender-biased language (*man*, *woman*, the generic *he*), some people overuse the word *person* in what often sounds a wordy, jargony way (for example, "The *persons* responsible for the accident have received a summons to traffic court"). Try to avoid it, or instead use *one*, or even *you* (see 4.4). In the plural, use *persons*

only when the number in question is small, say one or two or three ("Two *persons* refused to sign the petition") or when you want to emphasize the presence of *individuals* in a group ("Those *persons* wishing to attend the party should sign up now"), but even then the demonstrative pronoun *those* alone will often serve better ("*Those* wishing to attend . . ."). Otherwise, use *people,* which is normal even for referring to small numbers: "One or two *people* may object." (See also **man, woman, lady, etc.** and **individual.**)

**perspective** (See **in terms of.**)

**persuade** (See **convince, persuade.**)

**possible** (See **unique, etc.**)

**presently**
Since some people think that *presently* should mean only "in a short while, soon," and others think that it instead, or also, means "at present, currently, now," resulting in at least occasional ambiguity, many writers try to avoid the word altogether. Use the alternative terms and your meaning will be clear. (See also **momentarily.**)

**put forth** (See **set forth.**)

**quote**
In contexts that are at all formal, use this only as a verb; don't use it as a noun, equivalent to "quotation" or "quotation mark."

**raise, rise**
The verb *raise* is transitive, requiring an object: "I *raised* my hand; he *raises* horses." *Rise* is intransitive: "The temperature *rose* sharply; I *rise* each morning at dawn." If necessary, memorize their principal parts: *raise, raised, raised; rise, rose, risen.*

**real, realism, realist, realistic**
If necessary, use your dictionary to help you keep these words straight. The person who wrote that "Huxley's novel is not about *realistic* people" was at best being ambiguous: does *realistic* here mean "lifelike," or "facing facts"? The one who wrote "He based

his conclusions not on theory but on *realistic* observation" probably meant "observation of reality." (See also **material, materialistic**.)

**real, really** (See **very** and 9.2 [Real and really, sure and surely].)

**reason . . . is because**
Although this construction has long been common, especially in speech, many people object to it as (a) redundant, since *because* often means simply "for the reason that," and as (b) ungrammatical, since adverbial *because* should not introduce noun clauses after a linking verb (critics for the same reason object to *it is because, this is because*, and the like). However common such phrases may be, we suggest that you avoid them, especially in formal writing, since they are likely to draw criticism—especially *the reason is because*; instead write "the reason is that."

**reason why**
The *why* in this phrase is often redundant, as in "The reason *why* I'm taking Spanish is that I want to travel in South America." Check to see if you need the *why*.

**recommend**
When this transitive verb appears in a clause with an indirect object, that object must be expressed as a prepositional phrase with *to* or *for*, and it must follow the direct object:

✘   She recommended *me* this restaurant.

✘   She recommended *to me* this restaurant.

   She recommended this restaurant *to me*.

A number of other verbs fit the same idiomatic pattern as *recommend*. Among the most common are *admit, contribute, dedicate, demonstrate, describe, distribute, explain, introduce, mention, propose, reveal, speak, state*, and *suggest*. Note, however, that with several of these verbs, if the direct object is itself a noun clause, it usually follows the prepositional phrase:

   He admitted to me that *he had been lying*.

   She explained to me *what she intended to do*.

**regarding** (See **in terms of.**)

**relative, relativistic** (See **material, materialistic.**)

**rise, raise** (See **raise, rise.**)

**round** (See **unique, etc.**)

**scarcely** (See **can't hardly, etc.**)

**seeing as (how), seeing that** (See **being that, being as how.**)

**sensual, sensuous**

Although the meanings of these words overlap, and the two are often used interchangeably, *sensuous* is traditionally used to refer broadly to intellectual or physical pleasure derived from the senses, while *sensual*, on the other hand, usually refers to the gratification of physical—particularly sexual—appetites:

> Some Canadian poets, responding to the beauty of their natural environment, write *sensuous* poetry.

> We are discussing the *sensual* features of contemporary love poetry.

**set, sit**

*Set* (principal parts *set, set, set*) means "put, place, cause to sit"; it is transitive, requiring an object: "He *set* the glass on the counter." *Sit* (principal parts *sit, sat, sat*) means "rest, occupy a seat, assume a sitting position"; it is intransitive: "The glass *sits* on the counter. May I *sit* in the easy chair?"—though it can be used transitively in expressions like "I sat myself down to listen," "She sat him down at the desk." (See also **lie, lay.**)

**set forth**

As a stiff, unwieldy substitute for *express(ed)* or *present(ed)* or *state(d)*, this phrase is an attempt at sophistication that usually misfires. *Put forth* is similarly weak.

**shall, will; should, would** (See 6.5, 6.8 [Simple future], and 6.9 [Simple past].)

**she or he, her or his, she/he, s/he** (See 4.4.)

## simple, simplistic

Don't use *simplistic* when all you want is *simple*. *Simplistic* means "oversimplified, unrealistically simple":

> We admire the book for its *simple* explanations and straightforward advice.

> The author's assessment of the war's causes was narrow and *simplistic*.

Similarly, *fatalistic* does not mean the same as *fatal*. (See also **material, materialistic**.)

## since

*Since* can refer both to time ("*Since* April we haven't had any rain") and to cause ("*Since* she wouldn't tell him, he had to figure it out for himself"). Therefore don't use *since* in a sentence where it could mean either:

> ✘ *Since* you went away, I've been sad and lonely.

## sit, set (See set, sit.)

## so, so that, therefore

As a conjunction, *so* is informal but acceptable (see 12.1 [Joining sentences]); just don't overwork it. To introduce clauses of purpose and to avoid possible ambiguity, you will often want to use *so that* or *therefore* instead:

> He sharpened the saw *so that* it would cut the boards properly.

> She cleverly changed her story several times, *so that* we couldn't be sure what actually happened.

> She changed her story several times; *therefore* we couldn't be sure what actually happened.

## so . . . as, as . . . as

In strictly formal contexts, use *so* or *so . . . as* with negative comparisons; use *as* or *as . . . as* only with positive comparisons:

> Belinda was almost *as tall as* he was, but she was not *so* heavy.

> He was not *so* light on his feet as he once was, but he was *as strong as* ever.

## someplace (See anyplace, someplace.)

**somewheres** (See **anyways, etc.**)

**sort of** (See **kind of, sort of.**)

**specially** (See **especially, specially.**)

**square** (See **unique, etc.**)

**state**
*State* is a stronger verb than *say*; reserve *state* for places where you want the heavier, more forceful meaning of "assert, declare, make a formal statement."

**straight** (See **unique, etc.**)

**substitute**
Don't use *substitute* when you mean *replace*—i.e. don't follow it with *by* or *with*; use it only with *for*:

   ✘   The french fries were *substituted by* a tossed salad. (*replaced*)

      The server kindly *substituted* a tossed salad *for* the greasy french fries.

*Substitute* can also be used intransitively:

      Because he is off his game this year, Stanley has only *substituted*.

      Mere cleverness cannot *substitute* for common sense.

**sure, surely**
Don't use *sure* as an adverb. (See 9.2 [Real and really, sure and surely].)

**suspect, suspicious**
Though *suspicious* can mean *arousing suspicion*, it is sometimes best to reserve it for the person in whom the suspicions are aroused, using the adjective *suspect* for the object of those suspicions; otherwise ambiguity may result (unless the context makes the meaning clear):

   ✘   He was a very *suspicious* man.

      I thought his actions *suspect*.

He was *suspicious* of everyone he met.

All of us were *suspect* in the eyes of the police.

## tend, tends

This verb is often no more than a mushy filler. Don't say "My lunches *tend to* be healthy" when what you mean is "My lunches *are* healthy."

## therefore (See so, so that, therefore.)

## these (those) kinds (sorts), this kind (sort) (See 4.6.)

## think (See feel[s].)

## though, although (See although, though.)

## thusly

*Thusly* is nothing more than a pretentious-sounding error for *thus* (and see **muchly**).

## till, until, 'til

*Till* and *until* are both standard, and have the same meaning. *Until* is probably felt to be somewhat more formal, and (like the two-syllable *Although*) is usually preferable at the beginning of a sentence. The contraction *'til* is little used nowadays, except in markedly informal contexts, such as personal letters.

## too

Used as an intensifier, *too* is sometimes illogical; if an intensifier is necessary in such sentences as these, use *very*:

✗　I don't like my cocoa *too* hot.
　　I don't like my cocoa *very* hot.

✗　She didn't care for the brown suit *too* much.
　　She didn't care for the brown suit *very* much.

But often you can omit the intensifier as unnecessary:

She didn't care much for the brown suit.

(See **very**.)

**toward, towards**

These are interchangeable, but in North American (as opposed to British) English, the preposition *toward* is usually preferred to *towards,* just as the adverbs *afterward, forward* (meaning *frontward),* and *backward* are to their counterparts ending in *s.*

**true facts**

Any reference to *true facts* is an attempt to be emphatic that backfires into illogic. If there are such things as "true facts" or "real facts," what are "false facts" or "unreal facts"? Let the word *facts* mean what it is supposed to; trying to prop it up with *true* or *real* makes a reader or listener suspect it of being weak or insincere.

**type, -type**

Don't use *type* as an adjective or part of an adjective, as in "He is a very athletic *type* person." In any but a technical context, the word *type* has the ring of jargon, even when followed by the obligatory *of*; without the *of* it is colloquial at best. In general writing, if you can substitute *kind of* for *type of,* do so—but even then check to make sure you really need it, for often it is unnecessary, mere deadwood: "She is an intelligent [kind of] woman." As a hyphenated suffix, *-type* is similarly often unnecessary, as well as being one of the results of the impulse to turn nouns into adjectives: "This is a new-type vegetable slicer," or "He is a patriotic-type person." Avoid it. (See also **kind of, sort of.**)

**unique, absolute, necessary, essential, complete, perfect, fatal, equal, (im)possible, infinite, empty, full, straight, round, square, etc.**

In writing, especially formal writing, treat these and other such adjectives as absolutes that cannot logically be compared or modified by such adverbs as *very* and *rather.* Since by definition something *unique* is the *only one of its kind* or *without equal,* clearly one thing cannot be "more unique" than another, or even "very unique"; in other words, *unique* is not a synonym for *unusual* or *rare.* Similarly with the others: one thing cannot be "more necessary" than another.

Since *perfect* means "without flaw," there cannot be degrees of perfection. Colloquially, expressions of degree or comparison with these terms are fairly common, especially those like *round, square, full, empty,* and *straight.* But strictly speaking, a thing is either *round* or not; one tennis ball cannot be "rounder" than another. And so on. And note that you can easily get around this semantic limitation by calling one thing, for example, "more nearly perfect," "more nearly round," or "closer to round" than another, or by referring to something as "almost unique" or "nearly unique" (but you could simply call it "very rare" or "highly unusual").

**until** (See **till, until, 'til.**)

**usage, use, utilize, utilization**
The noun *usage* is appropriate when you mean customary or habitual use, whether verbal or otherwise ("British usage," "the usages of the early Christians"), or a particular verbal expression being characterized in a particular way ("an ironic usage," "an elegant usage"). Otherwise the shorter noun *use* is preferable. As a verb, *use* should nearly always suffice; *utilize,* often pretentiously employed instead, should carry the specific meaning "put to use, make use of, turn to practical or profitable account." Similarly, the noun *use* will usually be more appropriate than *utilization.* Phrases like *use of, the use of, by the use of,* and *through the use of* tend toward jargon and are almost always wordy.

**verbal, oral**
Although these words are commonly used interchangeably, you may want to preserve the still useful distinction between them. *Verbal* regularly means "pertaining to words," which could be either written or spoken. If you mean "spoken aloud," then *oral* is preferable. (In some special contexts *verbal* is often used to mean *oral* as opposed to written: "verbal contract, verbal agreement"—but even these usages can be ambiguous; *oral* and *written* would make the circumstances precisely clear.)

**very**

When revising, you may find that where you have used *very* you could just as well omit it. Often it is a vague or euphemistic substitute for a more precise adverb or adjective:

> It was *very* sunny today. (magnificently sunny?)

> I was *very* tired. (exhausted?)

> He was *very* intoxicated. (falling-down drunk?)

> Her embarrassment was *very* obvious. (It was either obvious or it wasn't; drop *very*, or change it to something like *painfully*.)

The same goes for *really* and *actually*. Such weak intensifiers sometimes even detract from the force of the words they modify.

Note that before some past participles, it is idiomatic to use another word (e.g. *much, well*) along with *very*:

> You are *very much* mistaken if you think I'll agree without an argument.

> Sharon is *very well* rehearsed for the role.

**virtually** (See **literally, virtually, figuratively.**)

**way, ways**

In formal usage, especially in writing, don't use *ways* to refer to distance; *way* is correct:

> We were a long *way* from home.

> They had only a little *way* to go.

**well** (See **good, bad, badly, well.**)

**when, where** (See **is when, is where.**)

**whereas** (See **while.**)

**while**

As a subordinating conjunction, *while* is best restricted to meanings having to do with time:

> *While* Vijay mowed the lawn, Honoree raked up the grass clippings.

> She played the piano *while* I prepared the dinner.

When it means *although (though)* or *whereas*, it can be imprecise, even ambiguous:

✘   *While* I agree with some of his reasons, I still think my proposal is better. (*Although* would be clearer.)

✘   *While* he does the lawn-mowing, she cooks the meals. (Fuzzy or ambiguous; *whereas* would make the meaning clear.)

And it is weakest of all when used as a substitute for *and* or *but*:

✘   The winning team guzzled champagne, *while* the losers sat quietly in their dressing room.

(See also **although, though.**)

**will, shall** (See 6.8 [Simple future].)

**-wise**
Just as *-ize* (or *-ise*) has long been used to turn nouns and adjectives into verbs, *-wise* has been used to turn them into adverbs, e.g. of manner or position: *clockwise, crabwise, lengthwise, edgewise, side-wise, likewise, otherwise*. But this suffix, in its sense of "with reference to" (and equivalent phrases), is so overused in modern jargon (*moneywise, sales-wise, personnel-wise*, etc.) that it is now employed mainly as a source of humour ("And how are you otherwise-wise?"). Therefore do not tack it onto nouns, for it produces such inanities as what a politician once announced: "We've just had our best month ever, fundraisingwise." It is acceptable in established words but not, or seldom, in new coinages. You can easily find a way to say what you mean without resorting to it (see **in terms of**):

✘   *Grammarwise*, Stephen is doing well.
     Stephen is doing well with grammar.

✘   *Insurance-wise*, I believe I am well enough protected.
     I believe I have enough insurance.

✘   This is the best car I've ever owned, *powerwise*.
     This car has more power than any other I've owned.

**with regard to** (See **in terms of.**)

**with respect to** (See **in terms of.**)

**woman** (See **man, woman, lady, etc.**)

**worthwhile**
Try to find a more precise and concrete way to express the desired meaning. "It was a very worthwhile experience" tells one very little (nor does the *very* succeed in propping up the weak *worthwhile*). Skip the vague statement; instead, describe or explain just what was so worthwhile about the experience. (See also section 54.)

**would, should** (See 6.5 and 6.9 [Past tense in independent clauses].)

# CHAPTER VII
# Principles of Composition

# INTRODUCTION

# Paragraphs, the Writing Process, and Argument

Earlier chapters discuss the primary units of communication—sentences—and the fundamental elements of expression that make up sentences: words, phrases, and clauses. The principles of unity, coherence, and emphasis that apply to sentences (see sections 18, 28, and 31) apply also to the larger units, the paragraph and the piece of writing as a whole. These larger units are the subject of this chapter, which also provides a guide to the writing process and advice on writing an argument.

# 62. KINDS OF PARAGRAPHS

A paragraph can be classified in two ways:

1.  according to its function in its larger context, or

2.  according to the kind of material it contains and the way that material is developed.

## 62.1 Functions of Paragraphs

Introductory, concluding, and transitional paragraphs are especially designed to begin or end a piece of writing or to provide links between major sections. Other paragraphs, the body paragraphs, contribute to the development of a topic.

## 62.2 Kinds of Paragraphs: Methods of Development

Body paragraphs can be classified according to the way their material is developed. There are several methods of development to choose from. The method(s) you use for any given paragraph will depend on the nature of your topic and on your audience and purpose. The principal methods are description, narration, definition, classification, analysis into parts, process analysis, comparison and contrast, cause

and effect, and example and illustration. The following questions
will help you approach your subject with these methods in mind. In
each question, "X" represents the topic being developed.

- *description*: What are the physical features of X?
- *narration*: What is the story/history of X?
- *definition*: What is X?
- *classification*: Into what categories or types can X be divided?
- *analysis*: What are the parts of X and how do they contribute to
  the whole of X?
- *process analysis*: What are the steps of X, or what are the steps
  leading to X?
- *comparison and contrast*: How is X similar to Y? How is X
  different from Y?
- *cause and effect*: What are the causes of or reasons for X? What
  are the effects or consequences of X?
- *example and illustration*: What are some concrete/specific
  examples or instances of X?

These methods of development are seldom mutually exclusive. Two
or more are often combined in a single paragraph, and a whole piece
of writing may use several. Even narration can be used in an expository (explanatory) work: for example, a case study may provide narrative evidence to support an observation.

Some methods are combined in other ways. For example, when
you are comparing or contrasting you are also necessarily classifying
and defining. And almost any method can be thought of as supplying
examples to support or clarify an assertion made early in a paragraph
or work. As long as you maintain the fundamental requirements of
unity and coherence, you can mix and combine these methods in any
way that will be effective.

To demonstrate the ways in which the questions we have listed
would operate in the development of a topic, consider the following
scenario.

Suppose that you were asked to write a short piece of 500 words
or so on the broad subject area of contemporary air travel. At first,
you might draw a blank in thinking about ways in which to focus
the topic to allow you to write something distinctive—something to
engage your own interest and to earn the respect and interest of your
potential readers. Applying the questions we have listed would very
likely help you to open up the possibilities for development.

The process would look something like this:

| | |
|---|---|
| SUBJECT: | air travel today |
| *narration:* | What is the story? Tell the story of recent air travel to the United States. |
| *analysis:* | What were the steps in the process of the journey? |
| *effect:* | What are the consequences of air travel? |

- the stress of travelling during times of heightened security/terrorism alerts
- the boredom of sitting for hours in the boarding lounge, the airline cabins, the line-ups for luggage
- cramped quarters and claustrophobia for those travelling economy class

| | |
|---|---|
| *comparison:* | What are the essential differences between travel to the US by air and travel by car, train, or bus? |
| *description:* | What might I describe to enhance my writing? |

- the terminal building
- the security gate or customs desk
- the cramped quarters in the airline cabin
- the noise of the aircraft, of fellow passengers

In this stage of the process, you might see the methods of definition, classification, process analysis, and example/illustration as being less promising. Keep in mind that you may return to them at a later point, for the process of thinking your way through a topic is recursive—back and forth—rather than linear.

Following is an example of one of the paragraphs that might result from this process:

| | |
|---|---|
| **narrative opening** | My most recent trip to New York City brought home to me the ways in which airline travel has changed for the worse since the events of |
| **analysis: the steps in the security process** | September 11, 2001. Concerns about security were evident from the moment we made our way to the security gates at Vancouver Airport. Passengers were asked to remove overcoats and shoes; their photo identification was studied carefully; every adult passenger was questioned |

about travel plans by members of the security

**time transition: "After a four-hour delay"** staff. After a four-hour delay in our departure time, armed air marshals apparently boarded the aircraft with us, and the cockpit was locked.

**effects of the process** These measures put many of us passengers on edge and added a large dose of nervousness to the boredom and claustrophobia long associated with cross-border flights in less dangerous times.

# 63–67 UNITY, COHERENCE, ORGANIZATION AND EMPHASIS IN PARAGRAPHS

All paragraphs, but especially body paragraphs, in order to be effective, require unity, coherence, and properly controlled emphasis. Writing a paragraph involves designing the best possible package to contain and convey your ideas. You have a sense of what point you wish to convey (your topic), and, usually early in the process, you have an array of items to include as well (your supporting ideas and evidence). You arrange your ideas and evidence in the package by ordering them logically, linking them to one another using strategies for coherence. You may well spend some time rearranging to make the package look the way you want it to—to give each item the proper emphasis.

# 63. PARAGRAPH UNITY

An effective body paragraph deals with one main idea; its singleness of purpose engages its readers by focusing their attention on that main idea. If a paragraph is disrupted by irrelevant digressions or unnecessary shifts in point of view or focus, readers will lose the thread of the discourse and become confused. In other words, a paragraph has unity when every sentence in it contributes to its purpose and nothing in it is irrelevant to that purpose.

# 64. PARAGRAPH COHERENCE

Though a paragraph is unified because every sentence contributes to the development of its single theme or idea, it could still come apart if it doesn't have another essential quality: coherence. Coherence is the connection of ideas. Some inexperienced writers assume that simply placing one sentence after another guarantees coherence. On the contrary, coherence is achieved only by carefully packing the contents of a paragraph and linking the ideas to one another. You can ensure coherence in your writing in two ways:

1. by carefully organizing your material, and
2. by using the transitional devices that create structural coherence.

# 65. PARAGRAPH ORGANIZATION

A body paragraph has a beginning, a middle, and an ending. Good organization means rational order. Typically, the beginning introduces the main idea, the middle clearly and logically follows from and develops the statement of that idea, and the ending is a natural conclusion that unobtrusively closes the discussion or provides a hook for the next paragraph. (See the Writing Tip in 65.1.)

## 65.1 The Beginning: Topic Sentences

Typically body paragraphs open with a statement of the main idea, called a topic sentence.

**Functions of topic sentences**
A good topic sentence indicates what the paragraph will be about. It is, in effect, a promise that the rest of the paragraph fulfills. If the paragraph is part of a larger piece of writing, the topic sentence will usually perform two other functions:

1. It will refer to the piece's main topic and at least suggest the relation of the paragraph to that topic.
2. It will provide a transition so that the new paragraph flows smoothly from the preceding paragraph.

# Writing Tip

## On Positioning Transitional Material

It is sometimes possible, but almost always difficult, to provide for-ward-looking material at the end of a paragraph. Don't struggle to get something transitional into the last sentence of a paragraph. The work of transition should be done by the first sentence of the next paragraph. In other words, tampering with a paragraph's final sentence merely for transitional purposes may diminish that paragraph's integrity and effectiveness. See 65.3.

### Efficiency of topic sentences

Since it has so much to do, a good topic sentence, even more than other sentences, should be efficient. Here is one that is not:

> The poet uses a great deal of imagery throughout the poem.

The sentence indicates the topic—the poem's imagery—but promises nothing more than to show that the poem contains a lot of it. But offering a long list of images wouldn't develop an idea; it would merely illustrate what is self-evident. Trying to revise this weak topic sentence, the writer inserted the adjective *good* before *imagery*; now the paragraph must at least try to show that the abundant images are good ones (not as easy a task as the writer may have thought). But the focus is still largely on the quantity of imagery, which is not where the focus should be. What is most important is the function of the imagery: What does the poet do with the imagery? Further thought might lead to a revision like this—a topic sentence that not only has more substance in itself but also suggests the approach the paragraph will take:

> The poem's imagery, most of it drawn from nature, helps to create not only the poem's mood but its themes as well.

A good opening topic sentence should be more than just a table of contents; it should be a significant part of the contents of the paragraph. Pay close attention to the formulation of your topic sentences, for they can help you achieve both unity and coherence not only in individual paragraphs but also in the piece as a whole (see 69.1–69.2).

### Notes on the placement of topic sentences

In many paragraphs, the development fulfills the promise made in an opening topic sentence. Or, by conscious design, a topic sentence may be placed at the end or elsewhere in a paragraph. Sometimes delaying a topic sentence can increase readers' interest by creating a little mystery to get them to read on. And stating a topic at the end of a paragraph takes advantage of that most emphatic position (see section 67). Note, for example, the paragraph in 65.2 [Coherence through orderly development]. The topic sentence identifies the topic, which has two elements. But the paragraph itself refers to "development" only at the end, where the short final sentence explicitly ties it all to the idea of coherence. That part of the topic, in other words, we delayed until the end, or climax.

A paragraph's topic, then, though single, may consist of more than one part. Similarly, it may not be stated all in one sentence. In this paragraph and the one preceding, for example, note that not until the end of the second sentence is the topic fully clear. It is not uncommon for a paragraph to have a second topic sentence, one that partly restates the topic and partly leads into the body of the paragraph.

And, rarely, a paragraph's topic may not be stated at all because the focal idea of a paragraph is clearly and strongly implied. This kind of paragraph occurs most often in narratives, where paragraphs begin in such a way that their relation to the preceding paragraph is sufficiently clear—perhaps indicated by no more than an opening *Then* or *When*. See also the Notes on Beginnings, 70.12.

## 65.2 The Middle

### Coherence through orderly development

A well-developed body paragraph fulfills the promise of its beginning. If, for example, you were writing a paragraph that began with the last example of a topic sentence above ("In the second stanza images of death begin the process that leads to the poem's ironic conclusion"), you would have to explain the process and the irony of the poem's conclusion, and you would have to show how images of death from the second stanza set that process in motion. To fulfill your promise effectively, then, you would have to decide how to organize your material. For example, you might first describe the irony of the conclusion and then analyze the images to show how they lead to that conclusion. Or you might start by analyzing the death imagery and then proceed to answer some questions that you could ask yourself: What effect do the images create? How does that effect contribute to the way the poem proceeds? How does that process lead to the conclusion? In other words, after considering the different possibilities, you would choose a way of presenting your material, and the order you choose to follow should be one that makes sense; one idea should lead logically to another until you reach your goal. Then your paragraph will be coherent.

## Patterns of development

Orderly development sometimes occurs automatically as one works through one's ideas in composing paragraphs. But most writers must give some conscious thought to how a particular paragraph can best be shaped. The most common patterns of development writers use to make their paragraphs orderly and coherent are the following:

- *spatial* (moving through space, such as top to bottom or left to right; used in describing physical space)
- *chronological* (moving through time; used in narration and process analysis)
- *climactic* (moving from the least important to most important point; used in much academic writing)
- *inverse pyramid* (moving from the most important to least important point; used in reportage/journalism)
- *inductive* (moving from data to assertions; often used in writing for sciences and social sciences)
- *deductive* (moving from assertions to supporting data or premises, often used in writing for the humanities)
- *block* (in a comparison of two items, a full discussion of the first item followed by a full discussion of the second item)
- *alternating* (in a comparison of two items, a back-and-forth discussion of the first and second items)

Further, some of the methods of development discussed above (see 62.2) themselves impose patterns on the arrangement of ideas in a paragraph. In addition to using narration and process analysis, which focus on chronological order, or description, with its focus on spatial order, one can move from cause to effect or from effect to cause, or from a statement about a whole to a division of it into parts (analysis), or from a statement about one thing to a comparison of it with another. As with the methods of development, these patterns are not mutually exclusive.

## 65.3 The Ending

As you compose and revise your drafts, the endings of your paragraphs will sometimes come naturally. But they are likely to do so only if, when you begin a paragraph, you know just where it is going. The concluding sentence of a paragraph, like all the others, should be a part of the whole (and see the Writing Tip in 65.1). In other words, the final sentence of a paragraph will most often be a statement growing out of the substance of the paragraph, a sentence that rounds off its paragraph in such a way that readers get the feeling of a satisfying close.

### Some advice for ending paragraphs

If a paragraph doesn't seem to be ending naturally, you may have to stop and think consciously about it. Here are a few pointers to help you do that:

1. A good ending may point back to the beginning, but it will not merely repeat it; if it repeats something, it will do so in order to put it in the new light made possible by the development of the paragraph.

2. A good ending sentence doesn't usually begin with a stiff "In conclusion" or "To conclude." In fact, sometimes the best way to end a paragraph is simply to let it stop, once its point is made. A too-explicit conclusion might damage the effectiveness of an otherwise good paragraph that has a natural feeling of closure at its end.

3. A good ending might have a slight stylistic shift that marks a paragraph's ending, perhaps no more than an unusually short or long sentence. Or an ending might be marked by an allusion or brief quotation, as long as it is relevant and to the point and not there simply for its own sake.

4. A good paragraph usually doesn't end with an indented ("block") quotation, or even a shorter full-sentence quotation that isn't set off. Even though you carefully introduce such a quotation, it will almost inevitably leave a feeling that you

have abandoned your paragraph to someone else. Complete such a paragraph with at least a brief comment that explains the quotation, justifies it, or re-emphasizes its main thrust.

# 66. STRUCTURAL COHERENCE

Careful organization and development go a long way toward achieving coherence. But you will sometimes need to use other techniques as well, providing links that ensure a smooth flow of thought from one sentence to another.

The main devices for structural coherence are parallelism, repetition, pronouns and demonstrative adjectives, and transitional words and phrases. Like the methods and patterns of development, these devices are not mutually exclusive: two or more may work together in the same paragraph, sometimes even in the same words and phrases.

## 66.1 Parallelism (See 17.3 and section 27.)

Parallel sentence structure is a simple and effective way to bind successive sentences. Similar structural patterns in clauses and phrases work like a call and its echo. But don't try to maintain a series of parallel elements for too long. If the echoes remain obvious, they will be too noticeable and will diminish in power as they get farther from the original. Parallelism, like any other device, should not be overdone.

## 66.2 Repetition

Like parallelism, repetition of words and phrases effectively links successive sentences. But the caution against overdoing is most applicable here. Repetition properly controlled for rhetorical effect can be powerful (as in Martin Luther King's famous "I have a dream" speech), but repetition, especially on paper, can also become evidence of a writer's limited vocabulary or ingenuity. Structure your repetitions carefully; don't put too many too close together. And generally use the device sparingly.

## 66.3 Pronouns and Demonstrative Adjectives

By referring to something mentioned earlier, a pronoun or a demonstrative adjective constructs a bridge within the paragraph between itself and its antecedent or referent.

# Writing Tip

## Using Pronouns and Demonstrative Adjectives to Create Unity and Coherence

It is also possible, of course, to use pronouns and demonstrative adjectives to create links between paragraphs, but avoid

- an ambiguous antecedent or referent, and
- a distant antecedent.

If you are far beyond the antecedent, or if more than one is possible, you risk confusing your readers rather than building coherence for them. Either way, straight repetition is preferable.

And make it a point to use demonstrative adjectives rather than demonstrative pronouns. Demonstrative adjectives are clear and can add emphasis. Pronouns are not emphatic; rather they can be weak and ambiguous (see 3.6, 5.3, 8.1, section 28).

## 66.4 Transitional Terms

Used strategically, transitional words and phrases can create a logical flow from one part or idea to another by indicating their relation. The best transitional signal for a particular spot in a discourse creates successful coherence. Here are some of the more common and useful transitional terms:

- terms showing addition of one point to another:

  | | | | |
  |---|---|---|---|
  | and | also | another | in addition |
  | further | besides | moreover | |

- terms showing similarity between ideas:

  | | | | |
  |---|---|---|---|
  | again | equally | in other words | in the same way |
  | likewise | similarly | | |

- terms showing difference between ideas:

  | but | although | conversely | despite |
  |---|---|---|---|
  | even though | however | yet | though |
  | in contrast | whereas | nevertheless | in spite of |
  | still | otherwise | on the contrary | on the other hand |

- terms showing cause and effect or other logical relations:

  | as a result | because | consequently | for |
  |---|---|---|---|
  | hence | of course | since | then |
  | therefore | thus | | |

- terms introducing examples or details:

  | for example | in particular | namely | specifically |
  |---|---|---|---|
  | for instance | to illustrate | that is | |

- terms expressing emphasis:

  | chiefly | especially | more important |
  |---|---|---|
  | indeed | mainly | primarily |

- terms showing relations in time and space:

  | after | afterward | at the same time | before |
  |---|---|---|---|
  | earlier | in the meantime | later | meanwhile |
  | simultaneously | then | while | subsequently |
  | behind | beyond | farther away | here |
  | nearby | in the distance | next | there |
  | to the left | | | |

These and other such words and phrases, occurring usually at or near the beginnings of sentences, are the glue that helps hold paragraphs together. But if the paragraph isn't unified in its content, and if its parts haven't been arranged to fit with one another, then even these explicit transitional terms won't give much structural coherence to your writing.

## Writing Tip

### On Avoiding Overuse of Transitions

Don't overuse transitional terms. If your paragraph already contains structural elements that make it coherent, it won't need any of these. Adding a transitional word or phrase to nearly every sentence will make writing stiff and mechanical sounding.

## 67. EMPHASIS IN PARAGRAPHS

Just as in a sentence, so in a paragraph the most emphatic position is its ending, and the second most emphatic position is its beginning (see 18.1). That is another reason the opening or topic sentence is so important a part of a paragraph. And an ending, because of its emphatic position, can make or break a paragraph.

But structure and diction are also important. Parallelism and repetition create emphasis. Independent clauses are more emphatic than subordinate clauses and phrases. Precise, concrete, and specific words are more emphatic than vague, abstract, and general ones. A long sentence will stand out among several shorter ones; a short sentence will stand out among longer ones. Keep these points in mind as you compose and revise your paragraphs; let emphasis contribute to the effectiveness of your writing.

## 68. PARAGRAPH LENGTH

There is no optimum length for a paragraph. The length of a paragraph will be determined by the requirements of the particular job it is doing. In narration or dialogue, a single sentence or a single word may constitute a paragraph. In a complex exposition or argumentative piece, a paragraph may go on for a page or more—though such long paragraphs are rare in modern writing. Most body paragraphs consist of at least three or four sentences, and seldom more than nine or ten. Transitional paragraphs are usually short, sometimes only one sentence. Introductory and concluding paragraphs will be of various lengths, depending on the complexity of the material and on the techniques of beginning and ending that the writer is using.

## 68.1 Too Many Long Paragraphs

If you find that you are writing many long paragraphs, you may be over-developing, piling more into a paragraph than its topic requires. Or you may not be weeding out irrelevant material. Or you may be dealing in one paragraph with two or more topics that should be dealt with in separate paragraphs. Any of these tendencies can damage the coherence of your writing. Generally, aim to give your reader a minimum of one paragraph break per page.

## 68.2 The Importance of Adequate Development

A common weakness among inexperienced writers is to settle for paragraphs that are too short to develop their topics sufficiently. The body of a paragraph should be long enough to develop a topic satisfactorily. Merely restating or summarizing the topic is not enough. If you find yourself writing many short paragraphs, you may not be adequately developing your main ideas. Or you may be endangering coherence by splintering your discussion into small parts: when you revise, check to see if two or more related short paragraphs can be integrated to form one substantial paragraph.

## 68.3 Variety

Try to ensure that any extended piece of writing you produce contains a variety of paragraph lengths: long, short, medium. The reader may become unengaged if all paragraphs are of a predictable length. (The same is true of sentences of similar length: see 17.1.) You should also try to provide a variety of patterns (65.2 [Patterns of development]) and methods of development (62.2) in your paragraphs. For example, parallelism, however admirable a device, would likely lose its effect if it were the basic pattern in several successive paragraphs.

Normally, then, the paragraphs that make up an extended piece of writing will vary in length. Ensure that each of your paragraphs is as long or as short as it needs to be to achieve its intended purpose. See also 69.3.

# 69. PRINCIPLES OF COMPOSITION: UNITY, COHERENCE, AND EMPHASIS

The principles of composition apply with equal validity to the piece of writing as a whole and to each of its parts: what holds true for the sentence and the paragraph also holds true for the entire work.

## 69.1 Unity

Like a sentence or a paragraph, any piece of writing should be unified. That is, everything in it should be about one topic. If your paragraphs are themselves unified and if you make sure that the opening sentences of each paragraph refer explicitly (or implicitly but unmistakably) to your overall subject (see 65.1 [Functions of topic sentences]), your piece of writing will be unified.

## 69.2 Coherence

There should be coherence not only between words and between sentences, but also between paragraphs. If the beginning of each paragraph provides some kind of transition from the preceding paragraph, the whole work will almost surely be coherent. The transitional words and phrases listed above (66.4) and others like them are often useful for establishing the necessary connections between paragraphs, but don't overdo it by using them to begin every paragraph. Often you can create the link by repeating a significant word or two from the preceding paragraph, usually from somewhere near its end, and sometimes you can make or strengthen the link with a demonstrative adjective, or even a pronoun (but see the Writing Tip in 66.3). Remember, though, that transitional words and phrases are meant to draw attention to links that exist in the content of consecutive paragraphs. Without an inherent connection between one paragraph and the next, not even explicit transitions will be effective. (See also 65.1, on topic sentences.)

## 69.3 Emphasis

Just as in a sentence or a paragraph (see 18.1 and section 67), the most emphatic position in a piece of writing is its ending, and the second most emphatic position is its beginning. That is why it is important to be clear and to the point from the beginning (see 70.12 [Direct, smooth, economical ...]), and why the ending of the piece should be forceful. Don't, for example, conclude by repeating your introduction or by summarizing your points. And since the last thing readers see is usually what sticks most vividly in their minds, writers often use climactic order, beginning with simple or less elaborate points and ending with more important or complex ones (see 65.2 [Patterns of development]).

Further, the length of a paragraph automatically suggests something about the importance of its contents. Although a short, sharp paragraph can be emphatic in its own way, generally a long paragraph will deal with a relatively important part of the subject. As you look over your work, check to make sure you haven't skimped on an important point, and also that you haven't gone on for too long about a relatively minor point (see section 68).

# 70. THE PROCESS OF PLANNING, WRITING, AND REVISING

No effective piece of writing can be a mere random assemblage of sentences and paragraphs. It must have a shape, a design, even if only a simple one. How does one get from the blank page to the desired finished product? By taking certain steps, because a piece of writing, like any other product, is the result of a process. The usual steps that a writer takes, whether consciously or not, fall into three major stages:

**Stage I: Planning**

- identifying the subject
- limiting the subject
- determining audience and purpose
- gathering data
- classifying and organizing the data
- outlining

**Stage II: Writing**

- writing the first draft

**Stage III: Revising**

- revising
- preparing the final draft
- editing and proofreading

Sometimes one or more steps may be taken care of for you; for example, if you are assigned a specific topic, finding and limiting a subject, and perhaps even determining audience and purpose, will already be taken care of. And often several parts of the process will be going on at the same time; for example, there is often a good deal of interaction among the activities in the planning stage. Sometimes the order will be different; for example, you may not be clear about your purpose until you have finished gathering and then classifying and organizing data. And sometimes in the revising stage, you may want to go back and rethink your purpose, or dig up more material, or even further limit or expand your topic. But all the activities have to happen somehow, somewhere, sometime, for a polished piece of writing to be produced.

And even though you may take some of these steps as a matter of course, relatively inexperienced writers should consider following them deliberately.

## 70.1 Identifying the Subject

An essential part of the writing process will involve identifying the subject that you are writing about. If research is involved, develop topics around researchable questions of current interest in the field and narrow them to fit your timeframe and the length expected by your reader.

In working out your research and preparing a writing plan, devise a reasonable timeline for research, planning, writing, revising, and editing. Consider the needs and expectations of your reading audience and the availability of a variety of electronic and non-electronic sources that are both reliable and current. Keep in mind that the use of Canadian sources may be important to your objectives and to your readers.

Try to find a subject that interests you, one that you will enjoy working with. Formulate a question or series of questions worth investigating and researching. Do not, in desperation, pick a subject that bores you, for you may handle it poorly, and probably bore your readers as well.

## 70.2 Limiting the Subject

Once you have a subject, limit it: narrow it to a topic that you can develop adequately within your timeframe. More often than not, writers start with subjects that are too big to handle. Seldom do they come up, right away, with a topic like what people's shoes reveal about their characters; they're more likely to start with some vague notion about footwear. To save both time and energy and to avoid frustration, be disciplined at this stage. If anything, overdo the narrowing, for at a later stage it's easier to broaden than it is to cut.

For example, let's say you wanted to write about "travelling"; that's obviously far too broad. "National travel" or "international travel" is narrower, but still too broad. "Travelling in Asia?" Better, but still too large, for where would you begin? How thorough could you be in a mere 500 or even 1,000 words? When you find yourself narrowing your subject to something like "How to survive on $20.00 a day in Tokyo" or "What to do if you only had 24 hours in Bangkok" or "Why I don't travel with my mother" or "The day my passport got stolen," then you can confidently look forward to developing your topic with sufficient thoroughness and specificity. (See also section 55.)

## 70.3 Considering Audience and Purpose

### Audience

When you write a personal letter, you naturally direct it to a specific reader. If you write a "Letter to the Editor" of a newspaper, you have only a vague notion of your potential readership, namely anyone who reads that newspaper, but you will know where almost all of them live, and knowing only that much could give you something to aim at in your letter. The sharper the focus you can get on your audience, the better you can control your writing to make it effective for that audience. Try to define or characterize your audience for a given piece of writing as precisely as possible.

In the absence of any other guideline, writing for your peers is not a bad idea. Your choice of the right tone and language to use and of what definitions and explanations to provide will often be appropriate if you keep an interested and serious but not fully informed audience in mind.

## Purpose

All writing has the broad purpose of communicating ideas. You will write more effectively if you think of each piece of writing as having one or more of the following purposes:

1. to inform

2. to convince or persuade

3. to enter into discussion or debate

4. to entertain

Most writers, however, face the challenge of writing for several purposes. For example, novelists' primary purpose may be to entertain their readers, but they may also seek to inform them with historically accurate details. A set of instructions will have the primary purpose of informing readers how to do something, but it may also be trying to convince them that this is the best way to do it. And in order to interest them more, it may also be written in a stimulating style. An entertaining or even whimsical piece may well have a satiric thrust or some kind of implicit "lesson" calculated to spark debate. And so on. Usually one of the four purposes will dominate, but several of the others will often be present as well. (And see section 71 below, on writing arguments.)

The clearer your idea of what you want to do in your writing, and why, and for whom, the better you will be able to make effective rhetorical choices. You may even want to begin by writing down, as a memo to yourself, a detailed description or "profile" of your audience and as clear a statement of your purpose as you can formulate. Tape this memo to the wall over your desk. If your ideas become clearer as the work proceeds, you can refine these statements. In any event, as you go through the process of writing, keep sight of your audience and your purpose.

## 70.4 Gathering Data

A piece of non-fiction writing can't survive on just vague generalizations and unsupported statements and opinions; it must contain specifics: facts, details, data, examples. Whatever your subject, you must gather material by reading and researching, conducting formal interviews, talking to others, or by thinking about your personal experience. And don't stop when you think you have just enough; collect as much information as you can within the time you have allotted for data gathering, even two or three times what you can use; you can select the best and bank the rest for future use.

### Brainstorming

If you are expected to generate material from your own knowledge and experience (instead of through formal research), you may, at first, have difficulty coming up with ideas. Don't be discouraged. Sit down with a pencil and a sheet of paper, write your topic in the centre or at the top, and begin jotting down ideas. Put down everything that comes into your head about it. Let your mind run fast and free. Don't bother with sentences; don't worry about spelling; don't even pause to wonder whether the words and phrases are going to be of any use. Just keep scribbling. It shouldn't be long before you've filled the sheet with possible ideas, questions, facts, details, names, examples. You may even need to use a second sheet. It may help if you also brainstorm your larger subject area, not just the narrowed topic, since some of the broader ideas could prove useful.

### Using questions

Another way to generate material is to ask yourself questions about your subject or topic and write down the answers. Start with the reporter's standard questions: *Who? What? Where? When? Why? How?* and go on from there with more of your own: What is it? Who is associated with it? In what way? Where and when is it, or was it, or will it be? How does it work? Why is it? What causes it? What does it cause? What are its parts? What is it a part of? Is it part of a process? What does it look like? What is it like or unlike? What is its opposite? What if it didn't exist? Such questions and the answers you get will make you think of more questions, and so on; soon you'll have more than enough material that is potentially useful. You may even find yourself writing consecutive sentences, since some questions prompt certain kinds of responses. For example, asking *What is it?* may lead you to begin defining your subject; *What is it like or unlike?* may lead you to begin comparing and contrasting it, classifying it, thinking of analogies and metaphors; *What causes it?* and *What does it cause?* may lead you to begin exploring cause-and-effect relations; *What are its parts?* or *What is it made of?* could lead you to analyze your subject; *How does it work?* or *Is it part of a process?* may prompt you to analyze and explain a process.

## 70.5 Classifying and Organizing the Data

### Classifying

As you brainstorm a subject and jot down notes and answers, you'll begin to see connections between one idea and another and start putting them in groups or drawing circles around them and lines and arrows between them. It is important to do this kind of classification when you have finished gathering material. You should end up with several groups of related items, which means that you will have classified your material according to some principle that arose naturally from it. During this part of the process you will probably also have discarded the weaker or less relevant details, keeping only those that best suit the topic as it is now beginning to take shape; that is, you will have selected the best.

# Writing Tip

## On Managing Groups of Details in Classifications

Try to classify your material in such a way that you end up with several groups, each of which will correspond to a separate major section of your piece of writing. Remember, though, that more than seven major sections may be unwieldy for both writer and reader. Similarly, an organization of only two major sections risks turning into two large lumps; if your material calls for organizing into only two sections, take extra care to ensure that the whole is unified and coherent.

## Organizing

Once you have classified your material into groups, put the groups into some kind of order. Don't necessarily accept the first arrangement that comes to mind; consider as many different arrangements as the material will allow, and then select the best one for your purpose and audience. (For the most common arrangements, see 65.2 [Patterns of development].) The order should be logical rather than accidental or arbitrary. Ideally, the groups and their details should fall into order naturally, resulting in an arrangement that is the most effective way of presenting the material.

## 70.6 The Outline

The most crucial part of the planning or "pre-writing" stage is the construction of an outline. During the early stages, you gradually increase your control over your piece of writing: you find and narrow a subject, you think about audience and purpose, you gather data and generate ideas, and you classify and arrange your material.

The ordered groups identified earlier become main headings, and the details that make up each group, if they aren't simply absorbed by the main heading, become subdivisions of it in various levels of subheadings. And though tentative sketches of a possible beginning and ending aren't essential to an outline, it's usually worth trying to think of something of the sort at this stage; you can easily change later if you think of something better.

Note the layout of an outline: numerals and letters are followed by periods and a space or two; subheadings are indented at least two spaces past the beginning of the first word of a main heading. Few outlines will need to go beyond one or two levels of subheading (see 70.10 #5).

## 70.7 The Importance of Outlining

An outline drawn up before you begin writing will usually save you both time and effort. Writing the draft will be easier and smoother because it follows a plan: you know where you're going. You can avoid such pitfalls as unnecessary repetition, digression, and illogical or otherwise incoherent organization. In other words, a good outline can be like a map that keeps the writer from taking wrong turns, wandering in circles, or getting lost altogether.

Keep in mind, too, that an outline should not be binding. If as you write and revise you think of a better way to organize your thoughts, or if some part of the outline proves clumsy when you try to set it down in paragraphs, or if you suddenly think of some new material that should be included, by all means go with your instincts and revise accordingly. And as you proceed, you may want to refine your argument to reflect changes in your ideas. The virtue of using an outline is that rather than drifting about rudderless, you are in control of any changes you make because you make them consciously and carefully, and you will have a record of your changes if you want to rethink them later.

## 70.8 Kinds of Outlines

Outlining of some kind is usually necessary. The method of outlining you use may be what makes most sense to you, or it may be one of the three common methods:

- *topic outline*: lays out headings and subheadings for each topic you will discuss
- *paragraph outline*: lists the proposed topic or opening sentences of successive paragraphs
- *sentence outline*: resembles a topic outline except that brief headings and subheadings are replaced by complete sentences

## 70.9 Sentence Outlines

The advantage of having to phrase each topic as a complete sentence is that you are unlikely to fool yourself into thinking you have something to say when in fact you don't. For example, imagine you are writing an article on various cuisines and, in a topic outline, you put down the heading "the new trends." But if you haven't been eating out recently, you might find when you sit down to write your draft that you have little or nothing to say. In a sentence outline, you are compelled to make a statement about the topic, in this case perhaps something like "Although people have their favourite meals at home, when it comes to eating out, they are willing to try different foods." With even such a vague sentence before you, you can more easily begin supplying details to develop your idea; the act of formulating the sentence guarantees that you have at least some ideas about whatever you put down.

Another virtue of a sentence outline is that, when properly handled, it is self-constructing. Our earlier example—"Although people have their favourite meals, when it comes to eating out, they are willing to try different food"—automatically leads into two subheadings: "A. people have their favourite meals," and "B. when it comes to eating out, they are willing to try different food." Such partial repetition is natural to a good sentence outline; it may seem stiff and clumsy, but it is a strength, since it fosters coherence and unity.

## 70.10 Constructing Sentence Outlines

The following are some guidelines for putting together a good sentence outline:

1.  Make every item from the main argument down to the last subheading a single complete major sentence.

2.  Use only simple or complex sentences; do not use compound sentences. Since the independent clauses of a compound sentence could themselves be written as separate sentences, having a compound sentence in your outline may mean that two or more headings are masquerading as one; consider making each clause a separate heading.

3.  In any kind of outline you need to supply at least two subheadings if you supply any at all. A subheading, by definition, implies division. For this reason, a heading cannot be subdivided into only one part as a subheading. If you find yourself unable to go beyond one subheading, it probably isn't a subdivision at all but an integral part of the main heading that should be incorporated into it.

4.  The headings or subheadings at each level should be reasonably parallel with each other; that is, I, II, III, etc. should have about the same level of importance, as should subheadings A, B, C, etc. under a given main heading, and 1, 2, 3, etc. under each of these. One way to help achieve this balance is to make the sentences at any given level as much as possible grammatically parallel.

5. Few outlines need to go beyond one level of subheading. Remember that headings and subheadings should mostly state ideas, propositions, generalizations; the supporting facts can be supplied at the writing stage and don't need to go into the outline. If you find yourself including several levels of subheading, you may already be itemizing your facts and details.

## Writing Tip

### On Managing the Number of Subheadings in an Outline

As with the major sections of your piece of writing, having more than six or seven subheadings under any one heading risks being unwieldy.

### 70.11 Writing the First Draft

Once you have a good outline to follow, the work of drafting becomes smoother and more purposeful. With the shape of the whole piece laid out, you can concentrate on the main tasks of drafting your piece of writing: finding the right words, generating the right kinds of sentences, and constructing good transitions and strong paragraphs.

## Writing Tip

### On Going from an Outline to a Draft

Sometimes a main heading and its subheading from the outline will become a single paragraph; sometimes each subheading will become a paragraph; and so on. The nature and density of your material will determine its treatment.

### 70.12 Notes on Beginnings

#### Postponing the beginning

Starting the actual writing can be a challenge: most writers have had the experience of staring at a computer screen or a blank sheet of paper for an uncomfortable length of time while trying to think of a good way to begin. If you have no beginning in mind at this point, don't waste time trying to think of one. Plunge right into the body paragraphs and write as rapidly as you can. Once you have finished writing the first draft, you'll have a better idea of what it is that needs to be introduced; you can then go back and do the beginning with relative ease. In fact, writers who write a beginning first often discard the original version and write a new one, either because the content demands a different kind of beginning or because in the midst of composing they thought of a better one.

### Beginning directly

Just as it isn't always a good idea to begin a final paragraph with "In conclusion," so it's generally not good practice to open routinely with something mechanical like "In this article I will discuss" or "This article is concerned with." On occasion, such as when you are presenting your writing as part of a conference or panel, it may be helpful to explain in advance what you will be speaking about, to provide the audience with what amounts to a brief outline (just as it is then often necessary to provide some summary by way of conclusion). But most writing doesn't require this kind of beginning and won't engage readers with such a stiff introduction. As a rule, then, don't talk about yourself; talk about your topic. Rather than begin by informing readers of what you are going to say (and then at the end reminding them of what you have said), start with something substantial and, if possible, attention-getting. Try to end with something similarly sharp and definitive.

### Direct, smooth, economical: some examples

Begin as directly, smoothly, and economically as you can. Here is an example of an ineffective beginning. That the writer was in difficulty is shown by the redundancy in the first sentence, the illogicality in the second sentence, and the vague reference and wordy emptiness of the third:

> Nowadays, in these modern times, different cultures celebrate different holidays in many different ways. Thanksgiving is filled with a seemingly endless variety of memories and emotions. I would imagine this is experienced by almost every family and mine is most certainly not an exception.

The writer's own revision proves that the difficulties were merely the result of floundering, trying too hard to make a beginning; had the beginning been written after the body paragraphs were complete, it might have taken this form:

> Holidays help define a family. In my family, where expectations are great, Thanksgiving brings out the best and worst of our individual characteristics.

## 70.13–70.15 The Final Steps

The product of rapid composition is a first draft. Although some first drafts may come close to being acceptable finished products, there are still three tasks to undertake before you should consider your piece final: revising, preparing the final draft, and proofreading.

### 70.13 Revising

Revision (literally meaning "scrutinizing again") is an extremely important stage of writing, far too often neglected by less experienced writers. Experienced writers revise a piece of writing at least two or three times. Many writers revise five or even ten or more times before they consider a piece to be finished.

Revise carefully and slowly, looking for any way to improve what you've written. Don't aim just to correct errors made in haste, but also to remove clutter and improve diction, sentence structure, punctuation, coherence, paragraphing, organization, and so on. Some writers find that going through a draft for one thing at a time is effective—for example, going through it looking only at paragraphing, then going through it again looking only at the structure and variety of sentences, then at punctuation, then at diction, and so on. And you will want to proofread carefully for those errors you know you tend to make.

Adopt the role of an observant and alert reader looking for strengths and pinpointing weaknesses and errors. To do this effectively, try to allow yourself a cooling-off period; wait as long as possible between the drafting and the revising—at least two or three days—so that you can look at your own work with more objectivity, as a dispassionate third-party reader would.

## 70.14 Preparing the Final Draft

When you are through revising a piece of writing, carefully prepare the final draft, the one that will be presented to your reader or readers. Once the work is out of your hands, it's too late to change anything; make sure it's in good shape when it leaves your hands. It should be neat, and it should be in the appropriate format for the kind of writing it is. For most formal writing, follow carefully the conventions listed and discussed in section 45.

## 70.15 Editing and Proofreading

Proofreading will have been taking place during revision, of course, and also during drafting, but go over what you consider to be the final version when you believe it is ready. This final proofreading will prove worthwhile; despite earlier careful scrutiny, you will probably discover not only typographical errors but also hitherto unnoticed slips in spelling, punctuation, and grammar.

Do your proofreading with exaggerated care. Read each sentence, as a sentence, slowly (and aloud whenever possible); but also read each word as a word; check each punctuation mark, and consider the possibility of adding some or removing some or changing some. Particularly when you proofread for spelling errors, do so as a separate process. You might consider doing this by starting at the end of your work and reading backward, one word at a time, so that you won't get caught up in the flow of a sentence and overlook an error.

Do not put full trust in any of the spelling, grammar, and style checks that are part of, or designed to be used with, word-processing programs. They can't possibly cover all the matters that require attention. And remember that spell checkers can't spot a misspelled word that happens to be the same as some other correctly spelled word—for example, *form* instead of *from*, or *through* instead of *though*; nor can they tell you that you've mistaken, say, *your* for *you're*, or *principal* for *principle*.

# 71. ARGUMENT: WRITING TO CONVINCE OR PERSUADE

Most of the principles of composition are even more important in argument than in other kinds of writing, though as we have suggested earlier (70.3 [Purpose]), other kinds of writing, especially exposition, often include an element of argumentation. But when your principal purpose is to convince or persuade, there are several additional points and principles to keep in mind. Here are some brief suggestions and some practical advice to help you write effective arguments. (See also section 61 [convince, persuade].)

## 71.1 Subject

When you are focusing on your subject for an argumentative piece of writing, keep in mind that there is no point in arguing about easily verifiable facts or generally accepted assumptions (2 + 2 = 4; the sky looks blue; good nutrition promotes good health; oil is a nonrenewable energy source). One cannot argue about facts, only about what the facts mean. Since an argument depends on logical reasoning, when you argue about opinions based on facts you will necessarily use factual data to support your contentions. A collection of unsupported opinions is not an argument but merely a series of assertions.

Similarly, one cannot logically argue about matters of taste. You can't argue that blue is a prettier colour than green; you can only assert that *you* find it prettier, for whatever reason. The subject of an argument should be something that is capable of verification, though the fact that it is being argued about at all indicates that its verification is not automatic or to be taken for granted.

## 71.2 Audience

When your purpose is to convince or persuade, your knowledge of your audience and your constant awareness of that audience are crucial. Consider, for example, how differently you would have to handle your material and your tone depending on whether you were writing to an audience of (a) people basically sympathetic to your position or (b) people likely to be hostile to your position. Since the effectiveness of an argument depends partly on your gaining or holding the confidence of your readers, or at least getting them to listen to you willingly and with a reasonably open mind, it is important that you avoid presenting anything that might keep them from listening.

Know your audience. Are your readers largely men? women? elderly? young? well-educated? middle-class? business people? students? politically conservative? "green"? wealthy? poor? artistic? sports lovers? car owners? family oriented? animal lovers? And so on. The more you know about your potential readers and their attitude toward your topic, the better you will know what choices to make so that you can clearly communicate your position and its value as an argument worth thinking about.

## 71.3 Evidence

When you are gathering material for an argument, look especially for concrete, specific, precise, factual data that you can use to support your generalizations (see 55.2). The effectiveness of your argument will, in part, depend on the quality and the quantity of the evidence you provide both to support your position and to counter your opposition. For example, try to find some statistics you can cite, or some expert you can quote (the appeal to authority), or some common experience or assumption about life that you can remind your readers of (the appeal to common sense). You may be able to make good use of your own experience or that of someone you know well.

But be sure that the evidence you gather and use is both reliable and relevant. Don't cite a rap artist as an authority on a medical question—unless she's studying for her M.D.; don't cite as support the results of an experiment that has been superseded by later experiments; don't discuss the style and upholstery of a car if you're arguing about which car provides the most efficient transportation.

## 71.4 Organization

Consider audience and purpose when laying out your material. You will find that an outline will often help you. Here are some specific points to keep in mind:

## Emphasis

Usually, you will want to save your strongest point or points for the end, the most emphatic position of your argument. But since the beginning is also emphatic, don't open with a weak or minor point. It is usually best to begin with strength and then deal with minor points and proceed to the end in the order of climax. (See also sections 18 and 67, and 69.3.)

## Thesis

In an argument, your thesis statement is in effect a proposition that you intend to support; you want to prove it, at least to the satisfaction of your readers. For that reason, it usually appears at the beginning, just as a formal debate begins with a reading of the proposition to be debated. Occasionally, however, you can delay your statement of the thesis until near the end, letting a logical progression of reasoning lead up to it. But don't try for this dramatic effect unless it will work better than stating your proposition up front; for example, consider whether your readers might be put off, rather than drawn in, by being kept in the dark about just what your proposition is. (See also 70.12 [Direct, smooth, economical ...].)

## Methods of development

Arguments can make use of any of the methods of development: narration (an illustrative anecdote), description (a detailed physical description of something it is important for readers to visualize clearly and perhaps feel emotion towards), comparison and contrast, analysis, and so on (see 62.2). But be careful with analogy: using an analogy as the central pillar of an argumentative structure is risky, for opponents can too easily challenge it and pull it apart (see 71.8 [False or weak analogy]); use analogy as an extra illustration or as one of several minor props. Definitions help establish a common ground between you and the reader. And give strong consideration to cause-and-effect analysis (*What caused it? What does it cause? What will it cause?*), often a mainstay of argument: you argue for or against something because of what has happened or is happening or will happen as a result of it.

## Patterns of development

Similarly, an argument can use any one or more of the common patterns of development (see 65.2 [Patterns of development]). An argument is likely, for example, to follow a logical progression, to move from general to specific or from specific to general, and to rise to a climax. But there is one further pattern that often occurs in argument: like a formal debate, many arguments move back and forth between *pro* and *con*, between statements supporting your proposition and statements refuting your opponent's position (see 71.6).

# 71.5–71.7 How to Argue: Reasoning Logically

## 71.5 Being Reasonable

Appeal to common sense; appeal to authority; above all, appeal to reason. Demonstrate your respect for your reader's intelligence by appealing to it; a reader is then more likely to respect you and your arguments. If you appeal to prejudices and baser instincts you may get through to a few, but thoughtful readers won't respond favourably to such tactics. Appeals to people's emotions (sympathy for the poor or sick, love of children, feelings of patriotism, fear of injury) can be effective additions to an appeal to reason, but they are not a valid substitute for it. Similarly, if you're conducting a reasoned argument you will usually want to adopt a moderate tone. Stridency and sarcasm will only win you points with readers who are already thoroughly in agreement with your position.

## 71.6 Including the Opposition

Be fair: bring in and address any major opposing points of view. Your readers are likely to be aware of these and will expect you to address them. If you try to sway your readers by mentioning only what favours your side, you will lose their confidence because they will conclude correctly that you are unfairly suppressing unfavourable evidence. By raising opposing points and doing your best to refute them convincingly, you will not only strengthen the logic of your argument but you will present yourself as a reasonable person, willing to concede that there is another side to the issue. Moreover, by taking on the discussion of both sides in a debate, you can often impart a useful back-and-forth movement to your argument, and you

can see to it that after refuting the final opposition point, you end on
your own strongest points.

## 71.7 Using Induction and Deduction

The two principal methods of reasoning, induction and deduction,
occur both separately and in combination in argument. You should
know how each works, and it sometimes helps to be aware of which
one you are using at any given point so that you can use it effectively.

### Induction

Inductive reasoning argues from the particular to the general. That is,
it uses specific examples to support a general proposition. A team of
chemists will argue that their new theory is correct by describing the
results of several experiments that point to it. If you want people to
vote for mayoral candidate A rather than B, you could point to several
instances of A's actions on behalf of the city while on city council and
also perhaps point to several instances of B's harmful decisions. If you
wanted to argue against a proposal to cut back on funding for the
athletic program at your community centre, you could cite the major
ways in which the program benefits the community; you could also
interview other residents to show that the majority agrees with you.

Inductive reasoning cannot prove anything; it can only establish
degrees of probability. Obviously the number of examples affects the
force of such arguments. If the chemists could point to only two successful experiments, the claim for their theory would remain weak;
if they could cite a hundred consecutive successes, their argument
would be convincing; there would be a strong likelihood that the
experiment would work again if tried for the hundred-and-first time.

Be rigorous in presenting your data, but also consider how much
detail your audience really needs. If, in a speech or a written argument, you detailed fifty noble acts of candidate A and fifty ignoble
acts of candidate B, you would probably lose your audience and
turn them against you and your proposition. You would do better
to describe a few actions on each side and try to establish that those
actions were representative of the two candidates' behaviour.

Similarly, if you interviewed residents about the athletic program at your community centre, you would need to talk to enough

of them for your sampling to be considered representative; if you polled only elite athletes, you could hardly claim that their opinions were typical. And though the sampling would have to be large for the results to be convincing, it would be the total number that would carry weight, not the detailed opinions of each individual member of the community.

In addition, you must be able to explain any notable exceptions among your examples, for these form the bases of possible opposition arguments. For example, if one of their experiments failed, the chemists would need to show that at that time their equipment was faulty, or that one of their ingredients had accidentally become adulterated. If candidate A had once voted to close a useful facility, you could try to show that financial exigency at that time left no choice, or that the facility, though generally perceived as beneficial, was in fact little used and therefore an unnecessary drain on the city's resources. If you explicitly acknowledge such exceptions and show that they are unimportant or atypical, they can't easily be used against you by a reader who disagrees with you.

## Deduction

Deductive reasoning argues from the general to the particular. It begins with facts or generally accepted assumptions or principles and applies them to specific instances. For example, we know that oil and other fossil fuels are nonrenewable energy sources that will presumably someday be depleted, and we also know that the world's energy needs are increasing exponentially. Basing their argument on those two facts, energy experts have concluded that it is increasingly important for us to discover or develop alternative sources of energy.

The standard way of representing the process of deductive thinking is the syllogism:

All mammals are warm-blooded animals. (major premise)

Whales are mammals. (minor premise)

Therefore, whales are warm-blooded animals. (conclusion)

Syllogistic reasoning is a basic mode of thought, though commonly in everyday thinking and writing one of the premises is omitted as "understood"; for example if a writer states "This chapter is due to my publisher tomorrow, so I'll have to finish it tonight," the assumed second premise ("I don't want to hand the chapter in late") goes without saying.

Deductive reasoning, unlike inductive reasoning, can establish proof, but only if the premises are correct and you follow the rules of logic. For example, if one of the premises is negative, the conclusion must be negative—and two negative premises cannot lead to a conclusion at all. The term common to both premises—called the "middle" term (in the foregoing example, *mammals*)—cannot appear in the conclusion. Most important, if the conclusion is to be an absolute certainty, this "middle" term must, in at least one of the premises, be all-inclusive, universal, or what is called "distributed"; that is, it must refer to all members of its class, usually with an absolute word like *all, every, no, none, always, never.* If instead it is qualified by a word like *some, most,* or *seldom,* the conclusion can only be a probability, not a certainty (and if both premises include such a qualifier, they cannot lead to a conclusion):

> Most mammals are viviparous.
> Whales are mammals.
> Therefore, whales are probably viviparous.

Here one could reason further that since whales are not among the oviparous exceptions (platypus, echidna), they are indeed viviparous.

For a conclusion to amount to certainty both premises must be true, or accepted as true:

> No mammals can fly.
> Whales are mammals.
> Therefore, whales cannot fly.

Here the conclusion is valid (the reasoning process follows the rules), but it is not sound, since the first premise with its categorical *no* excludes the bat, a flying mammal. Such a conclusion, even if true (as this one is), will be suspect because it is based on a false premise.

If one argues that

> All mammals are four-legged animals.
> Whales are mammals.
> Therefore, whales are four-legged animals.

the conclusion, however valid, is not only unsound but untrue as well. To be accurate, the first premise would have to refer to *some* or *many*; the conclusion would then have to be something like "whales may be four-legged animals." Here the absurdity is obvious. But it is not uncommon to hear something like "X must be anti-business; after all, he is in favour of preserving the rain forests." In such a case the absurdity may not appear so obvious, but in the syllogism underlying this reasoning the first premise would read something like "Anyone who argues for preserving the environment is against business"; again, changing "Anyone who argues" to the correctly qualified "Some people who argue" renders the conclusion unsound.

Be skeptical whenever you find yourself using—or thinking—absolute terms like *all* and *everyone* and *no one* and *must* ("Everyone benefits from exercise"; "Lawyers are overpaid"; "No one cares about the elderly"; "Vitamin E must be good for you"): you may be constructing an implicit syllogism that won't stand up, one that an opponent can turn against you. Use such qualifiers as *most* and *some* and *sometimes* when necessary; you won't be able to establish absolute proof or certainty, but you may still have a persuasive argument.

### Combining induction and deduction

Induction and deduction often work together. For example, when you cite instances from candidate A's record, you use induction to establish the general proposition of your candidate's worthiness. But then you implicitly turn to deduction, using that generalization as the basis for a further conclusion: "Candidate A has done all these good things for our city in the past; therefore when elected mayor he or she will do similar good things." (But would the unstated second premise—"A person who behaved in a certain way in the past will continue to behave that way in the future"—require some qualification?)

## 71.8 Detecting and Avoiding Fallacies

If you are mounting a counter-argument, it often pays to look for flaws in your opponent's reasoning, such as hidden assumptions and invalid syllogisms. There are several other kinds of recognized, and recognizable, logical fallacies to look for—and, of course, to guard against in your own writing. Most of them amount to either avoiding evidence or distorting evidence, or both, and some are related to or overlap with others. Here are the main ones to watch for:

### Argumentum ad hominem

*Argumentum ad hominem* means "argument directed at the person." It refers to an attempt to evade the issue by diverting attention to the person at the centre of the argument: "Mozart lived an amoral life; therefore his music is bound to be bad." Mozart's morality is irrelevant to a discussion of the aesthetic quality of his music. "My opponent is obviously not fit to be mayor; she never goes to church, and her daughter was arrested last year for shoplifting." Neither the candidate's non-attendance at church nor her daughter's arrest—whether or not she was guilty—necessarily has any bearing on the candidate's fitness for office. Such tactics, according to their degree of directness or nastiness, are referred to as innuendo or name-calling or mud-slinging.

A similar tactic, known as guilt (or virtue) by association, is an attempt to tarnish (or enhance) someone's or something's reputation through an association with another person or thing. This kind of argument often takes the form of an endorsement: "I always take my car to Caesar's Garage because my friend Manuel says they're great, and he knows a lot about cars." Many instances of this kind of argument turn out to be fallacious because the stated connection between the two things is either not real or irrelevant. A brand of soft drink is not necessarily better because a famous actor is paid to say it is, nor is a politician necessarily evil because he once had his picture taken with someone later convicted of a crime.

### Argumentum ad populum

*Argumentum ad populum* is an "argument directed at the people"—an attempt to evade the issue by appealing to mass emotion. Like *argumentum ad hominem*, this technique uses appeals to prejudices, fears, and other feelings not—or not clearly—relevant to the issue. Often by using what are called "glittering generalities," it calls upon large and usually vague, unexamined popular feelings about religion, patriotism, home and family, tradition, and the like. One version of it, called the "bandwagon" approach, associates mass appeal with virtue: if so many people are doing this or thinking that or drinking this or wearing that, it must be right or good.

## Red herring

A red herring is a false or misleading issue dragged across the trail to throw the dogs off the scent. The new matter may be interesting, but if it is fundamentally irrelevant to the question being argued, it is a red herring. *Ad hominem* arguments are red herrings, since they divert a reader's or listener's attention from the main question by injecting the issue of personality.

## Hasty generalization

A hasty generalization is a generalization for which there is insufficient evidence. It occurs when an arguer jumps to a conclusion that is based on relatively little proof, for example when a team of chemists formulates a theory with only two successful experiments to point to (see 71.7 [Induction]). Consider another example: just because you and a friend didn't like the food you were served once at a particular restaurant, you aren't justified in asserting that the food is always bad at that restaurant; maybe the regular chef was away that day. But if you've had several such experiences and can find other people who've had similar ones, you'll be closer to establishing that those experiences were typical and therefore sufficient to generalize upon.

## Begging the question

Begging the question is assuming as true something that needs to be proved: "The government should be voted out of office because the new tax they've just imposed is unfair to consumers." The arguer here is guilty of begging the question of the tax's unfairness, which needs to be established before it can be used as a premise.

Similar to question-begging is circular reasoning, in which a reason given to support a proposition is little or no more than a disguised restatement of the proposition: "Her consistently good cooking is easy to explain: she's an expert at all things culinary." This is the same as saying she is a good cook because she is a good cook.

## *Post hoc ergo propter hoc*

*Post hoc ergo propter hoc* means "after this, therefore because of this." It refers to oversimplifying the evidence by assuming that merely because B follows A in time, B must be caused by A. It's true that thunder is caused by lightning, but the subsequent power failure may have been caused not by the lightning but by a tree blown down across the power line. Think about common superstitions: if you always wear your green socks during an exam because once when you wore them you wrote a good exam and so you think they bring you good luck, you are succumbing to the *post hoc* fallacy. Consider another example: "As soon as the new government took office, the price of gasoline went up"; the price hike might have nothing to do with the new government, the timing being coincidental.

### Either-or

The either-or fallacy, also called "false dilemma," refers to an over-simplification of an issue by presenting it as consisting of only two choices when in reality it is more complex than that. Some questions do present two clear choices: one either gets up or stays in bed; either one is pregnant or one is not; either one votes in an election or one doesn't. But most arguable issues are not matters simply of black and white; there is often a large area of grey between the extremes. One doesn't have to vote for either A or B; one can perhaps find a third candidate, or one can stay home and not vote for anyone. "If you aren't for us, then you must be against us!" This common cry is false; one could be neutral, impartial, uninterested, or committed to a third option. "The administration at work is either indifferent to employees' needs or against employees in general." Neither unpleasant alternative is likely to be true. This insidious pattern of thinking underlies a good deal of what we think of as prejudice, bigotry, and narrow-mindedness: "If you don't attend a recognized religious institution, then you're not really religious," or "If you don't support the war, you're unpatriotic." Although it is sometimes tempting, don't oversimplify; acknowledge the rich complexity of most issues.

### Exaggerating the trivial

When you exaggerate the trivial, you distort the evidence by treating a minor point as if it were a major one. If the point is your own, discerning readers will infer that you lack substantial evidence and have had to fall back on weak arguments. If the point is an opposing one, the audience will infer that you can't refute major points and are trying to make yourself look good by demolishing an easy target. "We should all give more to charity because being generous can give us a warm feeling inside" may be worth mentioning, but not worth dwelling on. On the other hand, don't distort the evidence by trivializing opposition points that are important.

### False or weak analogy

A false or weak analogy occurs when one oversimplifies the evidence by arguing that because two things are alike in some features, they are necessarily alike in one or more others as well. You can say that learning to ride a bicycle is like learning to play the piano: once you learn, you seldom forget; but you would not go on to argue that one should have a bicycle tuned periodically or that one should mount a tail-light on the piano for safety while playing at night. Analogies can provide interesting and concrete illustrations; by suggesting similarities they can help define, clarify, explain, or emphasize something; see, for example, the analogy comparing an outline to a road map in 70.7. We would not expect our analogy to convince you of the importance of an outline, but we hope that, by adding its concrete touch, we help you to understand and perhaps to accept our assertions.

One fairly common argument claims that because city or provincial or other governments are in some ways similar to large business organizations, they need experienced business people to run them. The more similarities you can point to, the stronger the argument. The trouble with this and other arguments from analogy is that no matter how many specific similarities you can come up with, your opponents can usually keep ahead of you by citing an even greater number of specific and significant differences. After all, leading a government may be *like* running a business, but it is not the same thing.

### Equivocation

Equivocation involves using a term in more than one sense; being ambiguous, whether accidentally or intentionally: "It is only natural for intelligent people to reject this idea. And as science tells us, natural law is the law of the universe; it is the law of truth, and must be obeyed." Aside from the appeal to snobbery and self-esteem (we all like to think we are "intelligent," but just what is "intelligence"?) and the appeal to the prestige of "science" in the modern world (but just how infallible is science?) and the imposing but vague term *universe* and the glittering abstraction *truth,* do the two occurrences of the word *natural* correspond with each other? And is a natural *law* comparable to legislation passed by a government and enforced by police and the courts? Don't let the meanings of words shift as you move from one phrase or sentence to the next. Choose and use your words ethically and carefully.

## Non sequitur

Non sequitur means "it does not follow." When for whatever reason a general proposition does not follow logically from the particular examples cited to support it, or a conclusion does not logically follow from its premises, it is a non sequitur. The term would apply to any of the fallacies discussed above and also to such leaps of logic as "She can French braid hair; she'd make a good mother," and "I've had singing lessons for two years; I should get the lead role in the opera."

# CHAPTER VIII
# Documentation

There are several reasons why writers need to ensure proper documentation of their sources. Accurate citations for works of nonfiction ensure that you, the writer, are a genuine researcher who has done considerable work of investigating authorities in the field(s) pertaining to your subject matter. Through a bibliography, notes, or in-text citations, you are acknowledging your indebtedness to these particular sources and demonstrating that you are not claiming someone else's original ideas for your own. Documentation also lends weight to your statements and arguments by citing authorities to support them, and demonstrates the extent of your investigation of a topic. Finally, detailed citations enable an interested reader to pursue the subject further by consulting the works you have referenced.

Chapter VIII deals with the various ways that writers can acknowledge sources to avoid plagiarism and outlines the four dominant citation styles (Chicago, MLA, APA, and CSE) for various disciplines and types of published works.

# 72. ACKNOWLEDGING SOURCES

Notifying your reader that you are borrowing exact words or ideas from another source is part of your responsibility as a writer. To omit a citation and consequently claim someone else's writing for your own—whether intentional or not—is an unethical practice known as plagiarism (see 73.5). Throughout this chapter we will discuss the various methods of acknowledging sources and how to write proper citations. As you work though the research stage of your writing, ensure that you keep accurate notes for all material you may reference.

## 72.1 "Common Knowledge"

It is not necessary to provide documentation for facts or ideas or quotations that are well known, or "common knowledge"—such as the fact that Shakespeare wrote *Hamlet*, or that Hamlet said "To be or not to be," or that Sir Isaac Newton formulated the law of gravity, or that the story of Adam and Eve appears in the book of Genesis in the Bible, or that the moon is not made of green cheese. But if you are at all uncertain whether or not something is common knowledge, play it safe: it is far better to over-document and appear a little naive than to under-document and engage in plagiarism.

If a piece of information appears in three or more different sources, it qualifies as common knowledge and need not be documented. For example, such facts as the elevation of Mt. Logan, or the current population of the world, or the date of the execution of Louis Riel can be found in dozens of reference books. But it can be dangerous for a writer to trust to such a guideline when dealing with other kinds of material. For example, there may be dozens of articles, websites, and books referring to or attempting to explain something like a neutrino, or the red shift, or black holes, or discoveries at the Olduvai Gorge, or Jungian readings of fairy tales, or the importance of the human genome project, or deep structure in linguistic theory, or the warnings about bio-terrorism, or neo-Platonic ideas in Renaissance poetry, or the nature and consequences of the great potato famine, or the origin of the name *Canada*; nevertheless, it is unlikely that a relatively unsophisticated writer will be sufficiently conversant with such material to recognize and accept it as common knowledge. If something is new to you, and if you have not thoroughly explored the available literature on the subject, it is best to acknowledge a source.

When the question of common knowledge arises, ask yourself: common to whom? Your readers will probably welcome the explicit documentation of something that they themselves do not realize is, to a few experts, common knowledge. Besides, if at any point in your writing you give your readers cause to question your data, you will have lost their confidence. So be scrupulous: document anything about which you have the least doubt.

# 73. QUOTATION, PARAPHRASE, SUMMARY, AND PLAGIARISM

Quotation must be exact. A well-documented paraphrase, on the other hand, reproduces the content of the original, but in different words. Paraphrase is a useful technique because it enables writers to make use of source material while still using their own words and thus to avoid too much direct quotation. But a paraphrase, to be legitimate, should give clear credit at its beginning to the source and should not use significant words and phrases from an original without enclosing them in quotation marks. A paraphrase will usually be a little shorter than the original, but it need not be. A summary, however, is by definition a condensation, a boiled-down version that expresses only the principal points of an original source.

Direct quotation must be documented: a reader of a passage in quotation marks will expect to be told who and what is being quoted. But some writers make the serious mistake of thinking that only direct quotations need to be documented; on the contrary, it is important to know and remember that paraphrase and summary must also be fully documented. Failure to document a paraphrase or summary is plagiarism, a form of intellectual dishonesty that is illegal under Canadian Copyright Law.

To illustrate the differences between a legitimate and illegitimate use of source material, here is a paragraph, a direct quotation, from Rupert Brooke's *Letters from America*, followed by

1.   legitimate paraphrase,

2.   illegitimate paraphrase,

3.   combination paraphrase and quotation,

4.   summary, and

5.   a comment on plagiarism.

> Such is Toronto. A brisk city of getting on for half a million inhabitants, the largest British city in Canada (in spite of the cheery Italian faces that pop up at you out of excavations in the street), liberally endowed with millionaires, not lacking its due share of destitution, misery, and slums. It is no mushroom city of the West, it has its history; but at the same time it has grown immensely of recent years. It is situated on the shores of a lovely lake; but you never see that, because the railways have occupied the entire lake front. So if, at evening, you try to find your way to the edge of the water, you are checked by a region of smoke, sheds, trucks, wharves, storehouses, "depôts," railway-lines, signals, and locomotives and trains that wander on the tracks up and down and across streets, pushing their way through the pedestrians, and tolling, as they go, in the American fashion, an immense melancholy bell, intent, apparently, on some private and incommunicable grief. Higher up are the business quarters, a few sky-scrapers in the American style

without the modern American beauty, but one of which advertises itself as the highest in the British Empire; streets that seem less narrow than Montreal [sic], but not unrespectably wide; "the buildings are generally substantial and often handsome" (the too kindly Herr Baedeker). Beyond that the residential part, with quiet streets, gardens open to the road, shady verandahs, and homes, generally of wood, that are a deal more pleasant to see than the houses in a modern English town. (Brooke 80–81)

The parenthetical reference for this block quotation begins one space after the final punctuation mark. It includes the author's surname and the page numbers on which the original appeared. The complete bibliographical entry for Brooke's work would appear in the list of Works Cited as follows:

Brooke, Rupert. *Letters from America*. London: Sidgwick and Jackson, 1916.

(For more information about handling quotations, see section 43.)

## 73.1 Legitimate Paraphrase

During his 1913 tour of the United States and Canada, Rupert Brooke sent back to England articles about his travels. In one of them, published in the 1916 book *Letters from America*, he describes Toronto as a large city, predominantly British, containing both wealth and poverty. He says that it is relatively old, compared to the upstart new cities further west, but that nevertheless it has expanded a great deal in the last little while. He implies that its beautiful setting is spoiled for its citizens by the railways, which have taken over all the land near the lake, filling it with buildings and tracks and smell and noise. He also writes of the commercial part of the city, with its buildings which are tall (like American ones) but not very attractive (unlike American ones); one of them, he says, claims to be the tallest in the British Empire. (He pokes fun at Baedeker for being over-generous with his comments about the city's downtown architecture.) The streets he finds wider than those of Montreal, but not too wide. Finally, he compares Toronto's attractive residential areas favourably with those of English towns. (80–81)

This is legitimate paraphrase. Even though it uses several individual words from the original (*British, railways, tracks, American, British Empire, streets, residential, English town[s]*), they are a small part of the whole; more important, they are common words that would be difficult to replace with reasonable substitutes without distorting the sense. And, even more important, they are used in a way that is natural to the paraphraser's own style and context. For example, had the writer said "in the American style" or "the entire lake shore," the style (and words) would have been too much Brooke's. Paraphrase, however, does not consist in merely substituting one word for another, but rather in assimilating something and restating it in your own words and your own syntax.

The parenthetical reference contains only the page numbers, since the author is named in the text. Similarly, though it comes at the end of a long paragraph, it is clear because the paragraph begins by identifying its overall subject and because the writer has carefully kept Brooke's point of view apparent throughout by including him in each independent clause (a technique that also establishes good coherence): *Rupert Brooke, he describes, He says, He implies, He also writes, he says, He pokes fun, he finds, he compares.*

## 73.2 Illegitimate Paraphrase

An illegitimate paraphrase of Brooke's paragraph might begin like this:

> Brooke describes Toronto as a *brisk* kind of city with nearly *half a million inhabitants*, with some *Italian faces popping up* among the British, and with both *millionaires and slums*. He deplores the fact that the *lake front* on which *it is situated* has been *entirely occupied by the railways*, who have turned it into a *region of smoke and storehouses* and the like, and *trains that wander back and forth, ringing their huge bells* (80–81).

The parenthetical reference at paragraph's end does not protect such a treatment from the charge of plagiarism, for too many of the words and phrases and too much of the syntax are Brooke's own. The words and phrases we have italicized are all "illegitimate": a flavourful word like *brisk*; the intact phrases *half a million inhabitants* and *Italian faces popping up*, so little different from *pop up*; and so on. Changing *the railways have occupied the entire lakefront* to the passive *the lake-front . . . has been entirely occupied by the railways*, or *trains that wander up and down* to *trains that wander back and forth*, or *tolling . . . an immense . . . bell* to *ringing their huge bells*, does not make them the writer's: they still have the diction, syntax, and stylistic flavour of Brooke's original, and therefore constitute plagiarism.

Had the writer put quotation marks around "brisk," "Italian faces . . . pop[ping] up," "millionaires" and "slums," "lake front," "it is situated," "occupied," "a region of smoke," "trains that wander," and "bell[s]," the passage would, to be sure, no longer be plagiarism—but it would still be illegitimate, or at least very poor, paraphrase, for if so substantial a part is to be left in Brooke's own words and syntax, the whole might as well have been quoted directly: the writer would have done little more than lightly "edit" the original.

## 73.3 Paraphrase and Quotation Mixed

A writer who felt that a pure paraphrase was too flat and abstract, who felt that some of Brooke's more striking words and phrases should be retained, might choose to mix some direct quotation into a paraphrase:

> In *Letters from America*, Rupert Brooke characterizes Toronto as a "brisk," largely British city having the usual urban mixture of wealth and poverty. Unlike the "mushroom" cities farther west, he says, Toronto has a history, though he points out that much of its growth has been recent. He notes, somewhat cynically, that the people are cut off from the beauty of the lake by the railways and all their "smoke, sheds, trucks, wharves, storehouses, 'depôts,' railway lines, signals, and locomotives and trains" going ding-ding all over the place (80–81).

This time the context is very much the writer's own, but some of the flavour of Brooke's original has been retained through the direct quotation of a couple of judiciously chosen words and the cumulative list at the end. The writer is clearly in control of the material, as the writer of the preceding example was not. (See also 73.6.)

## 73.4 Summary

The purpose of a summary is to substantially reduce the original, conveying its essential meaning in a sentence or two. A summary of Brooke's passage might go something like this:

> Brooke describes Toronto as large and mainly wealthy, aesthetically marred by the railway yards along the lake, with wide enough streets and tall but (in spite of Baedeker's half-hearted approval) generally unprepossessing buildings, and a residential area more attractive than comparable English ones (80–81).

It is appropriate and usually preferable to refer to an author by name in your text—and the first time by full name, as in 73.1 and 73.3. If for some reason you do not want to bring the author's name into your text (for example if you were surveying a variety of opinions about Toronto and did not want to clutter your text with all their authors' names), then your text might read in part like this, with the author's surname tucked away in the parenthetical reference:

> Toronto was once described as "brisk," large, and encumbered with railways and tall but ugly buildings (Brooke 80–81).

## 73.5 Plagiarism

Had one of the foregoing versions of the passage not mentioned Brooke, nor included quotation marks, nor ended with documentation, it would have been plagiarism. Keep in mind that you are ethically bound to give credit twice—in the text of the written document and in the Works Cited list—to all sources of information you have used (both print-based and electronic). All of the following kinds of material require acknowledgement whether they are drawn from print sources or from the Internet:

- direct quotations—whether short or long
- your summaries and paraphrases of sources
- ideas, theories, inspirations drawn from a source
- statistical data compiled by institutions and other researchers
- graphic materials (diagrams, charts, photographs, illustrations, slides, film and television clips, audio recordings, video recordings, CD-ROMs, and DVDs)

Note that giving credit for this kind of material does not at all diminish your own work: it enhances the credibility of your claims and demonstrates just how much genuine research you have conducted.

## 73.6 Altering Quotations to Fit Context

When you include quoted material within one of your own sentences, you may well have to alter it in one way or another in order to incorporate it smoothly. That is, you may have to change the grammar, syntax, or punctuation of a quotation to make it conform to that of your own sentence. Note how the writers have altered the quoted material in the following examples. (See also 43.10.)

The original quotation (from Mary Shelley's *Frankenstein; or, The Modern Prometheus*):

> I am by birth a Genevese; and my family is one of the most distinguished of that republic. My ancestors had been for many years counsellors and syndics; and my father had filled several public situations with honour and reputation. He was respected by all who knew him for his integrity and indefatigable attention to public business. He passed his younger days perpetually occupied by the affairs of his country; a variety of circumstances had prevented his marrying early, nor was it until the decline of life that he became a husband and the father of a family.

(a)  altered for pronoun reference:

> Victor Frankenstein begins his story by stating that "[he is] by birth a Genevese; and [his] family is one of the most distinguished of that republic" (Shelley 31).

The first-person pronouns have been changed to third person in order to fit the third-person point of view in the sentence as a whole. The changed pronouns and the accompanying verb (*is* for *am*) appear in square brackets. (The opening *he is* could have been left outside the quotation, but the writer preferred to incorporate the parallelism within the quotation.)

(b)  altered for consistent verb tense:

> As we first encounter him in the description at the beginning of his son's narrative, Victor's father is a man "respected by all who [know] him for his integrity and indefatigable attention to public business" (Shelley 31).

The verb in square brackets has been changed from past to present tense to conform with the tense established by the *is* of the writer's sentence.

(c)  altered for punctuation:

> The first words of Victor Frankenstein's narrative—"I am by birth a Genevese" (Shelley 31)—reveal a narrator preoccupied with himself, his birth, and his nationality.

The semicolon of the original has been dropped to avoid its clashing with the enclosing dashes of the writer's own sentence.

(d) selective quotation:

> The first paragraph of Victor's narrative focuses more on Victor's
> father than on any other member of the Frankenstein family.
> Victor takes pains to describe him as a man of "honour and
> reputation . . . respected by all who [know] him for his integrity
> and indefatigable attention to public business" and "perpetually
> occupied by the affairs of his country" (Shelley 31). A first-time
> reader of the novel might well be forgiven for assuming that
> Victor's narrative will be more a tribute to his father than an
> account of his own creation of a monster.

Here, the writer has selected key words and phrases from the
opening paragraph of Victor Frankenstein's narrative in order
to make a point about the novel's focus. The ellipsis indicates
that material has been omitted in the interests of the writer's
own sentence structure.

# 74. DOCUMENTATION STYLE

In order to be effective, documentation must be complete, accurate,
and clear. Completeness and accuracy depend on careful recording of
necessary information as you do your research and take notes. Clarity depends on the way you present that information to your reader.
You will be clear only if your audience can follow your method of
documentation. Therefore, it is important that before you begin any
research project, you investigate the method of documentation you
need to use. There are four main methods:

1.  The note method, recommended by the *Chicago Manual of
    Style*;

2.  the name-page method, recommended by the Modern Lan-
    guage Association (MLA), and with wide use in the humanities;

3.  the name-date method, recommended by the American Psych-
    ological Association (APA), and used in some of the social and
    other sciences; and

4.  the number method, recommended by the Council of Science
    Editors (CSE), used mainly in the sciences.

Which method you choose will depend on what discipline you are writing in and the type of document you are preparing. But you should familiarize yourself with all of them, or at least with those you will most often encounter in your particular discipline.

## 74.1 The Note Method (Chicago Style)

*The Chicago Manual of Style* is the style guide used by the majority of North American publishers. If you are preparing a work (novel, short story, non-fiction book) for publication, it is safe to assume that your publisher will want references in note style. If in doubt, ask your editor what style to follow when preparing the manuscript for submission.

The note method, which uses either footnotes or endnotes and a bibliography, has traditionally been used in published books because it allows for less interruption during reading. Rather than cumbersome in-text citations, a superscript numbered note indicates unobtrusively to the reader that more information is available pertaining to the source, should the reader require it.

Notes—either footnotes or endnotes—should be single-spaced and formatted with either a first-line indent or a hanging indent. Although the note numbers in the text are superscript, the note numbers preceding each endnote or footnote are not. Notes should contain the name of the author, the name of the source, and the publisher and place of publication, as well as the page, chapter, or table number referred to if appropriate. If you are referring repeatedly to the same source, you can use the abbreviation "Ibid." and the page number for subsequent references, provided that there is no intervening reference to a different source. In cases where a different source intervenes, you can use a shortened citation, which should include enough information to lead the reader to the appropriate entry in the bibliography, and normally consists of the last name of the author and a shortened version of the title:

1. John Mercer and Kim England, "Canadian Cities in Continental Context: Global and Continental Perspectives on Canadian Urban Development," in *Canadian Cities in Transition: The Twenty-First Century*, ed. Trudi Buntin and Pierre Filion (Toronto: Oxford University Press, 2000), 59.

2. Ibid., 60.

3. Glen Williams, *Not For Export: The International Competitiveness of Canadian Manufacturing* (Toronto: McClelland & Stewart, 1994), 97.

4. Mercer and England, "Canadian Cities," 66.

All of the sources you have used in your writing, including those you may have consulted but not referred to directly, are listed in a Bibliography at the end of the document. A bibliography may not be required if full bibliographic information has been included in the endnotes or footnotes; however, a bibliography allows the reader to see in a single glance all of the sources you have used. If a bibliographic entry runs on more than one line, all subsequent lines should be indented by approximately one tab space.

The following examples illustrate the Chicago style for documenting sources in footnotes or endnotes (N) and in the bibliography (B), based on the sixteenth edition of *The Chicago Manual of Style*, 16th ed. (2010).

### A book by one author

N: 1.  Margaret MacMillan, *Paris 1919: Six Months that Changed the World* (New York: Random House, 2001), 322.

B:  MacMillan, Margaret. *Paris 1919: Six Months that Changed the World*. New York: Random House, 2001.

### A book with an editor or translator
If the book you are citing has an editor and no author, give the editor's name first, followed by "ed.":

N: 2.  William Toye, ed., *The Concise Oxford Companion to Canadian Literature* (Toronto: Oxford University Press, 2001), 17.

B:  Toye, William, ed. *The Concise Oxford Companion to Canadian Literature*. Toronto: Oxford University Press, 2001.

If the book has a translator or editor as well as an author, the author's name should come before the title, with the translator's or editor's name following the title:

N: 3.  Denyse Baillargeon, *Making Do: Women, Family and Home in Montreal During the Great Depression*, trans. Yvonne Klein (Waterloo: Wilfrid Laurier University Press, 1999), 16.

B:  Baillargeon, Denyse. *Making Do: Women, Family and Home in Montreal During the Great Depression*. Translated by Yvonne Klein. Waterloo: Wilfrid Laurier University Press, 1999.

## A book by two or more authors or editors

N: 4.  Kathy Latrobe, Carolyn Brodie, and Maureen White, *The Children's Literature Dictionary: Definitions, Resources, and Learning Activities* (New York: Neil-Schuman, 2002), 16.

B:  Latrobe, Kathy, Carolyn Brodie, and Maureen White. *The Children's Literature Dictionary: Definitions, Resources, and Learning Activities*. New York: Neil-Schuman, 2002.

If the book has more than three authors or editors, you can use the name of the first author or editor only, followed by "et al.":

N: 5.  Eva-Marie Kröller et al., eds., *Pacific Encounters: The Production of Self and Others* (Vancouver: Institute of Asian Research UBC, 1997), 126.

B:  Kröller, Eva-Marie, et al., eds. *Pacific Encounters: The Production of Self and Others*. Vancouver: Institute of Asian Research UBC, 1997.

## A multivolume work

N: 6.  Lucy Maud Montgomery, *The Selected Journals of L.M. Montgomery*, eds. Mary Rubio and Elizabeth Waterston, 4 vols. (Toronto: Oxford University Press, 1985–2004).

B:  Montgomery, Lucy Maud. *The Selected Journals of L.M. Montgomery*. Edited by Mary Rubio and Elizabeth Waterston. 4 vols. Toronto: Oxford UP, 1985–2004.

## A work by a government agency or a corporate author

N: 7.  Government of Canada, *Canada's Innovation Strategy: Canadians Speak on Innovation and Learning* (Ottawa: Government of Canada, 2002), 22.

B:  Government of Canada. *Canada's Innovation Strategy: Canadians Speak on Innovation and Learning*. Ottawa: Government of Canada, 2002.

## A work in an edited anthology

N: 8.  Al Purdy, "Say the Names," in *A New Anthology of Canadian Literature in English*, eds. Donna Bennett and Russell Brown (Toronto: Oxford University Press, 2002), 567.

B:  Purdy, Al. "Say the Names." In *A New Anthology of Canadian Literature in English*, edited by Donna Bennett and Russell Brown. Toronto: Oxford University Press, 2002, 567.

## A journal article

N: 9.  Patrick Harrigan, "The Schooling of Boys and Girls in Canada," *Journal of Social History* 23 (1990): 803–16.

B:  Harrigan, Patrick. "The Schooling of Boys and Girls in Canada." *Journal of Social History* 23 (1990): 803–16.

## A journal article available online

N: 10.  Deborah Weagel, "Musical Counterpoint in Albert Camus' *L'Etranger*," *Journal of Modern Literature* 25, no. 2 (2002): 141–45, http://muse.jhu.edu/journals/journal_of_modern_literature/v025/25.2weagel.html.

B:  Weagel, Deborah. "Musical Counterpoint in Albert Camus' *L'Etranger*." *Journal of Modern Literature* 25, no. 2 (2002): 141–45. http://muse.jhu.edu/journals/journal_of_modern_literature/v025/25.2weagel.html.

## A newspaper article

Since a newspaper may have several editions in a given day, and items may be moved or eliminated in various editions, page numbers should be omitted. If the section of the newspaper containing the article is identified, give its name, number, or letter.

N: 11.  J.B. MacKinnon, "Paradise Lost?: The Great Bear Rain Forest," Travel, *Globe and Mail*, July 26, 2003, sec. T.

B:  MacKinnon, J.B. "Paradise Lost?: The Great Bear Rain Forest." Travel, *Globe and Mail*, July 26, 2003, sec. T.

If the article is unsigned, begin with the title of the article. In the bibliography, however, the newspaper name comes first.

N: 12.  "Jordan's King Sacks Government, Appoints New PM Amid Street Protests," *Globe and Mail*, February 1, 2011.

B:  *Globe and Mail*. "Jordan's King Sacks Government, Appoints New PM Amid Street Protests." February 1, 2011.

## A newspaper article available online

N: 13.   "Hamas orders ban on folk tale book," *Jerusalem Post*, March 5, 2007, http:// www.jpost.com/Home/Article.aspx?id=53582.

B:        "Hamas orders ban on folk tale book." *Jerusalem Post*, March 5, 2007. http://www.jpost.com/Home/Article.aspx?id=53582.

## An anonymous article in a reference book

Notes that cite alphabetical entries in an encyclopedia, dictionary, or the like are named after "s.v." (*sub verbo*, "under the word").

N: 14.   *Canadian Oxford English Dictionary*, 2nd ed., s.v. "bibliophile."

## A website

Include as much information as possible when citing online content. Similar to unsigned articles, the website owner's name should appear first in the bibliography when no author is provided on the webpage.

While access dates used to be required for electronic sources, the sixteenth edition of *The Chicago Manual of Style* no longer recommends this practice due to the rapid rate at which online content changes. Furthermore, since most writers consult an electronic source several times over the course of their research, it is difficult to determine a single date to include in the citation. If you are preparing a manuscript for publication, check with your editor first before omitting access dates, as they are still used in certain disciplines.

# Research Tip

## On the Critical Evaluation of Internet Sources

The Internet is a largely unregulated source of information. You need to evaluate carefully and critically the websites you locate in your searches. You should not, as a rule, use as an authoritative source a personal website. You should look for sites produced and maintained by recognized public or private institutions; you should ascertain the professional credentials of the identified authors of the site. Finally, you should check that any site is current and recently updated, and you should look for detailed bibliographic information supporting the claims and evidence offered on the site.

When a website's publication date or revision date is unavailable, then it is helpful to include an access date for your readers.

N: 15.  Howard S. "Looking Forward to Starbucks Next Chapter," Starbucks Coffee, accessed January 5, 2011, http://www.starbucks.com/blog/looking-forward-to-starbucks-next-chapter.

B:      Gap Inc. "Social Responsibility." Accessed February 1, 2011. http://www.gapinc.com/socialresponsibility.

## A review

N: 16.  Anne Geddes Bailey, "Mourning Lessons," review of *Elizabeth Rex*, by Timothy Findley, *Canadian Literature* 174 (2002): 116–17.

B:      Bailey, Anne Geddes. "Mourning Lessons." Review of *Elizabeth Rex*, by Timothy Findley. *Canadian Literature* 174 (2002): 116–17.

## A lecture

B:      McLachlin, Beverly. "The Role of the Courts in a Modern Democracy." Paper presented at the Vancouver Institute, University of British Columbia, March 2000.

## A dissertation

B:      Rae, Ian Thomas. "Unframing the Novel: From Ondaatje to Carson (Michael Ondaatje, Anne Carson, George Bowering, Joy Kogawa, Daphne Marlatt)." PhD diss., University of British Columbia, 2003.

## A film

N: 17.  *Passchendaele*, directed by Paul Gross (Toronto: Alliance, 2008), DVD.

B:      *Passchendaele*. Directed by Paul Gross. Toronto: Alliance, 2008. DVD.

## An interview

N: 18.  The Dalai Lama, interviewed by Peter Mansbridge, *Mansbridge One on One*, CBC, April 14, 2008.

## A letter

N: 19.  Leacock to Carl Goldenberg, 20 March 1937, in *The Letters of Stephen Leacock*, ed. David Staines (Toronto: Oxford University Press, 2006), 335.

B:      Leacock, Stephen. *The Letters of Stephen Leacock*. Edited by David Staines. Toronto: Oxford University Press, 2006.

### An audio recording

N: 20.   Neil Gaiman, *Coraline*, read by author (Harper Children's Audio, 2002). CD.

B:      Gaiman, Neil. *Coraline*. Read by author. Harper Children's Audio, 2002. CD.

## 74.2 The Name–Page Method (MLA Style)

The name–page method is detailed in the seventh edition of the *MLA Handbook for Writers of Research Papers* (2009). This documentation style is largely used for academic research papers and articles in the humanities. The virtues of this method of citation over the note method are obvious: simplicity and efficiency. No footnotes or endnotes are needed. Using this method, you provide a short, usually parenthetical or in-text reference to each source as you use it in the body of your document. Then, you provide complete bibliographical information about all the electronic and non-electronic sources you have used at the end of the document, in a Works Cited list, alphabetized by surnames of authors or editors (or title, when no author is named).

The pages that follow illustrate examples of the basic patterns of MLA documentation: each in-text parenthetical reference is accompanied by its bibliographic entry (B) that would appear in the Works Cited list. (See also the examples in 73.1–73.4.) Note that parenthetical references are usually placed at the end of the sentence in which the citation occurs; but if a sentence is necessarily long and complicated, a reference may be placed earlier, immediately after the citation itself.

### A book by one author or editor

In-text:   The reaction in China to the end of World War I has been described by one historian as "popular rejoicing"— particularly among young people, who had "an uncritical admiration for Western democracy, Western liberal ideals, and Western learning" (MacMillan 322).

Note that when you don't mention the author by name in your actual sentence, the parenthetical reference includes the author's surname and a page reference, with no intervening punctuation, and that the page number is not preceded by the abbreviation "p." The closing period follows the parenthesis. If you can include the author's name and credentials in your text, however, the parenthetical reference will be shorter, the context of the quotation clearer, and the credibility of the point stronger.

In-text: The reaction in China to the end of World War I has been described by historian Margaret MacMillan as "popular rejoicing"—particularly among young people, who had "an uncritical admiration for Western democracy, Western liberal ideals, and Western learning" (322).

Words like "Ltd." and "Inc." can be omitted from the publisher's name, and the name can be shortened to a single word (like "Random" rather than "Random House").

The medium of publication—web, print, TV, DVD, etc.—appears after the date in the Works Cited list. This is a new requirement of the seventh edition of the *MLA Handbook*.

B: MacMillan, Margaret. *Paris 1919: Six Months that Changed the World*. New York: Random, 2001. Print.

## A book by two or more authors or editors

When you have more than one author or editor in a Works Cited entry, the names following the first name appear in first-name–last-name order.

In-text: One study of war literature for children concludes with the assertion that "young readers need narratives which explore the nature and experience of war if they are to make sense of the world they have inherited and the future they confront" (Agnew and Fox 179).

B: Agnew, Kate, and Geoff Fox. *Children at War: From the First World War to the Gulf*. London: Continuum, 2001. Print.

For a book by more than three authors, in the parenthetical reference supply the name of the author or editor whose name appears first on the title page of the work, followed by the Latin abbreviation *et al.* (for Latin *et alii*, "and others"). The abbreviation "eds." indicates that the names listed are those of the book's editors. The abbreviation "ed." is used following the name of a single editor.

In-text:   The articles in *Pacific Encounters: The Production of Self and Other* are ordered neither chronologically nor geographically, a deliberate strategy on the part of the editors (Kröller et al. 11).

B:   Kröller, Eva-Marie, et al., eds. *Pacific Encounters: The Production of Self and Others*. Vancouver: Institute of Asian Research UBC, 1997. Print.

## Two or more works by the same author

If you cite two different works by a single author in your writing, the in-text references must include title information to distinguish the two works. Note that the pattern calls for the author's surname and then a comma, followed by the distinctive word or phrase from the title and then the page number. There is no comma between the title word and the page number. While it is preferable to include all of the required information, the "n. pag." notation can be used when the referenced page is not numbered.

In-text:   Both novels—*Stanley Park* and *Story House*—begin with searching looks into the past. *Stanley Park*'s "Author's Note" recalls "January of 1953 [and] the skeletal remains of two children . . . found in Stanley Park" (Taylor, *Stanley* n. pag.). *Story House* begins with the cryptic chapter title, "17 Years Before the Beginning" (Taylor, *Story* 3).

The two works by Taylor would be listed alphabetically according to the titles. In this case, the title beginning with "Sta" would precede the title beginning with "Sto."

B:   Taylor, Timothy. *Stanley Park*. Toronto: Knopf, 2001. Print.

———. *Story House*. Toronto: Knopf, 2006. Print.

Note that the second entry does not repeat the author's name but rather marks it with three consecutive en-dashes followed by a period.

## A multivolume work

When you cite one volume from a work of two or more volumes, include the volume number in the parenthetical reference, followed by a colon and a space, and then the page number:

In-text:   In an entry dated 3 August 1908, she described her second book as "not nearly so good as *Green Gables*" (Montgomery 1: 338).

> B: Montgomery, Lucy Maud. *The Selected Journals of L.M. Montgomery.* Ed. Mary Rubio and Elizabeth Waterston. 4 vols. Toronto: Oxford UP, 1985–2004. Print.

The "UP" in the publication information is an abbreviation for "University Press." The date range "1985–2004" indicates that the first volume of the journals was produced in 1985 and the last volume in 2004.

### A work by a government agency or a corporate author

A government agency is one of the many branches or departments of government at the international, federal, provincial, or municipal level. A corporate author is a group, association, or institute of authors who are not named individually on the title page of a work.

> In-text: A ninety-two-page report published in 2002 offers the views of individual Canadians on our national strategies for innovation in the decade ahead (Government of Canada).

Here, there is no page number because the reference is to the report as a whole.

> B: Government of Canada. Canada's Innovation Strategy: Canadians Speak on Innovation and Learning. Ottawa: Government of Canada, 2002. Print.

### A work in an edited anthology

> In-text: The poem consists largely of a wonderful litany of Canadian place names "that ride the wind," as the speaker observes (Purdy 567; line 14).

In this parenthetical reference, the line number follows the name-page information and is separated from it with a semicolon.

> B: Purdy, Al. "Say the Names." *A New Anthology of Canadian Literature in English.* Ed. Donna Bennett and Russell Brown. Toronto: Oxford UP, 2002. 567. Print.

### A journal article

> In-text: Maria Ng begins her article on the challenges of writing a memoir with the comment: "To recount my birth is not as straightforward as naming a place and date" (35).

> B: Ng, Maria Noelle. "Mapping the Diasporic Self." *Canadian Literature* 196 (2008): 34–45. Print.

This particular journal uses only issue numbers. Were there a volume number as well, the issue number would follow it in the entry. For example, 19.2 would mean that the article appeared in the second issue of volume 19.

## A journal article available online

> B: Golovankha-Hicks, Inna. "Demonology in Contemporary Ukraine: Folklore or 'Postfolklore'?" *Journal of Folklore Research* 43.3 (2006): 219–40. *Project Muse*. Johns Hopkins UP, 2006. Web. 15 Jan. 2007.

## A newspaper article

> In-text: J.B. MacKinnon recalls this image from his trip to the Great Bear Rain Forest: "A herd of seals, their lives so perfect they no longer ate whole fish but only individual bites out of passing salmon" (T1).

> B: MacKinnon, J.B. "Paradise Lost?: The Great Bear Rain Forest." *Globe and Mail* 26 July 2003: T1+. Print.

In this example, the page number T1+ indicates that the article begins on page 1 of section T of the newspaper and then continues not on page 2 but later in the section.

Newspaper editorials are not ordinarily attributed to a particular writer/editor. Without an author, the title moves into the author position and is used in short form in the parenthetical in-text reference and in full form in the Works Cited entry.

> In-text: "Mr. Bush and British Prime Minister Blair are embroiled in rancorous controversies at home over how they built the case for war" ("Questions" A18).

> B: "Questions remaining about the war on Iraq." Editorial. *Globe and Mail* 26 July 2003: A18. Print.

## A newspaper article available online

> B: "Hamas orders ban on folk tale book." *Jerusalem Post*. Jerusalem Post, 5 March 2007. Web. 6 March 2007.

The article from the *Jerusalem Post* lists no author, and so the title of the article moves into the author position. Note that the Jerusalem Post (no italics) is listed as the publisher as well as the source.

Be aware that some online periodicals may have names different to those of their print versions:

> B: Faught, Brad. "A History of the Exam." *Macleans.ca*. Rogers Publishing, 13 Nov. 2006. Web. 8 Jan. 2007.

*Macleans.ca* is the online version of *Maclean's* magazine. The article was first posted in November 2006 and accessed in January 2007.

### An anonymous article in a reference book

> In-text: One of the most distinctive sights to be seen off the shores of Pacific Rim National Park Reserve is that of the grey whales "migrat[ing] past the park on their travels between Baja California and the Bering Sea" ("Pacific" 525).

> B: "Pacific Rim National Park Reserve." *Encyclopedia of British Columbia*. Ed. Daniel Francis. Madeira Park, BC: Harbour Publishing, 2000. 525. Print.

Because Madeira Park, the place of publication, is not widely known, the Works Cited entry includes "BC" (for British Columbia) to provide a fuller geographical marker. When including a province or state in the place of publication, two-letter postal abbreviations are used (e.g. AB for Alberta, SK for Saskatchewan, ME for Maine). The page number for the article follows the period that follows the year of publication.

### A website

The in-text reference patterns for electronic sources follow those for print sources. Include the last name of the author and, if it is available, the number of the page in the electronic document. If the document is not paginated, include the paragraph number(s) from which you are quoting, and use "par."—the abbreviation listed in the current edition of the *MLA Handbook*. If neither page nor paragraph is available, use "n. pag."—the abbreviation for "no pagination." If the document you are referring to does not have an author, then the in-text reference would begin with a key word from the title of the document.

A complete citation for an online source includes the same information used to cite a published source: the name of the author or editor, the name of the website or page, the publisher's name and date of publication, the volume and issue numbers (for online journals), and any relevant page references. Use the abbreviations "n. pag." (no pagination) whenever you are unable to provide the information.

> B: Dutton, Dennis, ed. *Arts and Letters Daily*. Chronicle of Higher Education, 18 Feb. 2009. Web. 24 Feb. 2009.

## A review

> In-text: The reviewer offers this insightful comment on the final moments of Timothy Findley's *Elizabeth Rex*: "Whether Findley's conclusion is a disappointment or a triumph will depend upon one's political conviction" (Bailey 117).

> B: Bailey, Anne Geddes. "Mourning Lessons." Rev. of *Elizabeth Rex*, by Timothy Findley. *Canadian Literature* 174 (2002): 116–17. Print.

## A lecture

> B: McLachlin, Beverly. "The Role of the Courts in a Modern Democracy." Vancouver Institute Lecture. University of British Columbia. 11 Mar. 2000. Lecture.

## An online dissertation

> B: Rae, Ian Thomas. "Unframing the Novel: From Ondaatje to Carson (Michael Ondaatje, Anne Carson, George Bowering, Joy Kogawa, Daphne Marlatt)." Diss. U of British Columbia, 2003. *ProQuest*, June 2003. Web. 27 July 2003.

## A film

Begin with the italicized title (unless you are emphasizing a particular contributor, such as the writer or director, or a performer), followed by the director, the distributor, and the date:

> B: *Passchendaele*. Dir. Paul Gross. Alliance, 2008. Film.

You may wish to include other information as well—whatever you think relevant to your use of the item; for example:

> B: Gross, Paul, writ., dir., and perf. *Passchendaele*. Perf. Caroline Dhavernas. Alliance, 2008. Film.

For a recorded film, the medium (DVD) replaces *Film* at the end of the Works Cited entry.

### A television program

B: "Adventurers and Mystics. 1540–1670." Writ. Hubert Gendron and Gene Allen. *Canada: A People's History*, Episode 2. CBC. 28 Oct. 2000. Television.

### An interview

This category includes interviews published in newspapers, magazines, books; interviews broadcast on radio or television; and interviews conducted by researchers themselves. In your text, include a parenthetical reference for a published interview; for a broadcast or for an interview you conduct for your own research include the necessary information, but without page numbers. In the Works Cited entry, include the identification "Interview" for a published or broadcast interview, and "Personal interview," "Telephone interview," or "Email interview" for one you conducted yourself.

(a)  A published interview

In-text: Thomas King describes his novel *Medicine River* as a book about "a very human side of Native life" (111).

B: King, Thomas. Interview. *Contemporary Challenges: Conversations with Canadian Native Authors*. Ed. Harmut Lutz. Saskatoon: Fifth House, 1991. 107–16. Print.

(b)  A broadcast interview

In-text: In a CBC interview in advance of the 2008 summer Olympics, the Dalai Lama spoke at length about the longstanding dispute between China and Tibet.

B: The Dalai Lama. Interview by Peter Mansbridge. *Mansbridge One on One*. CBC Newsworld. Toronto, 14 April 2008. Television.

(c)  Your own research interview

In-text: Professor Joseph Atkinson reported that ideas of innovation in the teaching of science in British universities are a relatively new concern among his colleagues.

B: Atkinson, Joseph. Email interview. 12 June 2003.

### A letter

B: Leacock, Stephen. "To John Murray." 10 January 1935. *The Letters of Stephen Leacock*. Ed. David Staines. Toronto: Oxford University Press, 2006. 249. Print.

## An audio recording

B:  Gaiman, Neil. *Coraline*. Perf. by Neil Gaiman. Harper Children's
    Audio, 2002. CD.

B:  Obama, Barack. *Dreams from My Father: A Story of Race and
    Inheritance*. Random House Audio, 2005. CD.

B:  Ryder, Serena, perf. "Sisters of Mercy." By Leonard Cohen. *If Your
    Memory Serves You Well*. EMI, 2006. CD.

## Citing more than one source

If you wish to cite more than one source in a single parenthetical
reference, simply write each in the usual way and separate them with
a semicolon:

In-text:  The First World War left Canadians "a deeply divided people
          who had inherited staggering debt," but it also "mark[ed] the
          real birth of Canada" (Morton 226; Gwyn xxi).

B:  Gwyn, Sandra. *Tapestry of War: A Private View of Canadians in
    the Great War*. Toronto: HarperCollins, 1993. Print.

B:  Morton, Desmond. "First World War." *The Oxford Companion
    to Canadian History*. Ed. Gerald Hallowell. Toronto: Oxford UP,
    2004. Print

## Using notes as well as parenthetical references

If circumstances demand, you may also use an occasional note along
with the name–page method. For example, if you think that a reference requires some comment or explanation, make it an endnote
rather than an obtrusive parenthetical reference. But keep such notes
to a minimum; if you cannot comfortably include such discursive
comments in your text, it may be that they aren't relevant after all.
Try to limit such notes to (a) those commenting in some useful way
on specific sources, such as a "See," "See for example," or "See also"
note, and (b) those listing three or more sources, which might be
unwieldy as a parenthetical reference.

In the text, insert a superscript numeral where you want to signal
the note (usually at the end of a sentence). Begin the note by indenting
five spaces, followed by a superscript numeral corresponding with the
one in the text, then another space, and then the note. The most recent
edition of *The MLA Handbook for Writers of Research Papers* recommends the use of endnotes over footnotes in such circumstances

as we have just described. If a note carries over to a second page, a line should separate the bottom of the body text from the note. If you use endnotes, put them on a separate page with the heading *Notes*, following the text and before the Works Cited list.

## 74.3 The Name–Date Method (APA Style)

The name–date system is common in the social sciences; the standard guide is the *Publication Manual of the American Psychological Association* (6th ed., 2010). Like the name–page method, it uses parenthetical references in the text, but instead of listing the author and the page in the source where the cited material occurs, it lists the author and the date of publication of the source. The practice is the same whether the source is print-based or electronic. Since in the behavioural and social sciences reference is quite often made to the argument or evidence presented by an entire work, page numbers are not always necessary:

> In-text:  There are many remarkable parallels between the way artists and scientists look at the world around us (Shlain, 1991).

But if you refer to a particular part of the source, or if you quote from it, supply the relevant page number or numbers:

> In-text:  As Leonard Shlain (1991) reminds us, "Space, time, and light are of profound interest to both the physicist and the artist" (p. 28).

Note that, as in the name–page method, if you name the author in the text, you don't include the name in the parenthetical reference.

In Reference lists in APA style, capitalize only the first letter of a book or article title, the first word after a colon or dash, and the first letter of all proper nouns. All other words begin with the lower case. The titles of periodicals are capitalized as they would be in MLA style. For titles appearing within the body of your work, capitalize all key words with the exception of prepositions, articles, and conjunctions. Authors' first and middle names are abbreviated to their first initial.

The following examples illustrate the APA style for documenting various types of material as both in-text citations and bibliographic entries (B).

## A book by one author

> In-text: John Helliwell (2002) provides an incisive analysis of the effects of globalization.

> B: Helliwell, J. (2002). *Globalization and well-being.* Vancouver: UBC Press.

## A translated work

> B: Levi, P. (2001). *The search for roots: A personal anthology* (P. Forbes, Trans.). London: Allen Lane.

## A work with two or more authors

> In-text: Although it is true that "the religious and secular customs of the community sometimes helped women who had been assaulted or harassed, nothing could lessen the impact of war on the countryside and its inhabitants" (Anderson & Zinsser, 1988, 1: pp. 115–116).

The fact that the citation comes from volume 1 of a two-volume work could also be noted in the References list. Note that in APA style an ampersand (&) rather than *and* separates two authors in a reference, that author and date are separated by a comma, that the abbreviations "p." and "pp." are used for "page" and "pages," and that all three digits of the closing page number are included.

If a work has two authors, list both names in each reference you make to the source. If it has three, four, or five authors, list all of them the first time, but only the first and *et al.* (not italicized or underlined) thereafter. If it has six or more authors, list only the first and *et al.* each time, including the first.

## A multivolume work

> B: Smelser, N.J., & Baltes, P.B. (Eds.). (2001). *International encyclopedia of the social and behavioural sciences* (Vols. 1–26). Amsterdam: Elsevier.

## A work by a government agency or corporate author

> B: Canadian Radio-Television and Telecommunications Commission. (1995). *Competition and culture on Canada's Information Highway: Managing the realities of transition.* Ottawa: CRTC.

## An article in an edited book

B: Kaplan, A. (2003). Women, film, resistance: Changing paradigms. In J. Levitin, J. Plessis & V. Raoul (Eds.), *Women filmmakers: Refocusing* (pp. 15–28). Vancouver: UBC Press.

## A journal article

B: Fabian, E. (2002). On the differentiated use of humor and joke in psychotherapy. *Psychoanalytic Review, 89*, 399–412.

## A journal article available online

If the article you are citing comes from an online source that is identical to a print edition, you can use the same format you would for a print version of the article, adding "Retrieved from" at the end of the citation, followed by the URL. No retrieval date is needed.

B: Weagel, D. (2002). Musical counterpoint in Albert Camus' L'etranger. *Journal of Modern Literature, 25*, 141–145. Retrieved from http://muse.jhu.edu/journals/journal_of_modern_literature/v025/25.2/weagel.html

## A newspaper article

B: Cosmonaut's plans for nuptials up in the air. (2003, July 19). *The Globe and Mail*, p. A14.

## A newspaper article available online

B: Hamas orders ban on folk tale book. (2007, March 5). *Jerusalem Post*. Retrieved from http://www.jpost.com/Home/Article.aspx?id=53582

## An article in a reference book

B: Fernandez, D. (2002). Rice cake of the Philippines. In A. Davidson (Ed.) *The Penguin companion to food* (pp. 792–797). London: Penguin.

## A website

B: Dutton, D. (2003, March 23). *Arts and letters daily*. Retrieved from http://www.aldaily.com

In APA style, the name of the person or organization that has provided the content of the site comes first. The date in parentheses is the date the material was last updated. Note that the URL is not contained in angle brackets, and the entry does not conclude with a period.

## A review

B: Cohen, L. (2003). Metaphor and alienation. [Review of the book *The age of immunology: Conceiving the future in an alienating world*, by A. David Napier]. *Anthropological Quarterly*, 76, 343–350.

## A lecture

B: McLachlin, B. (2000, March 11). *The role of the courts in a modern democracy*. Paper presented at the Vancouver Institute, University of British Columbia.

## A dissertation

B: Ing, N.L. (2002). *Dealing with shame and unresolved trauma: Residential school and its impact on 2nd and 3rd generation adults* (Unpublished doctoral dissertation). University of British Columbia, Vancouver.

## A film

B: Moore, M. (Writer/director). (2002). *Bowling for Columbine* [Motion picture]. United States: United Artists, Alliance Atlantis, & Dog Eat Dog Films.

## A letter

B: Tompkins, M. (2003, July 19). Quitting Iraq [Letter to the editor]. *The Globe and Mail*, p. A16.

## An audio recording

B: McFerrin, B. (2000). *The story of jazz* [CD]. The Netherlands: EMI Plus (Europe).

## 74.4 The Number Method (CSE Style)

Methods of documentation in the natural, physical, life, and applied sciences vary more than those in the social sciences and the humanities. Most of the sciences, and their scientific journals, use a form of the number method. The following guidelines, which are used by the Council of Science Editors, are based on the seventh edition of *Scientific Style and Format: The CSE Manual for Authors, Editors, and Publishers* (2006).

Superscript numbers in the text correspond to numbered references in a References section at the end of the document.

Hawking discusses black holes at some length.[3]

The reference may be to more than one source, listing the items in numerical order:

Several recent articles have discussed this continuing investigation.[4,7,18,21]

In the References list, these references are ordered according to the order in which they are first cited in the text. The information for each reference is presented in the following order:

1.  the note number, followed by a period and one space

2.  the author's last name, followed by initials without punctuation and then a period

3.  the title of the work, followed by the title of the source, with no underlining or italics or quotation marks; only the first word of the title and proper nouns are capitalized

4.  the place of publication, followed by a colon

5.  the name of the publisher followed by a semicolon

6.  the date of publication (or last update, if the source is online)

7.  the date the information was retrieved in year-month-day format (from an online source)

8.  the range or total number of pages (optional)

The following are some examples of entries as they would appear in the References section of a document in CSE style.

### A book by one author

1. MacMillan M. Paris 1919: six months that changed the world. New York: Random House; 2001. 288 p.

### A book with an editor

2. Case-Smith J, editor. Pediatric occupational therapy and early intervention. 2nd ed. Boston (MA): Butterworth-Heinemann; 1998. 324 p.

### A book by two or more authors

3. Agnew K, Fox G. Children at war: from the First World War to the Gulf. London: Continuum; 2001. 227 p.

## A multivolume work

4. Montgomery LM. The selected journals of LM Montgomery. Rubio M, Waterston E, editors. Toronto: Oxford Univ Pr; 1985–2004. 4 vol.

## A work in an edited anthology

5. Purdy A. Say the names. In: Bennett D, Brown R, editors. A new anthology of Canadian literature in English. Toronto: Oxford Univ Pr; 2002. p. 567.

## A journal article

5. Harrigan P. The schooling of boys and girls in Canada. J Soc Hist. 1990;23:803–16.

Note that the CSE uses abbreviations in names of journals.

## A journal article available online

6. Weagel D. Musical counterpoint in Albert Camus' L'etranger. J Mod Lit [Internet]. 2002 [cited 2003 Jun 13];25:141–45. Available from: http://muse.jhu.edu/journals/journal_of_modern_literature/v025/25.2weagel.html

## A newspaper article

7. MacKinnon JB. Paradise lost?: the Great Bear rain forest. Globe and Mail. 2003 Jul 26;Sect. T:1, 14.

In this example, the article begins on page T1 and continues on T14.

## A website

8. Centres of excellence for children's well-being [Internet]. Ottawa: Health Canada; 2001 Nov [cited 2003 Jul 1]. Available from: http://www.hc-sc.gc.ca/english/media/ releases/2000/2000_ 96ebk1 htm

## A lecture

9. McLachlin B. The role of the courts in a modern democracy. Proceedings of the Vancouver Institute; 2000 March; University of British Columbia.

## A dissertation

10. Ing NL. Dealing with shame and unresolved trauma: residential school and its impact on 2nd and 3rd generation adults (unpublished doctoral dissertation). Vancouver: University of British Columbia; 2002.

## An audio recording

11. McFerrin B. The story of jazz [CD]. The Netherlands: EMI Plus (Europe); 2000.

## 74.5 Some Abbreviations Commonly Used in Documentation and Notes (see also 46.7)

| | |
|---|---|
| abr. | abridgement |
| adapt. | adapted by, adaptation |
| anon. | anonymous |
| arch. | archaic |
| attrib. | attributed to |
| bk.; bks. | book; books |
| c., ca. | (Latin *circa*) about, approximately (with dates: c. 1737) |
| CD-ROM | compact disc read-only memory |
| cf. | compare |
| ch.; chs. | chapter; chapters (also chap.; chaps.) |
| col.; cols. | column; columns |
| comp. | compiler, compiled by |
| dir. | director, directed by |
| diss. | dissertation |
| distr. | distributor |
| DVD | digital videodisc |
| ed.; eds. | editor, edited by, edition; editors, editions |
| e.g. | (Latin *exempli gratia*) for example |
| email | electronic mail |
| esp. | especially |
| et al. | (Latin *et alii*) and others |
| etc. | (Latin *et cetera*) and so forth |
| ex. | example |
| f.; ff. | and the following page(s) or line(s), e.g. pp. 21ff. |
| fig.; figs. | figure; figures |
| fwd. | foreword, foreword by |
| ibid. | (Latin *ibidem*) in the same place |
| i.e. | (Latin *id est*) that is |
| illus. | illustrator, illustrated by, illustrations |
| introd. | introduction, introduced by |
| HTML | Hypertext Markup Language |
| KB | kilobyte |
| l.; ll. | line; lines |
| ms.; mss. | manuscript; manuscripts |
| n.; nn. | note; notes (usually with page numbers: 37n.; p.73, nn.2–4; or without periods: 37n, 73nn2–4) |

| | |
|---|---|
| natl. | national |
| N.B., n.b. | (Latin *note bene*) note well, take notice |
| n.d. | no date of publication given |
| no.; nos. | number; numbers |
| n.p. | no place of publication given, no publisher |
| n. pag. | no pagination |
| n.s. | new series |
| *OED* | *Oxford English Dictionary* |
| op. | opus, work |
| P | Press (see UP) |
| p.; pp | page; pages |
| par.; pars. | paragraph; paragraphs |
| perf. | performed by, performer |
| pl. | plate; plural |
| pref. | preface, preface by |
| prod. | producer, produced by |
| pub., publ. | publisher, published by |
| qtd. | quoted |
| q.v. | (Latin *quod vide*) which see |
| rev. | revision, revised, revised by, review, reviewed by |
| rpt. | reprint, reprinted by |
| sec., sect. | section |
| ser. | series |
| sic | (Latin) appears thus in the source (see 43.10) |
| st.; sts. | stanza; stanzas |
| supp.; supps. | supplement; supplements |
| sv. | (Latin *sub verbo*) under the word |
| trans. | translated by, translator |
| ts.; tss. | typescript; typescripts |
| U, Univ. | University |
| UP | University Press |
| URL | uniform resource locator (i.e. web address) |
| v. | (Latin *vide*) see |
| VHS | video home system |
| vol.; vols. | volume; volumes |
| vs. (v.) | versus (v. used in legal contexts) |
| writ. | written by, writer |
| www | World Wide Web |

# APPENDIX

# Reference Sources

Since many reference books—especially dictionaries, encyclopedias, and the like—are frequently updated in revised editions or with supplements, we omit dates of publication; we also omit names of authors, editors, and compilers, since often they, too, change or are added to in successive editions. Simply find and use the latest edition available—or select an earlier edition if it is more relevant to your topic. For many indexes and the like, we give the year when coverage began; that is, "*1938–*" means "from *1938* to the present." Take advantage of these older indexes: even if you're working on a current topic, you should go back at least a few years in search of relevant material. For resources that have moved in whole or in part to an online format, we have indicated so in brackets.

## Catalogues, Bibliographical Aids, and Reference Guides (General)

Use the sources to find full lists of works published by individual authors or complete records of periodicals by subject.

*Bibliographic Index: A Cumulative Bibliography of Bibliographies* (1938–)
*Books in Print*
*Canadian Books in Print*
*Cumulative Book Index*
*The Current Contents Address Directory. Social Sciences / Arts & Humanities*
*Gale Directory of Publications and Broadcast Media* (1869–)
*Guide to Reference Books*
*Guide to Reference Materials for Canadian Libraries*
*Guide to the Research Collections of the New York Public Library*

*Guide to the Use of Libraries and Information Sources*
*Microform Research Collections: A Guide*
*Scholarly Electronic Publishing Bibliography*
*The Standard Periodical Directory*
*Topical Reference Books*
*Union List of Scientific Serials in Canadian Libraries*
*Union List of Serials in the Social Sciences and Humanities Held by*
    *Canadian Libraries*
*World Guide to Libraries*

## Dictionaries and Other Word-Books

Some of these sources will provide information about regional dialects, foreign phrases, informal language, and slang.

*Abbreviations Dictionary*
*Acronyms, Initialisms, & Abbreviations Dictionary*
*Allusions: Cultural, Literary, Biblical, and Historical; A Thematic*
    *Dictionary*
*The American Heritage Dictionary of the English Language*
*Brewer's Dictionary of Phrase and Fable*
*Canadian Oxford Dictionary*
*Collins Canadian Dictionary*
*Concise Oxford Dictionary of Current English*
*The Concise Oxford Dictionary of English Etymology*
*A Dictionary of American English on Historical Principles*
*A Dictionary of Canadianisms on Historical Principles*
*A Dictionary of Modern English Usage*
*Dictionary of Newfoundland English*
*A Dictionary of Slang and Unconventional English*
*Dictionary of Word and Phrase Origins*
*An Etymological Dictionary of the English Language*
*Funk & Wagnalls New Standard Dictionary of the English Language*
*Gage Canadian Dictionary*
*Guide to Canadian English Usage*
*The Harper Dictionary of Foreign Terms*
*Merriam-Webster's Dictionary of English Usage*
*Modern American Usage: A Guide*
*The New Fowler's Modern English Usage*
*The New Oxford Thesaurus of English*
*The New Shorter Oxford English Dictionary on Historical Principles*
*Oxford Advanced Learner's Dictionary*
*Oxford Canadian Spelling*

*The Oxford Dictionary of English Etymology*
*Oxford Dictionary of Foreign Words and Phrases*
*The Oxford English Dictionary on Historical Principles*
*Paperback Oxford Canadian Thesaurus*
*Portmanteau Dictionary: Blend Words in the English Language*
*Practical English Usage*
*Random House Webster's Dictionary*
*Roget's Thesaurus* [online resource]
*Roget's 21st Century Thesaurus in Dictionary Form*
*Webster's Third New International Dictionary of the English Language*

## Quotations, Proverbs

*Bartlett's Familiar Quotations*
*Chambers Dictionary of Quotations*
*Colombo's New Canadian Quotations*
*The Macmillan Dictionary of Contemporary Quotations*
*The New Penguin Dictionary of Modern Quotations*
*The New Quotable Woman*
*The Oxford Book of Aphorisms*
*Oxford Dictionary of Literary Quotations*
*The Oxford Dictionary of Phrase, Proverb, and Quotation*
*The Oxford Dictionary of Thematic Quotations*
*Oxford Dictionary of Quotations*
*Random House Webster's Quotationary*

## Periodical and Other Indexes (General)

These sources provide lists of articles published in journals, magazines, and newspapers in particular subject areas.

*Academic Search Premier* (1965–)
*Alternative Press Index* (1973–)
*Arts and Humanities Citation Index* (1976–)
*Canadian Business and Current Affairs* (1982–)
*Canadian Newsstand* (1985–)
*Canadian Periodical Index Quarterly* (1920–)
*Directory of Scholarly Electronic Journals and Academic Discussion Lists* (2000–)
*Dissertation Abstracts; Dissertation Abstracts International*
*Humanities and Social Sciences Index* (1983–)
*LexisNexis Academic* (1975–)
*Poole's Index to Periodical Literature* (1802–1906)

*Readers' Guide Abstracts* (1983–)
*Répertoire analytique d'articles de revues du Québec* (1972–)
*Ulrich's International Periodicals Directory* (1979–)
*World News Connection*

## Book Reviews (General)

These sources provide lists of reviews written on works of fiction and non-fiction.

*American Reference Books Annual* (1970–)
*Book Review Digest* (1905–)
*Book Review Index* (1965–)
*Canadian Book Review Annual* (1975–)
*Children's Book Review Index*
*Combined Retrospective Index to Book Reviews in Humanities Journals 1802–1974*
*Combined Retrospective Index to Book Reviews in Scholarly Journals 1886–1974*
*An Index to Book Reviews in the Humanities* (1960–1990)
*The New York Times Book Review Index* (1896–)

## Encyclopedias (General)

These sources provide articles giving overviews of various topics in addition to basic bibliographical leads to additional sources.

*The Canadian Encyclopedia*
*The Encyclopaedia Britannica*
*Encyclopedia Americana*
*The New Encyclopedia Britannica*

## Collections of Facts and Opinions; Yearbooks; Chronologies; Atlases and Gazetteers

Some of these sources provide basic statistical, geographical, and historical data about Canada and other nations.

*The Annual Register: A Record of World Events* (1758–)
*Atlas of Exploration*
*Atlas of the World*
*Britannica Book of the Year* (1938–)
*Canada Year Book*
*Canadian Almanac & Directory* (1847–)

*Canadian Global Almanac* (1992–)
*Canadian News Facts* (1967–)
*Canadian Sourcebook* (1997–)
*Cultural Atlas of Africa*
*Demographic Yearbook; Annuaire démocratique* (1948–)
*The Europa World Year Book* (1926–)
*Facts on File: A Weekly World News Digest* (1940–)
*Historical Atlas of Canada*
*National Geographic Atlas of the World*
*The New York Public Library Desk Reference*
*The New York Times Almanac* (1969–)
*The Statesman's Yearbook* (1864–)
*The Times Atlas of the World*
*The Timetables of History*
*The World Almanac and Book of Facts* (1868–)
*World Opinion Update* (1997–)
*The Year Book of World Affairs*

## History, Politics

*America: History and Life* (1964–)
*The American Historical Association's Guide to Historical Literature*
*Annotated Bibliography of Canadian Demography* (1966–)
    [online resource]
*Australian Public Affairs Information Service: A Subject Index
    to Current Literature* (1945–2000)
*Bibliography of Asian Studies* (1971–) [online resource]
*Bibliography of British History*
*The Cambridge Ancient History*
*The Cambridge Medieval History*
*Canadian Annual Review of Politics and Public Affairs* (1971–)
*Canadian Foreign Relations Index* (1945–) [online resource]
*Canadian Research Index (Microlog)* (1982–) [online resource]
*China Facts and Figures Annual* (1978–)
*CPOL: Bibliography of Canadian Politics and Society* (1929–)
    [online resource]
*A Current Bibliography on African Affairs* (1962–)
*Current Geographical Publications* (1938–)
*Dictionary of Human Geography*
*Dictionary of Political Thought*
*Encyclopedia of British Columbia*
*Encyclopedia of Modern Asia*
*Encyclopedia of Newfoundland and Labrador*

*Encyclopedia of the Third World*
*Encyclopedia of Women Social Reformers*
*An Encyclopedia of World History*
*Foreign Affairs Bibliography*
*Government of Canada Publications*
*Historic Documents* (1972–)
*Historical Abstracts* (1955–)
*History* (1972–)
*Indian Reference Sources* (1988–)
*Index to House of Commons Parliamentary Papers*
*International Bibliography of Historical Sciences* (1926–)
*International Political Science Abstracts* (1951–) [online resource]
*Monthly Catalogue of United States Government Publications*
*A New Dictionary of Political Analysis*
*The Oxford Classical Dictionary*
*The Oxford Companion to Canadian History*
*The Oxford Companion to Canadian Military History*
*The Oxford Companion to Politics of the World*
*Peace Research Abstracts Journal* (1964–)
*Political Science: A Bibliographical Guide to the Literature*
*The Political Science Reviewer: An Annual Review of Scholarship*
*Polling the Nations* [online resource]
*Public Affairs Information Service (PAIS) Bulletin: Annual Cumulated
    Bulletins, Cumulative Subject Index* (1915–)
*The Times Atlas of World History*
*World Encyclopedia of Parliaments and Legislatures*
*World News Connection* [online resource]
*Yearbook of the United Nations* (1946–)

## Biography (General)

*Biography and Genealogy Master Index*
*Biography Index* (1946–)
*The Cambridge Biographical Dictionary*
*Canadian Who's Who* (1910–)
*Chambers Biographical Dictionary*
*Current Biography* (1940–)
*Dictionary of American Biography*
*Dictionary of Canadian Biography*
*Dictionary of National Biography* (British)
*International Who's Who* (1935–)
*Who Was Who*
*World Biography Index* [online resource]

## Science and Technology

*Abstracts of North American Geology* (1966–)
*ACM Digital Library* [online resource]
*Analytical Chemistry Handbook*
*Applied Science and Technology Abstracts* (1983–)
*Aquatic Sciences and Fisheries Abstracts* (1971–)
*Astronomy and Astrophysics Abstracts* (1969–2000)
*Black's Medical Dictionary*
*Biological Abstracts* (1926–)
*Biological and Agricultural Index* (1964–)
*British Technology Index* (1962–)
*The Cambridge Encyclopedia of Astronomy*
*The Cambridge Encyclopedia of Earth Sciences*
*Chemical Abstracts* (1907–) [online resource]
*CHEMnetBASE* [online resource]
*Collection of Computer Science Bibliographies* [online resource]
*Computer and Control Abstracts* (1969–)
*Concise Encyclopedia of Biology*
*Concise Encyclopedia of the Sciences*
*CRC Concise Encyclopedia of Mathematics*
*CRC Handbook of Chemistry and Physics*
*A Dictionary of Biology*
*A Dictionary of Earth Sciences*
*A Dictionary of Ecology*
*Dictionary of Ecology and Environmental Science*
*A Dictionary of Genetics*
*A Dictionary of Physics*
*Dictionary of Science and Technology*
*Dictionary of Scientific Biography*
*Ecology Abstracts* (1980–)
*Encyclopedia of Astronomy and Astrophysics*
*Encyclopedia of Bioethics*
*The Encyclopedia of Chemistry*
*Encyclopedia of Endangered Species*
*Encyclopedia of Environmental Science*
*Encyclopedia of Life Sciences* [online resource]
*The Engineering Index* (1884–)
*ENVIROnetBASE: Environmental Sciences Electronic Library*
    [online resource]
*Environment Abstracts* (1974–) [online resource]
*General Science Index* (1978–) [online resource]
*Great Canadian Scientists* [online resource]

*Grzimek's Animal Life Encyclopedia*
*Handbook of Writing for the Mathematical Sciences*
*History of Science* (1962–)
*Index Medicus* (1879–1997) [online resource]
*McGraw-Hill Basic Bibliography of Science and Technology*
*McGraw-Hill Encyclopedia of Environmental Science and Engineering*
*McGraw-Hill Encyclopedia of Science and Technology*
*The Merck Index* (1889–) [online resource]
*Oceanic Abstracts* (1966–)
*Penguin Dictionary of Geology*
*Physics Abstracts* (1903–)[online resource]
*Pollution Abstracts* (1981–) [online resource]
*Reader's Guide to the History of Science*
*The Timetables of Science: A Chronology of the Most Important People
    and Events in the History of Science*
*The Timetables of Technology: A Chronology of the Most Important
    People and Events in the History of Technology*
*Web of Science* [online resource]
*World Climate Report* [online resource]
*World Directory of Country Environmental Studies: An Annotated
    Bibliography of Natural Resource Profiles, Plans, and Strategies*
*The Zoological Record* (1864–)

## Social Sciences; Education

*Abstracts in Anthropology* (1970–) [online resource]
*Anthropological Index* (1957–) [online resource]
*Anthropological Literature* (1979–) [online resource]
*Bibliography of Asian Studies* (1971–) [online resource]
*Bibliography of Native American  Bibliographies (Bibliographies and
    Indexes in Ethnic Studies)*
*Biographical Dictionary of Psychology*
*Canadian Business and Current Affairs (CBCA) FullText Education*
    (1976–) [online resource]
*Canadian Heritage Info Network (CHIN)* [online resource]
*Contemporary Psychology* (1956–2004)
*Contemporary Women's Issues* (1992–) [online resource]
*Criminal Justice Abstracts* (1968–) [online resource]
*Criminology and Penology Abstracts* (1961–1980) [online resource]
*Current Anthropology* (1959–) [online resource]
*The Dictionary of Anthropology*
*A Dictionary of Education*
*A Dictionary of Psychology*

*A Dictionary of Sociology*
*Dictionary of the Social Sciences*
*Education Index* (1929–) [online resource]
*Encyclopedia of Educational Research*
*Encyclopedia of Human Behavior*
*Encyclopedia of Psychology*
*Encyclopedia of Social Work*
*ERIC (Education Resource Information Centre) Database* (1966–)
   [online resource]
*The Europa World of Learning* (1947–)
*First Nations Periodical Index* (1981–) [online resource]
*Health and Psychosocial Instruments* (1985–) [online resource]
*Humanities and Social Sciences Index* (1907–1984) [online resource]
*International Bibliography of Social and Cultural Anthropology* (1955–)
*International Bibliography of the Social Sciences* (1951–)
*International Bibliography of Sociology* (1951–)
*International Encyclopedia of the Social and Behavioral Sciences*
*LLBA (Linguistics and Language Behavior Abstracts)* (1973–) [online
   resource]
*MEDLINE Database* (1946–) [online resource]
*New Books on Women, Gender & Feminism* (1987–)
*Physical Education Index* (1970–) [online resource]
*PsycCRITIQUES* [online resource]
*Psychological Abstracts* (1927–2006) [online resource]
*PsycINFO List of Journals* (1987–) [online resource]
*Reader's Guide to the Social Sciences*
*RIE: Resources in Education* (ERIC) (1979–) [online resource]
*Social Sciences Citation Index* (1956–) [online resource]
*Social Sciences Index* (1974–)
*Sociological Abstracts* (1963–2005) [online resource]
*Women, Race, and Ethnicity: A Bibliography*
*Women's Studies Index* (1991–)
*Women Studies Abstracts* (1972–2009)
*Women's Studies International* (1972–) [online resource]

## Canadian Studies

*Artists in Canada* [online resource]
*Bibliography of Native North Americans* [online resource]
*Canadian Education Index* [online resource]
*Canadian MAS FullTEXT Elite* (1990–) [online resource]
*Canadian Music Periodical Index* [online resource]
*Canadian Periodical Index Quarterly* [online resource]

*Canadian Research Index: Microlog* (1979–) [online resource]
*CBCA (Canadian Business and Current Affairs) Index* (1982–)
     [online resource]
*CHIN (Canadian Heritage Information Network)* (1955–) [online
     resource]
*CIHM (Canadian Institute for Historical Microreproductions)* [online
     resource]
*ICAR (Inventory of Canadian Agri-Food Research)* [online resource]
*Index to House of Commons Parliamentary Papers* [online resource]

## Economics and Business

*ABI/Inform: Abstracted Business Information* (1970–) [online resource]
*Business Periodicals Index* (1958–) [online resource]
*Business Source Elite* (1984–) [online resource]
*The Cambridge Economic History of Europe*
*CBCA (Canadian Business & Current Affairs) Fulltext Reference* (1982–)
     [online resource]
*Country Reports* [online resource]
*Economics Selections: Cumulative Bibliography* (1954–62)
*EconLit* (1969–) [online resource]
*Economic Abstracts* (1953–) [online resource]
*International Bibliography of Economics* (1952–) [online resource]
*Macmillan Dictionary of Marketing and Advertising*
*The McGraw-Hill Dictionary of Modern Economics: A Handbook of
     Terms and Organizations*
*The McGraw-Hill Encyclopedia of Economics*
*National Bureau of Economic Research* (1994–) [online resource]
*The Penguin Dictionary of Economics*
*Survey of Economic and Social History in Canada* (1976–)
*Transport* (1988–)

## Philosophy, Religion, Mythology, Folklore

*The Anchor Bible Series*
*The Anchor Yale Bible Dictionary*
*ATLA (American Theological Library Association) Database* (1949–)
     [online resource]
*A Bibliography of Canadian Folklore in English*
*Brewer's Book of Myth and Legend*
*Bulfinch's Mythology*
*Catholic Almanac Online* (1904–) [online resource]
*The Concise Encyclopedia of Western Philosophy and Philosophers*

A Concordance of the Qur'an
Cruden's Complete Concordance to the Old and New Testaments
Cyclopaedia of Biblical, Theological, and Ecclesiastical Literature
A Dictionary of the Bible [online resource]
Dictionary of Chinese Mythology
A Dictionary of Christian Biography
A Dictionary of Hinduism
Dictionary of Non-Christian Religions
A Dictionary of Western Mythology
Encyclopaedia of the Hindu World
Encyclopedia of Bioethics
The Encyclopedia of Eastern Philosophy and Religion: Buddhism,
     Hinduism, Taoism, Zen
The Encyclopedia of Islam
Encyclopedia Judaica [online resource]
An Encyclopedia of Occultism & Parapsychology
The Encyclopedia of Philosophy
An Encyclopedia of Religion
Encyclopedia of Religion and Ethics
The Encyclopedia of Unbelief
Everyman's Dictionary of Non-Classical Mythology
Funk & Wagnalls Standard Dictionary of Folklore, Mythology, and Legend
The Global Anabaptist Mennonite Encylopedia Online [online resource]
The Golden Bough: A Study in Magic and Religion
A Handbook of Greek Mythology
Harper's Bible Dictionary
Index to Book Reviews in Religion [online resource: incorporated
     in the the ATLA Religion Database (ATLA RDB)]
Index to Fairy Tales, Myths, and Legends (1926–)
Index Islamicus [online resource]
Index to Jewish Periodicals (1963–) [online resource]
International Standard Bible Encyclopedia
The Interpreter's Dictionary of the Bible
Larousse World Mythology
The Macmillan Bible Atlas
Motif-Index of Folk-Literature: A Classification of Narrative Elements
     in Folktales, Ballads, Myths, Fables, Mediaeval Romances, Exempla,
     Fabliaux, Jest-Books and Local Legends
The Mythology of All Races
Nelson's Complete Concordance of the Revised Standard Version Bible
The New Bible Dictionary
The New Cambridge History of Islam

*New Catholic Encyclopedia*
*A New Dictionary of Christian Theology*
*The New Interpreter's Bible*
*The New Standard Jewish Encyclopedia*
*The Oxford Dictionary of the Christian Church*
*The Oxford Dictionary of Philosophy*
*The Oxford Dictionary of Saints*
*The Penguin Dictionary of Religions*
*The Philosopher's Index* (1967–) [online resource]
*A Popular Dictionary of Sikhism: Sikh Religion and Philosophy*
*A Rationalist Encyclopaedia*
*A Reader's Guide to the Great Religions*
*Religion Index* (1949–) [online resource]
*The Shambhala Dictionary of Buddhism and Zen*
*Who's Who in Egyptian Mythology*
*Young's Analytical Concordance to the Bible*

## The Arts

*Art and Architecture in Canada: A Bibliography and Guide to the
    Literature*
*ARTbibliographies Modern* (1974–) [online resource]
*Arts & Humanities Citation Index* (1978–) [online resource]
*Art Index* (1929–) [online resource]
*Art Index Retrospective* (1929–84) [online resource]
*Baker's Biographical Dictionary of Musicians*
*Bibliography of the History of Art* (1978–) [online resource]
*Canadian Music Periodical Index*
*CHIN (Canadian Heritage Information Network)* (1955–) [online resource]
*Concise History of Western Music*
*The Concise Oxford Dictionary of Ballet*
*The Concise Oxford Dictionary of Music*
*The Concise Oxford Dictionary of Opera*
*Design and Applied Arts Index* (1973–) [online resource]
*A Dictionary of Canadian Artists*
*A Dictionary of Musical Terms*
*A Dictionary of Symbolism: Cultural Icons and the Meanings Behind Them*
*A Dictionary of Symbols*
*The Encyclopedia of Dance and Ballet*
*The Encyclopedia of Jazz*
*Encyclopedia of Music in Canada*
*Encyclopedia of Painting*
*Encyclopedia of Popular Music*

Encyclopedia of World Architecture
Encyclopedia of World Art
The Focal Encyclopedia of Photography
The Grove Dictionary of Art
Guide to the Literature of Art History
The Harvard Concise Dictionary of Music and Musicians
Index to Canadian Legal Literature (1987–) [online resource]
The International Center of Photography Encyclopedia of Photography
The International Cyclopedia of Music and Musicians
International Index to Music Periodicals [online resource]
McGraw-Hill Dictionary of Art
Music Index (1949–1998) [online resource]
The New Encyclopedia of the Opera
The New Grove Dictionary of Music and Musicians
The New Oxford History of Music
The Oxford Companion to Music
The Oxford Companion to the Decorative Arts
RILM Abstracts of Music Literature (1969–) [online resource]
Sculpture Index: Sculpture of Europe and the Contemporary Middle East
Symbols and Legends in Western Art
Who's Who in Opera: A Guide to Opera Characters
World Painting Index

## Drama, Film, Television

Annual Index to Motion Picture Credits (1993–)
The Brock Bibliography of Published Canadian Plays in English 1776–1978
Canada on Stage: Canadian Theatre Review Yearbook
Catalogue of Canadian Plays (1995–) [online resource]
The Complete Encyclopedia of Television Programs (1947–79)
Contemporary Dramatists (1973–)
Contemporary Theatre, Film, and Television (1984–1998)
The Encyclopedia of World Theater
Film Canadiana (1980–)
The Film Encyclopedia
Film Literature Index (1973–) [online resource]
Film Review Index (1986–) [online resource]
The Film Studies Dictionary
Filmmaker's Dictionary
Halliwell's Filmgoer's Companion
A History of English Drama
International Bibliography of Theatre (1982–1999)
International Index to Film Periodicals (1972–2008)

*International Motion Picture Almanac* (1941—2009)
*International Television Almanac* (1956–1986)
*International Television and Video Almanac* (1987–)
*Magill's Survey of Cinema*
*MLA International Bibliography* (1963–) [online resource]
*Motion Picture Guide*
*The New York Times Film Reviews* (1913–)
*The New York Times Theater Reviews* (1920–)
*The Oxford Companion to the Theatre*
*The Performing Arts: A Guide to the Reference Literature*
*Play Index* (1949–1987)
*Radio and Television: A Selected, Annotated Bibliography*
*Television Drama Series Programming: A Comprehensive Chronicle*
    (1959–1986)

## Literature and Language

*ABES (Annotated Bibliography for English Studies)* [online resource]
*Abstracts of English Studies* (1958–1971)
*Annual Bibliography of Commonwealth Literature* (1964–)
*Annual Bibliography of English Language and Literature* (1920–)
    [online resource]
*Arts and Humanities Citation Index* (1989–) [online resource]
*Benét's Reader's Encyclopedia*
*A Bibliography of the English Language from the Invention of Printing
    to the Year 1800*
*The Bloomsbury Guide to Women's Literature*
*Calendar of Literary Facts*
*The Cambridge Bibliography of English Literature*
*The Cambridge Companion to Canadian Literature*
*The Cambridge Companions to Literature series*
*The Cambridge History of English Literature, 1660–1780 (The New
    Cambridge History of English Literature)*
*Canadian Periodical Index Quarterly* (1988–) [online resource]
*Children's Book Review Index* (1975–)
*Children's Literature Abstracts* (1973–)
*Children's Literature Review: Excerpts from Reviews, Criticism &
    Commentary on Books for Children and Young People*
*A Complete and Systematic Concordance to the Works of Shakespeare*
*Comprehensive Shakespeare Dictionary* [CD-ROM]
*The Concise Oxford Dictionary of Literary Terms*
*Contemporary Authors New Revision* (1962–)

Contemporary Literary Criticism (1973–2008)
Dictionary of Literary Biography
A Dictionary of Literary Terms and Literary Theory
An Encyclopedia of British Women Writers
Encyclopedia of Literature in Canada
Encyclopedia of World Literature in the 20th Century
The Feminist Companion to Literature in English: Women Writers from
    the Middle Ages to the Present
Fiction Catalog (1908–)
A Glossary of Literary Terms
A Handbook to Literature
A History of the English Language
Humanities and Social Sciences Index (1907–1984) [online resource]
Index to Children's Poetry
International Companion Encyclopedia of Children's Literature
International Medieval Bibliography Online (1967–) [online resource]
Letters in Canada (1935–)
Linguistic Bibliography (1939–) [online resource]
Linguistics and Language Behavior Abstracts (1967–) [online resource]
Literary Criticism Index
Literary History of Canada: Canadian Literature in English
A Literary History of England
Literary History of the United States
Macmillan History of Literature Series
Magill's Guide to Science Fiction and Fantasy Literature
MLA International Bibliography (1963–) [online resource]
New Literatures Review (1975–)
The Oxford Companion to African American Literature
The Oxford Companion to American Literature
The Oxford Companion to Australian Literature
The Oxford Companion to Canadian Literature
The Oxford Companion to Canadian Theatre
The Oxford Companion to Children's Literature
The Oxford Companion to Classical Literature
The Oxford Companion to the English Language
The Oxford Companion to English Literature
The Oxford Companion to Fairy Tales
The Oxford Companion to French Literature
The Oxford Companion to German Literature
The Oxford Companion to Irish Literature
The Oxford Companion to New Zealand Literature
The Oxford Companion to Shakespeare

*The Oxford Companion to Spanish Literature*
*The Penguin Dictionary of British and American Women Writers 1660–1800*
*Poetry Index Annual (1982–1990)*
*Poetry by Women to 1900: A Bibliography of American and British Writers*
*Post-Colonial Literatures in English: General Theoretical Comparative, 1970–1993*
*Princeton Encyclopedia of Poetry and Poetics*
*Selective Bibliography for the Study of English and American Literature*
*The Short Oxford History of English Literature*
*Short Story Index (1953–)*
*Short Story Index: Collections Indexed, 1900–1978*
*Victorian Database* [online resource]
*World Shakespeare Bibliography (1945–2002)* [online resource]
*The World Encyclopedia of Comics*
*The Year's Work in English Studies (1919–)* [online resource]
*The Year's Work in Modern Language Studies (1929–)*

## Sports and Games

*Dictionary of the Sport and Exercise Sciences*
*Encyclopedia of Sports Medicine*
*Encyclopedia of Sports Science*
*Encyclopedia of World Sport: From Ancient Times to the Present*
*Information Sources in Sport and Leisure*
*International Encyclopedia of Women and Sports*
*The Oxford Companion to Sports and Games*
*SPORTDiscus* [online resource]
*Sport Search*
*Whitaker's Olympic Almanack: An Encyclopedia of the Olympic Games*

# Index